The Idea

The Idea of Design

A *Design Issues* Reader

edited by

Victor Margolin and Richard Buchanan

The MIT Press

Cambridge, Massachusetts

London, England

The contents of this book were first published in Design Issues (ISSN 0747-9360), a publication of The MIT Press. Except as otherwise noted, copyright in each article is owned by the Massachusetts Institute of Technology.

Richard Buchanan, "Wicked Problems in Design Thinking," vol. 8, no. 2, (Spring 1992): 5–21; Yves Deforge, "Avatars of Design: Design Before Design," vol. 6, no. 2, (Spring 1990): 43–50; Alain Findeli, "Moholy-Nagy's Design Pedagogy in Chicago (1937–1946)," vol. 7, no. 1, (Fall 1990): 4–19; Jorge Frascara, "Graphic Design: Fine Art or Social Science?", vol. 5, no. 1, (Fall 1988): 18–29; Victor Papanek, "The Future Isn't What It Used To Be," vol. 5, no. 1, (Fall 1988): 4–17; Rudolph Arnheim, "Sketching and the Psychology of Design," vol. 9, no. 2, (Spring 1993): 15–19; Richard Buchanan, "Myth and Maturity: Toward a New Order in the Decade of Design," vol. 6, no. 2, (Spring 1990): 70–80; Martin Krampen, "Semiotics in Architecture and Industrial/Product Design," vol. 5, no. 2, (Spring 1989): 124–140; Ann Tyler, "Shaping Belief: The Role of Audience in Visual Communication," vol. 9, no. 1, (Fall 1992): 21–29; Martin Solomon, "The Power of Punctuation," vol. 6, no. 2, (Spring 1990): 28–32; Mihaly Csikszentmihalyi, "Design and Order in Everyday Life," vol. 8, no. 1, (Fall 1991): 26–34; S. Balaram, "Product Symbolism of Gandhi and Its Connection with Indian Mythology," vol. 5, no. 2, (Spring 1989): 68–85; Clive Dilnot, "The Gift," vol. 9, no. 2, (Spring 1993): 51–63; Klaus Krippendorff, "On the Essential Contexts of Artifacts or On the Proposition that 'Design Is Making Sense (of Things),'" vol. 5, no. 2, (Spring 1989): 9–38; Rajeswari Ghose, "Design, Development, Culture, and Cultural Legacies in Asia," vol. 6, no. 1, (Fall 1989): 31–48; Tony Fry, "A Geography of Power: Design History and Marginality," vol. 6, no. 1, (Fall 1989): 15–30; Takuo Hirano, "The Development of Modern Japanese Design: A Personal Account," vol. 7, no. 2, (Spring 1990): 54–62; A. Cheng, "Line," vol. 7, no. 2, (Spring 1990): 5–16; Gert Selle, "Untimely Opinions (An Attempt to Reflect on Design)," vol. 6, no. 2, (Spring 1990): 33–42; Tomas Maldonado, "The Idea of Comfort," vol. 8, no. 1, (Fall 1991): 35–43; Barbara Usherwood, "The Design Museum: Form Follows Funding," vol. 7, no. 2, (Spring 1991): 76–87; Abraham Moles, "Design and Immateriality: What of It in a Post Industrial Society?" vol. 4, no. 1–2, (Special Issue 1988): 25–32; Victor Margolin, "Expanding the Boundaries of Design: The Product Environment and the New User," vol. 4, no. 1–2, (Special Issue): 59–64.

Fourth printing, 2000

Selection and introduction; copyright© 1995 by the Massachusetts Institute of Technology.

Library of Congress Cataloging-in-Publication Data
The idea of design/edited by Victor Margolin and Richard Buchanan
          p. cm.—(A Design issues reader)
     ISBN 0-262-63166-0 (alk. paper)
0.1 Design.   I. Margolin, Victor.   II. Buchanan, Richard.
NK1525.I34   1995
745.4—dc209   5-24675
                                                                        CIP

To our families
Sylvia and Myra
and
Barbara, Stephanie and Rick

Contents

Section III

Design and Culture

Acknowledgments

We are indebted to the following individuals who have contributed their editorial skills, insights, time, and passion to *Design Issues* during the period of publication from which the essays in this anthology were drawn: Leon Bellin, Stephen Bloom, Marco Diani, Dennis Doordan, John Heskett, Martin Hurtig, and Lawrence Salomon. We also acknowledge others for their efforts on behalf of the journal during the same period: John Cullars, Bonnie Osborne, and Faith Van Alten. In addition we would like to thank Karen Moyer for her design assistance. The School of Art and Design at the University of Illinois at Chicago (under the directorship of Martin Hurtig, then Susan Sensemann, and finally Judith Kirshner) served as the original home for *Design Issues* and sustained the journal for its first nine volumes (1984–1993). *Design Issues* is now edited at the Department of Design at Carnegie Mellon University and published by The MIT Press.

Introduction

The essays collected in this anthology represent an important shift of focus in how the idea of design is explored in contemporary discourse. For earlier writers like Adolf Loos, Walter Gropius, and Edgar Kaufmann, Jr., the object or artifact attracted central attention. Loos critiqued the presence of excessive ornament as a distraction from the experience of formal qualities, while Gropius, in his Bauhaus manifesto of 1919, proclaimed the cathedral as the emblematic object that would embody the spiritual values of the age. Properly conceived, the object was an instrument for improving social life and bringing order, reason, and expressive vitality to everyday experience. It carried enormous symbolic weight, and battles were fought over the proper form of the object as an expression of personal vision, aesthetic sensibility, and cultural values. In later years, the "good design" debate revolved around issues of how the form of objects could enhance the quality of life. Rationalist design discourse of the 1950s and 1960s promulgated a spare formal order as a design ideal, whether manifested in Swiss typography or in unobtrusive products like the Braun stereo sound system. Even reactions against those formal restrictions by Pop designers in the 1960s or Memphis designers and *new-wave* typographers in the 1980s nonetheless emphasized the objects themselves rather than the complex thought processes that led to them or the situations in which they were used and given meaning.

The emphasis is reversed in design discourse of the 1980s and 1990s. Objects remain important as a symbolic location of experience, but writers increasingly focus attention on the psychological, social, and cultural contexts that give meaning and value to products and to the discipline of design practice. This shift is not based on the suspiciously tidy and ideologically convenient division between modernism and postmodernism that some writers proposed in the early 1980s. Rather, it is guided by the recognition that objects are situated in a variety of ways that were not clearly understood or adequately explored by the designers, historians, critics, and theorists who established the precedents for the field of design earlier in this century. As a consequence, contemporary design discourse does not represent a radical break with the past. Instead, it represents a broadening of the scope of design to include issues and problems that were often embedded in earlier practice and speculation but were seldom developed in depth.

The essays assembled here are primarily examples of design criticism and theory, with occasional ventures into philosophical issues that bear on the understanding of design. However, it is important to place this work in its proper relationship with design history because historical materials are included from time to time in many of the essays. Where history seeks to reproduce and interpret concrete events as they actually occurred—recognizing that *events* and *actually occurred* are highly ambiguous terms whose meanings are essentially contested in design history—criticism and theory seek to explain, on the basis of the study of many instances of design in a variety of circumstances, the nature of design processes, practices, and products. Philosophic speculation, to the degree that it occurs in these essays, serves to anchor criticism and theory in the further investigation of general principles of human experience. Such reflection, whether it is critical, theoretical, or philosophic, sometimes emerges from the personal experience of historical events or from the consideration of historical materials, but the direction of investigation is toward the understanding of contemporary problems and toward ideas that will affect future practice and the general understanding of design.

However, this book is not an effort to establish a monistic vision of design. It is not based on a single unifying concept of design or on the prospect of a single philosophy of design. Rather, it is based on a belief in the value of radical systematic pluralism: the principled cultivation of a sustained conversation among individuals with widely differing perspectives on the natural and human-made world. Pluralism keeps alive the ongoing search for truth and understanding by focusing inquiry on common problems encountered in experience—in this case, the experience of the human-made—rather than on the technical refinement, fine points, and stylistic polish of a single theory. Pluralism sustains the ecology of culture, maintaining a gene pool of diverse ideas and methods that enables us to avoid entrapment in dogma by forcing our attention to features of the world that might otherwise be ignored by doctrines that are conceived too narrowly—as it seems all doctrines eventually prove to be.

Despite the enthusiasm with which it has been embraced by theorists of the postmodern, radical pluralism is not an invention belonging to the late twentieth century. The concept of systematic pluralism that lies behind this book has its precedent in the works of John Dewey, Scott Buchanan's *Possibility* (published in 1927), and the works of the two greatest American rhetoricians of the twentieth century, Kenneth Burke and Richard McKeon. These individuals recognized that "terministic screens" mediate our experience of the world, but that the resolution of semantic problems is only a step on the way toward engaging significant problems of inquiry.

Design is an area of both semantic problems and significant inquiry. The semantic problems come from the range of intellectual and practical perspectives on the human-made world that have helped to shape design thinking in the twentieth century. From its beginning, design discourse has reflected a wide variety of ideas

The Idea of Design

and methods and a broad diversity of philosophical assumptions, and it has been difficult for readers to disentangle the various perspectives from the substantive problems that writers sought to address. This has contributed to ideological disputes among the schools of design and has slowed the development of design studies as a meeting ground for significant inquiry. However, as the semantic differences among participants become more familiar, there is a new possibility for productive conversation. The purpose of this anthology is to move design discourse toward the discussion of common themes, rather than merely sustain ideological differences. Ideological differences will take care of themselves. The challenge is to show how discussion may become more productive by learning what different perspectives have to offer to the community of inquirers as new insights into design.

Accordingly, the essays in this volume are organized in three sections, each representing an important area of new inquiry that expands the scope of design thinking. There are many connections and interdependencies among these sections, but each section develops its own set of themes and offers a distinctive orientation toward the complexity of design in the contemporary world. Essays in the first section address the culture of design. They are investigations of designers and the arts and disciplines of design thinking and design practice. Essays in the second section address the meaning of products, with special emphasis on how meaning is socially constructed through interactions between users and the human-made world. Finally, essays in the third section address the broad relations between design and culture, placing design and Euro-centric visions of design in the context of world culture.

Reflecting on Design

Among the many themes explored in this section, three stand out as particularly significant for revealing the trend of contemporary design discourse. The first theme is the nature of the discipline of design and its relationships with other disciplines and bodies of knowledge. The second theme is the connection between contemporary reflection and historically situated ideas and practices of design. The third theme is the direction of new practices and lines of research in the conception, planning, and presentation of design ideas.

In the first essay, Richard Buchanan explores the discipline of design as a new form of rhetoric suited to an age of technology. He argues that design is a liberal art of technological culture, concerned with the conception and planning of all of the instances of the artificial or human-made world: signs and images, physical objects, activities and services, and systems or environments. The conception or invention of new design ideas is explained through the "doctrine of placements," while the planning of products requires the integration of knowledge from many fields and disciplines, directed toward the solution of wicked problems of indeterminacy. He argues that the three great expressions of design thinking in the twentieth century—engineering, marketing, and the forms of graphic and industrial design—are distinguished by the modality or qualification of their arguments: Engineers argue from necessity, marketing experts argue from contingency, and graphic and industrial designers argue from a vision of possibility. Contemporary approaches to design increasingly recognize the interdependence of these modalities of argument in the development of successful products.

Similarly, Yves Deforge seeks to establish a new humanistic approach to design. He also argues that designers are concerned with conceiving and realizing ideas in products. However, Deforge begins by studying the avatars of design—early engineers—in order to distinguish the utilitarian and sign functions that he believes all designers must explore in the creation of material products. He argues that all of the technical capacities of the engineer-designer must "dissolve" into a single technical capacity. This capacity, Deforge observes, unfortunately tends to be reductive, threatening the new breed of designers with a loss of the former strength and originality of design: a vision of the world, based on the ascendancy of humanity over nature. Deforge's hope is that consumers may become more involved in the conception of products so that a new possibility may emerge: the engineer-designer-consumer.

While Deforge begins with the avatars of design and Buchanan anchors his inquiry in the cultural and philosophical revolution that occurred at the beginning of the twentieth century, Alain Findeli turns to Moholy-Nagy and the New Bauhaus in Chicago between 1937 and 1946. He examines design education and the changing pattern of supporting studies, tracing Moholy-Nagy's effort to introduce general education and science into the curriculum in order to encourage individuality and social responsibility among his students. Although this project was cut short by financial difficulties and the untimely death of Moholy-Nagy, Findeli argues that it can be adapted to the new circumstances of design, helping prepare designers for the increasing complexity of their work, particularly with regard to aesthetic and ethical issues.

Some of the new problems of aesthetics, ethics, and human values are discussed by Jorge Frascara and Victor Papanek. Both authors point toward the need for the discipline of design to find ways of incorporating the practical consequences of knowledge gained from the social sciences. Frascara argues that excessive emphasis on aesthetics has distracted graphic designers from reaching a clearer understanding of communication and social significance as equally important factors in assessing the quality of their work. He urges designers to consider the performance of their work in terms of changes produced in the audience, recognizing the wide array of functions performed by graphic design in contemporary life. Graphic design should be based, he argues, on the study of human communication. This would shift "the designer's center of attention from the interrelation of visual components to that between the audience and the design, recognizing the receiver as an active participant in the construction of meaning." Turning from graphic to industrial design, Papanek identifies a problem that appears to be symmetrical to that raised by Frascara. Instead of excessive emphasis on aesthetics, Papanek observes excessive emphasis on "high-tech functionalism that disregards human psychic needs at the expense of clarity." His essay attempts to demonstrate the vast amount of new and useful information that is now available in the social sciences but is often ignored or neglected by designers—and, implicitly, ignored in design education.

Although design thinking in the contemporary world must be based on knowledge gained from many fields and disciplines, the core of design thinking remains the ability to conceive, plan, and present ideas about products. Knowledge may be a source of inspiration, practical constraint, or criteria for evaluation, but knowledge is useless unless it is transformed in the designer's imagination into ideas and images, visions of the world that may be effectively communicated to others. This is the subject of Rudolf Arnheim's essay on sketching and the psychology of design. Taking as his point of departure the idea of sketching as a kind of dialectic, an idea proposed by architect Gabriela Goldschmidt, Arnheim discusses the relation between mental images and visual representation in the design process. He implicitly argues that the nature and functions of sketching in design deserve much more attention than they have received in the past—despite numerous "how to" books—and that sketching is a design tool of remarkable flexibility that individuals trained in the logocentrism of Western culture have failed to examine in proper depth. In effect, Arnheim reminds us that the new discipline of design, although it requires sophisticated knowledge and communicative ability, can never be based on words alone: Design is a discipline of vision, both literally and metaphorically.

Efforts to shape a new discipline of design and better prepare designers to work effectively in contemporary circumstances are signs of the changing culture of design. As Jorge Frascara points out, design has evolved into sophisticated practice in a piecemeal fashion, without the benefit of much theoretical speculation. This issue is addressed in more detail in the final essay of this section: a discussion by Richard Buchanan of the problems raised (and the problems ignored) at one recent international design conference. In this essay, Buchanan focuses attention on the nature and value of design studies as a complement to traditional design education and to new forms of design practice. He provides a framework for how diverse kinds of knowledge can be brought into design thinking in support of the development of a new discipline of design.

The Meaning of Products

Although the first section emphasizes the designer and the discipline of design thinking, the following section focuses the experience of the human beings who use products. Despite the best efforts of designers to determine the precise nature of products in order to effect their "designs upon the world," the career of products in human experience depends as much on the ability of human beings to make sense of the artificial world as it does on the intentions of the designer. The meaning of products is constructed through personal interactions that are not entirely within the control of designers.

Two themes in this section indicate the direction of contemporary investigations of the meaning of products. The first theme is interaction itself. It is expressed in the idea that human beings are not passive recipients of product messages, but rather are active participants in shaping meaning. The second theme is that the construction of meaning, although subject to the contingencies and vagaries of personal interest and attention, is disciplined and systematic, not random. This is expressed in the idea that although human users may not be conscious of the art of reading and interpreting the products around them, a variety of arts or disciplines do exist and may be articulated clearly by critics and others who explore how products gain meaning in one's personal and social life. Once again, pluralism is the hallmark of contemporary discourse in this area of investigation. The writers explore semiotics, grammar, rhetoric, logic, and dialectic, as well as social psychology, phenomenology, and product semantics, in an effort to understand the meaning of products.

In the first essay of this section, Martin Krampen introduces the concept of ecological semiotics in order to focus on the reciprocal relationships between humans and their built environment. He proposes the term *affordance*, coined by James J. Gibson in *The Ecological Approach to Visual Perception*, as the appropriate ecological equivalent of meaning, relating the different scales of architectural and industrial design through physiognomic qualities. What follows is a study of the physical and social affordances provided by products of different scales, with subtle implications for how the concept of affordance may be extended into the study of graphical user interfaces.

In the next essay, Martin Solomon continues the theme of grammatical analysis begun by Krampen, but without direct reference to the concept of affordance. He demonstrates how the designer's attention to the subtle qualities of punctuation in typography may guide a reader through the dynamics of the reading process, not only affecting typographic clarity, but supporting the entire feeling of a visual design. On first reading, Solomon's essay may appear to be a return to formalist considerations—the interaction of visual components in typography—but this would be a misreading of his intent. Solomon is making the passage from a formalist design aesthetic to the problems of rhetorical engagement with readers; the resources of grammar and punctuation serve communicative goals that, by extension, may reach to the new "reader-based" communication theory.

Graphic designer Ann Tyler takes a different approach to the problem of meaning. She turns explicitly to rhetoric in order to explore the delicate dynamic negotiation that takes place between the designer and his or her audience in effective visual communication. Instead of developing an art of interpretation like Krampen's ecological semiotics, Tyler focuses on an art of persuasion directed toward the different communicative ends of moving an audience to action, teaching, and exhibiting values. Like Frascara, Tyler tries to move the discussion of graphic design beyond formalism to a consideration of social significance. Her approach focuses on the arguments of visual communication, with formal devices (such as those discussed by Solomon or by writers who have taken from rhetoric merely the figures of speech) placed in the context of interactive argumentation.

Krampen, Solomon, and Tyler view interaction with users and audiences from the perspective of the designer—with the user as a kind of "implied audience" in the designer's method. In contrast, the prominent social psychologist Mihaly Csikszentmihalyi, author of *Flow: The Psychology of Optimal Experience*, turns directly to ordinary people to assess the meaning of art and design in their lives. This is a provocative project; it initially appears to demolish the pretensions of designers—particularly some of the modernists—who believe that they can impose order on otherwise chaotic environments. However, in the course of extensive interviews with "normal" people, Csikszentmihalyi discovers a subtle connection between the high arts and kitsch. Specifically, he explains how objects are assimilated into personal, private lives and are given symbolic meaning as expressions of the order of private experiences. Objects take on symbolic value with reference to one's personal history: "The meaning of our private lives is built with these household objects." Yet he suggests further that public art and design perform an analogous function for society as a whole: "The high arts help create order in the thoughts and feelings a given society has about itself." The artist and designer are able "to condense, in a given moment of historical time, the expressive striving of a great number of people."

S. Balaram builds on the theme of product symbolism and rhetoric by shifting our attention to Indian culture. He discusses the importance of rhetoric in Indian life for the creation and transmission of mythologies, with particular reference to Gandhi and Krishna. Then, in a very persuasive argument, he demonstrates how successful artifacts symbolically mediate between the stable mythological heritage of a culture and the fast-changing socioeconomic contexts of their use. He argues that the semantic meaning of products can both support and interpret the powerful mythologies of a rich culture such as that of India. This essay presents one of the most effective renderings of the relatively recent concept of product semantics, which was developed by Reinhart Butter and Klaus Krippendorff. As Balaram shows, product semantics is neither new nor dependent on the concepts of semiotics developed in the West. It is an element in the broader current of rhetorical thinking that links western and eastern cultures.

This theme is continued in the next essay, but in place of the art of rhetoric we see the art of dialectic as it is employed in contemporary phenomenology. In contrast to rhetoric, which reveals our motives and the designs we make on others, dialectic points toward the design or pattern of relationships, the harmonies and disharmonies, that we discover in the world. Gift giving is both a private and a public act. It is the focus of a set of mysterious dialectical issues that are probed by Clive Dilnot, who explores the phenomenological dimensions of the gift in human culture. What makes this essay a useful contribution to understanding the meaning of products are the paradoxes surrounding the act and the object. Is the gift the act of giving or is it the object given, and if it is the object given, then surely the object has more meaning in the context of a human relationship than a designer can begin to imagine. Dilnot's focus on the meaning of a gift implies many questions about the meaning of any product in the context of social processes. Indeed, Dilnot suggests that the act of giving could become the chief analogy for defining the character of all of the things that we make.

In the final essay of this section, Klaus Krippendorff returns to an emphasis on the designer as the maker of meaning. In this case, he seems to assume, as many designers do, that designers are surrogates for the user: The way a designer makes meaning is the way a user will reconstruct meaning. However, it is precisely this assumption that Krippendorff seeks to address. "No one can presume that form (the designer's objectified meaning) and (the user's) meaning are the same; hence, the need for product semantics to study how they relate." He explains the concept of product semantics and its relation to traditional semiotics, with emphasis on analytic and cognitive models of communication represented in a variety of schematic diagrams. The goal is to provide a corrective to thoughtless self-expression in design that fails to properly engage human users by ignoring how they make meaning through products. Designers are part of a broad ecological process, but their success depends upon their ability to understand "the hidden governance of collectively shared archetypes and mythologies whose meanings must be respected, grasped, tapped, and drifted with." This essay is one of the original, and probably the best, expositions of product semantics of the 1980s.

The meaning of products—what it is, how it is constructed, and under what principles—was often neglected as a problem in earlier design discourse. The essays in this section do not bring closure to this new effort. Rather, they open up possibilities for

The Idea of Design

further investigation in a variety of directions. Both designers and the general public can gain from a better understanding of what, how, and why products mean.

Design and Culture

The essays in the final section address the culture in which designers and communities of users function. Because the traditions of anthropology and cultural theory have paid insufficient attention to design as a cultural practice, its effects on individuals and the world at large have been little understood. Yet we do not live without products, and we shape our lives with the products that are available to us. Design thus operates culturally in a number of significant ways. First, products embody notions of identity that are socially recognized and thus become tokens in the symbolic exchange of meaning. Second, products become instruments for individual and collective action that ranges from the provision of essential needs to hobbies and pastimes. Third, products as tokens of economic exchange are central to the formation of global trade patterns and the accumulation of capital. Design policies are therefore integral to debates about national economic and social development, just as design philosophies and values on an individual and group level shape our reflections on how we might live.

Design as an element of planning policy and a means to reflect on the quality of life are both themes that are taken up in the essays included in this section. A new element in design discourse is the emergence of voices from cultures from which little was previously heard, particularly in Asia and Latin America. This has been prompted in part by the awareness of tensions that have arisen since the end of World War II from attempts to impose ideologies of western industrial progress on developing nations. Rajeshwari Ghose addresses this problem in her essay when she discusses the struggle to define a strategy of design that is appropriate to the conditions of life in India. Currently, she says, the "discourses on design are so overpowered by dominant first world methodologies that we must wait quite a while for new approaches to evolve and be cogently articulated." Ghose recognizes that many Asians hope to modernize their countries through paradigms of design that arrive from the first world. However, she sees the main task of the Asian designer as bringing some semblance of order into a fragmented environment in which continuities of traditional practices and methods coexist with the discontinuities of innovation. As Ghose makes clear, this can create a schizophrenic situation whereby Asian designers espouse the virtues of intermediate technology at international conferences while satisfying the demand for high-priced luxury goods from the affluent upper classes at home.

In her assessment of the issues that are central to the development of new design practices in Asia, Ghose employs a center-periphery model in which the center is occupied by developed first world nations that export the rationality of modernization to those on the periphery. Tony Fry also uses this model to characterize the difficulties of writing a design history of Australia, a country that has traditionally been perceived as marginal to design practice. Although Australia is not considered a developing country in an economic sense, Fry recounts an aspect of its history that illustrates comparable behavior in cultural terms. He points out in his case study of the Ford assembly plant in Geelong, Victoria, that Australians drew their own sense of design from an American model. Fry relates the dominance of American technology in Australia to Australia's exclusion from the master narratives of design history. He uses the example of the Ford plant to espouse a politics of marginality that must be engaged to redress the imbalances that he finds prevalent in design history.

Takuo Hirano's experience as one of Japan's first industrial designers provides a different scenario of engagement with western design and technology than Fry describes in Australia. Rather than succumb to a foreign influence, the Japanese used the techniques of American designers and manufacturers to build their own economy. In a period of forty years Japan went from "a country in which there were no designers, much less design education, to one where currently there are large numbers of designers and myriad design education opportunities." Initially trained as a craftsman, Hirano became a leader in this transformation. He chronicles the government's shift away from sending students abroad to building up its own system of design education. Unlike the Australian experience with Ford, Japan's encounter with Western design and technology led to a strong national production system in which design plays a central part.

In contrast to Hirano's emphasis on design as an instrument of modernization, A Cheng conveys the depth and richness of line as a traditional design principle in Chinese culture, making the point that line is an essential part of Chinese identity. He shows how widespread line is in different forms of artistic practice, such as ink painting, architecture, and creating shadow puppets. The recognition of this depth and the pervasiveness of a common principle in many different cultural forms is a good indicator of what is at stake and how much might be lost when design principles and methods are adapted from one culture to another.

Gert Selle does not see the same aesthetic stability in German culture that A Cheng claims for the traditional Chinese arts, nor is he satisfied with the kind of design that becomes a mark of identity for large numbers of people. He argues that most people derive their understanding of design from discount furniture chains and mail-order catalogs. For Selle, the politics of design are embodied in the striving to produce authentic objects. Making a Manichaean distinction between authentic and inauthentic products, he favors objects like Mario Bellini's Divisumma calculator, with which the user can establish a full sensual and emotional relation. The alternative, he says, is an empty aestheticism.

As Tomás Maldonado argues, objects not only shape feelings of identity, they also regulate human behavior. He focuses on comfort, which he finds to be a value that is far from innocuous. Along with privacy and hygiene, he claims, comfort is a control mechanism that helps in "structuring, and in the final analysis, stabilizing daily life in capitalist society." Objects become part of environments, such as domestic interiors, and these environments contribute to the construction of human consciousness and values. The modern kitchen, designed on the basis of an industrial model, became a site of production rather than a place to socialize. Likewise the bathroom reinforced notions of privacy and a different relation to one's body. Maldonado exposes a hidden politics of material culture that links objects of daily life to regimes of social order and control.

The theme of control is also evident in Barbara Usherwood's critique of London's Design Museum, which was written shortly after the museum opened in July 1989. Just as Maldonado finds political meaning in the design of the domestic interior, Usherwood claims an underlying ideological message in the seemingly neutral displays of the Design Museum. The intent of the museum, she argues, is to promote a better educated consumer, but she also points out the connection between the kinds of goods sold by Sir Terence Conran, the museum's principal donor, and those on display in the exhibits. She sees no signs of pluralism in the museum's exhibition philosophy, particularly in its Study Collection, nor does she find any sense of history's contingency in the descriptive labeling of the objects.

The Design Museum, however, is anchored in material culture which some cultural theorists believe is becoming marginal as we move into a period in which increasing attention is being paid to immateriality as manifested in such forms as virtual reality and the Internet. Sociologist Abraham Moles counters this claim by noting that "the seductive immateriality of today's world" rests firmly on a foundation of material support whose reliability and stability the designer must maintain. Moles refuses to identify the designers of immaterial culture as a new avant-garde by emphasizing that immaterial experiences, with their illusion of perfection, are only possible because of material equipment that is vulnerable to malfunction and deterioration.

The social organization of product maintenance, which was an ongoing theme of Moles's work, is also central to Victor Margolin's essay. Margolin expands the subject matter of design to include all of the elements that are required for a product to remain operative. He suggests that designers locate individual objects within a larger "product environment" that must also be designed. This environment includes the instruction manuals, help lines, replacement parts, and repair services that are necessary to sustain a working relationship with a complex product like a computer or an automobile.

When elements of the product environment are not available to support the product, the product itself suffers.

Conclusion

The authors in this anthology include designers, historians, rhetoricians, architects, psychologists, communications theorists, sociologists, philosophers, and semioticians. What we intend to demonstrate through the remarkable diversity of themes they have addressed is how fruitful the results can be when different perspectives are brought into relation in a spirit of shared concern for common problems. A design discourse based on a commitment to radical pluralism can open up new vistas for thought and enable us to circumvent the cul-de-sacs that arise when reflection becomes too rigid.

Contemporary design problems cut across many traditional specializations and disciplines, yet there is a tendency among some who study design to wish it institutionalized in the same manner as other subjects, following the model of the old learning. There are others, however, who see in design a path to the new learning, a path toward a better integration of theory, practice, and production. Unfortunately, design is often poorly understood and is regarded merely as an area of commercial application—a curiosity, a place of trade activity—instead of being regarded as a resource and a place for interdisciplinary collaboration that can give new life and purpose to the conception and planning of products.

To support this more fruitful regard for design, *Design Issues*, from which the essays in this anthology have been drawn, has, since its inception in 1984, consistently promoted a new place for thought where scholars and practitioners with different experiences and modes of reflection can share an interest in understanding design in all its ramifications. What some scholars are now calling "design studies" is not an effort to remove speculation on design from the day-to-day problems of design practice. If discussion moves, for a time, away from the design studio, it does so only to return with new ideas and understanding. The essays in this anthology indicate how diverse and productive a pluralistic field of design studies can be. They point toward a new culture of design that is connected in a variety of ways with other specializations of learning. If the essays are any indication, design is more like a site of research than an institutionalized profession, offering fresh opportunities to understand what it means to be human in the contemporary world and, at the same time, bringing theoretical understanding into direct relation with practice and production. Those who are able to integrate the abundance of new thought that can be brought to bear on common problems will create a new world without ignoring the past or neglecting the value of knowledge. This is the idea of design.

Victor Margolin
Richard Buchanan

Section I

Reflecting on Design

Wicked Problems
in Design Thinking
Richard Buchanan

This essay is based on a paper presented at "Colloque Recherches sur le Design: Incitations, Implications, Interactions," the first French university symposium on design research held October 1990 at l'Université de Technologie de Compiègne, Compiègne, France.

Introduction

Despite efforts to discover the foundations of design thinking in the fine arts, the natural sciences, or most recently, the social sciences, design eludes reduction and remains a surprisingly flexible activity. No single definition of design, or branches of professionalized practice such as industrial or graphic design, adequately covers the diversity of ideas and methods gathered together under the label. Indeed, the variety of research reported in conference papers, journal articles, and books suggests that design continues to expand in its meanings and connections, revealing unexpected dimensions in practice as well as understanding. This follows the trend of design thinking in the twentieth century, for we have seen design grow from a *trade activity* to a *segmented profession* to a *field for technical research* and to what now should be recognized as a new *liberal art of technological culture.*

It may seem unusual to talk about design as a liberal art, particularly when many people are accustomed to identifying the liberal arts with the traditional "arts and sciences" that are institutionalized in colleges and universities. But the liberal arts are undergoing a revolutionary transformation in twentieth-century culture, and design is one of the areas in which this transformation is strikingly evident.

To understand the change that is now underway, it is important to recognize that what are commonly regarded as the liberal arts today are not outside of history. They originated in the Renaissance and underwent prolonged development that culminated in the nineteenth century as a vision of an encyclopedic education of *beaux arts, belles lettres,* history, various natural sciences and mathematics, philosophy, and the fledgling social sciences. This circle of learning was divided into particular subject matters, each with a proper method or set of methods suitable to its exploration. At their peak as liberal arts, these subject matters provided an integrated understanding of human experience and the array of available knowledge. By the end of the nineteenth century, however, existing subjects were explored with progressively more refined methods, and new subjects were added to accord with advances in knowledge. As a result, the circle of learning was further divided and subdivided, until all that remained was a patchwork quilt of specializations.

1   From Richard McKeon, "The Transform-
    ation of the Liberal Arts in the
    Renaissance," *Developments in the Early
    Renaissance*, ed. Bernard S. Levy (Albany:
    State University of New York Press,
    1972),168–69.

2   Neo-positivism, pragmatism, and various
    forms of phenomenology have strongly
    influenced design education and practice in
    the twentieth century. If design theory has
    often tended toward neo-positivism, design
    practice has tended toward pragmatism
    and pluralism, with phenomenologists in
    both areas. Such philosophical differences
    are illustrated in the split that developed
    between the theoretical and studio courses
    at the Hochschule für Gestaltung (HfG) Ulm
    before its closing. The split between theory
    and practice in design is an echo of the
    difference between the predominantly neo-
    positivist philosophy of science and the
    exceptionally diverse philosophies of prac-
    ticing scientists. Design history, theory, and
    criticism could benefit from closer attention
    to the pluralism of views that guide actual
    design practice.

3   Walter Groupius was one of the first to
    recognize the beginnings of a new liberal art
    in design. In an essay written in 1937, he
    reflected on the founding of the Bauhaus as
    an institution grounded on the idea of an
    architectonic art: "Thus the Bauhaus was
    inaugurated in 1919 with the specific object
    of realizing a modern architectonic art,
    which like human nature was meant to be
    all-embracing in its scope. . . . Our guiding
    principle was that design is neither an intel-
    lectual nor a material affair, but simply an
    integral part of the stuff of life, necessary for
    everyone in a civilized society." *Scope of
    Total Architecture* (New York: Collier Books,
    1970), 19–20. The term "architectonic," in
    this case, transcends the derivative term
    "architecture" as it is commonly used in the
    modern world. Throughout Western culture,
    the liberal arts have similarly been described
    as "architectonic" because of their integra-
    tive capacity. Groupius appeared to under-
    stand that architecture, regarded as a liberal
    art in its own right in the ancient world, was
    only one manifestation of the architectonic
    art of design in the twentieth century.

4   John Dewey, *The Quest for Certainty: A
    Study of the Relation of Knowledge and
    Action* (1929; rpt. New York: Capricorn
    Books, 1960), 290–91.

Today, these subject matters retain an echo of their old status as liberal arts, but they flourish as specialized studies, leading to the perception of an ever more rich and detailed array of facts and values. Although these subjects contribute to the advance of knowledge, they also contribute to its fragmentation, as they have become progressively narrow in scope, more numerous, and have lost "connection with each other and with the common problems and matters of daily life from which they select aspects for precise methodological analysis."[1] The search for new integrative disciplines to complement the arts and sciences has become one of the central themes of intellectual and practical life in the twentieth century. Without integrative disciplines of understanding, communication, and action, there is little hope of sensibly extending knowledge beyond the library or laboratory in order to serve the purpose of enriching human life.

The emergence of design thinking in the twentieth century is important in this context. The significance of seeking a scientific basis for design does not lie in the likelihood of reducing design to one or another of the sciences—an extension of the neo-positivist project and still presented in these terms by some design theorists.[2] Rather, it lies in a concern to connect and integrate useful knowledge from the arts and sciences alike, but in ways that are suited to the problems and purposes of the present. Designers, are exploring concrete integrations of knowledge that will combine theory with practice for new productive purposes, and this is the reason why we turn to design thinking for insight into the new liberal arts of technological culture.[3]

Design and Intentional Operations

The beginning of the study of design as a liberal art can be traced to the cultural upheaval that occurred in the early part of the twentieth century. The key feature of this upheaval was described by John Dewey in *The Quest for Certainty* as the perception of a new center of the universe.

> The old center of the universe was the mind knowing by means of an equipment of powers complete within itself, and merely exercised upon an antecedent external material equally complete within itself. The new center is indefinite interactions taking place within a course of nature which is not fixed and complete, but which is capable of direction to new and different results through the mediation of intentional operations.[4]

What Dewey describes here is the root of the difference between the old and new liberal arts, between specialization in the facts of a subject matter and the use of new disciplines of integrative thinking.

Dewey observes, however, that the meaning and implications of the new direction are still not fully understood.

Nowadays we have a messy conjunction of notions that are

Reflecting on Design

consistent neither with one another nor with the tenor of our actual life. Knowledge is still regarded by most thinkers as direct grasp of ultimate reality, although the practice of knowing has been assimilated to the procedure of the useful arts;—involving, that is to say, doing that manipulates and arranges natural energies. Again while science is said to lay hold of reality, yet "art" instead of being assigned a lower rank is equally esteemed and honored.[5]

Carrying these observations further, Dewey explores the new relationship between science, art, and practice. He suggests in Experience and Nature that knowledge is no longer achieved by direct conformity of ideas with the fixed orders of nature; knowledge is achieved by a new kind of art directed toward orders of change.

But if modern tendencies are justified in putting art and creation first, then the implications of this position should be avowed and carried through. It would then be seen that science is an art, that art is practice, and that the only distinction worth drawing is not between practice and theory, but between those modes of practice that are not intelligent, not inherently and immediately enjoyable, and those which are full of enjoyed meanings.[6]

Although the neo-positivists courted Dewey for a time, it was apparent that his understanding of the development of science in the twentieth century was quite different from their understanding.[7] Instead of treating science as primary and art as secondary, Dewey pointed toward science as art.

The consideration that completes the ground for assimilating science to art is the fact that assignment of scientific status in any given case rests upon facts which are experimentally produced. Science is now the product of operations deliberately undertaken in conformity with a plan or project that has the properties of a working hypothesis.[8]

What Dewey means by "art" in this context is crucial to understanding the new role of design and technology in contemporary culture.

After a period in which natural knowledge progressed by *borrowing* from the industrial crafts, science entered upon a period of steady and ever-accelerated growth by means of deliberate invention of such appliances on its own account. In order to mark this differential feature of the art which is science, I shall now use the word "technology." . . . Because of technologies, a circular relationship between the arts of production and science has been established.[9]

What Dewey defines as technology is not what is commonly understood in today's philosophy of technology. Instead of meaning knowledge of how to make and use artifacts or the artifacts themselves, technology for Dewey is an art of experimental thinking. It is, in fact, intentional operations themselves carried out in the

5   John Dewey, *Experience and Nature* (1929; rpt. New York: Dover Publications, Inc., 1958), 357.

6   Dewey, *Experience and Nature*, 357–58.

7   The neo-positivist *International Encyclopedia of Unified Science*, which included Charles Morris's Foundations of the Theory of Signs, also included Dewey's Theory of Valuation. However, Dewey's Logic was ignored or ridiculed by neo-positivist logicians and grammarians.

8   John Dewey, "By Nature and By Art," *Philosophy of Education (Problems of Men)* (1946; rpt. Totowa, New Jersey: Littlefield, Adams, 1958), 288.

9   Dewey, "By Nature and By Art," 291–92.

sciences, the arts of production,[10] or social and political action. We mistakenly identify technology with one particular type of product—hardware—that may result from experimental thinking, but overlook the art that lies behind and provides the basis for creating other types of products.

From this perspective, it is easy to understand why design and design thinking continue to expand their meanings and connections in contemporary culture. There is no area of contemporary life where design—the plan, project, or working hypothesis which constitutes the "intention" in intentional operations—is not a significant factor in shaping human experience. Design even extends into the core of traditional scientific activities, where it is employed to cultivate the subject matters that are the focus of scientific curiosity. But perceiving the existence of such an art only opens the door to further inquiry, to explain what that art is, how it operates, and why it succeeds or fails in particular situations. The challenge is to gain a deeper understanding of design thinking so that more cooperation and mutual benefit is possible between those who apply design thinking to remarkably different problems and subject matters. This will help to make the practical exploration of design, particularly in the arts of production, more intelligent and meaningful.

However, a persistent problem in this regard is that discussions between designers and members of the scientific community tend to leave little room for reflection on the broader nature of design and its relation to the arts and sciences, industry and manufacturing, marketing and distribution, and the general public that ultimately uses the results of design thinking. Instead of yielding productive integrations, the result is often confusion and a breakdown of communication, with a lack of intelligent practice to carry innovative ideas into objective, concrete embodiment. In turn, this undermines efforts to reach a clearer understanding of design itself, sometimes driving designers back into a defense of their work in the context of traditional arts and crafts. Without appropriate reflection to help clarify the basis of communication among all the participants, there is little hope of understanding the foundations and value of design thinking in an increasingly complex technological culture.

The Doctrine of Placements

By "liberal art" I mean a discipline of thinking that may be shared to some degree by all men and women in their daily lives and is, in turn, mastered by a few people who practice the discipline with distinctive insight and sometimes advance it to new areas of innovative application. Perhaps this is what Herbert Simon meant in *The Sciences of the Artificial*, one of the major works of design theory in the twentieth century, when he wrote: "the proper study of mankind is the science of design, not only as the professional component of a technical education but as a core discipline for every liberally educated man."[11] One may reasonably disagree with aspects of Simon's positivist and

---

10 For Dewey, the arts of production, include the fine arts. He makes no sharp distinction between fine and useful arts.

11 Herbert A. Simon, *The Sciences of the Artificial* (Cambridge: M.I.T. Press, 1968), 83

empiricist view of design as a science[12] (as one may disagree with the pragmatic principles that stand behind Dewey's observation of the importance of intentional operations in modern culture),[13] but there is little reason to disagree with the idea that all men and women may benefit from an early understanding of the disciplines of design in the contemporary world. The beginning of such an understanding has already turned the study of the traditional arts and sciences toward a new engagement with the problems of everyday experience, evident in the development of diverse new products which incorporate knowledge from many fields of specialized inquiry.

To gain some idea of how extensively design affects contemporary life, consider the four broad areas in which design is explored throughout the world by professional designers and by many others who may not regard themselves as designers. The first of these areas is the design of *symbolic and visual communications*. This includes the traditional work of graphic design, such as typography and advertising, book and magazine production, and scientific illustration, but has expanded into communication through photography, film, television, and computer display. The area of communications design is rapidly evolving into a broad exploration of the problems of communicating information, ideas, and arguments through a new synthesis of words and images that is transforming the "bookish cultures" of the past.[14]

The second area is the design of *material objects*. This includes traditional concern for the form and visual appearance of everyday products—clothing, domestic objects, tools, instruments, machinery, and vehicles—but has expanded into a more thorough and diverse interpretation of the physical, psychological, social, and cultural relationships between products and human beings. This area is rapidly evolving into an exploration of the problems of construction in which form and visual appearance must carry a deeper, more integrative argument that unites aspects of art, engineering and natural science, and the human sciences.[15]

The third area is the design of *activities and organized services*, which includes the traditional management concern for logistics, combining physical resources, instrumentalities, and human beings in efficient sequences and schedules to reach specified objectives. However, this area has expanded into a concern for logical decision making and strategic planning and is rapidly evolving into an exploration of how better design thinking can contribute to achieving an organic flow of experience in concrete situations, making such experiences more intelligent, meaningful, and satisfying. The central theme of this area is connections and consequences. Designers are exploring a progressively wider range of connections in everyday experience and how different types of connections affect the structure ot action.[16]

The fourth area is the design of *complex systems or environments for living, working, playing, and learning*. This includes the tradi-

12 Although Simon's The Sciences of the Artificial is cited repeatedly in design literature because of its definition of design, it is open read with little attention given to the full argument. A careful analysis from the standpoint of industrial design would be a useful contribution to the literature. Such a reading would reveal the positivist features of Simon's approach and help to explain why many designers are somewhat disenchanted with the book. Nonetheless, it remains an exceptionally useful work.

13 See Richard Buchanan, "Design and Technology in the Second Copernican Revolution," *Revue des sciences et techniques de la conception* (*The Journal of Design Sciences and Technology*), 1.1 (January 1992).

14 The phrase "bookish culture" is used by literary critic George Steiner and is a theme in a forthcoming book by Ivan Illich, *In the Vineyard of the Text*.

15 The design of material objects includes, of course, new work in materials science, where a highly focused form of design thinking is evident.

16 Some of the psychological and social dimensions of this area are illustrated in works as diverse as George A. Miller, Eugene Galanter, and Karl H. Pribram, *Plans and the Structure of Behavior* (New York: Holt, Rinehart and Winston, 1960); Lucy Suchman, *Plans and Situated Actions: The Problem of Human Machine Communication* (Cambridge: Cambridge University Press, 1987); and Mihaly Csikszentmihalyi, *Flow: The Psychology of Optimal Experience* (New York: Harper & Row, 1990).

tional concerns of systems engineering, architecture, and urban planning or the functional analysis of the parts of complex wholes and their subsequent integration in hierarchies. But this area has also expanded and reflects more consciousness of the central idea, thought, or value that expresses the unity of any balanced and functioning whole. This area is more and more concerned with exploring the role of design in sustaining, developing, and integrating human beings into broader ecological and cultural environments, shaping these environments when desirable and possible or adapting to them when necessary.[17]

Reflecting on this list of the areas of design thinking, it is tempting to identify and limit specific design professions within each area—graphic designers with communication, industrial designers and engineers with material objects, designers-cum-managers with activities and services, and architects and urban planners with systems and environments. But this would not be adequate, because these areas are not simply categories of objects that reflect the results of design. Properly understood and used, they are also *places of invention* shared by all designers, places where one discovers the dimensions of design thinking by a reconsideration of problems and solutions.

True, these four areas point toward certain kinds of objectivity in human experience, and the work of designers in each of these areas has created a framework for human experience in contemporary culture. But these areas are also interconnected, with no priority given to any single one. For example, the sequence of signs, things, actions, and thought could be regarded as an ascent from confusing parts to orderly wholes. Signs and images are fragments of experience that reflect our perception of material objects. Material objects, in turn, become instruments of action. Signs, things, and actions are organized in complex environments by a unifying idea or thought. But there is no reason to believe that parts and wholes must be treated in ascending rather than descending order. Parts and whole are of many types and may be defined in many ways.[18] Depending on how a designer wishes to explore and organize experience, the sequence could just as reasonably be regarded as a descent from chaotic environments to the unity provided by symbols and images. In fact, *signs*, *things*, *actions*, and *thoughts* are not only interconnected, they also interpenetrate and merge in contemporary design thinking with surprising consequences for innovation. These areas suggest the lineage of design's past and present, as well as point to where design is headed in the future.

It is easy to understand that industrial designers are primarily concerned with material objects. But the research reported in design literature shows that industrial designers have found new avenues of exploration by thinking about material objects in the context of signs, actions, and thoughts. For example, some have considered material objects communicative, yielding reflections on

17 One of the early works of systems engineering that influenced design thinking is Arthur D. Hall, *A Methodology for Systems Engineering* (Princeton, New Jersey: D. Van Nostrand Company, 1962). For more recent developments in systems thinking, see Ron Levy, "Critical Systems Thinking: Edgar Morin and the French School of Thought," *Systems Practice*, vol. 4 (1990). Regarding the new "systemics," see Robert L. Flood and Werner Ulrich, "Testament to Conversations on Critical Systems Thinking Between Two Systems Practitioners," *Systems Practice*, vol. 3 (1990), and M. C. Jackson, "The Critical Kernel in Modern Systems Thinking," *Systems Practice*, vol. 3 (1990). For an anthropological approach to systems, see James Holston, *The Modernist City: An Anthropological Critique of Brasilia* (Chicago: University of Chicago Press, 1989).

18 Compare the Platonic, Aristotelian, and classic materialist treatments of parts and wholes. These three approaches to the organization of experience are well represented in twentieth century design thinking. For example, see Christopher Alexander, *Notes on the Synthesis of Form* (Cambridge: Harvard University Press, 1973).

the semantic and rhetorical aspects of products. Others have placed material objects in the context of experience and action, asking new questions about how products function in situations of use and how they may contribute to or inhibit the flow of activities. (Of course, this is a significant shift from questions about the internal functioning of products and how the visual form of a product expresses such functioning.) Finally, others are exploring material objects as part of larger systems, cycles, and environments, opening up a wide range of new questions and practical concerns or reenergizing old debates. Issues include conservation and recycling, alternative technologies, elaborate simulation environments, "smart" products, virtual reality, artificial life, and the ethical, political, and legal dimensions of design.

Comparable movements are evident in each of the design professions: their primary concern begins in one area, but innovation comes when the initial selection is repositioned at another point in the framework, raising new questions and ideas. Examples of this repositioning abound. For example, architecture has traditionally been concerned with buildings as large systems or environments. For nearly twenty years, however, a group of architects have aggressively sought to reposition architecture in the context of signs, symbols, and visual communication, yielding the postmodern experiment and trends such as deconstructionist architecture. Oxymorons such as "deconstructionist architecture" are often the result of attempts at innovative repositioning. They indicate a desire to break old categories, as in the now familiar and accepted "constructivist art" and "action painting." The test, of course, is whether experiments in innovation yield productive results, judged by individuals and by society as a whole.[19] Some experiments have fallen like dead leaves at the first frost, swept away to merciful oblivion. At present, the results of deconstructionist architecture are mixed, but the experiment will continue until individuals or groups reposition the problems of architecture and shift general attention toward new questions.[20]

A strikingly different repositioning is now beginning in the profession of graphic design and visual communication. In the late nineteenth and early twentieth centuries, graphic design was oriented toward personal expression through image making. It was an extension of the expressiveness of the fine arts, pressed into commercial or scientific service. This was modified under the influence of "communication theory" and semiotics when the role of the graphic designer was shifted toward that of an interpreter of messages. For example, the graphic designer introduced emotional colorings of corporate or public "messages" or, in technical terms, the graphic designer "coded" the corporate message. As a result, the products of graphic design were viewed as "things" or "entities" (material texts) to be "decoded" by spectators.[21] Recently, however, a new approach in graphic design thinking has begun to question

19 Such judgments are the measure of objectivity in contemporary design thinking. Without objectivity to ground the possibilities discovered in design, design thinking becomes design sophistry.

20 Architect Richard Rogers seeks to reposition the problems of architecture in a new perception of multiple overlapping systems, rejecting the notion of a system as "linear, static, hierarchical and mechanical order." According to Rogers: "Today we know that design based on linear reasoning must be superseded by an open-ended architecture of overlapping systems. This 'systems' approach allows us to appreciate the world as an indivisible whole; we are, in architecture, as in other fields, approaching a holistic ecological view of the globe and the way we live on it." *Architecture: A Modern View* (New York: Thames and Hudson Inc., 1991), 58. Rogers's notion of "indeterminate form" derives not from the ideas of literary deconstruction but from his innovative view of multiple systems. For more on Rogers's pointed criticism of postmodern architecture from the perspective of multiple systems, see *Architecture: A Modern View*, 26.

the essentially linguistic or grammatical approach of communications theory and semiotics by regarding visual communication as persuasive argumentation. As this work unfolds, it will likely seek to reposition graphic design within the dynamic flow of experience and communication, emphasizing rhetorical relationships among graphic designers, audiences, and the content of communication. In this situation, designers would no longer be viewed as individuals who decorate messages, but as communicators who seek to discover convincing arguments by means of a new synthesis of images and words.[22] In turn, this will shift attention toward audiences as active participants in reaching conclusions rather than passive recipients of preformed messages.

What works for movements within a design profession also works for individual designers and their clients in addressing specific problems. Managers of a large retail chain were puzzled that customers had difficulty navigating through their stores to find merchandise. Traditional graphic design yielded larger signs but no apparent improvement in navigation—the larger the sign, the more likely people were to ignore it. Finally, a design consultant suggested that the problem should be studied from the perspective of the flow of customer experience. After a period of observing shoppers walking through stores, the consultant concluded that people often navigate among different sections of a store by looking for the most familiar and representative examples of a particular type of product. This led to a change in display strategy, placing those products that people are most likely to identify in prominent positions. Although this is a minor example, it does illustrate a double repositioning of the design problem: first, from *signs to action*, with an insight that people look for familiar products to guide their movements; second, from *action to signs*, a redesign of display strategy to employ products themselves as signs or clues to the organization of a store.

There are so many examples of conceptual repositioning in design that it is surprising no one has recognized the systematic pattern of invention that lies behind design thinking in the twentieth century. The pattern is found not in a set of categories but in a rich, diverse, and changing set of *placements*, such as those identified by signs, things, actions, and thoughts.

Understanding the difference between a category and a placement is essential if design thinking is to be regarded as more than a series of creative accidents. Categories have fixed meanings that are accepted within the framework of a theory or a philosophy, and serve as the basis for analyzing what already exists. Placements have boundaries to shape and constrain meaning, but are not rigidly fixed and determinate. The boundary of a placement gives a context or orientation to thinking, but the application to a specific situation can generate a new perception of that situation and, hence, a new possibility to be tested. Therefore, placements are sources of

21 Although still a common and useful way of studying visual communication, this approach has lost some of its initial force in actual design practice because it has moved into personal idiosyncrasy and a search for novelty, which often distracts one from the central tasks of effective communication. This is evident, for example, among those graphic designers who have made pedestrian readings of deconstructionist literary theory the rationale for their work. Visual experimentation is an important part of graphic design thinking, but experimentation must finally be judged by relevance and effectiveness of communication. For a discussion of the limits of semiotics and design, see Seppo Vakeva, "What Do We Need Semiotics For?," *Semantic Visions in Design*, ed. Susann Vihma (Helsinki: University of Industrial Arts UIAH, 1990), g-2.

22 Swiss graphic designer Ruedi Ruegg has recently spoken of the need for more fantasy and freedom in graphic design thinking. Based on his approach, one might argue that efforts to introduce deconstructionist literary theory into graphic design have often led to a loss of freedom and imagination in effective communication, contrary to the claims of its proponents.

Reflecting on Design

new ideas and possibilities when applied to problems in concrete circumstances.[23]

As an ordered or systematic approach to the invention of possibilities, the doctrine of placements provides a useful means of understanding what many designers describe as the intuitive or serendipitous quality of their work. Individual designers often possess a personal set of placements, developed and tested by experience.[24] The inventiveness of the designer lies in a natural or cultivated and artful ability to return to those placements and apply them to a new situation, discovering aspects of the situation that affect the final design. What is regarded as the designer's style, then, is sometimes more than just a personal preference for certain types of visual forms, materials, or techniques; it is a characteristic way of seeing possibilities through conceptual placements. How-ever, when a designer's conceptual placements become categories of thinking, the result can be mannered imitations of an earlier invention that are no longer relevant to the discovery of specific possibilities in a new situation. Ideas are then forced onto a situation rather than discovered in the particularities and novel possibilities of that situation.[25]

For the practicing designer, placements are primary and categories are secondary. The reverse holds true for design history, theory, and criticism, except at those moments when a new direction for inquiry is opened. At such times, a repositioning of the problems of design, such as a change in the subject matter to be addressed, the methods to be employed, or the principles to be explored, occurs by means of placements. Then, history, theory, or criticism are are "redesigned" for the individual investigator and sometimes for groups of investigators.[26] As the discipline of design studies adds a reflective and philosophic dimension to design history, theory, and criticism, positive consequences are possible. Historians, for example, may reconsider the placement of design history as it has been practiced throughout most of the twentieth century and work to discover other innovative possibilities. Discontent with the results

---

23 The concept of placements will remain difficult to grasp as long as individuals are trained to believe that the only path of reasoning begins with categories and proceeds in deductive chains of propositions. Designers are concerned with invention as well as judgment, and their reasoning is practical because it takes place in situations where the results are influenced by diverse opinions.

24 Some placements have become so common in twentieth-century design that they hardly attract attention. Nonetheless, such placements are classic features of design thinking, and in the hands of a skilled designer retain their

inventive potential. Designer Jay Doblin sometimes employed a cascade of placements stemming from the basic placement "intrinsic/extrinsic." Doblin's placements serve as a heuristic device to reveal the factors in design thinking and product development. Other placements are described by Doblin in *Innovation, A Cook Book Approach*, n.d. (Typewritten.) With different intent, Ezio Manzini recently argued that the designer needs two mental instruments with opposite qualities to examine a design situation: a microscope and a macroscope. The mental microscope is for examining "how things work, down to the smallest

details," particularly in regard to advances in materials science. A further series of placements fill out the microscope to give it efficacy. See Ezio Manzini, *The Materials of Invention: Materials and Design* (Cambridge: M.I.T. Press, 1989), 58.

25 The ease with which placements are converted into categories should make any designer or design educator cautious in how they share the conceptual tools of their work. The placements that might shape an innovative approach for the founder of a school of design thinking often become categories of truth in the hands of disciples or descendants.

26 Thomas Kuhn was interested in the repositionings that mark revolutions in scientific theory. His study of this phenomenon, perhaps contrary to his initial expectations, has helped to alter the neo-positivist interpretation of the history of science. But Kuhn's "paradigm shifts" were never developed to their fullest intellectual roots in rhetorical and dialectical invention, which are based on the theory of topics. Chaim Perelman has developed an important contemporary approach to what is called here the doctrine of placements. See Chaim Perelman and L. Olbrechts-Tyteca, *The New Rhetoric: A Treatise on Argumentation* (Notre Dame: University of Notre Dame Press, 1969). See also, Stephen E. Toulmin, *The Uses of Argument* (Cambridge: Cambridge University Press, 1958) for a modern discovery of dialectical topics. Although remote from the immediate interests of designers, these works are cited because they deal with practical reasoning and have important bearing on aspects of design theory, including the logic of decision making discussed in Simon's *The Sciences of the Artificial.*

27 In order to solve such problems, more attention should be given to the various conceptions of design held by designers in the past. This would reposition design history from material objects or "things" to thought and action. In other words, what designers say and do, the history of their art as philosophy and practice. For a discussion of the subject matter of design history, see Victor Margolin, "Design History or Design Studies: Subject Matter and Methods," *Design Studies*, vol. 13, no. 2 (April 1992): 104–16.

28 The phrase "non-dimensional images" refers to all images created in the mind as part of design thinking and, in particular, to the various schematizations of conceptual placements (e.g., hierarchical, horizontal, or in matrix and table form) that may aid invention.

of current design history suggests that new repositionings are called for if the discipline is to retain vitality and relevance to contemporary problems.[27]

The doctrine of placements will require further development if it is to be recognized as a tool in design studies and design thinking, but it can also be a surprisingly precise way of addressing conceptual space and the non-dimensional images from which concrete possibilities emerge for testing in objective circumstances.[28] The natural and spontaneous use of placements by designers is already evident; an explicit understanding of the doctrine of placements will make it an important element of design as a liberal art.

All men and women require a liberal art of design to live well in the complexity of the framework based in signs, things, actions, and thoughts. On one hand, such an art will enable individuals to participate more directly in this framework and contribute to its development. On the other, professional designers could be regarded as masters in its exploration. The ability of designers to discover new relationships among signs, things, actions, and thoughts is one indication that design is not merely a technical specialization but a new liberal art.

The Wicked Problems Theory of Design

Recent conferences on design are evidence of a coherent, if not always systematic, effort to reach a clearer understanding of design as an integrative discipline. However, the participants, who increasingly come from diverse professions and academic disciplines, are not drawn together because they share a common definition of design a common methodology, a common philosophy, or even a common set of objects to which everyone agrees that the term "design" should be applied. They are drawn together because they share a mutual interest in a common theme: the *conception and planning of the artificial*. Different definitions of design and different specifications of the methodology of design are variations of this broad theme, each a concrete exploration of what is possible in the development of its meanings and implications. Communication is possible at such meetings because the results of research and discussion, despite wide differences in intellectual and practical perspectives, are always connected by this theme and, therefore are supplemental. This is only possible, of course, if individuals have the wit to discover what is useful in each other's work and can cast the material in terms of their own vision of design thinking.

Members of the scientific community, however, must be puzzled by the types of problems addressed by professional designers and by the patterns of reasoning they employ. While scientists share in the new liberal art of design thinking, they are also masters of specialized subject matters and their related methods, as found in physics, chemistry, biology, mathematics, the social sciences, or one of the many subfields into which these sciences have been divided.[29]

This creates one of the central problems of communication between scientists and designers, because the problems addressed by designers seldom fall solely within the boundaries of any one of these subject matters.

The problem of communication between scientists and designers was evident in a special conference on design theory held in New York in 1974.[30] This conference was interesting for several reasons, the most significant directly related to the content of the meeting itself. Reviewed in one of the initial papers,[31] the "wicked problems" approach to design proved to be one of the central themes to which the participants often returned when seeking a connection between their remarkably diverse and seemingly incommensurate applications of design.[32] Also significant was the difficulty that most of the participants had in understanding each other. Although an observation of an outsider on the dynamics of the meeting, it is an excellent example of a "wicked problem" of design thinking.

The *wicked problems* approach was formulated by Horst Rittel in the 1960s, when design methodology was a subject of intense interest.[33] A mathematician, designer, and former teacher at the Hochschule für Gestaltung (HfG) Ulm, Rittel sought an alternative to the linear, step-by-step model of the design process being explored by many designers and design theorists.[34] Although there are many variations of the linear model, its proponents hold that the design process is divided into two distinct phases: *problem definition* and *problem solution*. *Problem definition* is an *analytic* sequence in which the designer determines all of the elements of the problem and specifies

29 This list could also include the humanistic disciplines and the fine arts, because there is as much difficulty in communicating between some traditional humanists and designers as between designers and scientists. This is evident in the persistent view that design is simply a decorative art, adapting the principles of the fine arts to utilitarian ends, held by many humanists.

30 William R. Spillers, ed., *Basic Questions of Design Theory* (Amsterdam: North Holland Publishing Company, 1974). The conference, funded by the National Science Foundation, was held at Columbia University.

31 Vladimer Bazjanac, "Architectural Design Theory: Models of the Design Process," *Basic Questions of Design Theory*, 3–20.

32 Graph theory, developed by the mathematician Frank Harary, also served to connect the work of researchers in many areas. It was reported by the organizers that Harary, who attended this conference and delivered the paper "Graphs as Designs," suggested that the basic structure of design theory could be found in his work on structural models. Whether or not Harary made such a suggestion, it is possible to see in graph theory, and, notably, the theory of directed graphs, a mathematical expression of the doctrine of placements. Comparison may establish a surprising connection between the arts of words and the mathematical arts of things, with further significance for the view of design as a new liberal art. "Schemata" are the connecting link, for placements may be schematized as figures of thought, and schemata are forms of graphs, directed or otherwise. For more on graph theory see F. Harary, R. Norman, and D. Cartwright, *Structural Models: An Introduction to the Theory of Directed Graphs* (New York: Wiley, 1965).

33 A series of conferences on Design Methods held in the United Kingdom in 1962, 1965, and 1967, led to the formation of the Design Research Society in 1967, that today continues to publish the journal *Design Studies*. Parallel interest in the United States led to the establishment of the Design Methods Group in 1966, which published the *DMG Newsletter* (1966–71), renamed the *DMG-DRS Journal: Design Research and Methods*, and then renamed in 1976 and published to the present as *Design Methods and Theories*. For one attempt to describe and integrate a set of methods used in design thinking, see J. Christopher Jones, *Design Methods: Seeds of Human Futures* (1970; rpt New York: John Wiley & Sons, 1981). Many of the methods Jones presents are consciously transposed from other disciplines. However, they all can be interpreted as techniques for repositioning design problems, using placements to discover new possibilities.

34 Rittel, who died in 1990, completed his career by teaching at the University of California at Berkeley and the University of Stuttgart. For a brief biographical sketch, see Herbert Lindinger, *Ulm Design: The Morality of Objects* (Cambridge: M.I.T. Press, 1990), 274.

35 Bazjanac presents an interesting comparison of linear models and the wicked problems approach.

36 The phrase wicked problems was borrowed from philosopher Karl Popper. However, Rittel developed the idea in a different direction. Rittel is another example of someone initially influenced by neo-positivist ideas who, when confronted with the actual processes of practical reasoning in concrete circumstances, sought to develop a new approach related to rhetoric.

37 The first published report of Rittel's concept of wicked problems was presented by C. West Churchman, "Wicked Problems," *Management Science*, vol. 4, no. 14 (December 1967), B-141–42. His editorial is particularly interesting for its discussion of the moral problems of design and planning that can occur when individuals mistakenly believe that they have effectively taken the "wickedness" out of design problems.

38 See Horst W. J. Rittel and Melvin M. Webber, "Dilemmas in a General Theory of Planning," working paper presented at the Institute of Urban and Regional Development, University of California, Berkeley, November 1972. See also an interview with Rittel, "Son of Rittelthink," *Design Methods Group 5th Anniversary Report* (January 1972), 5–10; and Horst Rittel, "On the Planning Crisis: Systems Analysis of the First and Second Generations," *Bedriftsokonomen*, no. 8: 390–96. Rittel gradually added more properties to his initial list.

39 Weltanschauung identifies the intellectual perspective of the designer as an integral part of the design process.

all of the requirements that a successful design solution must have. *Problem solution* is a *synthetic* sequence in which the various requirements are combined and balanced against each other, yielding a final plan to be carried into production.

In the abstract, such a model may appear attractive because it suggests a methodological precision that is, in its key features, independent from the perspective of the individual designer. In fact, many scientists and business professionals, as well as some designers, continue to find the idea of a linear model attractive, believing that it represents the only hope for a "logical" understanding of the design process. However, some critics were quick to point out two obvious points of weakness: one, the actual sequence of design thinking and decision making is not a simple linear process; and two, the problems addressed by designers do not, in actual practice, yield to any linear analysis and synthesis yet proposed.[35]

Rittel argued that most of the problems addressed by designers are *wicked problems*.[36] As described in the first published report of Rittel's idea, *wicked problems* are a "class of social system problems which are ill-formulated, where the information is confusing, where there are many clients and decision makers with conflicting values, and where the ramifications in the whole system are thoroughly confusing."[37] This is an amusing description of what confronts designers in every new situation. But most important, it points toward a fundamental issue that lies behind practice: the relationship between *determinacy* and *indeterminacy* in design thinking. The linear model of design thinking is based on *determinate* problems which have definite conditions. The designer's task is to identify those conditions precisely and then calculate a solution. In contrast, the *wicked-problems* approach suggests that there is a fundamental *indeterminacy* in all but the most trivial design problems— problems where, as Rittel suggests, the "wickedness" has already been taken out to yield determinate or analytic problems.

To understand what this means, it is important to recognize that *indeterminacy* is quite different from *undetermined*. Indeterminacy implies that there are no definitive conditions or limits to design problems. This is evident, for example, in the ten properties of *wicked problems* that Rittel initially identified in 1972.[38]

1 *Wicked problems* have no definitive formulation, but every formulation of a *wicked problem* corresponds to the formulation of a solution.

2 *Wicked problems* have no stopping rules.

3 Solutions to *wicked problems* cannot be true or false, only good or bad.

4 In solving *wicked problems* there is no exhaustive list of admissible operations.

5 For every *wicked problem* there is always more than one possible explanation, with explanations depending on the *Weltanschauung* of the designer.[39]

Reflecting on Design

40   This property suggests the systems aspect of Rittel's approach.

41   Rittel's example is drawn from architecture, where it is not feasible to rebuild a flawed building. Perhaps the general property should be described as "entrapment" in a line of design thinking. Designers as well as their clients or managers are often "entrapped" during the development phase of a new product and are unable, for good or bad reasons, to terminate a weak design. For a brief illustration of entrapment in the product development process of a small midwestern company, see Richard Buchanan, "Wicked Problems: Managing the Entrapment Trap," *Innovation*, 10:3 (Summer, 1991).

42   There is one case in which even the subject matters of the sciences are indeterminate. The working hypotheses of scientists invariably reflect distinctive philosophic perspectives on and interpretations of what constitutes nature and natural processes. This is a factor in accounting for the surprising pluralism of philosophies among practicing scientists and suggests that even science is shaped by an application of design thinking, developed along the lines of Dewey's notion of "intentional operations." Even from this perspective, however, scientists are concerned with understanding the universal properties of what is, while designers are concerned with conceiving and planning a particular that does not yet exist. Indeterminacy for the scientist is on the level of second-intention, while the subject matter remains, at the level of first-intention, determinate in the manner described. For the designer, indeterminacy belongs to both first- and second-intention.

43   For a brief discussion of different conceptions of subject matter on this level held by three contemporary designers, Ezio Manzini, Gaetano Pesce, and Emilio Ambaz, see Richard Buchanan, "Metaphors, Narratives, and Fables in New Design Thinking," *Design Issues*, vol. 8, no. 1 (Fall, 1990): 78–84. Without understanding a designer's view of subject matter on the general level, there is little intelligibility in the shifts that occur when a designer moves, for example, from designing domestic products to graphic design or architecture. Such shifts are usually described in terms of

6   Every *wicked problem* is a symptom of another, "higher level," problem.[40]

7   No formulation and solution of a *wicked problem* has a definitive test.

8   Solving a *wicked problem* is a "one shot" operation, with no room for trial and error.[41]

9   Every *wicked problem* is unique.

10 The *wicked problem* solver has no right to be wrong—they are fully responsible for their actions.

This is a remarkable list, and it is tempting to go no further than elaborate the meaning of each property, providing concrete examples drawn from every area of design thinking. But to do so would leave a fundamental question unanswered. *Why are design problems indeterminate and, therefore, wicked?* Neither Rittel nor any of those studying *wicked problems* has attempted to answer this question, so the *wicked problems* approach has remained only a description of the social reality of designing rather than the beginnings of a well-grounded theory of design.

However, the answer to the question lies in something rarely considered: the peculiar nature of the subject matter of design. Design problems are "indeterminate" and "wicked" because design has no special subject matter of its own apart from what a designer conceives it to be. The subject matter of design is potentially *universal* in scope, because design thinking may be applied to any area of human experience. But in the process of application, the designer must discover or invent a *particular* subject out of the problems and issues of specific circumstances. This sharply contrasts with the disciplines of science, which are concerned with understanding the principles, laws, rules, or structures that are necessarily embodied in existing subject matters. Such subject matters are undermined or under-determined, requiring further investigation to make them more fully determinate. But they are not radically indeterminate in a way directly comparable to that of design.[42]

Designers conceive their subject matter on two levels: general and particular. On a *general level*, a designer forms an idea or a working hypothesis about the nature of products or the nature of the humanmade in the world. This is the designer's view of what is meant, for example, by the "artificial" in relation to the "natural." In this sense, the designer holds a broad view of the nature of design and the proper scope of its application. Indeed, most designers, to the degree that they have reflected on their discipline, will gladly, if not insistently, explain on a general level what the subject matter of design is. When developed and well presented, these explanations are philosophies or proto-philosophies of design that exist within a plurality of alternative views.[43] They provide an essential framework for each designer to understand and explore the materials, methods, and principles of design thinking. But such philosophies do not and cannot constitute sciences of design in the sense of any natural, social or humanistic science. The reason for this is simple: design is fundamentally concerned with the particular, *and there is no science of the particular.*

In actual practice, the designer begins with what should be called a *quasi-subject matter*, tenuously existing within the problems and issues of specific circumstances. Out of the specific possibilities of a concrete situation, the designer must conceive a design that will lead to *this* or *that* particular product. A *quasi-subject matter* is not an undetermined subject waiting to be made determinate. It is an indeterminate subject waiting to be made specific and concrete. For example, a client's brief does not present a definition of the subject matter of a particular design application. It presents a problem and a set of issues to be considered in resolving that problem. In situations where a brief specifies in great detail the particular features of the product to be planned, it often does so because an owner, corporate executive, or manager has attempted to perform the critical task of transforming problems and issues into a working hypothesis about the particular features of the product to be designed. In effect, someone has attempted to take the "wickedness" out. Even in this situation, however, the conception of particular features remains only a possibility that may be subject to change through discussion and argument.[44]

This is where placements take on special significance as tools of design thinking. They allow the designer to position and reposition the problems and issues at hand. Placements are the tools by which a designer intuitively or deliberately shapes a design situation, identifying the views of all participants, the issues which concern them, and the invention that will serve as a working hypothesis for exploration and development. In this sense, the placements selected by a designer are what determinate subject matters are for the scientist. They are the *quasi-subject matter* of design thinking, from which the designer fashions a working hypothesis suited to special circumstances.

This helps to explain how design functions as an integrative discipline. By using placements to discover or invent a working hypothesis, the designer establishes a *principle of relevance* for knowledge from the arts and sciences, determining how such knowledge may be useful to design thinking in a particular circumstance without immediately reducing design to one or another of these disciplines. In effect, the working hypothesis that will lead to a particular product is the principle of relevance, guiding the efforts of designers to gather all available knowledge bearing on how a product is finally planned.

But does the designer's working hypothesis or principle of relevance suggest that the product itself is a determinate subject matter? The answer involves a critical but often blurred distinction between design thinking and the activity of production or making. Once a product is conceived, planned, and produced, it may indeed

43 the designer's "personality" or "circumstances," rather than the continued development of a coherent intellectual perspective on the artificial.

44 Failure to include professional designers as early as possible in the product development process is one of the sources of entrapment in corporate culture. Professional designers should be recognized for their ability to conceive products as well as plan them.

Reflecting on Design

become an object for study by any of the arts and sciences—history, economics, psychology, sociology, or anthropology. It may even become an object for study by a new humanistic science of production that we could call the "science of the artificial," directed toward understanding the nature, form, and uses of humanmade products in all of their generic kinds.[45] But in all such studies, the activities of design thinking are easily forgotten or are reduced to the kind of product that is finally produced. The problem for designers is to conceive and plan what does not yet exist, and this occurs in the context of the indeterminacy of *wicked problems*, before the final result is known.

This is the creative or inventive activity that Herbert Simon has in mind when he speaks of design as a science of the artificial. What he means is "devising artifacts to attain goals" or, more broadly, "doctrine about the design process."[46] In this sense, Simon's science of the artificial is perhaps closer to what Dewey means by technology as a systematic discipline of experimental thinking. However, Simon has little to say about the difference between designing a product and making it. Consequently, the "search" procedures and decision-making protocols that he proposes for design are largely analytic, shaped by his philosophic view of the determinacies that follow from the natural laws that surround artifacts.[47]

For all of the insight Simon has in distinguishing the artificial as a domain of humanmade products different from objects created by natural processes, he does not capture the radical sense in which designers explore the essence of what the artificial may be in human experience.[48] This is a synthetic activity related to indeterminacy, not an activity of making what is undetermined in natural laws more determinate in artifacts. In short, Simon appears to have conflated two sciences of the artificial: an inventive science of design thinking which has no subject matter aside from what the designer conceives it to be, and a science of existing humanmade products whose nature Simon happens to believe is a manipulation of material and behavioral laws of nature.[49]

---

45 The earliest example of this science is Aristotle's *Poetics*. Although this work is directed toward the analysis of literary productions and tragedy in particular, Anstotle frequently discusses useful objects in terms of the principles of poetic analysis. "Poetics," from the Greek word for "making," is used by Aristotle to refer to productive science or the science of the artificial, which he distinguishes both from theoretic and practical sciences. Few investigators have recognized that poetic analysis can be extended to the study of making "useful" objects. When designer and architect Emilio Ambaz refers to the "poetics of the pragmatic," he means not only esthetic or elegant

features of everyday objects, but also a method or discipline of analysis that may contribute to design thinking.

46 Simon, *The Sciences of the Artificial*, 52–53.

47 For Simon, the "artificial" is an "interface" created within a materialist reality: "I have shown that a science of artificial phenomena is always in imminent danger of dissolving and vanishing. The peculiar properties of the artifact lie on the thin interface between the natural laws within it and the natural laws without." Simon, *The Sciences of the Artificial*, 57. This is one expression of the positivist or empiricist philosophy that guides Simon's theory of design.

48 For Simon, the equivalent of a wicked problem is an "ill-structured problem."

For Simon's views on how ill-structured problems may be addressed, see "The Structure of Ill-Structured Problems," *Models of Discovery* (Boston: D. Reidel, 1977), 305–25. This paper has interesting connections with the doctrine of placements because placements may be used to organize and store memories, and Simon is particularly concerned with the role of long-term memory in solving ill-structured problems. But Simon's methods are still analytic, directed toward the discovery of solutions in some sense already known rather than the invention of solutions yet unknown.

Design is a remarkably supple discipline, amenable to radically different interpretations in philosophy as well as in practice. But the flexibility of design often leads to popular misunderstanding and clouds efforts to understand its nature. The history of design is not merely a history of objects. It is a history of the changing views of subject matter held by designers and the concrete objects conceived, planned, and produced as expressions of those views. *One could go further and say that the history of design history is a record of the design historians' views regarding what they conceive to be the subject matter of design.*

We have been slow to recognize the peculiar indeterminacy of subject matter in design and its impact on the nature of design thinking. As a consequence, each of the sciences that have come into contact with design has tended to regard design as an "applied" version of its own knowledge, methods, and principles. They see in design an instance of their own subject matter and treat design as a *practical demonstration* of the scientific principles of that subject matter. Thus, we have the odd, recurring situation in which design is alternately regarded as "applied" natural science, "applied" social science, or "applied" fine art. No wonder designers and members of the scientific community often have difficulty communicating.

Design and Technology

Many problems remain to be explored in establishing design as a liberal art of technological culture. But as it continues to unfold in the work of individual designers and in reflection on the nature of their work,[50] design is slowly restoring the richer meaning of the term "technology" that was all but lost with the rise of the Industrial Revolution. Most people continue to think of technology in terms of its *product* rather than its form as a *discipline of systematic thinking*. They regard technology as things and machines, observing with concern that the machines of our culture often appear out of human control, threatening to trap and enslave rather than liberate. But there was a time in an earlier period of Western culture when technology was a human activity operating throughout the liberal arts.[51] Every liberal art had its own *technologia* or systematic discipline. To possess that technology or discipline of thinking was to possess the liberal art, to be human, and to be free in seeking one's place in the world.

Design also has a *technologia*, and it is manifested in the plan for every new product. The plan is an argument, reflecting the deliberations of designers and their efforts to integrate knowledge in new ways, suited to specific circumstances and needs. In this sense, design is emerging as a new discipline of practical reasoning and argumentation, directed by individual designers toward one or another of its major thematic variations in the twentieth century: *design as communication, construction, strategic planning,* or *systemic integration.*[52] The power of design as deliberation and argument lies in overcoming the

49 Although Simon's title, *The Sciences of the Artificial*, is a perfecdy adequate translation of what we have come to know in Western culture as Aristotle's Poetics, Simon seems unaware of the humanistic tradition of poetic and rhetorical analysis of the artificial that followed from Aristotle. This is not an antiquarian issue, because the study of literary production—the artificial formed in words—prefigures the issues that surround the study of the artificial in all other types of useful objects. Aristotle carefully distinguished the science of the artificial from the art of rhetoric. When Aristotle comes to discuss the thought that is presented in an artificial object such as a tragedy, he pointedly refers the reader to his treatise on the inventive art of rhetoric for the fullest elaboration of the issue. However, Simon deserves less criticism for overlooking this connection than humanists who have been amazingly neglectful, if not scornful, of the rise of design and technology in the twentieth century.

50 One example of such reflection is the interdisciplinary conference "Discovering Design," organized by R. Buchanan and V. Margolin and held at the University of Illinois at Chicago in 1990. The collected papers from this conference have been published as *Discovering Design: Explorations in Design Studies* (Chicago: University of Chicago Press, 1995).

51 Richard McKeon, "Logos: Technology, Philology, and History" in *Proceedings of the XVth World Congress of Philosophy: Varna, Bulgaria, September 17–22, 1973* (Sofia: Sofia Press Production Center, 1974), 3:481–84.

limitations of mere verbal or symbolic argument—the separation of words and things, or theory and practice that remains a source of disruption and confusion in contemporary culture. Argument in design thinking moves toward the concrete interplay and interconnection of signs, things, actions, and thoughts. Every designer's sketch, blueprint, flow chart, graph, three-dimensional model, or other product proposal is an example of such argumentation.

However, there is persistent confusion about the different modes of argumentation employed by the various design professions. For example, industrial design, engineering, and marketing each employ the discipline of design thinking, yet their arguments are often framed in sharply different logical modalities. Industrial design tends to stress what is *possible* in the conception and planning of products; engineering tends to stress what is *necessary* in considering materials, mechanisms, structures, and systems;[53] while marketing tends to stress what is contingent in the changing attitudes and preferences of potential users. Because of these modal differences in approaching design problems, three of the most important professions of design thinking are often regarded as bitter opponents in the design enterprise, irreconcilably distant from each other.[54]

What design as a liberal art contributes to this situation is a new awareness of how argument is the central theme that cuts across the many technical methodologies employed in each design profession. Differences of modality may be complementary ways of arguing—reciprocal expressions of what conditions and shapes the "useful" in human experience. As a liberal art of technological culture, design points toward a new attitude about the appearance of products. Appearance must carry a deeper, integrative argument about the nature of the artificial in human experience. This argument is a synthesis of three lines of reasoning: the ideas of designers and manufacturers about their products; the internal operational logic of products; and the desire and ability of human beings to use products in everyday life in ways that reflect personal and social values. Effective design depends on the ability of designers to integrate all three lines of reasoning. But not as isolated factors that can be added together in a simple mathematical total, or as isolated subject matters that can be studied separately and joined late in the product development process.

The new liberal art of design thinking is turning to the modality of *impossibility*. It points, for example, toward the impossibility of rigid boundaries between industrial design, engineering, and marketing. It points toward the impossibility of relying on any one of the sciences (natural, social, or humanistic) for adequate solutions to what are the inherently *wicked problems* of design thinking. Finally, it points toward something that is often forgotten, that what many people call "impossible" may actually only be a limitation of imagination that can be overcome by better design thinking. This is not thinking directed toward a technological "quick fix" in hard-

52 For Rittel's view of argumentation in design, see Rittel and Webber, *Dilemmas*, 19. Also discussed in Bazjanac, "Architectural Design Theory: Models of the Design Process," *Basic Questions of Design Theory*. Students report that late in his career Rittel came to recognize the affinity between his approach and rhetoric.

53 The necessary is sometimes referred to as "capacity" or "capability" in engineering. For a useful introduction to engineering design, see M. J. French, *Invention and Evolution: Design in Nature and Engineering* (Cambridge: Cambridge University Press, 1988).

54 Philip Kotler, the internationally recognized expert on marketing, has suggested that what many industrial designers object to in marketing should not be regarded as marketing itself, but as bad marketing. For new developments in marketing, see Philip Kotler, "Humanistic Marketing: Beyond the Marketing Concept," *Philosophical and Radical Thought in Marketing*, eds. A. Fuat Firat, N. Dholakia, and R. P. Bagozzi (Lexington, MA: Lexington Books, 1987).

ware but toward new integrations of signs, things, actions, and environments that address the concrete needs and values of human beings in diverse circumstances.

Individuals trained in the traditional arts and sciences may continue to be puzzled by the neoteric art of design.[55] But the masters of this new liberal art are practical men and women, and the discipline of thinking that they employ is gradually becoming accessible to all individuals in everyday life. A common discipline of design thinking—more than the particular products created by that discipline today—is changing our culture, not only in its external manifestations but in its internal character.

---

55 "Neoteric" is a term often associated in Western culture with the emergence of new liberal arts. Neoteric arts are arts of "new learning." For a discussion of neoteric and paleoteric liberal arts, see Richard Buchanan, "Design as a Liberal Art," *Papers: The 1990 Conference on Design Education, Education Committee of the Industrial Designers Society of America* (Pasadena, CA, 1990).

Reflecting on Design

Avatars of Design:
Design Before Design
Yves Deforge

Inasmuch as the purpose of this article is to draw the reader's attention to "the avatars of design" and particularly to "design before design," an appropriate approach is to isolate the term *design* temporarily and to consider very generally the fact that every technological object, that is, every object produced by human beings with a certain technical nature, always has two *functions*: utilitarian and sign. From the consumer's point of view, an object may have great utility and little value as a sign, or the contrary; what was utilitarian can become sign and vice versa. All determinations are possible and include those in which utility as itself is considered a sign (of purity, perfection, completion) and those in which the object serves no purpose: a useless object, a decorative object, an esthetic object.

From the viewpoint of production, the discussion can be summed up by two positions: *production* of a sign is involved and imposed on utilitarian production. For example, effective and light, beautiful and solid, perfectly fulfilling their utilitarian function—thus appear the Viking ships, which sailed under certain conditions with so many men on board.[1] This is a twentieth-century judgment, marked by some addition to the past. Such a judgment is also found in respect to other old ships, pottery, or tools. But perhaps for the Vikings, that utilitarian function, acquired at the cost of many trials and shipwrecks, was insufficient in the eyes of their contemporaries, so they added a sign function: vivid colors, purple or black sails.

All the war ships of the seventeenth and eighteenth centuries are marked by that double *function* of utility and sign. The utilitarian *function* was provided by the shipbuilders and carpenters, who strove to construct seaworthy vessels. The sign *function* was applied by specialized artists, sculptors, and decorators, whose mission was to make the menacing power and the grandeur of kings manifest.[2] Sometimes, they overburdened the structures of the ships to the extent that they forfeited their utility. An example is the warship Wasa, which capsized in Stockholm harbor the day it was launched.

Another example of a dual function is that of ancient physical instruments.[3] The artisans who produced these knew how to blend the utilitarian and sign functions intimately. The splendid decorations and Latin emblems that adorn these pieces are not superfluous embellishments; they arise in some way from the utilitarian function and underline or illustrate it. But we twentieth-century consumers, who no longer know very well what purpose these astrolab, armillary spheres, or quadrants for sighting serve, see only the sign (*Figure 1*).

1   "De l'archéologie à la navigation, la réplique d'un bateau Viking," *Chasse–Marée: Revue d'Histoire et d'Ethnologie Marine*, no. 30, 1987.

2   For example, Pierre Puget (1620–1694); see "Pierre Puget, Sculpteur du Roi à l'Arsenal de Toulon, Artiste ou Ingénieur?," *Revue Historique des Armées*, no. 1, 1974, 45–68.

3   Maria Luisa Bonelli Righini and Thomas Settle, *The Antique Instruments at the Museum of History of Science at Florence* (Florence: Arnaud, 1978).

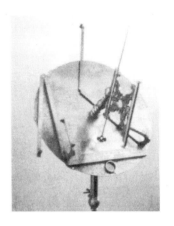

Figure 1

Considering what happens historically in production, the materialization of the utilitarian and sign functions results in two kinds of work: A single technical capacity [*technicité*] is that of the artisan who both conceives *and* realizes the work with imagination, taste, memory, and skill, sometimes aided by sketches, molds, or original or adapted models. Examining the grills in the doors, windows, and balconies of the old houses in the Marais section of Paris, for example, uncovers how intimately the ironworkers of the seventeenth century were able to blend the functions of utility and sign; less known is the fact that this ironwork is almost all copied from "collections of models" established by artists.[4] However, all the artisan-masters of that period received instruction in the academies and the guild schools, so they could make their own models and "give the sign" to their own productions. At present, some professional schools still provide this double technical capacity of utility and sign. The numerous trades that are referred to as *artisanat d'art* (sculptors, restorers, jewelers, bookbinders) have this capacity. The practitioners made (and continue to make) the reputation of the Parisian artistic handicrafts, when they are not mass-produced mechanically.

Two different types of technical capacity occur in succession: the work of the designer who gives the project its general look, including sign and utility, and that of the practitioners who realize the design. Easily recognizable are such classic pairs as architects/builders and stylists/sheet iron-workers. These divisions of labor have always occurred in order to produce *projects of great size*: pyramids, temples, castles, and cathedrals. The complexity of these objects and the time required for construction exceeded any individual's capacity to master both the conceptualization and its realization. Some support for reflection, a reference, a plan preserving the general outline of the project at its time of conception—a model or a design—was necessary.

Elsewhere I presented the hypothesis that such a reference point was necessary to produce important harmonious wholes collectively.[5] Until the nineteenth century, the production of these referential models was done *by artists*. In the literature of the time, designers were called architects or engineers, as they are today, but their "technical" formation was chiefly artistic. Their role consisted of graphically expressing a *design*, that is, an artistic goal bearing a sign function for the whole. Their technical capacity was limited to using a compass and ruler to execute the projects in conformity with what they knew of esthetics, harmony, and proportion: in short, they followed the rules of art.[6]

Proportions were a way of taking into account the results of what was known about the toughness of building materials or the equilibrium of constructions. These were especially important in obtaining *harmonious* constructions. The architects or engineers would have been hard put to do this; the realization of the de-

4 These collections are always consulted by local craftsmen at the Forney Library on Figuier rue in the Marais district of Paris.

5 Yves Deforge, *Le Graphisme Technique, son Histoire et son Enseignement* (Seyssel: Champ Vallon, 1981).

Reflecting on Design

signer's prescriptions was the business of the technicians, who worked with their own technologies. For example, the plans for Strasbourg cathedral, executed by different architects from the twelfth to the fifteenth centuries, were designs in the sense that they communicated the general intention for the cathedral, respecting the Golden Number and "divine proportions" *(Figures 2 and 3)*.[7] The architects also studied the proportions of similar older structures that were still standing, because they knew that monumental structures that did not respect proper proportions had an unfortunate tendency to collapse. Comparing the designs for the Strasbourg cathedral with reality, notable differences are apparent. Particularly, the spire on the right, on the marshy side, was not built, because its construction was judged too risky by the builders.

Renaissance engineers produced innumerable "theaters of machinery," whose use was related to hydraulics.[8] These ingenious machines could not be built as the technical means to make the parts and transfer motion—the action of gears and endless screws —to the parts was lacking. Another problem was the inability to build in the dimensions required. The proposed operation of these devices, is often antimechanical, which is the case with Leonardo da Vinci's famous inventions. This flaw matters little, as the design (intention) of Renaissance designers was not to define realizable machines, but rather to illustrate utopias that could eventually be

6   On that question of proportions, numerous theses have been developed. See Deforge, *Le Graphisme Technique* and see chapter 6 for a memoir, Albert Dürer, *Traité des proportions,* edited by Pierre Vaisse (Paris: Hermann, 1964).

7   André Fischer, *Das Geheimnis des Strasburger Munster* (Strasbourg: Fischer Verlag, 1963).

8   Bertrand Gille, *Les Ingenieurs de la Renaissance* (Paris: Hermann, 1964).

Figure 2

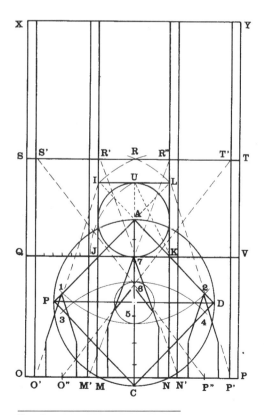

Figure 3

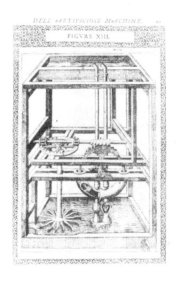

Figure 4

realized (flying, submarine travel, dominating and exploiting the forces of nature) and to give them all the signs of the impressive *(figure 4)*.

At the conceptual stage, accumulated technical capacity permits the treatment of both utilitarian and sign functions. It also entirely defines the object so that only the execution remains. Such is the structure of classical industrial production with planners on one side and *executants* on the other. That structure, which appeared toward the middle of the nineteenth century, was based on the fact that technological capitalism had the disposition to increase and become formalized as a result of the labor of technologists, mechanics, and scientists of that period.

Except for rare cases, the corpus of nineteenth century models used in relation to the conceptualization of objects corresponding to the utilitarian function was formed *inductively* by examining the dimensions and solutions of construction problems adopted by the builders. Thus, a logical conclusion could be that this technical capacity normally returned to the realizers, but, actually, the opposite has taken place:

- The engineers' training gradually has commanded their greatest skills.
- The know how of the builders has gone into the machines.
- The builders consequently have become executants. This is the well-known process of dichotimization.[9]

During the transition period, which lasted in some cases until the beginning of the twentieth century, the training of engineers still included the knowledge of construction technology or industrial science, as well as *an initiation into the knowledge of styles* and to academic art design. This training let them conceive of interesting ensembles in which the sign function was manifested by forms and decorations inspired by classical styles or by the imitation of architectural effects. The capacity of engineers to "give the sign" to their concepts was sustained by their artistic formation; the intensive employment of structures in cast-iron, particularly amenable to decoration, contributed to this education. This educational trend was the epoque of the "mechanization of decoration"[10] that would find its apogee in Hector Guimard's Paris metro entrances at the end of the century. Even if the doric typewriters, steam engines with fluted columns, or gothic frameworks seem surprising *(Figure 5)*, credit should be given to the engineer-designers of these large technical objects who made the praiseworthy and sincere effort "to give the sign" to their concepts, even before industrial design existed.

The Universal Exposition at the Crystal Palace in London, 1851, and the expositions that followed have been occasions not only to demonstrate responses to technological problems, but also to disclose the signs of the industrial art that was being sought. The machinery tools presented at the time of these expositions were

9   Yves Deforge, *Technologie et Génétique de l'Objet Industriel* (Paris: Maloine, 1985).
10   Siegfried Giedion, *Mechanization Takes Command* (New York: Oxford University Press, 1948).

Reflecting on Design

Figure 5

appraised for their utilitarian and sign functions by juries that equally appreciated their elegance, as much as their ingenuity, and utility. The case was not the same with the small industrial objects then beginning to proliferate. With some asperity, artists of the period denounced the ugliness of these objects and called for "the reconciliation of art and industry" while there was still time. Perhaps these artists were reacting to their elimination from the process of conceptualization. That is the sense of such movements as the Deutscher Werkbund or the Bauhaus. Very opportunely, some firms that had the means, such as the AEG in Germany, engaged artistic consultants whom they involved in the process of conceptualization. In most cases, however, artists were confined to the activities of styling or streamlining, which limited them to working with existant products to render them more esthetically pleasing and easier to market.

Thus was born the concept of industrial design. For Tomás Maldonado, "design is a creative activity that consists in determining the formal properties of objects that are produced industrially."[11] The skill of that definition lies in the fact that it involves design in the conceptual process (probably to differentiate it from applied design in which design is applied as a trimming to the products) and makes clear that industrial design requires a *specific technical capacity*.

When the debate as to the possibility of a science of industrial design that can be included in the engineering sciences opened around 1900, the engineer-designers—fortified by their recently conquered technology—abandoned all artistic claims and maintained that they did not need them to conceive of beautiful and significant products. *Beauty is rational*; it arises from the strict adaptation of any object to its utilitarian function or to the strict application of calculations. The great works of metallic art from the end of the nineteenth century, including Roebling's Brooklyn Bridge, Fowler and Baker's Firth of Forth Bridge, and particularly the Eiffel Tower, are good examples of technical capacity that is sure of itself and of its triumphant functionalism. Even in 1887 when work on the Eiffel Tower had scarcely begun, artists protested "with all their strength, with all their indignation, in the name of disregarded French taste, in the name of threatened French art and history, against the erection in the very heart of our capital of the useless and monstrous Eiffel tower."[12] To which Eiffel replied, "I believe that my calculations produce results that conform to the secret conditions of harmony . . . I claim that the curves of the four arrises of the monument, *such as my calculations have furnished them*, will give a great impression of strength and beauty."[13] Applied design was no longer possible in that perspective. The only concession Eiffel would authorize was the application of a few zinc decorations on the first story, where they would not disturb the total effect.

But the Eiffel Tower, first perceived as a gigantic sign of technical capacity, did not have any utilitarian function. To balance the

11 Tomás Maldonado is the author of a definition of design adopted by the International Council of Societies of Industrial Design (ICSID).

12 René Boirel, *Théorie Générale de l'Invention* (Paris: Presses Universitaires de France, 1961) and chapter 3, Deforge, *Technologie et Génétique*.

13 Danielle Quarante, *Elements de Design Industriel* (Paris: Maloine, 1985).

utilitarian and sign functions, Eiffel spoke of "the function of power" or "the function of endurance," and he endeavored for the remainder of his life to find some practical use for his tower as a meteorological station, a laboratory for aerodynamic studies and especially, in 1906, for electromagnetic waves. That example poses the very timely question of the relation between design and objects defined by a careful play of circumstances and conceived by *the application of deductive models*.

If the chassis of an automobile is conceived by an engineer, sent through a blast-furnace, and streamlined to lower the CX, what is left for the designer of the chassis, who is asked to intervene *after* the structure is defined? The condition is the same with an airplane, a racing vessel, and all objects, big or small, where physical relations react very strongly with the environment. When the engineer Tupelev was accused of copying the supersonic airplane Concorde with his TU 144, he very logically replied that, having to solve the same problems using the same deductive models and the same sort of calculations as the French and English team, he could only design the same aircraft.

On the other hand, if design is *a condition* of the problem to be solved and if deductive models integrate that condition, then one is in the presence of a design *implied in the conceptualization* and *implied in the education* of engineers and architects. The condition is that the technical capacity of the engineers and architects includes *the capacity to respond scientifically to both the function of utility and the function of sign*; this means that every conceptualizing of the object as use and as sign is based on deductive models.

Such is, in its extreme position, the claim of industrial design, according to the following:
- metaphysical design ("divine proportions")
- symbolic design (forms that speak)
- artistic design (applied and decorative art)
- functional design (utility and nothing but)

Industrial design, noting the importance of the sign function, proposes that the engineer possess a *double technical capacity*: that of the engineer and that of the designer. The engineer's great merit is to make tools of the trade (for example, analytical methods for forms and colors) that did not formerly appear in the engineer's panoply available to the designer. This, however, is also a weakness, because the formalization of industrial design, as with ergonomy and conduit design, and ergonomy and construction interpenetrating, dissolves into a single technical capacity. This single technical capacity of the engineer-designer at its extreme position hits upon a conception using a computer that deals equally with utilitarian and sign functions.[14] That integrative tendency *is also a reductive tendency*. Design reduced to the limits of technical capacity loses what had formerly been its strength and originality: a vision of the world, a

14   Yves Deforge, *L'Oeuvre et le Produit* (Seyssel: Champ Vallon, 1990).

choice for society, a leading *ideology* to which all techniques were submitted. That originality is what the "design before design" of the Renaissance engineers supplied when the engineers announced the ascendancy of humanity over nature. There are other examples as well: the Shakers when, in the image of the life they wanted to lead, they preached the rigorous simplicity of forms; William Morris, when he argued for socialism to publicize the return to guild-like organizations of artisans; and the founders of the Bauhaus from the first manifesto in 1919 on the reconciliation of the arts and trades until the formalism of the 1930s.

The question must then be asked, what ideologies could arouse concepts of products for today and tomorrow? It could be the scrupulous respect for cultural, ethnic, religious, and environmental diversities that produce alternative design and, in its strongest form, *interactive design*. This situation occurs when the *consumers* of the sign and utilitarian functions intervene directly in the conceptualizing of the product, fashioning it according to their needs and tastes, combining elements or modules. Nothing is imposed; all is proposed. Interactive design is now possible thanks to the informing of the production process and management that permits infinite suppleness in modular combinations, such as that seen in architectural kits and beginning to be seen in automobiles produced in batch production. Each product is then a work unique to the designer-consumer (of use and sign).

Yet the strongest ideology is certainly born from a realization of the dangers with pollution and the depletion of resources that are confronting society. *Ecological design* must be an example of an ideology that inspires the conceptualization of products. A small example worked on in the 1960s illustrates this point. The instructions given to the engineer were to design a disposable lighter with the capacity of a large box of matches and no more expensive. Moreover, it had to be esthetically pleasing, as they said then, ergonomic, and safe. A contemporary engineer-designer would have a whole arsenal of means available to address the problems involved; the computer, work on a CRT screen, research methods bearing on the utilitarian and sign functions, and so forth. The engineer from the 1960s, who did not have these means, nonetheless had to address these problems successfully as his lighter was always commercialized with some variations.

Nonetheless, neither the engineers of the 1960s nor the engineer-designers of today, whether they make small or large objects, seemingly innocent or eminently dangerous objects, are accustomed or able to pose this question: they make good products, but do they perform good actions?

Designing a disposable lighter is to participate in the waste of human labor and the energetic capital of the earth. That may appear minimal in the case of a lighter, but if all the materials thrown out daily in millions of lighters, washing machines, or cars are added up, the situation assumes the dimensions of an ecological catastrophe. It is then an evil action.

Of course the question posed reaches well beyond rational conceptualizations and the design of form and color. It is an ethical question, an old question, that technology has always avoided by extricating itself from responsibility but to which design in its final avatar must answer, not by piling technology upon technology but by a deliberate ideology.

Translated from the French by John Cullars

Moholy-Nagy's Design Pedagogy in Chicago (1937–46)
Alain Findeli

1   A good example of this situation is the CIRA Conference held in January 1989 under the title: "Design at the Crossroads," *CIRA Seminar Series Monograph* 2 (Evanston: Northwestern University, May 1989).

2   Although the author believes that the current historiography of the Bauhaus is missing some important points central to its philosophy, the general history of this institution and the main features of its pedagogical principles are assumed to be known by the reader. Frank Whitford's *Bauhaus* (London: Thames and Hudson, 1984) and Gillian Naylor's *The Bauhaus Reassessed* (New York: Dutton, 1985) provide the reader of English with a reasonable general overview of this history. The history of the American Bauhaus, however, (New Bauhaus, School of Design, Institute of Design) is still incomplete. The history of its founding is exhaustively related in Lloyd C. Engelbrecht's unpublished dissertation, *The Association of Arts and Industries: Background and Origins of the Bauhaus Movement in Chicago* (Chicago: University of Chicago, 1973), an abstract of which appeared in the catalog of the Centre George Pompidou's *László Moholy-Nagy* exhibition (Paris: CCI, 1976). The first complete monograph on the subject is the Bauhaus Archiv's catalog of the anniversary exhibition, *50 Jahre new bauhaus* (Berlin: 1987). Sibyl Moholy-Nagy's biography of her husband provides a very lively, although very personal, general framework to this period, *Moholy-Nagy: Experiment in Totality* (Cambridge: MIT Press, 1950, second edition, 1969). Additional information is provided in chapter I.2 of J. S. Allen's *The Romance of Commerce and Culture* (Chicago: The University of Chicago Press, 1983) and the general Chicago background is summarized by J. Fiske Mitarachi in "Dramatis Personae," *ID* 5 (October 1956): 69–80. Finally, a comprehensive survey of its first ten years (1937–46) is to be found in book II of the author's *Du Bauhaus à Chicago: les années d'enseignement de László Moholy-Nagy* (Paris: Université de Paris VIII, 1989).

Anybody who has been confronted with design education would readily admit that proposing a satisfactory definition of *design* is a rather risky, if not impossible, enterprise. Its definition indeed depends on whether design is considered to be an idea, a knowledge, a project, a process, a product, or even a way-of-being. Its fundamental characteristics may also vary according to the historical and geographical, that is, cultural context. Nevertheless, this endemic philosophical impasse has neither impeded the expansion and the sophistication of the design professions (graphic, industrial, architectural design, and so forth) in the twentieth century, nor the proliferation of theoretical treatises on design in the past two or three decades.[1] The situation becomes more problematic, however, when it comes to defining what design *education* could and should be. Indeed, it would be rather odd to imagine that a reliable design education program could be put together without an underlying model of design.

Actually, these models usually do exist but rarely, if ever, are they explicit or conscious. Whatever they may or may not be, they have one characteristic in common: they insist upon the multidisciplinary nature of design and they consider that design is to be found somewhere at the intersection of technology, art, and science. As a consequence, any design school will have a curriculum reflecting these various disciplines.

The German Bauhaus, founded by Walter Gropius in 1919, represents an important and significant endeavor toward devising both a general definition of design and a method of design education in the twentieth century. Although Gropius resigned in 1928 and the Bauhaus was closed in 1933, it was to be reborn in 1937 in Chicago under the name of the New Bauhaus.

The purpose of this essay is to propose a critical survey of the pedagogical method developed by Moholy-Nagy, founder and first director of the American Bauhaus in Chicago, from the original principles of the Bauhaus. This method will be validated by placing it in a more general philosophical context, namely Goethe's *Naturphilosophie* and Dewey's pragmatics. In the conclusion, this article shall draw some consequences regarding the future of design education and practice. But as an introduction to the essay, a short historical updating about the New Bauhaus might be helpful.[2]

New Bauhaus (1937–38), School of Design (1939–44), Institute of Design (1944–present)

The possibility of opening a Bauhaus in Chicago had been offered to Walter Gropius by the Association of Arts and Industries in 1937. Having already accepted a position at Harvard, Gropius suggested László Moholy-Nagy as the best candidate for the mission. Then active in England as a graphic and exhibition designer after his exile from Berlin, Moholy-Nagy took up the challenge with great enthusiasm. In June 1937, he was invited by Mrs. Stahle, executive secretary of the Association, to cross the Atlantic on the first ship available, so that the new school could be opened for the coming fall semester. Three months is a rather short time for building the complete program of a design school, but such a detail was certainly not perceived as an obstacle by the fiery Moholy-Nagy *(figure 1)*. The program of the New Bauhaus was first made public in September 1937, in a two-hour lecture he gave to an audience of 800 people packed in the ballroom of the chic Knickerbocker Hotel.[3] Opened on October 18, 1937, the New Bauhaus-American School of Design was to be short lived: a complex set of causes, among which the 1938 stock market minicrash was the most obvious, led the Association to withdraw its financial support in August 1938. To Moholy-Nagy and his colleagues, this decision came as a shock; however, instead of disbanding, they managed to raise enough private money and good will to rent a loft in downtown Chicago and to reopen as the School of Design in Chicago in February 1939. Student enrollment increased slowly, teachers were hard to find on the low salaries—if any at all—that were offered, and economic conditions worsened when the United States entered World War II.

Figure 1
First draft of New Bauhaus curriculum, drawn by Moholy-Nagy while crossing the Atlantic, August 1937. (Source: Hattula Moholy-Nagy Collection.)

3   In this opening speech, Moholy-Nagy described the content and intentions of the course. Only fragments remain of this manuscript in the archives, but a good summary appeared as an article by Moholy-Nagy: "Why Bauhaus Education?," *Shelter* (March 1938), 7–21.

Nevertheless, the first graduation ceremony took place in May 1942, with five successful students: Juliet Kepes, Myron Kozman, Nathan Lerner, Charles Niedringhaus, and Grace Seelig.[4] Meanwhile, Walter Paepcke, the president of the Container Corporation of America, began to develop a real passion for Moholy-Nagy's endeavors and convinced him to modify the school's administrative structure and reorient its pedagogical program to bring it more in line with the priorities of Chicago's skeptical businessmen. In March 1944, Paepcke became president of the board of the newly named Institute of Design (ID), with Moholy-Nagy as acting director. As a first consequence, the school was granted college-level accreditation and moved the faculty to new premises. With great difficulty, Paepcke and Moholy-Nagy managed to sustain the Institute of Design through the war years, despite a lack of students, the departure of some of the best teachers, and the rationing of materials. Unfortunately, these difficult years had exhausted Moholy-Nagy, who was never to reap the fruits of his venture as he expected and deserved. Three months before his untimely death in November 1946, the enrollment was close to 600 day and night students and the faculty numbered 28 teachers and assistants.

As indicated previously, the general structure of the course of study was based on Bauhaus principles: after a one-year requisite Preliminary Course, later renamed the Foundation Course in 1945, each student was to choose a three-year specialized workshop (*figure 2*). In 1938, the proposed workshops were the following: in Light, Product Design, Modeling, Color, Stage, Weaving, and Architecture, the latter leading into a two-year master's program. In approximately 1945, the Light workshop split into two parts: one

Figure 2
Structure of the first program of the New Bauhaus, September 1937. (Source: Ray Pearson collection.)

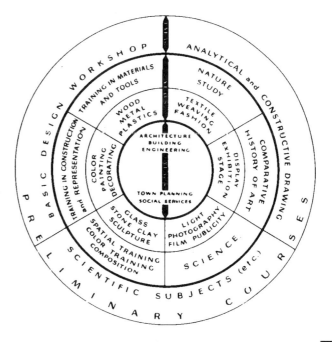

4   Described in a letter from Moholy-Nagy to Robert J. Wolff, June 7, 1942, Archives of American Art.

became the Photo and Film workshop, while the other merged with the Color workshop to constitute the Graphic Design workshop. After this reorganizing, there remained only four workshops in 1946: Product Design, Graphic Design, Photography and Film, and Architecture.

In 1949, under the directorship of Serge Chermayeff, the ID became part of the Illinois Institute of Technology (IIT). In 1955, the Architecture workshop finally disappeared from the curriculum, as it constituted an obvious annoyance to Mies van der Rohe's already established Architecture Department at IIT. The other three workshops remain at present as the main departments of the Institute of Design.

Although Moholy-Nagy considered the fundamentals of Bauhaus education still to be valid for the New Bauhaus, he nevertheless realized that the North American context and the evolution of science and technology would require some modifications in content. Two important additions were made to the original idea:

1 The domain of the artistic component of the curriculum was extended to the more technological arts, such as photography, film, and kinetic and light sculpture, and to nonvisual arts, such as music and poetry.

2 To the two basic elements of the formula that Gropius made famous ("Art and Technology: a New Unity"), Moholy-Nagy added a third element: science. As a consequence, the curriculum included a series of courses in physical, life, human, and social sciences, the coordination of which was entrusted to Charles Morris from the Department of Philosophy at the University of Chicago.

Before entering into a critical examination of the underlying theoretical and pedagogical principles of this program, some general remarks can be made as guidelines to understanding Moholy-Nagy's viewpoint and, indeed, any other school's explicit or implicit philosophy.

Schematically, two main ingredients are necessary to set up any educational program: a curriculum and a pedagogical method to transmit its content. The relationship between content and pedagogy determines two opposite poles between which even school necessarily hesitates or oscillates. In a design school, if the emphasis is on the curriculum, that is, if the school is content-oriented, the characteristic profile is vocational; if, on the contrary, pedagogics predominates, that is, if the school is process-oriented, the profile is, as Sir Herbert Read rightly put it, humanistic.[5] This intrinsic polarity is responsible for the kind of schizophrenia every design school has experienced since the Bauhaus was founded, revealing itself in oppositions such as theory/practice, art/technology, and the like. Indeed, the discipline of design has to be considered as paradoxical in essence, and any attempt to eliminate one pole to the benefit of the other inevitably distorts its fundamental nature. To perceive this

5   Herbert Read, *Education Through Art* (London: Faber & Faber, 1943), *passim.* This is one of the most penetrating works on the subject of design education, another one being Friedrich Schiller's *Letters on the Aesthetic Education of Man* (1795). John Dewey's contribution will be discussed later in this text.

Reflecting on Design

dualism as a dialectic, to transform this antagonism into a constructive dynamic, unquestionably constituted Moholy-Nagy's fundamental issue and philosophy in Chicago.

The Preliminary Course and its underlying didactics

The Preliminary Course is doubtless the most publicized feature of the Bauhaus pedagogy. Its principles are widely known, even if sometimes misunderstood. They have recently been subjected to heavy criticism, not all of it unjustified.[6] In Moholy-Nagy's words, this one-year course "offers a test of the student's abilities, . . . helps shorten the road to selfexperience, . . . embodies briefly the essential components of the training given in the specialized workshops, [and] gives [the student] ample opportunity to make a careful choice of his own field of specialization later."[7] More concretely, it can be outlined as follows: there are two main categories or aspects every designer or artist has to consider, one being the plastic elements (line, shape, color, texture, structure, volume, motion, space, and so forth) and the other, the specific tools and materials used to create form (brush, pen, power tool, camera, pigment, paper, clay, wood, plastics, and so forth). The Preliminary Course set out to familiarize the students with these two categories through carefully designed assignments and to allow them to choose the workshop where their talent and latent aptitudes, which the course had revealed, were likely to blossom in the following three years (*see figure 2 above*).

To meet these objectives, two general types of problems were identified and submitted to the students. In the first type, the student was asked to explore one specific plastic element in different media. For example, the expressive potentialities of texture were tested and experienced through drawing with pencil, pen, and brush; photography and printing; and through working with hand- and power tools (in different materials); as well as haptically, visually, and musically. In the second type, the process was reversed. Here the students were invited to explore the expressive potentialities of the various plastic elements with only one medium of their choice (*figure 3*). According to Moholy-Nagy, the underlying methodological axiom was the following: "Anyone who has experienced the mechanics of work in one medium, peculiar unto itself, will be capable of working successfully in other media too."[8] This last set of exercises led to the full comprehension of a medium's capacity, given that the proposed problems were of an artistic type, without the restriction of a specific function attached to the object. Incidentally, this latter feature later encountered the most criticism. However, the fact that the main objectives of the course were to rid every student of fear and self-consciousness, "the most serious psychological hindrances in life,"[9]—and to make "man, not the product, . . . the end in view,"[10] meaning that the object should be secondary to the process, should be remembered. This is precisely why only those schools that are

6   See, for example, Mark Gelernter, "Reconciling Lectures and Studio," *Journal of Architectural Education* 41/2 (Winter 1988): 46–52.

7   "Educational Program," *The New Bauhaus. American School of Design*, 1937–38 bulletin, The University of Illinois at Chicago Library, Special Collections.

8   László Moholy-Nagy, *Vision in Motion* (Chicago: Paul Theobald, 1947), 35.

9   Moholy-Nagy, *Vision in Motion*, 26.

10 László Moholy-Nagy, *The New Vision* (New York: Brewer, Warren & Putnam, Inc., 1930), 13.

Figure 3
The methodological structure of the
Preliminary Course in Chicago.

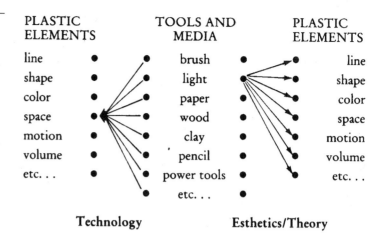

product- or profession-focused tend to criticize and misunderstand this kind of heuristic process called *maieutics*.

Superficially, these two types of problems seem symmetrical, one being the mirror-image of the other. But in reality, they are richer in content than apparent at first glance. A closer examination reveals that the first type of problem (one plastic element treated in various media) deals with the *technological* side of the design process, whereas the second type (one medium exploring all the plastic elements) pertains to the *esthetical/theoretical* aspect of design. The above diagram *(figure 3)* summarizes the pedagogical principles of the course, where Gropius's famous title "Art and Technology: A New Unity" is readily recognizable.

Reviewing the course of the students from a phenomenological point of view, the following remarks can be made: throughout the Preliminary Course, each student experienced a progression leading from an unconscious state to full awareness through three successive stages: (1) observation, perception, and description; (2) systematic exploration and analysis; and (3) conscious manipulation and action, leading to the eventual mastery of *design*. This whole structure seems considerably more sophisticated than at the original Bauhaus. It results from the introduction of the scientific courses into the curriculum. By transforming the art/technology polarity into the ternary system of art/science/technology, Moholy-Nagy tried to confer a scientific profile on the design process. According to his model, design ends up being the result of a dynamic relationship between art and science, revealed and materialized through technology. By introducing the scientific method into the basic structure of the Bauhaus curriculum, Moholy-Nagy made his program the first and most ambitious of its kind.[11]

The specialized workshops and organic functionalism
A thorough development of the theoretical and methodological foundations of all four previously identified workshops is beyond the scope of such an essay. The Product Design workshop shall be

11 I already noted that Charles Morris of the University of Chicago was in charge of the implementation of the scientific curriculum; he also taught "Intellectual Integration," a kind of introduction to epistemological evolution. A concise description of his theoretical model of the design process is given in his article, "Science, Art and Technology," *Kenyon Review* I (Fall 1939): 409–23.

discussed as an example. It was headed by Moholy-Nagy himself and assisted by such talented persons as James Prestini, Charles Niedringhaus, Nathan Lerner, Eugene Bielawski, and others, and its methodology would most adequately be called organic *functionalism*.[12]

Moholy-Nagy wanted this workshop to operate similar to a laboratory in which research would be conducted on new materials and techniques. Its program was composed of three components that were to be integrated in every project:[13]

- the problem of design
- the design of the problem
- the execution of design

The theoretical and philosophical aspects of design are easily recognized in the first component; the methodological, in the second; and the communicational and technological, in the third. This essay shall focus on the second component, the methodology of design.

Moholy-Nagy considered Louis Sullivan's famous dictum "form follows function" as an adequate guiding principle. However, it had to be interpreted in a new fashion:

> After a million years of trial and error, nature has produced well-functioning shapes, but human history is much too short to compete with nature's richness in creating functional forms. Nevertheless, the ingenuity of man has brought forth excellent results in every period of his history when he understood the scientific, technological, esthetic, and other requirements. This means that the statement, "form follows function," has to be supplemented; that is, form also follows—or at least it should follow— existing scientific, technical and artistic developments, including sociology and economy.[14]

The kind of functionalism Moholy-Nagy was promoting went beyond the materialistic model described and favored by Hannes Meyer at the Bauhaus, which was one of the major reasons for Moholy-Nagy's violent resignation in 1928.[15] According to Moholy-Nagy, one should take nature, the great designer, as an example; however, whereas nature has plenty of time to operate and to make the right selection after many trials and errors, the designer has to proceed more quickly with his or her project. This reality is why techno-scientific knowledge and esthetic judgment have to be developed and strengthened; they represent the human counterpart of nature's time-consuming processes.

This kind of biological analogy is a deep-seated fascination for humankind;[16] teleology, the art of adapting the proper means to a prescribed purpose, and evolutionism are its underlying scientific paradigms; *biotechnique*, the art of adapting natural structures and processes to technical artifacts, is the application of this analogy to

12 The Photo and Film workshop was also headed by Moholy-Nagy, with the assistance of James Brown, Robert Delson, Bob Graham, Eugene Idaka, William Keck, Nathan Lerner, Frank Levstik, Frank Sokolik, Edward Rinker, and Leonard Nederkorn. Its esthetical and technological principles derive widely from Moholy-Nagy's numerous publications on this subject. The Graphic Design workshop became the *oeuvre* of György Kepes, Moholy-Nagy's fellow Hungarian, associate, and close friend. Its basics are to be found in Kepes's still essential book, *Language of Vision* (Chicago: Paul Theobald, 1944) where Charles Morris's largely commented semiotical model is clearly apparent. The Architecture workshop was headed by George Fred Keck, followed by Ralph Rapson, assisted by Robert B. Tague and Jan Reiner. Its main concerns were industrialization and public housing, but, due to the war conditions, it never functioned at full capacity.

13 *Product Design*, mimeograph (2 pages), School of Design (1942), Ray Pearson Collection.

14 Moholy-Nagy, *Vision in Motion*, 33.

15 See Moholy-Nagy's declaration and imaginary interview in Krisztina Passuth, *Moholy-Nagy* (Paris: Flammarion, 1984), 395–98.

16 In his well documented book, *The Evolution of Designs* (Cambridge: Cambridge University Press, 1979), Philip Steadman leads us through the history of the teleological idea in the nineteenth and twentieth centuries. The evolution of this idea in American architectural design is examined in detail by Mark Mumford in "Form Follows Nature: The Origins of American Organic Architecture," *Journal of Architectural Education* 42/3 (Spring 1989): 26–37.

design. Moholy-Nagy was introduced to biotechnique through the book *The Plants as Inventors*,[17] written by the Hungarian biologist and theosopher Raoul Francé, active in Berlin at the turn of the century. Here are some excerpts from this work: "There is for everything, be it a concrete thing or a thought, only one form that corresponds to the nature of that thing;" "To every process belong, by necessity, fundamental forms of change;" "Every event has its necessary form;" "Every process produces for itself its technical form . . . every energy its form of energy" *(figure 4)*.[18]

The highly seductive power of such catch-phrases and their effect on Moholy-Nagy can easily be imagined. Particularly enlightening is the distinction Francé establishes between *shape* and *form* (a very classical scholastic theme, without which Sullivan's formula is incomprehensible), where the shape is inferred from the activity and the form from the purpose of an organism, so that "all natural forms are crystallized processes." Moreover, nothing could have delighted

Figure 4
Excerpts of Raoul Francé's *The Plants as Inventors* (two photographs).

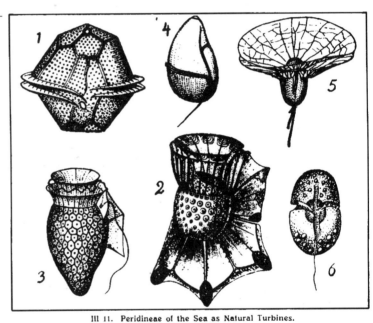

Ill 11. Peridineae of the Sea as Natural Turbines.
1. Goniodoma acuminatum. 2. Ornithocercus magnificus. 3. Dinophysis acuta. 4. Gymnodinium spirale. 5. Ornitho cercus splendidus. 6. Gymnodinium rhomboides.

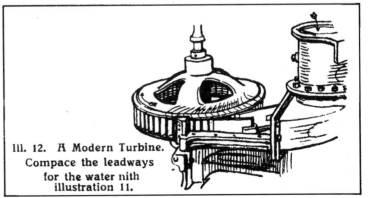

Ill. 12. A Modern Turbine.
Compace the leadways
for the water nith
illustration 11.

17 Raoul Francé, *Die Pflanze als Erfinder* (Stuttgart: Kosmos, 1920) translated as *The Plants as Inventors* (New York: A. and Ch. Boni, 1923).

18 Francé, *The Plants as Inventors*, 11, 12, 13.

Reflecting on Design

the constructivist artist Moholy-Nagy more than Francé's assertion that the fundamental technical forms of the natural world are contained in but seven elementary forms: the crystal, the globe, the plane, the pole, the ribbon, the screw, and the cone. The number seven bore a symbolic meaning in Francé's Platonistic and theosophy-inspired *Weltanschauung*. Moholy-Nagy reading this kind of literature and at the same time having on his faculty, as responsible for the intellectual and scientific courses, Charles Morris, one of the finest representatives of Rudolf Carnap's and Otto Neurath's logical positivism of the *Wienerkreis* is paradoxical. Paradoxical, but not necessarily contradictory, remembering Moholy-Nagy's own description of the Bauhaus: "*Bauhaus* is a coined word. It means 'building house,' not only in a material, but also in a philosophic sense."

This attempt toward a conciliation of the vitalist-spiritualist philosophy of Raoul Francé and the rationalist-positivist philosophy of the *Wienerkreis* and its American counterpart, The Unity of Science Movement, is the outgrowth, on the theoretical level, of the paradoxical essence of design.

Our notion of organic functionalism becomes clearer now. The functionalist aspect denotes a careful analytic, essentially scientific process whereby the students gather all pertinent information about their design problems in order to define the function that the design has to perform, not only in purely material and technological terms, but also in biological, psychophysical, and social terms, insists Moholy-Nagy. The organic aspect on the other hand is what makes the method phenomenological instead of strictly rationalistic and positivistic; this synthetic stage of the design process is achieved by *intuition*, because the complexity of the problem is beyond the reach of the sequential and verbalized process of the intellect.

Gestalt psychologists have confirmed the presence of both types of perception (analytic-focused, synthetic-holistic), and György Kepes has presented a convincing application of this model to visual perception in his book, *Language of Vision*.[19] In other words, the organic-functionalist method has to proceed from eyesight to insight for a proper outline of the design problem: "The vividness of this inner visualization is a measure of the designer's ingenuity," writes Moholy-Nagy, adding: "The unique ability of the genius can be approximated by everyone if only its essential feature be apprehended: the flashlike act of connecting elements not obviously belonging together." He further explains that "if (this) methodology were used generally in all fields we would have the key to our age—*seeing everything in relationships*." Long before the term *creativity* and the rather exaggerated confusing writings around it invaded the literature on design, and more than two generations before systems theory and phenomenology actually proved to be the essential paradigms of contemporary science, Moholy-Nagy, quite intuitively, made them the fundamental methodological principles of the design process. This method had been revealed to him by a

19   Kepes, *Language of Vision*.

deep meditation on cubist painting and by the practice of the most representative technique of twentieth-century esthetics (and epistemology): the collage.

Goethe, Dewey, and Moholy-Nagy

The model and method of organic functionalism, which Moholy-Nagy developed intuitively, refer implicitly to two major philosophical systems. The humanistic anti-materialism recalls Goethe's epistemological system; the methodological aspects refer to John Dewey's pragmatic philosophy.

The first philosophical attacks against the epistemological principles of empiricism and rationalism were undertaken by the German *Naturphilosophie*, of which Goethe was representative. Goethe was particularly interested in developing a new method of scientific investigation, which he described in his botanical treatises and his study on color. Trying to find an intermediate solution between the extreme and opposed methods of materialism and idealism, he proposed the term of *Anschauende Urteilskraft* (contemplative judgment) to describe the most adequate attitude suitable for apprehending natural phenomena; intuition was to be the only way to attain their essence.[20]

Moholy-Nagy's new vision and vision in motion are exactly the kind of vision Goethe was referring to. The reference to the *Naturphilosophie* is clearly noticeable when Moholy-Nagy applies this design method to his own pedagogy, which is a design problem of its own. First, he insisted on hiring only teachers who were also artists; his reasoning was that the teacher had to be familiar with the intuitive process, which is indeed inherent in artistic practice. Second, the student was considered as a living organism, both physically and spiritually, instead of an empty box to be filled with skill and knowledge. Creative potentialities were not to be gathered or imposed from outside the individual, but rather to be developed from inside, provided there was an adequate environment to do so. Goethe, however, pretended that the solution to a problem lay in the problem itself, in the phenomenon itself, not within the experimenter. The experimenter is only there to guide and to help the phenomenon disclose its true nature; in the same way, the teacher should be there only to help the students discover and then master their potentialities, because, according to Moholy-Nagy, "everybody is talented." This type of method was essentially nondirective, noninterventionist, and, in brief, nonviolent.[21]

Dewey's philosophical influence upon Moholy-Nagy was even more direct. When Elkan Powell, president of the Association of Arts and Industries, closed the New Bauhaus in 1938, Charles Morris tried to convince Robert Hutchins, president of the University of Chicago, to accommodate Moholy-Nagy's New Bauhaus. Given the profound disagreement between Hutchins and Dewey, upon whose pragmatic philosophy Morris drew to

20 Goethe's endeavors were despised and ignored by the scientific community of his time. Recalling one contemporary anatomist, he writes: "This remarkable man did not realize however that there is seeing and seeing, that the spiritual eyes had to work in constant and vivid alliance with the bodily eyes, otherwise one is faced with the danger of seeing and yet of seeing nothing," Goethe, *La métamorphose des plantes* (Paris: Triades, 1975), 171 (My translation).

21 The best interpreter of Goethe's philosophy and epistemology in the twentieth century was Rudolf Steiner (1861–1924). The pedagogic principles he developed for his Waldorf Schools seem to be most pertinent to our technological era. Although Steiner only visited The Bauhaus once for a lecture, there is a considerable affinity between the Waldorf and the Bauhaus pedagogies. Steiner's architectural work, on the other hand, usually classified as expressionist, is more exactly described by the Wrightian designation of *organic*, which bears the same meaning in the present essay. Most of the books of Moholy-Nagy's personal library have been lost or given to the Institute of Design. Very few remained in his private collection; among them: Goethe's *Farbenlehre*, considerably annotated.

Reflecting on Design

construct his theory of semiotics, this was hopeless. When Moholy-Nagy went to New York in November 1938, Morris gave him a letter of introduction to Dewey. In the letter he sent to Morris after the visit, Dewey recalls:

> I had a very interesting conference with Dr. Moholy-Nagy. I enjoyed meeting him both for his personality and for his unusual intellectual penetration. . . . He is such an unusual person that it seems to me very probable that he will succeed in doing what he wants to if sufficient time is taken for him to become adequately acquainted.[22]

During the visit, Dewey gave Moholy-Nagy his book, *Experience and Education*, which had just been published. Indeed, Dewey's *Art as Experience* was a compulsory textbook in the Product Design workshop of the ID. Innumerable parallels could be drawn between Moholy-Nagy's pedagogical principles and Dewey's powerful philosophy. Moholy-Nagy found in Dewey's work the theoretical foundation and justification of his own pedagogy. The experimental aspect (in Dewey's instrumentalist sense) of the course of study in Chicago is but one of the numerous examples of the analogy between both pedagogical and methodological models. Dewey's fundamental theoretical model is relativistic: no human phenomenon can be considered without its general physical and social environment. What Dewey calls a situation is constituted by the interactions between the individual (or the group) and the environment. *Situation* and *interaction* are Dewey's keywords; he calls them internal and external conditions, respectively. This simple model is instrumental in every discipline: psychology, education, sociology, political science, and so forth. An experience, in Dewey's terms, is a set of situations; the structure of the set, its *gestalt*, decides whether the experience is meaningful or not for the individual. Consequently, education is the art of conceiving situation sets susceptible to promote the growth of personality, that is, the art of proposing a meaningful "continuum of experience." To avoid the excesses of classical education, which focuses mainly on external conditions and, therefore, leads to coercion, and of progressive education, which focuses mainly on internal conditions and, therefore, leads to laxity, the educator has to produce a dynamic interaction between both extremes. Dewey's image of the mind as an active process rather than a thing in itself, also inspired by William James's psychology, is very evocative and helps to explain the basics of his educational method. The distinction between content-oriented (vocational) and process-oriented (humanistic) schools can be found in Dewey's differentiation between *work* and *occupation*:

> So far as the external result is held in view, rather than the mental and moral states and growth involved in the process of reaching the result, the work may be called manual, but cannot rightly be termed an occupation. Of course the

22 Copy of letter, John Dewey to Charles Morris, December 2,1938, Ray Pearson collection.

tendency of all mere habit, routine, or custom is to result in what is unconscious and mechanical. That of occupation is to put the maximum of consciousness in whatever is done.[24]

No clearer description could be given of Moholy-Nagy's intentions in Chicago.

Discussion

When Moholy-Nagy took up the challenge of rebuilding the Bauhaus in Chicago in 1937, he decided to maintain the same pedagogical principles he and his colleagues had put into practice in the German Bauhaus, but found it necessary to update the content of the program and the design method used in the workshops. Therefore, the major changes consisted not only in the introduction of scientific courses, but also and more important, in the promotion of a method of analysis of design problems adapted to the still-emerging scientific and philosophical paradigms of the twentieth century.

The changes conformed to the original aims of the Bauhaus, with the following difference: whereas Gropius sought the global model of a new society or, more accurately, of a new community, the advent of which would be accelerated by the new architecture, Moholy-Nagy believed that a new *individuality* was a prerequisite condition for a new society. This was even truer for future designers and architects due to the responsibilities inherent in their professions. For, just as Dewey considered that philosophers had to commit themselves within their sociocultural environment, so Moholy-Nagy averred that through their own practice, artists and designers should be *engagés*. His main concern, therefore, was to devise a pedagogical method that would encourage, in priority, the sense of responsibility within the students. Hence he insisted on a process-oriented education leading to an inner transformation, to a conversion, of the students.

How and why did the pedagogy and the design method that Moholy-Nagy promoted in Chicago (esthetic education, organic functionalism) guarantee the students a heightened sense of social responsibility? And more fundamentally, can ethical and moral values be induced by a pedagogical method based on esthetic education and by a less positivistic, more organic (systemic) design method? A deeper, phenomenological, inquiry into Moholy-Nagy's methodological premises will further clarify the first issue.[24] The conclusion will approach, if only superficially, the second issue, by placing it in our contemporary context.

In his book *Von Material zu Architektur*,[25] Moholy-Nagy discusses the progression of the arts from the simplest material quality of the sense of touch, through the successive stages of surface (painting, photography), volume (sculpture), and space (architecture), to the most ethereal quality of space-time. If taken literally, this process seems to be irrelevant to the practice and teach-

23   John Dewey, "The Pychology of Occupations" in *The School and Society* (Chicago: The University of Chicago Press, 1900, reprinted 1956),132–33.

24   For a more elaborate division of this aspect, see the author's "László Moholy-Nagy: Alchemist of Transparency," *The Structurist* 27/28 (1987/88): 4–11 and "László Moholy-Nagy, alchimiste de la transparence," in *Du Bauhaus à Chicago*, book 1, 230–72.

25   László Moholy-Nagy, *Von Material zu Architektur* (Bauhausbuch #14, 1929) translated as *The New Vision*, first English edition 1930 (see note10); revised and enlarged edition (New York: W. W. Norton Co., 1938).

Reflecting on Design

ing of design today, for the apparent emphasis it places on formal aspects. Formalism is the main accusation Moholy-Nagy, and the Bauhaus in general, have had to face; an accusation that may have been well-founded in some cases. But the significance of the above-mentioned progression unveils itself in a different light if taken symbolically. Moholy-Nagy gives some clues in this direction. His starting point is that everybody is capable of doing his or her best, provided the opportunity is granted; but *before* this opportunity is actually made available, no judgment should be made about an individual's personality and capacity. Such an opportunity is provided by the Preliminary Course: "The acquisition of technique and skills increases the expressive power of the individual; and with the accumulation of experiences his intellectual status is refined. The refinement in turn affects his emotional existence."[26] This process suggests the distillation of a crude material into a more subtle substance, each cycle yielding purer immateriality. The last step to be attained is the "growth of the individual within the group," and Moholy-Nagy called the artists-designers *integrators*, persons who, within their activity, are actually capable of expressing their cultural epoch on the highest level *(figure 5)*. To reach that ultimate level of transparency one must dissolve oneself (or, more accurately, one's self) into the phenomenological world. This view has of course nothing in common with the conventionally accepted image of the artists as detached individuals, secluded in their ivory tower. In Moholy-Nagy's mind, there is no contradiction in being *both* a good professional designer and a great artist.

Dr. Conrad Sommer, deputy director of the Mental Hygiene Service of the State of Illinois, who co-sponsored the Occupational Therapy course given at the ID in 1943–44, recognized the close analogy between Moholy-Nagy's educational approach and psychoanalysis in that they both reach down into the unconscious.[27] The closest and most striking analogy of this process is the timeless and traditional initiatory process practiced by the alchemists: by mastering crude matter technologically in order to refine it, alchemists also

Figure 5
Moholy-Nagy critquing student's work.
(Source Ray Pearson collection.)

26 Moholy-Nagy, *Vision in Motion*, 35.
27 The objectives of the Occupational Therapy course are described in Moholy-Nagy's article, "Better than Before," *The Technology Review* 46/1 (November 1943): 3–8. Dr. Sommer's declaration is published at length in *Vision in Motion*, 72.

Findeli, *Moholy-Nagy's Design Pedagogy in Chicago (1937–46)*

acted on their own consciousness and transformed it into a more precious—a wiser—entity.

Conclusion

The technological changes experienced in the postmodern era raise great hopes as to future emancipation of humankind. Dematerialization, one of the most noticeable and commented features of so-called postindustrial technology, may symbolically represent the unchaining of culture from the material constraints of nature.[28] However, there are now more than sufficient reasons for us to be a little more critical about the consequences of the Promethean frenzy of our century. All these radical changes doubtless have a significant influence upon design practice and, hence, on design education.

There is no question that the content of a design curriculum should be updated, as a result of the sometimes rapid technological evolution. But unless the fact that humankind undergoes as rapid a change on the biological level, as our material environment is considered, there is no reason why the pedagogical methods should *automatically* be modified at the same rate. In other words, a careful distinction should be made between the content of a design program and the pedagogical principles that are fit to transmit it.

28   For these questions, see for instance *Modernes et aprés: les immateriaux* (Paris: Autrement, 1985) and also *Design Issues* IV, nos. I & 2 (Fall 1988), special issue: "Designing the Immaterial Society."

This article has alleged that the first factor pertained mainly—but not exclusively—to the technological aspect of design, whereas the second factor dealt with its methodological and philosophical presuppositions. This distinction was a mere analytical commodity, the central practical educational issue still consisting in finding the adequate coordination between both factors.

In this respect, Moholy-Nagy's own presuppositions in Chicago may still have some relevancy today. At least, they deserve some second thought. The following premonition, written in 1946, gives an idea of his acute understanding of the wide-ranging problematics of design:

> The coming of an 'electronic age' brings the stringencies of the profit system into even greater conflict with the potentialities such an age has for richer sociobiological economy. . . . The need for this coordination makes more pertinent than ever the social obligations of the designer as a designer.[29]

Professional responsibility of architects, engineers, and designers is usually expressed in terms of technical performances of the produced objects, as well as, but more seldom, in terms of physical security of their users. At present, this is no longer sufficient, as every technical object or system may have, and indeed has, considerable anthropological and cultural (in a general sense) implications and consequences. Who else but the designers in the first place should be aware of these problems? More than half a century ago, Moholy-Nagy warned:

> To be a designer means not only to sensibly manipulate techniques and analyze production processes, but also to accept the concomitant social obligations. . . . Thus quality of design is dependent not alone on function, science, and technological processes, but also upon social consciousness.[31]

The general pedagogical approach of Moholy-Nagy, if correctly adapted to the new circumstances, still constitutes a valid preparation toward the tasks that await future designers; the new vision he fostered should bring them to a proper understanding of the complexity and intricacy of their time. The reason for its relevancy is that it was supported by adequate methodological and philosophical premises. In other words, if design is to survive our "paradigm shift" or "epistemological (r)evolution," it has to develop from a purely technical and skilled knowledge into a science, in the widest philosophical meaning of this time. This concept is precisely why the general curriculum of design schools should, in the future, be based on a general philosophy of design and as such derive, not only from techno-scientific considerations, but also from esthetic and ethical considerations.

29 Moholy-Nagy, *Vision in Motion*, 55.
30 Ibid., 56.

Beware of Steps

High Voltage

Corrosive

No Open Flame

Figure 1
Symbols for safety, an area left aside when graphic design is only viewed as an esthetic activity.

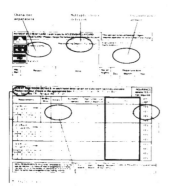

Figure 2
Structuring communication by design: design of forms based on human factors has been shown to make a difference that conventional designers trained in art schools had not achieved before applied psychologists took the lead. A user-performance-based approach where the analysis of the communication process is at the center.

Figure 3
Design beyond esthetics: alphabet for the learning disabled by J. Frascara and T. M. Nelson. Widely tested, it has proved to out perform other initial reading alphabets as a learning tool.

Graphic Design: Fine Art or Social Science?
Jorge Frascara

I thank the editors of *Design Issues* and particularly Victor Margolin, for their useful comments to my initial manuscript. The present version has very much benefited from their advice.

Toward a theoretical backbone for graphic design

Graphic design has existed long enough for its role in society to be easily understood. However, unlike architecture, literature, or the fine arts, it has developed without much theoretical reflection. It has evolved into a sophisticated practice in a piecemeal fashion, with scattered efforts aimed at the development of subareas, such as posters or books, but without either the critical apparatus in literature or the discussion present in architecture.

The aspect of graphic design that has attracted some discussion is visual style. But this discussion of style has several flaws:

- It overemphasizes the importance of the visual structure within an esthetic context.
- It omits problems of appropriateness.
- It leaves out certain areas of graphic design, such as signage, forms, timetables, maps, and educational material (*figures 1, 2, 3*).
- It omits the importance of ideas in the communication process, not distinguishing between visual creation and visual manipulation.
- It avoids problems of performance related to visual perception.
- It omits problems related to the impact that graphic communication has on the public's attitudes and ideas.

These flaws have led to several distortions, the most important brought about by the praise of modern avant-garde typography. How long will the praise of El Lissitzky continue? True, he made a strong impact on a few typographic designers whose work in graphic design was closely related to the practice of art and looked very similar to their paintings or the paintings of avant-garde artists of the time. However, was Lissitzky's contribution really positive? His visual language was tremendously abstract (*figure 4*), as inappropriate to mass communication as Schwitters's graphics using Pelikan ink motives were inappropriate for the product (*figures 5 and 6*). Pelikan ink, used for line drawing and calligraphy, was presented, surrounded by geometric typography, black and red bars, and rectangles. Not only did that imagery not express the product, but it did not even relate to the logo or the label. Why did

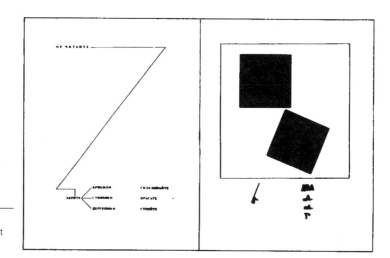

Figure 4
El Lissitzky, *Of Two Squares*, 1920. Abstract language directed at children.

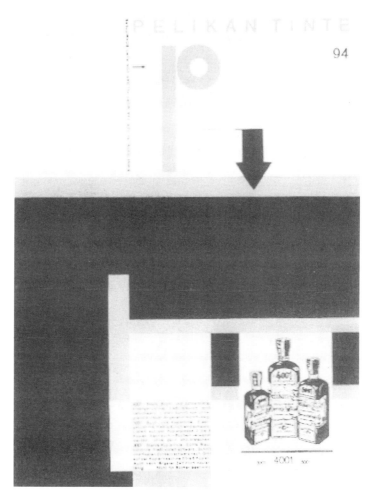

Figure 5
The pre-modern Pelikan logo: appropriateness of language with clear reference to the drawing ink medium.

Schwitters's designs include Pelikan ink bottles when the designs really related to constructivism, not to Pelikan.

Lissitzky was *interested* in improving communication, as his writing shows. This article, however, questions the apparent success of his works reproduced in design history books. He and other

Figure 6
Kurt Schwitters: Design with Pelikan ink. A case where the created image has nothing to do with the product or its label.

MERZ
1
HOLLAND
DADA

JANUAR 1923
HERAUSGEGEBEN VON KURT SCHWITTERS
HANNOVER - WALDHAUSENSTRASSE 5

Figure 7
Kurt Schwitters: Expression that is appropriate on the cover of the first issue of *Merz*.

Figure 8
Vilmos Huszar: Logo for *De Stijl* journal. A case of spontaneous appropriateness in visual style usual among artists who express their own ideas.

avant-garde artists made a major impact on the visual development of graphic design, but they also raised the importance of their esthetic approach to a point where the communication link with the common denominator they were addressing broke down. They seem not to have been aware that communication requires the sharing of codes. Although designers need not rely totally on the stereotypes, they cannot disregard the codes of the public; they should work with the public and improve its visual and conceptual language as much as possible, without breaking the communication link.

Lissitzky worked on a wide range of projects, some of them possibly less flashy and more useful than others, but the Lissitzky worshiped by many contemporary designers and design historians is the person who produced the quasi-abstract, constructivist, red and black pieces.

Although the quality of Lissitzky's, Schwitters's, and van Doesburg's designs in their own exhibitions *(figures 7 and 8)*, ideas, and publications can be praised, the fact that they failed to realize that their visual language was not appropriate in all possible cases must be acknowledged. The same is applicable to other artists who did some graphic design. Joan Miró was perfectly skillful in the promotion of his own exhibition *(figure 9)*, but Albers's promotion for a Lincoln Center Film Festival says a lot about Albers and little, if anything, about a film festival *(figure 10)*.

The excessive importance given to the avantgarde movement in the context of graphic design history is based on the failure of theory to recognize graphic design as something other than an art form. Furthermore, as an art form, graphic design is viewed only from an esthetic perspective, without enough consideration of communication and social significance. Surely, esthetics is important, but it is by no means the sole measure for quality.

Discussion should start with a working definition. Graphic design *is the activity that organizes visual communication in society*. It is concerned with the efficiency of communication, the technology used for its implementation, and the social impact it effects, in other words, with social responsibility. The need for communicative efficiency is a response to the main reason for the existence of any piece of graphic design: *someone has something to communicate to someone else*. This involves, to a greater or lesser extent, a perceptual and a behavioral concern.

The perceptual concern involves visual detection problems sometimes and communication problems all the time. Problems of detection and communication include visibility, legibility, and esthetics. The behavioral concern has to do with the way graphic communications affect the attitudes and conduct of their audiences. Advertising design is expected to make people buy products or services; political or ideological propaganda is expected to affect people's beliefs and actions; regulatory signs on highways are intended to organize the flow of traffic; teaching aids are supposed

Figure 9
Joan Miró: Galerie Maeght. Another example
of appropriateness of style.

Figure 10
Josef Albers: 10th New York Film Festival.
The poster expresses a lot of Albers and little
if anything about films. A case of communication failure.

to improve learning performance; bank notes are designed to make
forgery difficult and identification of one denomination from another
easy. This is the real measure of the performance of any and every
piece of graphic design and the proof that graphic design cannot be
understood in isolation but only within a communication system.

Social responsibility in graphic design is the concern for the
following:

- The impact that all visual communication has in the
  community and the way in which its content influences
  people.
- The impact that all visual communication has in the visual
  environment.
- The need to ensure that communications related to the
  safety of the community are properly implemented (*figure
  11*). This brief summary shows that the practice of graphic

design transcends the realm of esthetics. Pursuing the identification of the pioneers of graphic design in this context and seeing in what way El Lissitzky compares to Edward Johnston (*figure 12*) or to Jan Tschichold (*figure 13*) is therefore worthwhile. Interesting results might also be derived from comparisons between the contributions of Armin Hofmann and Giovanni Pintori when the focus of attention moves from a specific esthetic conception to communication efficiency. Although Hofmann created a beautiful style (*figures 14 and 15*), Pintori had a greater flexibility and a better understanding of the importance of appropriateness and created a feeling for Olivetti that still exists after 30 years (*figure 16*).

Although the concepts of communication and technological efficiency are common denominators for all areas of graphic design, several internal differences, depending on the subarea, need devel-

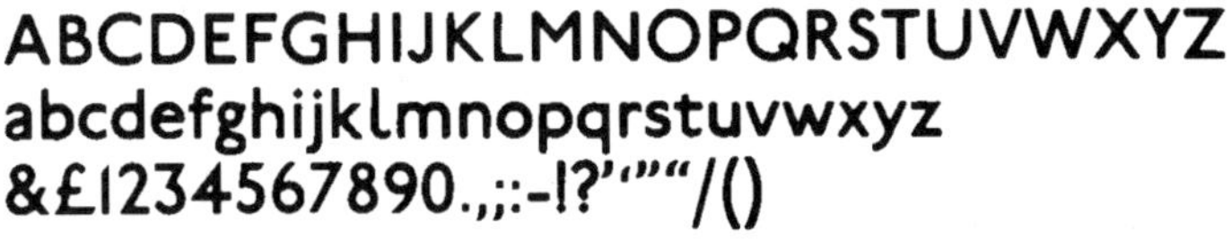

Figure 11   A case of lack of professional responsibility: actual size of a label for a contact cement container showing directions for use and warnings about toxicity (black type on red ground in the original).

Figure 12   Edward Johnston: London Underground type 1916. A no-nonsense typography for signage. A step ahead in communication at a time when ornament and self-expression were the common alternatives.

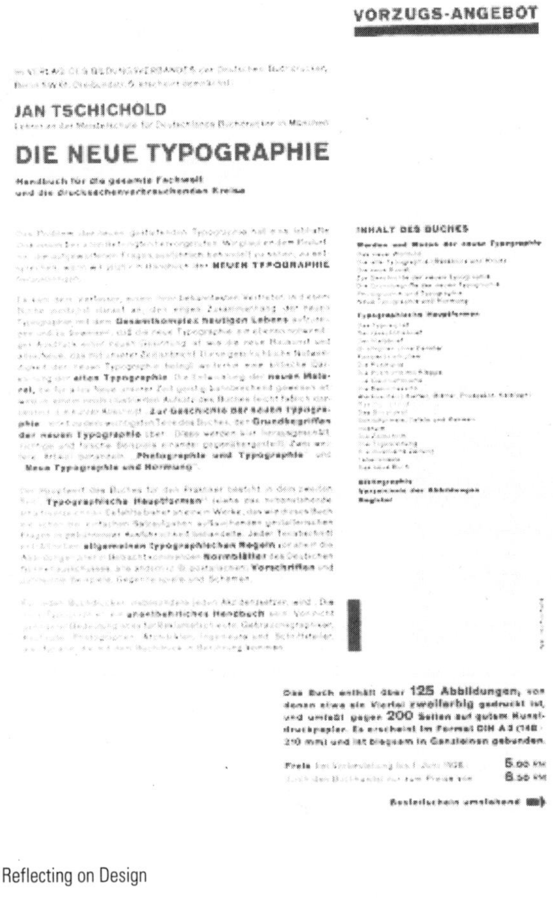

ABCDEFGHIJKLMNOPQRSTUVWXYZ
abcdefghijklmnopqrstuvwxyz
&£1234567890.,;:-!?'""'/()

Figure 13
Jan Tschichold: Die neue typographie. A new approach to typographic design that combined esthetics with a strong concern for the organization of information.

oping. The things graphic designers should know to promote the sale of cookies are very different from those they need to know to teach a five-year-old how to read. Every time a graphic designer really wishes to achieve the objectives of the communication proposed, the cross-disciplinary nature of the profession becomes apparent.

Graphic designers are always in need of active dialogue with their clients and with other professionals—be it with an editor, a manager, a marketing expert, or an educator—to really make the best of their practice. This certainly has important implications in relation to the evaluation of graphic design quality and to the education of graphic designers.

The problem of quality in graphic design

Further to the working definition of graphic design advanced above, a definition for quality in graphic design is also necessary: *Quality in graphic design is measured by the changes it produces in the audience.* The movement away from esthetics and stylistic innovation as determinants of quality started when investigations related to perceptual psychology, particularly the Gestalt school, provided some theoretical concepts for visual fundamentals courses in art schools. These concepts replaced intuitive rules for what was called

Figure 14
Armin Hofmann: Advertisement for Herman Miller 1962. Coincidence between the graphic designer's style and the product announced.
Figure 15
Armin Hofmann: An abstract composition intended to represent insects. A strong esthetic paradigm does not allow communication efficiency.
Figure 16
Giovanni Pintori: Poster for Olivetti 82 Diaspron 1958. Technological precision and modern elegance in the development of a successful corporate identity.

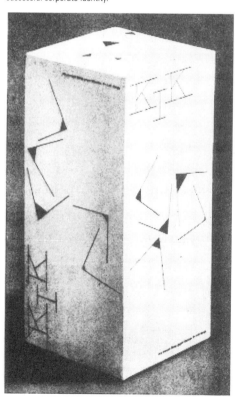

composition. This involved a rationalization of part of the design process and was parallel to developments in the study of legibility. The studies in legibility were the expression of an interest that went beyond the esthetic structure of the visual field and stepped into a concern for communication efficiency.

This concern represented a new factor in the measurement of quality in design. The 1950s and 1960s saw a growing interest in communication throughout the field. The works of Paul Rand and Josef Müller-Brockmann are two different expressions of this concern *(figures 17 and 18).* Research on labeling of equipment, instruction strategies, and information panels, developed by the United States armed forces since World War II introduced a concern for communication efficiency simultaneous with the development of information theory, communication theory, and semiotics. Signs became signage systems and logos became corporate identities. Buildings, fashion, and life-styles started to be analyzed in communication terms. In addition, the receivers of graphic design messages were then discovered as an active part of the communication process. However, these receivers initially were perceived basically as decoders.

The objective of graphic designers was to produce clear communications. Only designers in the advertising business were concerned with other elements in the performance of their designs: namely, sales. At least as far back as the 1950s, it became clear that clients' accounts depended on clients' success and that advertising design was a contributing factor to the success of a business. The

Figure 17
Paul Rand: Cover design for the American Institute of Graphic Arts. The rebus as a way of communicating to graphic designers.
Figure 18
Joseph Müller-Brockmann: Poster for a campaign against noise pollution. The strength of form as a vehicle for communication (typography in red in the original version).

concern for sales and persuasion in the advertising field led to the constitution of multidisciplinary teams of managers, writers, sociologists, psychologists, and designers who contributed to the establishment of marketing as an indispensable component of the advertising field.

Although understanding the importance of changes in public attitudes as a consequence of design has so far been limited to advertising, a closer look at the whole field of graphic design might suggest that specific changes in attitudes and conduct are, indeed, the final aim of graphic design in most areas. It has been said many times that the designer is a problem solver of visual communications and of clients' needs. *But the solution to a client's need is not the production of the visual communication; it is the modification of people's attitudes or abilities in one way or another.* This modification can be a *change*, as in switching from one product to another or in quitting smoking; a *reinforcement*, as in the case of exercising more, giving more money to charities, or drinking more milk; or a *facilitation*, as in the case of reducing the complexity of reading, operating a machine, or orienting oneself in a new place.

The quality of the designs produced in relation to the above examples will be determined by the number of people who switch to the desired product, who quit smoking, and so forth. Clarity and beauty do not necessarily determine objective achievement, whereas they usually contribute to success. If graphic designers wish to be recognized as problem solvers, it is indispensable that they concern themselves with the results of their work measured by achievement of the objectives that generated the need for the production of the visual communication in question.

I am not advocating the demise of esthetics. Esthetic appropriateness and quality are certainly of high importance, both as factors that affect performance and as responsibilities designers have to the community. My proposition is to place the concept of quality in context and to establish its relativity, as well as to clarify that the esthetic quality of a design does not determine its *overall* quality.

This thesis has wide implications both in terms of the practice of the profession and of education for it. In the case of *practice*, specialists other than graphic designers are required to interpret public responses, to evaluate design performance, and to advise regarding appropriate modification of the communication strategies when better results are desired. The experts required for this task may vary from one professional area to another, but, in general, they should presumably come from the fields of marketing, sociology, psychology, and education, disciplines whose main concerns are the behavior of individuals and groups, and the problems of interpreting, quantifying, and qualifying information, as well as to a greater or a lesser extent, applying the information to practical ends.

The implications for graphic design *education* are just as obvious: the traditional art school cannot provide a full answer.

Obviously, the thesis here contends that the designer's job is not finished when the design is produced and delivered, but that evaluation must be an integral part of the design process. In a safety symbols project, for example, the design problem is not the production of symbols but the development of an effective communication strategy for the prevention of accidents. It is not enough for the symbols to be beautiful, clear, and visible; these are useful factors, but the real measure of the quality of the design lies in its contribution to the reduction of accidents.

At best, these considerations will make the evaluation of design quality clearer and will better equip designers to contribute more efficiently to the solution of clients' problems. And not just communication problems, because as already indicated, the final objective of every communication design is some kind of behavioral change in a target population that occurs *after* the communication has taken place.

The education of graphic designers

A basic duality of graphic design becomes apparent when the formation of practitioners is considered: what skills do they need to develop? Graphic design is both a rational and an artistic activity. The decision-making process in graphic design alternates between the consideration of objective information and intuitive leaps. The goal of practitioners should be to base their decisions as much as possible on objective information, but the nature of the field always requires a certain degree of artistic intuition, that is, of decisions made by designers on the basis of experience that is difficult to quantify or explain rationally. (Graphic design in this case is comparable to marketing or psychoanalysis. All are activities in which a body of knowledge has to be applied to specific situations that relate to human behavior.)

The balance between artistic and rational elements in the practice of graphic design poses an interesting challenge to design educators, a challenge that calls for the development of visual sophistication and intuitive abilities to express concepts visually, along with a rational capacity for processes of analysis and synthesis. In addition, graphic designers need skills to listen and interpret the needs and concepts of people in other fields and enough flexibility of mind and visual resources to produce efficient communications.

No school could attempt to deal with all of these requirements in every area of professional practice. Advertising, information, illustration, editorial, signage, and education design are areas that demand different backgrounds, training, and aptitudes and require both specialized instructors and motivated students for each. Reducing the scope of a program to include only some of the professional areas would be admissible. A school might choose not to deal with three-dimensional design, that is, packaging, signage, and exhibitions; another might concentrate on advertising, which might be excluded by still another.

Whereas, making the above choices would be desirable, removing any of the concerns that should be present in all graphic design work would not be advisable. The teaching should represent all levels of the activity, that is, the emotional and the rational, the communicative, the technological, and the awareness of the social context.

In most cases, emphasis has been placed on the visual aspect in education. There has also been a focus on education as a process of transmission of information and the development of personal skills and style. This trend has led to a reduction of the concerns appropriate to graphic design.

In this context, an important distinction can be made between undergraduate and graduate education in graphic design. Undergraduate education must be centered on developing individual student's skills; graduate education should do the same at a higher and more conceptual level, while also contributing to the advancement of knowledge in the field.

Research and advancement of knowledge in graphic design require the support of senior educational institutions. Professional practice does not usually allow for research time, and, when research is developed, practitioners do not share information with others. Market research in advertising is very common, but it is case specific and difficult to apply to different situations. Perception psychologists develop basic and applied research of wider application, but many times psychological research is so removed from reality that placing its results in applied contexts requires additional research efforts.

I am not supporting the idea that universities should directly serve industry, but that those interested in the advancement of knowledge cannot expect from industry inquiries other than those connected to its immediate benefit. It therefore follows that visual communication problems that relate to noncommercial human needs have only the university as a resource for developing solutions. There is a need to work on several fronts:

- Reference centers where existing information can be stored and retrieved should be developed.
- More information should be generated through two kinds of research activities: experimental, and critical discussion of both present and past work.
- Communication networks should be developed among researchers, leading, at best, to coordinating efforts and, at worst, to avoiding duplication.

Graduate programs in graphic design should either work along the preceding lines or generate design solutions for specific projects that clearly surpass the usual level of quality in the professional field and that become models of excellence for practicing graphic design. This practical work however, should be developed hand in hand with a sound, theoretical analysis of design solutions.

Although due regard should be paid to visual sophistication, and although design solutions cannot be based solely on the rational organization of objective information, the profession needs to move away from being a purely artistic endeavor toward becoming one in which visual solutions are based as much as possible on explicable decision processes.

In order to direct graduate graphic design studies toward the development of new knowledge, educators should conceive them as qualitatively different from undergraduate studies and not as mere continuation, whatever the increased degree of complexity and ambition might be. In undergraduate studies, the teachers instruct and create learning situations that help students make discoveries and develop their skills, but those discoveries and that development do not necessarily expand either the knowledge of the instructors or the advancement of the profession as a whole. Students can make new, surprising, and exciting syntheses, and teaching at the undergraduate level is therefore not necessarily repetitious, but the central task is the learning process of the students who require some years before they can make significant contributions to the profession. Nevertheless, undergraduate studies should not be seen as a mere preparation for integration into industry; in other words, undergraduate studies should not be merely job training, nor is it possible to believe that four years is all that is needed for a professional education. Undergraduate programs should aim at graduating persons who are ready to begin a professional career and whose conceptual preparation will allow them to progress rapidly and to enrich the practice of the profession.

Developing an awareness of the essential problems of graphic design in undergraduates is important. Graphic design is first and foremost *human communication*. A graphic designer is a person who constructs a pattern in order to organize the communication link between the piece of design and the viewer. In most cases, graphic designs are meant to be seen or read. These activities happen in time, as well as in space. Although designers work in two dimensions or in sequences of two-dimensional pieces for the most part, the enactment of these pieces occurs over time. As with the playwright or the composer, the designer produces a piece (score, play) that only comes into full existence when the communication with the audience takes place.

My emphasis on this aspect shifts the designer's center of attention from the interrelation of visual components to that between the audience and the design, recognizing the receiver as active participant in the construction of the message. It follows that decisions relating to visual aspects of the design should be based not only on compositional concerns, but also, and chiefly, on the study of human communication. This emphasis on the receiver within the conventional scheme of transmitter-receiver opposition places visual communication design opposite to the romantic conception of art as self-expression, thus avoiding one of the distorting conceptions of the profession.

Given the above, the time has come to understand that the education designers cannot be satisfied by the resources of traditional art schools and that several branches of psychology, verbal communication, sociology, computing science, marketing, and other disciplines should be called upon to develop in students the required awareness. This seems to be the only choice if a theoretical understanding of graphic design is to develop and if the field is to take on the responsibility for the conception and production of effective and conscientious communications and for the education of graphic designers. This specific operational dimension must be qualified by a concern for professional and social responsibility that includes ethics and esthetics.

The Future
Isn't What It Used To Be
Victor Papanek

Many designers are trying to make the design process more systematic, scientific, and predictable, as well as computer-compatible.
Their attempts to rationalize design by developing rules, tax-
onomies, classifications, and procedural design systems are extreme
examples of trying to provide design with a respectable scientific-
sounding theoretical background or, at least, a theory-like structure
that smacks of science. Their approach stands for reason, logic, and
intellect but such a method leads to reductionism and frequently
results in sterility and the sort of high-tech functionalism that disregards human psychic needs at the expense of clarity.

Other designers follow feeling, sensation, revelation, and
intuition. This is often called "seat-of-the-pants" design. Their work
is not reductionist but is stifling in its rich romanticism, substituting
sentimental passion for responses to human needs.

Rather than attempting a synthesis between such divergent
views, this article will show that both groups neglect important new
insights that are being developed in other domains and will demonstrate that there is an enormous amount of data available about how
people relate to their environment esthetically and psychophysio-
logically. Much of these data are still unknown to designers, architects, and planners as the data come from such diverse fields as
ergonomics, ecology, archeology, psychiatry, cultural history, anthropology, biology, ethology, and human geography.

The first part of this paper, "The Microbes in the Tower,"
describes some of this information that leads to new conclusions
about human responses to an increasingly technological environment. The second part, "Toward a Biotechnology of Communities,"
presents several observations on community planning, arranged in
a somewhat kaleidoscopic manner.

The microbes in the tower
Many overlapping sorts of evidence—mainly research findings by
public health and public safety researchers; discoveries about how
the human mind, emotions, and thinking functions; and personal
experiences in many different settings—have recently enlarged the
understanding of the rich and subtle ways in which people interact
with their everyday surroundings. The offices, roadways, parks,
train stations, airports, and other places (manufactured or natural)
that people work or live in, move through, and seek out for play or
relaxation, are not just a given: a backdrop that can be ignored.

The kind of sunlight (compare a July morning in Greece to the autumnal sun setting over Stockholm), the chemical composition of the air (contrast the birch-scented breeze on an island in the Finnish archipelago with the heady aroma of Frangipani and jungle vines on Bali or the plastic air in a shopping mall); and colors, spaces, shapes, materials, views, sounds, and odors affect everyone's physical well being, mental ability and cognitive grasp, sense of self, humanity, and, by extension, understanding of humanity's pressing problems and unfinished business.

Some examples may serve. Experiments in psychology and psychiatry at Yale University have demonstrated that some smells cause blood pressure changes similar to those achieved through meditation: the scent of spiced apple reduces blood pressure drastically. Biometeorologists and microbiologists have found that unscented air containing a certain amount of small-air ions (clusters of molecules with a negative electrical charge) lower the quantity of serotonin in the midbrain. Serotonin is a hormone associated with anxiety. The response of another brain-body system to the environment has been followed: some of the light entering the eyes in bright sunlight bypasses the cortex entirely and directly acts upon the hypothalamus, the spinal cord, and the pineal gland. There it suppresses the production of a hormone called melatonin, which affects moods, fertility, and many other body functions. For decades there has been awareness that a certain red-orange color will kick several psychophysiological systems dealing with aggression and sexuality into high gear. Recent studies in color therapy and photobiology, however, seem to show that "passive pink" (the bubble-gum color) has an almost immediate affect on aggressive behavior. A berserk teenager, when placed in a two by three-meter passive-pink cell will calm down within minutes and may, after a quarter hour or so, be lying on the floor, ready to go to sleep.[1]

Inasmuch as humans have always responded to air, smells, light, and colors, why have we only now managed to get significant data on these responses? Only since the war have a majority of people in the western world moved indoors, protected from bright sunshine and sealed off hermetically from the waterfalls, forests, rivers, and mountains that carry large amounts of small-air ions. In technologically developed countries, most people spend much of their time inside buildings under artificial lighting, with fixed windows, breathing recycled air. Especially in Canada and the United States, once-a-week shopping patterns and speculative land use have resulted in enormous, enclosed shopping malls. These malls are finding an increasing secondary use as jogging and walking spaces year-round, gossiping places for the elderly, and ideal hang-outs for teenagers—all in a climate-controlled environment. Dr. Richard Wurtman, a professor of brain and cognitive sciences at Massachusetts Institute of Technology, says, "We are all unwitting subjects of a long-term experiment on the effects of artificial lighting

---

1   Robert Ornstein, *The Healing Brain* (New York: Simon & Schuster, 1987).

on our health." Therefore, we must take conscious responsibility for creating manufactured environments that won't damage the performance of our brain-body systems even more.

Without going into more detail, certain facts about how humans relate to their environments have emerged. Dr. John H. Falk, a biologist and ecologist, is an expert on human responses to grass. He spent approximately 20 years researching landscape preferences with people of all ages from Africa, India, Europe, and America. The subjects' backgrounds included every kind of human habitat from savannah to mountain terrain, from desert to rain forest.

Photographs of different landscapes were shown to Falk's subjects. Not surprisingly, they liked best the environments they were used to—a reaction that might be explained as a purely cultural phenomenon. But unexpectedly, Falk also found a deep, innate preference for a grass landscape, even among people who had never experienced a grassland setting in their lives. Dr. Falk theorizes that, because the most extensive grasslands in the world are the savannahs of East Africa where human beings first evolved, we may have a genetically transmitted predisposition for the milieu of our species' birth and early development. Habitat preference may be tied to anatomy: walking upright, using hands to carry tools, the opposable thumb, binocular vision. Evolving to walk across the spongy texture of grass may even explain why—although we have the technology to make any floor surface—many people prefer the grass analog of rugs. Carpets from Persia and Pakistan are actually hand-knotted representations of formal gardens done in silk.

This innate and imprinted preference for grasslands may also help by providing an internal guide to our optimal level of environmental stimulus, the kind of complexity we need—in the things we touch, sniff, listen to, look at, feel against our skin or underfoot—to be our best. "Any reduced or raised level of stimulus may impair our functioning."

Dr. Falk's ideas are directly related to other fairly recent research fields. The development of the mammalian brain's shape, size, structure, and function is intimately linked to early sensory experience. (The negative effects of this are now all too well known from the performance of black children from slums and ghettos in the United States and the United Kingdom.) Furthermore, the beauty of human surroundings has been demonstrated to have a profound influence on human behavior and job performance.[2]

Without giving in to reductionist reasoning, neuroanatomical experiments with rats at the University of California at Berkeley have shown that when a young rat is put in an enriched environment (one with more playmates and toys) its cerebral cortex begins thickening within a few days; whereas, the cortex of a young rat in an impoverished milieu actually shrinks. Even old rats with an equivalent human's age of 75 to 90 years old grow bigger brains in an enriched environment. The brains of rats raised in a seminatural

2   Some of the material about Dr. Falk's findings are cited in two articles by Tony Hiss in *The New Yorker:* "Reflections," Part I (June 22,1987): 45–68, and Part II (June 29,1987): 73–86.

outdoor environment grow bigger still and, moreover, raise the animal's general intelligence. "The ambient lighting, noise, and odor, all appear to influence behavior positively," one researcher remarks.[3]

But Dr. Falk and others think that humans may have other unborn predispositions to parts of the natural landscape other than grasslands. A preference for water in the landscape seems innate in all people. Dr. Stephen Kaplan and Dr. Rachel Kaplan, psychologists at Michigan University believe that humans may have an imprinted preference for winding paths that provide "mystery" and "give the impression that one could acquire new information if one were to travel deeper into the scene."[4] This liking for winding paths, mystery, wishing to "travel deeper into the scene," has been used successfully for millennia in Japanese gardens and, more recently, in English landscape architecture. An argument could be made that it also informs *haptic* satisfaction we derive from viewing a painting or a boxing match.

In their book, the Kaplans write: "Mystery . . . is somewhat unexpected in the context of psychology. Perhaps for this reason there has been an inclination to translate it into a more familiar concept, such as 'surprise.' A critical difference between mystery and surprise, however, is that in a surprise the new information is present and it is sudden. In the case of mystery, the new information is not present; it is only suggested or implied. Rather than being sudden, there is a strong element of continuity. The bend in the road, the brightly lighted field seen through a screen of foliage—these settings imply that the new information will be continuous with, and related to, that which has gone before. Given this continuity one can usually think of several alternative hypotheses as to what one might discover."[5]

Jay Appleton, a geographer at Hull University in England, has used the words *prospect* and *refuge* to describe two more human desiderata in landscapes: both are enablers to survival and functioning. *Prospect* means a broad, sweeping vista, an outlook point from which we can take in visual information from many miles around without hindrance. *Refuge* means a hiding place where, secure in concealment, we can observe without being seen, gaining information in safety. Our concepts of *snug* in English, *cosy* in American, *gemütlich* in German, or *hyggelig* in Danish relate to this feeling.

We also seek environments that are easy to read, that is, landscapes that look as if they could be explored extensively without getting lost. The Kaplans consider such open landscapes with distinctive natural landmarks to provide legibility.

To summarize, environments speak to us in a number of ways, which can be listed in order of magnitude. These universal environmental elements consist first of those that are inborn, innate—the archetypal elements that apparently rise from the collective unconscious of humanity. These include a clear preference for

3 Ornstein, *The Healing Brain.*
4 Stephen Kaplan and Rachel Kaplan, *Cognition and Environment: Functioning in an Uncertain World* (New York: Praeger 1982).
5 Kaplan, *Cognition and Environment.*

grasslands, water, winding paths that embody mystery, places of refuge, and lookout points forming prospects. Add to these legibility, because, as the landscape architect William M. C. Lam has pointed out, we look to the environment for information regarding survival, sustenance, orientation, defense, and stimulation.

Then there are culturally conditioned elements. These are tied to specific cultures, yet change slowly with time. In his early books *The Silent Language* and *The Hidden Dimension*, Dr. Edward Hall established the science of proxemics. People walk through life within an invisible proxemic bubble. The shape and size of the bubble is culturally determined. The simplest example is the distances individuals maintain between each other during conversations. Northern Europeans tend to face one another at a distance of about three feet, Southern Europeans narrow this distance by a third, whereas some North Africans face each other at only ten inches. Another example: in Chad or the Cameroons, a conversation partner will bathe you in clouds of cigarette smoke because it is considered friendly. Such actions would be considered thoughtless in Europe, whereas in the United States smoking is now considered an antisocial act by many.[6]

Locally conditioned elements in the environment, distinct from cultural elements, may depend on climate and life-styles. These too may change in time. As a small boy in Austria, I would go to school on skis; I was delighted when, years later, I could commute on skis in Oslo. The flat landscapes of Holland and Denmark lend themselves to bicycling, just as the extensive canals and freezing temperatures of Ottawa provide an environment that delighted us when we were able to skate to and from work.

Personal elements are signifiers in the environment of events that have individual or familiar meaning. Someone looks out the window and says, "My great great grandfather planted that oak tree in 1790, when he was a boy." Or, "This is where I first kissed a girl," or, "My uncle once worked for that newspaper."

There is also the question of beauty in the environment. Approximately 30 years ago, Dr. Abraham Maslow, one of the founders of humanistic psychology, conducted some of the first experiments on the effects that a beautiful environment has on human functioning. He built three rooms: a "beautiful," an "average," and an "ugly" room. The ugly one was designed to look somewhat like a janitor's room, with a naked, hanging light bulb, an old mattress on the floor, battleship-grey walls, ripped window shades, trash, brooms, mops, and a good deal of dust and litter. The beautiful room had large windows, a superbly woven Navajo rug on the floor, off-white walls, paintings and sculpture, indirect lighting, a bookcase, a soft armchair, and a wooden desk. The average room had, according to the experimenters, "the appearance of a clean, neat, 'worked-in' office, in no way outstanding enough to elicit any comments."

6   In addition to my own observations, I refer the reader to O. Michael Watson's *Proxemic Behavior* (The Hague: Mouton, 1970), as well as Edward T. Hall's *The Silent Language* (Garden City, NY: Doubleday, 1959) and *The Hidden Dimension* (Garden City, NY: Doubleday, 1966).

Reflecting on Design

Volunteers were handed photographs of people and asked to report if the faces displayed energy and well-being. The volunteers were supervised by three examiners (who were themselves unaware of the real objective of the experiment). The true purpose was to study people's reactions to their environments. The results showed that the volunteers found energy and well-being in faces when seeing them in the beautiful room, but found fatigue and sickness in the same faces viewed in the ugly room. The behavior of the examiners (unaware of the intent of the test) also varied: they brusquely rushed through interviews in the ugly room, exhibiting "gross behavioral changes" while working there and complaining of monotony, fatigue, headache, hostility, and irritability. Strangely, even though their job performance and work satisfaction were over and over again influenced by where they worked, they failed to notice this fact even once. *They were completely unaware that their activities were in such a close relationship to the appearance of the rooms*, although they realized that they preferred not to work in the ugly room. Reactions by both volunteers and examiners to the average room were closer to the ugly than to the beautiful room.[7]

Often a cure for a problem has to begin before the sickness is recognized or proper diagnosis is possible. Beginning around 1830, doctors studying urban diseases realized that, as more and more people lived together in cities, local springs and wells could no longer be clean and pure. First, they noticed that people got sick more in the new cities than in villages. Next, they realized that in certain city areas, people got sick more often. Finally, doctors discovered that bacteria that had entered specific wells could cause cholera in those who drank from those wells. Eventually, such discoveries led to today's protected reservoirs and water filtration systems. These nineteenth-century public health officials started research methods still being used: finding correlations between two kinds of unintended changes: fluctuations in people's health or mental functions that point back to specific changes in the environment.

What makes this search important is the understanding that changing the environment—carelessly or in good faith—can catastrophically damage some as yet unsuspecting internal mechanism. Now that the need for clean water is self-evident, the fact that it took nearly 100 years to find this out should be remembered. Much of the public health changes were made *before the actual causes were fully understood.*[8]

One can only wish that we would stop the lethal effects of acid rain on forests, and the hole in the ozone layer over the Antarctic, without the plunderers that run most governments arguing endlessly about the precise percentages of damage done by industry vis-a-vis motorcars.

Recently, public health researchers have found that a relatively new use of water—in the central air conditioning systems of tall buildings—causes infections and may contribute to the sick-

7   Abraham H. Maslow, *Toward a Psychology of Being* (Princeton: Van Nostrand Reinhold Company, 1968), especially Part V: "Values."

8   Hiss, *The New Yorker.*

building syndrome. Symptoms range from headache to sore throat, wheezing, and shortness of breath. This is transmitted simultaneously in airborne and waterborne ways and can also be contracted on lengthy flights in aircraft.

Contemporary office and residential buildings are tightly sealed structures, usually with fixed windows. The integrated heating, ventilating, and air-conditioning systems reduce heating and cooling expenses (and energy use) by using the same recycled air over and over. Soon this stable air in sealed buildings will contain fungi, bacteria, and gases produced by most of the manufactured materials. Textiles for carpets and upholstery are increasingly made of plastics. These materials and the adhesives used to apply them release what a medical epidemiologist calls "a variety of volatile organic compounds" that cause eye irritations and infections of the upper respiratory tract. (Fluorescent lighting also causes irritations of the respiratory tract in ways not yet fully understood.)[9]

The problems of sealed buildings are compounded by "cooling-tower drift," the presence in the air of water droplets so tiny they can penetrate, unnoticed, deep in a person's lungs. Sometimes the fresh air intake of one high-rise building is so close to the cooling tower of another sealed building that drift will transmit bacteria growing in the cooling tower water more efficiently than breathing outdoor air. One such infection is already well known, Legionnaires' Disease. According to the Third International Conference on Indoor Air Quality and Climate, Stockholm, 1986, most sealed buildings are in a sick condition at least part of the time and should be written off as failures.

Although many of the connections among places, experiences, and health have yet to be discovered, some designers, architects, and planners have begun treating their own experiences to places in the same manner as midnineteenth-century clean water activists. They fight to prevent the demolition of buildings and communities, knowing that the destruction of an historic section will lead to psychological damage and even death of older people, *even though the exact mechanisms are not yet understood.*

This has not just to do with beauty of design, but the character of a place, the quality of life, its flavor, and ambience. It deals with human scale rather than metropolitan scale. "There is abundant evidence to show that high buildings can actually damage people's minds and feelings," says Christopher Alexander.[10]

TOWARD A BIOTECHNOLOGY OF COMMUNITIES

On centering communities

André Gide, a world-renowned author and a communist most of his life, visited Leningrad some years ago. Afterward, he deeply offended his Russian hosts by saying, "What I loved most in

9   For this and the following observations, see also Robert A. Levine, *Culture, Behavior and Personality* (Chicago: Aldine Publishing Company, 1973), as well as Irenäus Eibl-Eibesfelt, *Stadt und Lebensqualität* (Stuttgart: Deutsche Verlags-Anstalt, 1985), especially Parts I & II, written with Harry Glück.

10 Christopher Alexander, *A Timeless Way of Building* (New York: Oxford University Press, 1979).

Reflecting on Design

Leningrad was St. Petersburg."[11] Gide was not trying to insult his Russian friends. The reason he loved the St. Petersburg in Leningrad was that it was not built by modern planners and designers.

Cities, towns, villages, and groups of communities that were designed hundreds of years ago obviously are based upon some basic purpose of living that eludes current designers. Previous ages possessed one great advantage, a precise moral aim that gave meaning and direction to all planning and design. Classical antiquity pursued harmony; the middle ages strove for mystic fulfillment; the Renaissance, the elegance of proportions; more recent times, the enlightenment of humanism. The people of each period knew exactly what they wanted.

What then is the purpose of contemporary planners? Earlier builders knew what they were doing, because they executed the cultural imperatives of their society as their minds conceived them. In contrast, modern designers nourish public taste and have tried desperately to find out what that taste is. To help in this quandary designers use research staffs and questionnaires. What do they discover when at last their work is complete? That those for whom they have built, after one look, move back toward those parts of cities built hundreds of years ago.

There has (until very recently) been no such thing as a changing purpose in planning settlements. That old towns are charming and new ones are not is because city planners of former times—ancient Greece, medieval city states, the heart of Amsterdam, London, Paris, or Vienna—did not pursue *different* aims as their age changed, but instinctively always worked toward the one unchanging purpose that has always made people desire to live in urban centers in all human communities.

Aristotle expressed this purpose, saying that men form communities not for justice, peace, defense, or traffic, but for the sake of the good life, the *Summum Bonum*. This good life has always meant the satisfaction of four basic social desires, desires to which earlier designers have always given material and structural shape. These desires are *conviviality, religiosity, intellectual growth,* and *politics*. Therefore, the nucleus of cities, with all the variations in styles, consisted always of the same basic structures. Taverns, sports arenas, and theaters were built to satisfy conviviality; churches or temples, to facilitate religiosity; museums, zoos, libraries, and schools, to help intellectual growth; and city halls, political temperament. And because the satisfaction of these four community-shaping desires required an economic base, these structures were naturally and organically grouped around the marketplace, creating and serving the fifth communal activity: trade and commerce.

If a new region is to be successfully developed, decentralized, and open-ended to many different possibilities, some interventions are simple. What will be needed is the construction of focal

11 Cited by Leopold Kohr in *The Overdeveloped Nations: The Diseconomies of Scale* (New York: Schocken Books, 1977).

points at primitive crossroads: a sidewalk cafe, a restaurant serving excellent meals, a little concert hall or theater, a charming church, a well-designed meeting hall.

To sum up the success of old and the failure of modern community design in one sentence: ancient planners, recognizing the invariable Aristotelian purpose of why people live in communities, put all their talent into the building of the communal nucleus: inns, churches, and city halls. The rest of the settlement then followed naturally. In contrast, modern designers are forever building the rest of the city. But without a nucleus nothing can be held together. There are difficulties now in conceptualizing a nucleus, since we have become convinced—falsely—that every age has a different purpose; but, by the time we might discover our own, it will have run through our hands like sand.

On traffic

Modern civilization lives with traffic jams everywhere. The only question is what causes them? Too narrow streets? Streets have been widened, and jams have become worse. Too few traffic arteries? Traffic arteries have multiplied, and tieups have become more frequent. Urban density? Cities have exploded outward into suburbs and exurbs, *reducing* density, yet the gridlock has increased in proportion. Bad planning? International experts have made plans, and when implemented, jams have grown. Too little thought? Actually, the reverse is true: *too much thought*. Modern planners are so concerned about traffic that they have stopped thinking about anything but the fastest movement of cars and the attendant problems, as if the only function of the city is to serve as a racetrack for drivers between petrol pumps and hamburger stands. Los Angeles is at present the ultimate example of not much thought about traffic dislodging common sense. The result? What might have become an elegant city has instead become the first city that incorporates *rural* distances into its tormented traffic-choked *urban* sprawl.

What most planners have overlooked in their rush to eliminate all obstacles to traffic is that they are removing the most precious obstacle to traffic: the community itself. The function of a community, unlike that of a petrol station or a snack bar in the countryside, is to act as a goal, not as a passage point; an end, not a means; a stop, not a flow; a place to get out, not for driving through. This is why most good cities exist where the flow of traffic was bound to stop: at the base of mountains or at their top, on the bend of rivers, on the shores of lakes or oceans, or—in the case of some of the most spectacular, such as Venice, Stockholm, Amsterdam, Bangkok, San Francisco, or Manhattan—in the midst of canals and lagoons, or on the tips of thin islands where any movement beyond is restricted in all directions.

What designers must do if they want to improve the quality

Reflecting on Design

of modern life is to follow two guidelines: first, they must reverse their current hierarchy of values and give less, not more, thought to traffic planning and, instead, concentrate on trade and community planning. Second, designers must turn to a new set of experts. Inasmuch as the foremost city planners are responsible for the most glaring obscenities (Brasilia, Canberra, Ottawa, and the new towns of post-war England, to mention a few), the "new" experts will be found in the genius of the past. The field must look back in humility to study not what is the latest in Los Angeles or Milano, but what is oldest in Boston or Siena.

On site and beauty

One tried-and-true method to keep a community from turning into a speedway is the inclusion of squares into the road network. These squares act as traffic obstacles, and, at the same time, become enhanced by parks, statues, sculpture, music pavilions, seating, water fountains, and venerable trees.

Yet such is the paradoxical nature of communities that once a town attains both commercial desirability and esthetic attractiveness, it begins to act like a magnet and drains people from other communities. This drift toward centralization has to be fought, because even the most beautiful community, once involved in this cumulative process, will attract so much trade and attendant traffic that it will head toward perpetual decay.

Received wisdom explains site selection through the interplay of four determinants: distance from markets, raw material sources, transport, and labor pool. The esthetic factor, distance from a convivial center appealing to the senses, is ignored.

This fifth location determinant, the esthetic modifier, is not just equal in strength to any of the other four, but can be stronger than all others combined. This can be demonstrated positively whenever a new factory opens in the countryside. A sort of magnet begins to operate; instead of firmly anchoring the new plant to the ground, it draws people back to the city. The manager usually starts by deciding to subject himself to hour-long commuting daily, rather than face the meaningless idleness of the countryside. The workers usually follow as soon as they can afford to do so. Some, indeed, prefer unemployment and a richly convivial existence against a background of exciting architecture, theaters, galleries, inns, and a sparkling nightlife.

This esthetics of site has been overlooked, because modern location theory originated at a time during the nineteenth century when virtually all cities, towns, and villages possessed it to such an extent that the esthetic assets of each were cancelled out by the almost equal beauty of the others. Even the most remote western villages in Colorado boasted an opera house 100 years ago, as well as museums and decent inns. Austria-Hungary had so many glamorous small capital cities— most of them with their own operas, palaces, theaters, courts, and universities—that each had enough central force to hold beauty in balance across the land.

Location

Just as birds choose the ideal location for their nests with their strongly developed siting instincts and without the help of design consultants, so do certain human groups. Living and working in barrios in Brazil, Colombia, and Venezuela, one is struck by the paradox that the rich have luxury flats in high-rise towers at the base of a valley that is frequently choked by pollution, noise, and traffic, whereas the poor live in slums on mountain sides overlooking the city, the ocean, or the mountains. Even the large barrio just north of Guadalajara in Mexico is more pleasantly situated than the city. At Boroka in Papua, New Guinea, the slums are individual homes set on stilts in one of the most beautifully sheltered ocean bays just outside Port Moresby. The high level of social happiness that exists in these slums often surprises visitors. They are medically unhealthy and poverty is great, yet their inhabitants have solved many social and urban problems. There is no loneliness for the old, no lack of supervision for children. But, the high degree of social happiness aside, what slum dwellers demonstrate from a design viewpoint is that they are one of the five lucky categories of people endowed with a wonderful sense of location. The other four categories are, or were, the aristocrats, the innkeepers, the military, and the church. And a direct result of their well-developed "bump of location" is that where these favored groups pitch their tents, it is good to live. And where it is good to live, it is also beautiful to live.

On certain magic numbers

Beginning to do anticipatory design for an entirely new region that does not even exist as yet, designers instinctively look for some guideposts on which to base assumptions. Nothing is as frustrating to a designer than to begin with a complete *tabula rasa*, without any constraints or limitations. Reassuringly, there are many guideposts dealing with the ergonomics of communities. If architects, designers, and planners have neglected to use these facts in their work, it is because they are unaware that there is an emerging body of knowledge that deals primarily with human scale. These magic numbers are based on physical, psychological, and species abilities.

Our biogenetic heritage governs expectations of size, weight, distance, speed, and time. Old measurements, such as mile, pound, yard, foot, and stone, reflect what persons can lift or carry easily and how they use their bodies as templates for measure. The *eidetic image* that people carry with them through life provides another system for judging harmonious relationships and scale. Invented measuring systems, such as the meter, are as meaningless as is time shown by a digital watch. Le Corbusier published two books of incredibly sloppy and inaccurate mathematics, trying to fit the meter system to human perceptions, and failed.

Perception and *gestalt* mechanisms provide still more of a basis for magic numbers: all we have seen growing in nature since we were born reflects the Fibonacci series and thus deeply affects our concept of esthetics.

Eye-rotation and distance recognition yield ideal distances for houses from the street, house heights, and so forth. Experienced spaces, that is, our familiar and personal experiences, help determine what size a bedroom, a kitchen, or a restaurant should be. This is modified by cultural constraints: rooms in traditional Japanese farmhouses tend to be larger than in England, yet the Japanese rooms are multifunctional. Single-function bathrooms in the United States are palpably bigger than in the Scandinavian countries, but much space is wasted.

Terrain and climate influence distance measurements, as do driving, walking, and riding distance: the distances between villages reflect how far a man could walk in a day carrying a load (obviously in mountainous countries such as Switzerland, Papua, New Guinea, or Colombia, towns are closer together). How far a horse could be ridden or a cart driven in a day also affects spacing.

As far as the size of communities is concerned, here, too, some natural, magic numbers exist. They are determined by human's collective unconscious regarding group size, which in turn is affected by tribal life-styles, climate, even incest taboos in tribal societies that limit the number of people within an area.[12]

What are some of these magic numbers? Ideally, a private house should be half as tall as it is set back from the street, perhaps 32 feet tall and 60 feet from the road. Assuming a height of 32 feet, then 60 feet would give us a satisfyingly wide building, speaking esthetically. Physiological optics tell us that in looking at others, 50 feet is the limit to the distance at which facial expressions can be recognized; gender, outlines, gait, and basic contours can be identified at circa 450 feet. At 1,000 feet we can no longer make *any* identifications.[13]

These numbers may seem pedantic and completely useless, unless they are applied to real-world situations. For example, in plazas of many different periods, styles, and cultures, nearly everywhere the major axis of the square is the same length. Thus, the major axis of the square at the Acropolis is 480 feet long, St. Peter's in Rome is 435, *place* Vendome is 430, Amalienborg is 450, and Piazza San Marco is 422 feet in length. Although the large square at the imperial city in Beijing measures 9,000 feet, each unbroken segment is just 470 feet long. There is some inherently pleasing and esthetically appealing scale at work here, especially if other squares, piazzas, and plazas are added only to find that almost without exception, they measure between 420 and 580 feet.

To this we can relate numbers of commuter distances; that is, how far office workers will walk to sit in a public plaza at lunchtime or how far residents will walk willingly to reach a park. In the United States, these distances are about three city blocks, or a

12 The foregoing material is also explored in Victor Papanek, *Design for Human Scale* (New York: Van Nostrand Reinhold Company, 1983), and in *Seeing the World Whole: Interaction Between Ecology and Design* (University of Kansas, Fifth Inaugural Lecture, 1982).

13 The following material is largely developed from H. Maertens, *Der Optische Maasstab oder die Theorie and Praxis des Aesthetischen Sehen* (Berlin: Ernst Wasmuth, 1884).

three-minute walk. This not only suggests that office neighborhoods function much as residential areas do, but also something about ideal size again. If people will walk three minutes to reach a central gathering point, then a neighborhood is, in effect, about six minutes' walking time wide; or, in linear terms, five or six blocks, which is between 1,500 and 1,625 feet. Europeans and Asians will walk a little farther, resulting in Doxiades' "kinetic field," with a ten minute or 2,500-foot radius (twice the length of a typical plaza).[14]

Magic numbers and community size[15]

Professor George Murdoch of Yale University has studied more than 250 societies of different kinds and found that magic numbers operate here, as well. Aboriginal dialectical tribes, Amazonian Indian groups, and Peruvian and Tupi-Guarani hunting bands usually number between 400 and 600 individuals. Iroquois Indian longhouses accommodated 500, and excavated villages from Mesopotamia and Anatolia numbered 400 to 600 residents. So-called intentional religious communities in the United States during the eighteenth and nineteenth centuries usually had about 500 members, as did hippie communes 20 years ago. The average-size elementary school in several countries has 500 students in some 40,000 school systems.

These numbers hold steady even among primates: a tribe of Gelada baboons in Ethiopia will number 500 members, as will the snow monkeys of Japan. When groups of Langur monkeys in India exceed 500 in number, the tribe splits up.

Thus, a community size averages 450 to 600 individuals. However, in business groups working closely together some minor stresses appear only when the group exceeds 750; the "trouble threshold" appears at 1,200.

Behavioral scientists consider 250 people to constitute a small neighborhood, 1,500 a large one, and 450 to 1,000 constitute a social neighborhood.

From these numbers we can go further: with the objective being a benign, neighborly way of life, rich in interconnections and cultural stimuli, we can say that communities will consist of 400 to 1,000 people (the ideal is 500), common neighborhoods will accommodate roughly 5,000 to 10,000 residents (or 10 to 20 face-to-face communities), and the ideal city will house 50,000 souls (or 10 to 20 common neighborhoods). Special functional reasons may decrease city size to 20,000 or increase it to 120,000; beyond that lies social chaos.

We can provide some historical underpinnings for this. The major cathedral towns of Europe—Chartres, Avignon, Köln, Canterbury, Siena, Padua, Rheims, and Salisbury—each housed approximately 10,000 inhabitants at the height of their flowering. At the time of the Renaissance, the major universities, located in Bologna, Paris, Oxford, and Cambridge, had a faculty and student population of 20,000 to 35,000. The Florence of Leonardo and

---

14 Many of these figures are cited in Kirkpatrick Sale's, *Human Scale* (New York: Coward, McCann & Geoghegan, 1980).

15 Most of the material in this section rests on Konrad Lorenz, *Der Abbau des Menschlichen* (München: R. Piper, 1983), and Leopold Kohr, *Die Kranken Riesen: Krise des Zentralismus* (Wien: F. Deuticke, 1981).

Much of the material in this paper is based on my own experiences in many countries, interviews with people and researchers, reading, and observation. Besides the sources cited in the text, I should mention:
Christopher Alexander, et al., *A Pattern Language: Towns, Buildings, Construction* (New York: Oxford University Press, 1977).
Christopher Alexander, et al. *The Production of Houses* (New York: Oxford University Press, 1985).
Kevin Lynch, *The Image of the City* (Cambridge: MIT Press, 1960).
Yi-Fu Tuan, *Landscapes of Fear* (New York: Pantheon Books, 1979).
William H. Whyte, *The Social Life of Small Urban Spaces* (Washington, DC: Conservation Foundation, 1980).
These writers are in no way responsible for any conclusions I have reached.

Reflecting on Design

Botticelli built cathedrals, theaters, palaces, and public gardens with a population of 40,000. Michelangelo's Rome held 50,000. The musically, artistically, and architecturally exciting Germany of Dürer, Cranach, and Holbein during the fifteenth century listed its 150 large cities. In the first census, each had about 35,000 residents.

There is much more knowledge becoming available than would be suspected. It comes from many different disciplines, yet designers are the logical people to use and apply it. Whatever other definitions may come to mind, basically designers, planners, or architects work best as synthesists.

Sketching and the Psychology of Design
Rudolf Arnheim

The following considerations are suggested by an excellent essay of Gabriela Goldschmidt, "The Dialectics of Sketching" (1991), for whose publication anybody interested in visual design should be most grateful. The author, an Israeli architect, undertakes to answer the question, "What kind of reasoning does sketching represent?" The question arises because sketching does not consist simply of representing on paper the images held in the designer's mind; it consists rather in a dialectic process, "the oscillation of arguments which brings about gradual transformation of images ending when the designer judges that sufficient coherence has been achieved."[1]

This most relevant question points to psychological issues that aroused my interest. It reminded me of one of the classics on the subject of visual perception, Ernst Mach's treatise *The Analysis of Sensations*, first published in 1886.[2] Mach, a physicist, realized that scientists have no other access to the material world than what is transmitted to them by the senses, particularly the sense of vision. Therefore, the physicist must know what exactly the information generated by vision is and by what rules perception operates. The physicist's vital concern with perception parallels that of architects, who are also dealing with the world of physical matter. They, too, have no other access to what they want to achieve or the means by which to achieve it than what their senses make available to them. In what follows, I am relying on Goldschmidt's essay and on Mach's treatise.

Goldschmidt describes the process of creative design as an interaction of arguments and moves. Arguments are the labors of the designer's mind, the explorations of the task and the reasoning about it. Moves are the physical motions engendered by the arguments. Moves are what psychologists call the behavioral aspects of human activity. The architect's moves produce the drawings and they supply essential new food for the arguments. The drawings are tangible visual percepts, and it is their relation to the arguments that is the principle concern of the present discussion.

Mental images derive from optical percepts, but they are not identical copies of them. Mach describes them as necessary completions and elaborations of percepts. They differ from the optical percepts recorded by the eyes by their reduced intensity. They are fugitive, easily wiped off the slate of memory and, therefore, they offer a freedom not granted to optical percepts, especially in their dealings with space. Mental images can handle visual objects as though they were weightless. They can display them with ease from

1   Gabriela Goldschmidt, "The Dialectics of Sketching," *Creativity Research Journal* 4:123–43. See also, Gabriela Goldschmidt, "Criteria for design evaluation: a process-oriented paradigm," in Y. E. Kalay, ed., *Evaluating and Predicting Design Performance* (New York: Wiley, 1992). In this article I have not referred to this second paper.

2   Ernst Mach, *The Analysis of Sensations and the Relation of the Physical to the Psychical* (New York Dover, 1959, trans. into English). In my quotations I have somewhat altered the translation in keeping with my reading of the original, *Die Analyse der Empfindungen und das Verhältnis des Physischen zum Psychischen* (Darmstadt: Wissensch, Buchgesellschaft, 1985, reprint from original text of 1886).

any angle or at any distance, as long as the person's visual imagination is sufficiently concrete. They can ignore gravity, if they so choose. Optical percepts, of course, can also skip from image to image. In this respect, they resemble computers and are even surpassed by them. Computers combine the concreteness of drawings with a lightfootedness letting them run through any number of variations, but computers can also be accused of a seductive irresponsibility, that allows them to ignore the tangible conditions of materials as well as perceptual experience. Percepts, in turn, remain committed to the physical objects of which they are projections, whereas mental images depend much more loosely on the percepts from which they derive by the remnants of memory.

A telling difference between drawings made "from memory" and drawings made from models is also relevant here. Drawings done by artists from a model, whether or not they are intended as faithful copies, show accidental features that are typically observed, not invented. Drawings from mental images, on the other hand, rely on generalities, on the simplifications that remain in memory as abstractions from the multiplicity of individual experiences. Architects and designers, of course, rely on perceived models only in the more indirect sense of what they have seen of other people's work, historical or contemporary examples. But unless they actually copy such examples—a Renaissance villa or a chair exhibited in a furniture exhibition—they, too, rely on more or less dim recollections, extracts of what they have seen. Something very similar holds for scientific problem solving. "Perception, physical experience, and conceptual idealizations" says Mach, "are the three driving forces cooperating in scientific geometry."[3]

Creative designing always involves the solution to a problem, the carrying out of a task, and, therefore, the image unfolding in the mind always refers to a goal image. This final objective manifests itself at some degree of abstraction. Supplied by the designer or by the program imposed upon him or her, the goal image may be as intellectual as, say, the mere notion that the end product ought to be hierarchically structured rather than coordinative or that it should depict the interconnection of two separate entities. But because all abstract thinking relies on some perceptual referent,[4] even the most abstract theme is tied from the beginning to concrete images. These images supply the designer with the primary nucleus from which the actual structure develops.

As long as the guiding image is still developing it remains tentative, generic, vague. This vagueness, however, is by no means a negative quality. Rather it has the positive quality of a topological shape. As distinguished from geometrical shapes, a topological shape stands for a whole range of possibilities without being tangibly committed to any one of them. Being undefined in its specifics, it admits distortions and deviations. Its pregnancy is what the designer requires in the search for a final shape.

3   Mach, *The Analysis of Sensations and the Relation of the Physical to the Psychical*, 194.
4   Rudolf Arnheim, *Visual Thinking* (Berkeley: University of California Press, 1969).

This same vagueness is frequently apparent in the designer's sketches. "I like fuzzy stuff," said one of the designers interviewed by Goldschmidt. "I can see things in it more than I can in the harder-lined things." A sketch is a reflection of the guiding mental image; but it is not, and cannot be, identical with it, and this difference is precisely what makes it a precious instrument for the designer.

By making a sketch, the designer supplies the mental image with the assistance of an optical image, which has all the properties of such visual percepts. It is as tangibly concrete as all other things exposed to the eyes. Even when left vague, it shows that vagueness with a desirable precision. It persists objectively, while mental images are dependent on the willfulness of the mind, which makes them come and go. Although the sketch stands for a passing stage of the design process, it stops that process and makes the designer examine at leisure what has been done and in what direction the further work must proceed.

The mental image, then, is always underlaid, in Mach's beautiful phrase, by "the dark image of the persistently constant"—*das dunkle Bild des Beständigen*—namely, the goal image prevailing throughout the process of problem solving. Since, however, this goal is not given but only aimed at, it is only potentially present in the image at this particular stage. The goal is perceived as inherent in the attained phase of the process; and this is the case at both levels, the mental image and its reflection in the drawing. Here, then, is the dialectic process, rightly stressed by Goldschmidt. It does not take place between the drawing and the mental image but rather between the goal image and its realization, at both levels—the mental percept and the optical percept, the imagination and the sketch.

Thus far, I have referred only quite broadly to the unfolding of the design process, which leads from the primary nucleus to the completed work. But exactly in what way does this process come about? Does the work grow like a plant or in some other fashion? Obviously, it starts with an analysis of the given task. In a most concrete case, the designer is asked to work from a given plan such as, in Goldschmidt's experiment, the outline of a building for a branch library. Goldschmidt asserts that the analysis consists in parsing the given form into its smallest items, thereby offering the designer a supply from which he or she can select and which he or she can arrange appropriately. Such a description, however, is psychologically insufficient. It resembles too much the way a computer operates when, for example, it goes about finding the best strategy for playing chess. In that case, the machine has been supplied with the largest possible number of moves permitted on the chess board and with the sequences to which they can lead. From this supply the computer extracts quite mechanically the one best suited for a particular constellation of the game to lead to victory. Such a method, however—even if it leads eventually to defeating the masters—is of purely practical value. As an image of what happens in the mind of the human player it is a pitiful caricature of productive thinking. In design, such a procedure may be used occasionally. The designer quoted above reports that "sometimes I just get a lot of lines out of the whole assortment, and then I start to see things in it."[5] Such an assortment can be supplied by a computer, but again it is essential to distinguish between the instrument and the guiding mind. The procedure would be nothing better than a groping in the dark unless it were directed by the shape of the intended theme. What, then, is the nature of this theme?

Another of Goldschmidt's designers answers this question when he says that what is needed for the formal theme of an architectural solution is "a center, an axis, or a direction."[6] Now this is exactly what I have described in *Art and Visual Perception*[7] as the structural skeleton, namely the property that makes the pattern distinct, organized, identifiable. Such a structural skeleton constitutes the character of not only any meaningful design but in fact of any percept whatever. It is the sine qua non of all perception. In a sketch, a designer may indicate it by a pattern of axial lines.

Once such a structural skeleton has been arrived at in the mental image of the designer or on paper, it must be fleshed out; and here one can proceed by two methods, organization from below or organization from above. This difference often applies in architecture to that of proceeding from the inside out or proceeding from the outside in. In the first case, the architect may get together all the components needed for the building and arrange them sensibly. In the second case, starting from the outside, he or she may design a compact, simple, and attractively shaped whole. If, however, one of these procedures is applied one-sidedly, the result may be either an agglomeration of volumes, unreadable as a visual whole, or a fortress or monument, whose inner components are awkwardly lumped and squeezed to make do with the available space. An ideal solution has been developed by nature in the human or animal body, where a suitable arrangement of organs is held together by a symmetrical, coherent, and well-balanced whole.

A tentative skeleton may require a radical restructuring. Such a "Copernican switch" occurred, for example, during the designing of Le Corbusier's Carpenter Center for the Visual Arts at Harvard, as can be traced from the architect's sketches.[8] The guiding idea was that of a building that would defy the fortress-like closeness of other buildings on the New England campus. The idea was to be symbolized visually by a building that, although of an overall cylindrical shape, consisted of two studio units, separated and traversed by an S-shaped ramp that allowed pedestrian traffic to flow through the building. A problem for the architect was how to unify the two components in a coherent whole. The structural skeleton, as tentatively drawn, foresaw two kidney-shaped units, facing each other like mirror images, which did look separate but did not

5   Goldschmidt, "The Dialectics of Sketching," 129

6   Goldschmidt, "The Dialectics of Sketching," 134.

7   Rudolf Arnheim, *Art and Visual Perception* (Berkeley: University of California Press, 1974), 92.

8   Eduard F. Sekler and William Curis, *Le Corbusier at Work* (Cambridge: Harvard Unviersity Press, 1978).

congeal to a whole. By an ingenious act of restructuring, Le Corbusier turned one of the shapes upside-down, creating a windmill-like rotatory symmetry that combined separation and unity. The students of the Carpenter Center nicknamed the result "two pianos copulating."

As this example shows, a building cannot be formed without its relationship to the environment being considered, unless it be completely self-contained, as a piece of furniture can possibly be. Here again, the relation runs in two directions. It radiates from the inside of the building toward the surroundings as a set of outlets, but it is also determined by the outside through the various inputs converging toward the building. The building itself may demand no more than enough breathing space, such as the parvis of a cathedral, to let its visual powers exert themselves freely. Or it may have to adapt itself closely to the style and functional demands of its neighbors.

The function and nature of sketches is inseparable from that of the design it serves. The creative process of designing, being an activity of the mind, cannot be directly observed. The sketches, done for the eyes and directed by them, make some of the design plans visible. They not only supply the designer with tangible images of what his or her mind is trying out in the dimness of its own freedom, but they also permit the observer or theorist to catch a few stop-motion glimpses of the flow of creation.

Myth and Maturity: Toward a New Order in the Decade of Design
Richard Buchanan

"The industrial design profession has established a place for itself in a phenomenally short time. It is widely accepted as a useful service. But it is also still in the process of realizing its full potential as a service to a society going through a series of tremendous transformations."

—George Nelson[1]

"To be human a man must understand what has been accomplished and what can be accomplished by the arts of man."

—Richard McKeon[2]

Colin Forbes and a distinguished executive committee recently organized the first Stanford Design Forum: an invited gathering of CEOs, design managers, designers, and cultural leaders with an active interest in promoting design awareness and effectiveness in the contemporary world. Intended to be international in scope, the forum will be held in London in 1990 and perhaps Tokyo in 1991; in 1988 the participants came from Europe, Asia, and the United States. The goal of the forum, as Forbes explains, is to maintain an informal international network of people who meet from time to time to discuss major issues and to formulate general policies in response to them.[3]

The issues identified for the first meeting of the forum, held in September 1988, were the role of design as a corporate strategy, the relationship of design and international trade, and methods for communicating the importance of design to the general public. There were no formal papers but the discussions are reported in a narrative by Jeffrey Meikle, a design historian commissioned by the forum to provide a background sketch and a general survey of the issues and views represented at the meeting. Though spontaneous conversation seldom follows a simple, logical line of development, Meikle succeeds in representing the event in a straightforward, literal account that manages to incorporate glimpses of different perspectives through a mosaic of quotations. A more incisive interpretation of the contrasting positions taken on each issue may better serve future meetings of the forum, but he deserves credit for supplying suitable historical material and comments that otherwise help to illuminate the discussion for those who did not attend.

As might be expected in such a meeting where the establishment of a network of personal relationships was the primary objec-

1   George Nelson, "'Captive' Designer vs (?) 'Independent' (!) Designer," in his *Problems of Design* (New York: Whitney Publications, Inc., 1965), 30.

2   Richard McKeon, "The Liberating Arts and the Humanizing Arts in Education," in *Humanistic Education and Western Civilization: Essays for Robert M. Hutchins*, Arthur A. Cohen, ed. (New York: Holt, Rinehart and Winston, 1964), 159.

3   Jeffrey Meikle, *Design in the Contemporary World*, publication prepared from the proceedings of the Stanford Design Forum, Stanford, CA, September 1988 (n.p.: Pentagram Design, AG, 1989).

tive, there were interesting observations on recent experience but nothing especially new regarding the issues themselves. (Randy McAusland covered much of the same ground, though with different examples, in his László Moholy-Nagy Lecture.[4]) However, this is no criticism of the forum, for its significance lies more in the event than in originality of content: an influential group has come forward at the right time to send a message of design's importance for the business community and the general public in the 1990s.

One of Meikle's contributions is to place this message in a meaningful historical context. He compares the situation of industrial design in the 1920s and 1930s, when entrepreneurial consultant designers operated with a degree of independence from corporate structure, with the situation after World War II, when design professionals were absorbed within corporate structures to staff newly formed design departments.[5] By becoming part of the formal structure, designers often lost their voice in significantly affecting decisions about products.

> Unfortunately American industry capitalized on the success of the design decade of the 1930s by transforming industrial design into a routine business function and effectively smothering its innovative energy during the years after World War II.[6]

The loss of voice was more than metaphoric. This same period saw the rise of increasingly specialized design publications in which designers spoke to other designers about narrow technical matters rather than to a broader audience of potential clients. (This doubtless advanced the professionalization of design, but at a cost in general understanding that few expected design would have to pay in the coming years.)

After a gradual resurgence in the 1970s and 1980s, design is again poised to play a greater role in industry throughout the world. Placing the pragmatic theme of economic competitiveness within a broader theme of cultural expression and transformation, Meikle writes:

> More than competitive need, powerful as that is, now drives the emergence of the 1990s as a design decade that parallels and eventually could rival the 1930s. The designers of that former era not only boosted consumption; they also interpreted the larger culture by giving it material shape and thereby transforming it. Before their arrival on the scene, manufactured goods had received humdrum aesthetic treatment, either anonymously neutral or inappropriately ornate, at the hands of product engineers. But engineers had failed to give inherent, self-evident, or emotionally satisfying forms to a host of new products— such as automobiles, washing machines, refrigerators,

4   Randolph McAusland, "Is America Design Illiterate?" (paper presented as the first László Moholy-Nagy Lecture of the Institute of Design IIT, Chicago, IL, June 20, 1989).

5   Meikle's account leans heavily toward a history of design in the United States. The situation in Europe was somewhat different, but this does not weaken the main point of the argument if we keep in mind the industrial strength of the United States in the postwar period.

6   Meikle, *Design*, 26.

toasters, and radios. By recognizing that innovative mass-produced goods of a self-conscious machine age needed an evocative modern idiom, designers transcended the old clumsiness and enabled people to become comfortable with modernity by consuming its products in reassuring forms. By contrast, designers of the 1950s and 1960s had only to refine and tinker with the mass-produced material environment that had emerged during the 1920s and 1930s.[7]

The differences between the 1930s and the 1990s are significant in many respects—for example, growth of a so-called information age atop the machine age, a new level of worldwide economic competition, and so forth. But the similarities are strong enough to show why the message of the Design Forum is important as we enter the 1990s: deliberate attention to design innovation helped business and society during a difficult period in the past, and it can do so today if we recognize its potential worth.

To support the new design movement, the forum emphasizes two general policies: promotion of effective management and application of design by the business community; and promotion of public awareness of design. While the executive committee explains that the forum will undertake no specific projects, it recommends sixteen specific actions needed to reach the general public, better educate design managers and corporate executives, and improve the education of designers. Among these, several are of direct interest to design studies:

- Encourage international design expositions in different countries, revealing social, cultural, historical, and commercial aspects on a scale to generate spontaneous activity.
- Encourage the making of films and videos on design, including work of contemporary and historical designers. Integrate design management courses into the basic MBA curricula.
- Instill greater awareness of business needs and practices by requiring design students to study design management. Encourage courses on design theory, history, and criticism at universities with business schools.
- Encourage academic chairs of design theory, history, and criticism.
- Establish awareness of existing sources of information for research on design, its commercial effectiveness, and its cultural influence.

Of the full set of sixteen recommendations, most are obvious and all are worthwhile. Again, novelty of content here is less important than a timely expression of concrete actions that can and should be taken by a variety of individuals and institutions to advance design in the 1990s. The fact that some of these actions are already

7   Meikle, *Design*, 27–28.

being pursued speaks to the effectiveness of design advocacy over the past five or ten years. The efforts of the forum will likely encourage more action in the future.

Promotion and advocacy, however, have their limits. Will the field of design achieve its hoped-for success in the coming decade? The answer to this question is not as clear as one might wish. Despite the enthusiasm demonstrated in the Design Forum and other recent efforts to promote design consciousness, there is a subtle undercurrent of uncertainty that deserves serious attention. It is not uncertainty about the talent of individual designers: there are many imaginative designers in the world today who have much to say; if they can be heard, business and the general public will gain. It is uncertainty about the field of design: (1) its powers and limits, (2) how it relates to other practical and academic disciplines, and (3) the appropriate criteria for evaluating its results.

These were not the official themes of the forum. After all, effective promotion depends on identifying topical themes to which a broad audience can easily relate (corporate strategy and international trade for the business community, methods of promotion and education for those in cultural institutions). But a good argument could be made that they were the actual themes behind the topical discussions. More important, one could extend the argument to suggest that they will be the major themes of design in the 1990s, no matter what other topical issues attract immediate attention. For example, discussions of design as corporate strategy hinge on different views of what design can actually do for business and what conditions limit its effectiveness —precisely issues of the power and limits of design. Similarly, discussions of design shift uneasily among art, esthetics, engineering, human factors, management, and a variety of other disciplines, each of which is well established today and rests on a compelling body of theory and research for which there is no equivalent in design. Finally, discussions of promotional methods and education turn on issues of the perceived value of design for various constituencies—again, issues of evaluating the potential accomplishments of design. The point is that efforts to promote design consciousness inevitably lead back to fundamental unresolved questions about the field itself. These questions will persist in the next decade, framed in the context of the problems of the 1990s. They will be answered either outside the field by default to circumstances and competing interests or inside the field by careful, knowledgeable reflection.

The moral of Meikle's history ought to be made explicit. Economic competitiveness is the immediate driving force behind the resurgence of design today. Appropriately, much of the practical discussion of design in the next few years will likely involve precise, well-focused business issues and the problems that arise from better integration of design in the manufacturing process. But cultural issues (in both the humanistic and social science meanings of the term "culture") are more fundamental for the long-term prospects of the field. If there are not strong, well-reasoned positions about the nature and practice of design today, the voice of the design profession will lack authority in addressing the problems of the coming decade.

There are essentially two kinds of cultural issues involved in design. One is the role of design in interpreting and expressing culture at large. This is an exciting area for speculation, history, and criticism. Exploratory beginnings have been made by individuals in a variety of disciplines. However, as an antidote to excessive enthusiasm there is this sobering perspective.

> [Design] cannot transform a dark brown little life into a large, brightly colored one—only the person living the life can do that. It is not a vitamin pill or a sulfa drug. It reaches its full potential when it is experienced by a person fully equipped to understand and enjoy what it has to communicate. But such a person has no need of it for enrichment, for he is already rich. This, I think, is why people like Einstein and Picasso seem to ignore its more general manifestations—they are busy making good designs of their own and need no further distraction.
>
> The purpose of good design is to ornament existence, not to substitute for it.[8]

Design may be one of the new liberal arts of modern culture, but we should keep in mind its place within the complete circle of liberal arts that humanize and equip people to find meaning and value in their experience.

More important at the moment, however, is another kind of cultural issue: the culture of design, by which one means the ideas and disciplines of thinking and working that distinguish the field of design from other fields, giving it a well-grounded place in the modern world. It is the culture of design that causes uncertainty today not only in design practice but in the education of future designers.

Some of the problems of design education were expressed at the Stanford Design Forum by Arnold S. Wasserman, Vice President of Corporate Industrial Design and Human Factors at the Unisys Corporation. His comments are reported by Meikle as follows:

> In his [Wasserman's] opinion, the profession suffers "in a quantitative world" from its qualitative, "arts & crafts" orientation. Lacking the ability to judge its own performance in terms that the rest of the world can understand, design does not have even the tools to evaluate itself on its own terms. Scholarship has produced no "body of knowledge" to be imparted to practitioners. At least in Wasserman's view, design "lacks culturally contextual history, theory, research, and criticism." As a result, he argues, "our schools . . . train design technicians, we do not

8   Nelson, "Good Design: What Is It For?" in his *Problems*, 13. "Albert Einstein lived in a drab, ill-furnished little house on a side street in Pnnceton. Can you see this man's life enriched or deepened in the slightest by immersion in good, modern design?"

educate design professionals. " . . . [A]side from "a scatter-ing of obligatory courses on design history" and "some worthwhile work in design methodology at IIT and design semantics at Ohio State," not much has reached students. They are thus hampered when they begin their careers not only by insufficient acquaintance with business culture but by a lack of awareness of their own design culture.[9]

This is surely a puzzling and troubling situation after nearly seventy years of supposed growth in the field. Yet, the explanation must lie partly in design culture itself, for the profession did not form through an ongoing interplay of practice and detached reflection.

George Nelson once observed that industrial design "is the only profession that became a myth before it reached maturity."[10] Myth still influences design thinking in many ways, substituting for the serious reflection that is one of the characteristics of a mature profession. It is found, for example, in acceptance of the tacit premises that often guide design practice and education. It is found in outmoded conceptions of how design relates to other disciplines such as art and engineering. And it is found in antagonism toward theory and speculation: the reluctance of many designers to engage in frank theoretical discussions of the emerging field that they are helping to advance. Design culture is such that few designers are willing to step back from day-to-day practice and admit the sense in which their current ideas are speculative and theoretical, requiring reexamination in the light of new problems.[11] Thus, design lacks that tradition of ongoing reflection and debate which transforms a recognizable practical activity into a defensiblefeld with ideas and methods that can be systematically communicated to outsiders and to its own students.

The irony, of course, is that many of the "mythic" figures of modern design shaped our present attitudes by challenging and overturning notions about the field as it existed in their time. But they did so at a time when explicit reflection on the bases of design was less important than pioneering initiative. The early figures of twentieth-century design gained access to the highest levels of business decision making by displaying natural talents: common sense, an ability to identify opportunities for innovation in practice and production, and intuitive skill in persuasive communication. We now call them designers, but in many ways they initially defied categorization because they worked at the boundaries of what was then regarded as design practice. They had the instincts of great salesmen. Indeed, many came from theater, advertising, museums, and publishing, where promotion and sales were a vital part of the territory.[12] Their success in affecting product lines is well known. But they also changed the understanding of design in three essential ways: (1) extending its influence into new subject matters, (2)

9   Meikle, *Design*, 57. Omitted from this passage is Meikle's reminder that scholars have in fact begun in the past ten years to provide useful work in history, theory, and criticism. He cites the journal *Design Issues* and the new British *Journal of Design History* as well as a sampling of recent scholarly books. However, this does not weaken Wasserman's argument.

10   Nelson, "A New Profession?" in his *Problems*, 51.

11   George Nelson reports that his presentation of the lecture "Ends and Means" at the Chicago Institute of Design in the 1950s precipitated a near riot during the question-and-answer session. He had argued that the superb technical skills of designers were being used to convey "the most mediocre of ideas." See Nelson, *Problems*, 34.

12   Nelson, *Problems*, 53.

exploring new ways of thinking about the artificial world, and (3) discovering new purposes and goals for design thinking. Their shortcoming was this: they did not discuss these contributions in a way that was properly detached from publicity and promotional efforts. They helped to create a new profession, but they did not make it a mature discipline.

This points to one of the obvious but unremarked differences between design in the 1930s and the 1990s. In the 1930s, design had been a recognizable professional activity for little more than ten years. The "mythic" figures of the 1920s and 1930s—if they were even conscious of their historic role in shaping design—could honestly think of themselves as the originators of a field.[13] They had no need to give articulate theoretical explanations of what they were trying to accomplish because there was no theoretical context or history of a field with ideas that were directly relevant to their innovations. They demonstrated their ideas almost entirely through practice, leaving it for others to interpret and draw conclusions. In the 1990s the design profession does have a past. It is a past that strongly influences current thinking. It affects the ability of designers to adjust to new circumstances. And the new circumstances require adjustments in design thinking: the problems of industry and society have shifted and grown more complex in our understanding; knowledge of physical and human nature have greatly expanded; and other disciplines such as management, marketing, and engineering have attained higher levels of sophistication in theory and practice, with correspondingly stronger voices in decision making that enable them to demand and expect clear answers about what the field of design can actually accomplish today.[14]

These circumstances pose what may be a key question for the profession: will the resurgence of design in the 1990s succeed if it is based only on ideas about the field carried over from the 1930s with minor tinkering in subsequent decades? Two answers can be anticipated. Some will argue that the natural talents of individual designers served the profession well enough in the past (though it is a mythic past), and such talents are adequate to the challenges of the present. Others will argue that the problems of the 1990s require new ideas and new knowledge to supplement natural talent: the design profession must respond in new ways to the changed environment.

If the former view is correct, all is well. The year 2000 will see a strong profession with unsmothered energy and a distinctive voice. If the latter view is correct, the 1990s promise to be a challenging and uncertain decade, shaped by a debate that will energize the design community in ways not seen in the past, revealing new points of view among those who make, use, and study products.

For this debate to be productive, four conditions are necessary. (1) There will have to be a willingness to rethink the bases of design in the context of new problems. (2) There will have to be

13 One wonders, in reading materials from the time, if they even realized that they were creating a new field.

14 The strength of such disciplines and their consequent ability to pose tough questions about the *what, how,* and *why* of design was evident in a productive conference held at Northwestern University in January 1989. See Marco Diani and Victor Margolin, eds., *Design at the Crossroads: A Conference Report,* CIRA Seminar Series Monograph, No. 2 (Evanston, IL: Center for Interdisciplinary Research in the Arts, 1989).

more reflection on where design has been and where it is going. (3) There will have to be new, well-grounded explanations of the nature and practice of design, supplemented with diverse types of research. (4) There will have to be incisive explanations about the specific ways design can address the issues that will be important to industry and society. Without serious reflection—amounting to a redesign of design—the opportunities of the 1990s could disappear as quickly as short-term successes are achieved. Design could mimic the post–World War II period and again be buried in corporate and social structures that have no inherent obligation to supply the rationale for a profession that cannot speak clearly for itself.

At this point we should turn explicitly to design studies and consider its possible contribution to the decade of design. Since design studies is something quite new in the design community, it may be worthwhile to address this theme through a few preliminary questions.

Does a discipline of design studies exist today?

It exists only in an early formative stage, incomplete in many respects. It certainly exists in no significant institutional form and probably not in the conception of any single individual. Where it does exist is in the combined efforts of many people—designers, design historians, and scholars in a variety of existing disciplines— to begin reflecting on the nature of design and the human-made products created through deliberate planning. Design studies is emerging today for the same reasons that the design profession is experiencing a resurgence: immediate problems of integrating design into industry and long-term cultural questions about the role of design in the modern world and its potential for contributing to human experience. There is a growing awareness that we have very little knowledge about design and that a deep cultural bias has caused us to ignore what may prove to be one of the important arts of our time. A strong discipline of design thinking—if not the particular products created by that discipline today— could be one of the valuable legacies of the twentieth century.[15]

What is design studies?

The central theme of design is the conception and planning of the artificial. Design provides the thought which guides the making of all products, whether by individual craftsmanship or mass-production techniques: (1) material objects, (2) verbal and visual communications, (3) organized activities and services, and (4) complex systems or environments for living, playing, working, and learning. Virtually all definitions of design today are variations of this theme, each intended to draw out a different aspect or emphasize different possibilities of its meaning in accord with different (usually tacit) theoretical or philosophical assumptions.[16] Design studies is reflection on the conception and planning of the artificial. It seeks to

15 Architecture was such a legacy of the ancient world. In the Roman period, it was accorded the status of a liberal art, comparable to mathematics, music, grammar, rhetoric, and logic. From that art, which included some of the features of design thinking as we know it today, have come disciplines such as engineering and the science of mechanics. See Galileo's description of the constant activity in the Venetian arsenal, where the construction of many types of instruments and machines suggested to his mind "a large field for investigation." Galileo Galilei, *Dialogues Concerning Two New Sciences*, tras. Henry Crew and Alfonso de Salvio (New York: Dover Publications, 1954), 1.

16 For example, Herbert Simon's definition emphasizes *action*, which is fundamentally related to his theories of management science: "Everyone designs who devises courses of action aimed at changing existing situations into preferred one." Herbert A. Simon, *Sciences of the Artificial* (Cambridge: The MIT Press, 1969), 55. In his early work, John Heskett employs a more traditional definition, emphasizing the visual appearance of products as things: "design, the conception of visual form." John Heskett, *Industrial Design* (New York: Oxford University Press, 1980), 7. Designer Emilio Ambasz gives a descriptive but intellectually powerful definition, emphasizing poetic (is it really Platonic?) *thought*: "It has always been my deep belief that architecture and design are both myth-making acts." Emilio Ambasz, *Emilio Ambasz: The Poetics of the Pragmatic* (New York: Rizzoli International Publications, 1988), 24. Finally, George Nelson's definition emphasizes design as *communication*: "Every design is in some sense a social communication, and what matters is . . . the emotional intensity with which the essentials have been explored and expressed." Nelson, *Problems*, "Design as Communication," 6.

17 Vitruvius gave the best description of the relation between work and understanding when he wrote the foundation text for the art of architecture. The attention to understanding and explanation as an essential part of practice goes far to explain the high status given to architecture throughout Western history. Vitruvius, *The Ten Books on Architecture*, trans. Morris Hicky Morgan (New York: Dover Publications, 1960), 5. (This translation leaves much to be desired.)

18 For a further discussion of this idea, see Richard McKeon, "The Uses of Rhetoric in a Technological Age: Architectonic Productive Arts," in his *Rhetoric: Essays in Invention and Discovery*, Mark Backman, ed. (Woodbridge, CT: Ox Bow Press, 1987), 2.

19 Several years ago I noticed that a sizable number of students in my advanced courses on classical and modern rhetoric were Stanley Tigerman's architecture students. At the end of one term I was invited by some of these students to attend the annual "critique" of work by graduating students. As Tigerman and a small group of prominent architects from around the country observed the student presentations and asked probing questions, much as skeptical clients would, I realized the extent to which rhetorical thinking (skill in argumentation, use of the topics of invention, and so forth) was essential to successful practice in the supposedly "mute" art of architecture. The art of effectively explaining a design idea remains one of the most neglected areas of design practice and education. Most accounts of this activity excel in being pedestrian.

20 See the earlier quotation from George Nelson, where he suggests the sense in which intellectual and purely artistic work are also instances of design. (Note 8.) This particular meaning of "design" has a long legitimate standing in Western culture.

21 A useful and highly relevant discussion of the relation between the particular and general can be found in one of the foundation texts ("the green bible") that significantly contributed to establishment of the new field of sociology in the twentieth century. Robert E. Park and Ernest W. Burgess, eds., *Introduction to the Science of Sociology* (1921; Chicago: University of Chicago Press, 1970),11.

make explicit the diverse assumptions that guide design and to examine their consequences in the past, present, and future.

How is design studies related to the practice of design and the making of products?

Making involves two components. The first is the actual work of fabrication, where the regular and repeated exercise of the hand or machine forms materials in accord with the conception and plan of a design. The second is the ability to explain and demonstrate the results of fabrication based on reasons or principles. The ability to explain is an integral part of making: it enables the maker to judge the progress of work at each stage and, equally important, persuade colleagues, clients, and consumers that a particular product is effective for a given situation.[17] Makers who possess only the skills of work simply practice a trade at the direction of others. Those who also understand and can explain the basis of their work are "architectons"—master craftsmen, master builders, architects, engineers, and, in general, those who are capable of directing their own work and the work of others.[18]

In similar fashion the practice of design involves two components. The first is the actual work of conception and planning that is appropriate to a particular type of product. The second is the ability to explain the results of designing based on reasons or principles. Once again the ability to explain is an integral part of practice: it enables the designer to judge the progress of work at each stage and persuade colleagues and clients that a particular design is effective for a given situation.[19] Designers who possess only the skills of work are technicians; they practice a trade, not a profession. Designers who reach a position of authority among their colleagues and clients are usually those who can perform the actual work of designing and also explain the basis of their work to others in a manner that is pragmatically meaningful. Designers who are only skillful in explaining the reasons behind design are not designers at all in the sense we are now considering but critics and scholars. If they are designers, they are designers of communication, criticism, or other aspects of the field of design.[20]

Design studies as a whole is concerned with systematic understanding of the ideas lying behind design practice and making. It pursues understanding through two broad types of inquiry. The first is directed toward ideas in particular circumstances, whether in the past, present, or future. This includes study of the history of design; criticism of current practice; and speculative inquiry that may bear on future practice, often taking the form of research that draws on the ideas and methods of other disciplines such as psychology, management, anthropology, semiotics, and so forth. The second type of inquiry is theoretical and philosophical, directed toward general understanding of the theme of design in the diversity of its meanings, connections, and implications.[21] Traces of this type of inquiry are often found in short reflections, prefaces, and introductions to the other types of design inquiry, where those engaged in design studies have attempted to make explicit the assumptions on which their own work is based. Traces are also found in lectures, books, and other writings by designers themselves. In most cases keen interpretive work is needed to understand the philosophical positions that are expressed and to project their concrete implications. This is an important task for design studies as it attempts to clarify its own foundations as well as gain understanding of the field of design.

What makes design studies systematic is the attempt to focus attention on basic issues in the nature and practice of design. Three issues are central: (1) the subject matter of design, (2) the methods of design thinking and working, and (3) the purposes or goals sought in design. Virtually all questions about design can be formulated in terms of one or another of these issues and understood more clearly as a result.[22] However, the difficulty of the task is evident. The ideas lying behind design practice vary widely from designer to designer, revealing a pluralism of perspectives that is often as confusing to members of the design community as it is to other people. Design studies seeks to clarify this otherwise highly desirable pluralism by investigating the rationale for different positions and how these positions affect the field of design.

Design studies itself is inevitably a pluralistic enterprise. The diversity of perspectives in design practice is mirrored in a growing diversity of approaches to the study of design.[23] What unifies this diversity, however, is the recognition of common problems about the nature and practice of design that cut across different theoretical perspectives. To the extent that individuals are more interested in advancing our understanding of these problems than in asserting the superiority of a particular theory, design studies will continue to grow. Differences of approach will be supplementary, each adding a different dimension of understanding to the field. At the moment this is the case. Where long-established fields are now experiencing fragmentation along the lines of warring schools of divergent thought, design studies seems to display the enthusiasm that comes from recognition of a new unmapped domain. As long as this continues (the prospects for a decade of design in the 1990s suggest that it will for some time), differences of approach will likely be productive and convergent, serving to unify the discipline.

What is the purpose of design studies?

The conventional and easily defended response is that design studies is directed toward two goals: knowledge and improved design practice. These are valid reasons for pursuing design studies and serve well for explaining what design studies can contribute to design in the 1990s. But there is another reason that motivates inquiry into design: the possibility of helping to shape a new art of

22 For a discussion of these issues, see Richard Buchanan, "The Design of Design: Reflections and Conference Summary," in Diani and Margolin, *Design at the Crossroads*, 10–18.

23 For a brief discussion of the pluralism of methods in design studies, see Richard Buchanan, "A Response to Klaus Krippendorff," *Design Issues* 2 (Fall 1985), 72–74. For a discussion of the strengths and weaknesses of pluralism in the contemporary world, see "Pluralism and Its Discontents," a special issue of *Critical Inquiry*, 12 (Spring 1986). This contains essays by Wayne C. Booth Haydon White, W. J. T. Mitchell, Richard McKeon, and others.

design thinking that will be more flexible and successful in assisting production, leading to a larger proportion of products that are economical, efficient, and consonant with human values.

The obstacles to such an art are cultural rather than conceptual. Elements of the solution lie immediately at hand and would be obvious except for the cultural orientation of modern life that inclines toward increasing fragmentation of knowledge and the superiority of the "theoretical" sciences over productive arts.[24] The art of design as it exists today is pulled simultaneously in three directions by jealous guardians. It is pulled toward art and esthetics because many designers are properly concerned with the form and appearance of products. It is pulled toward engineering and the natural sciences because many designers are properly concerned with making products that work. And it is pulled toward the human sciences because many designers are properly concerned with communication and the relations between products and people. The purpose of design studies is to find a center among these tensions and, thereby, establish the identity of design thinking in the modern world. To the degree that this is accomplished in the 1990s, design studies will have made a useful contribution.

---

24 A similar view is argued by Herbert Simon in a chapter entitled "The Science of Design." See Simon, *Sciences of the Artificial*, 55–58.

The Meaning of Products

Semiotics in Architecture and Industrial/Product Design
Martin Krampen

The Problem

This investigation points out commonalities and differences between semiotics of architecture and semiotics of industrial/product design. We shall try to understand what the meanings of buildings and designed objects might be. My focus is, therefore, on architectural and product semantics. While a linguistic approach to meaning is genuinely, semiotic, semiotics is broader than linguistics. Verbal meaning must, therefore, be distinguished from other meanings such as those of buildings and other artifacts. As a matter of fact, the meaning of verbal and other signs of communication might turn out to be only a subclass of the meaning carried by human instruments in general, namely the subclass of instruments serving communication.[1]

In order to study their meanings, I single out of the entire ecology of human instruments those called "buildings" and "designed artifacts." I call this approach "ecological semiotics," and argue that such an ecological perspective more adequately reflects the reciprocal relationship of humans and their built and artifactual environments than the treatment of buildings and designed things as abstract objects detached from our bodies. In order to solve our problem, I first define some fundamental concepts of the ecological approach, then sketch an ecological semiotics with special regard to the surfaces and surface layouts of buildings and artifacts, and finally point out some differences between the meaning of buildings and of designed products as they result from human scale.

Background of the problem: some fundamental concepts

The first and most important concept to be defined is *ecology*. I use this term exactly in the sense the biologist Ernst Haeckel gave it when he introduced it in 1866: "Ecology is the general science that studies the relationship between the organism and its external environment."[2] In this instance, the organism in question is the human one. What we want to study then is the relationship between humans and their (external) architectural and product environment.

The next important concept to be defined is *scale*. There are important differences between the scales of the world of physicists and those of our human environment. The world of the physicist ranges from galaxies to atoms. Our lived-in visible environment is composed of all we must see in order to act successfully. In fact, we do see what we must see. This is not a tautology but the result of the evolution our visual system in concert with the other perceptual

1   Luis J. Prieto, "Signe et Instrument," in *Littérature, Histoire, Linguistique, Recueil d'Études Offert à Bernard Gagnebin* (Lausanne: Editions l'Age d'Homme, 1973).

2   Ernst Haeckel,"Generelle Morphologie der Organismen, *Allgemeine Entwicklungsgeschichte der Organismen*," Vol. II (Berlin: Reimer, 1866): 286.

systems has undergone through millenniums. So we see landscapes, mountains, trees, plants, animals, and people. We also see the buildings and artifacts constructed by humans. Our environment ranges from textures measurable in millimeters to objects measurable in meters to landscapes measurable in kilometers. We cannot see galaxies and atoms.

A further concept of importance to the understanding of the ecological approach to meaning is the *reciprocity* of all organisms and their environments. Organism and environment form an inseparable whole. No organism exists without its environment, and there would be no environment without the organism; the best symbol for the organism-environment reciprocity is the well-known Chinese figure of Yin and Yang. Whenever we see in our environment what we must see in order to act successfully, we see parts of ourselves "in the picture": our nose, our hands, our feet are always present if we look at a building or other artifact. This has definite consequences for the scale of our environmental experience: we cannot escape from our visual environment.

To conclude this survey of fundamental ecological concepts, I note favorably James Gibson's proposal that our terrestrial habitat is best described by its medium, its substances, and the surfaces that separate the substances from the medium.[3]

The gaseous atmosphere is the *medium* of many animals, including humans; it permits locomotion, seeing, hearing, and smelling. Fish have another medium: water. *Substances* are matter in a solid or semisolid state. They differ in hardness, viscosity, density, elasticity, plasticity, and so forth; but they do not permit motion through them. All substances have *surfaces* that are laid out in the environment. Surfaces and their layouts tend to resist deformation. Depending on the substance they delimit, surfaces have different textures and pigments. Surfaces have a shape; they may be more or less lit and absorb or reflect the illumination that falls on them.

Ecological semiotics: the theory of affordances
The environment of the organism is meaningful with respect to the organism and its scale. For example, a rock 45 cm high affords seating to the grownup wayfarer or a table to the accompanying child.

The concept *affordance*—a term coined by Gibson—is the ecological equivalent of meaning. The idea that the meaning of a thing has a physiognomic quality (e.g., the emotions that appear in a person's face) stems from Gestalt psychology. Kurt Koffka writes about prescientific behavior: "To primitive man each thing says what it is and what he ought to do with it: a fruit says, 'eat me;' water says, 'drink me;' thunder says, 'fear me;' and woman says, 'love me.'"[4] But even for modern man the handle "wants to be grasped," and objects "tell us what to do with them."[5] Koffka called this the "demand character" of things, his translation of Kurt Lewin's German term *Aufforderungscharakter*, which was translated into

3   James J. Gibson, *The Ecological Approach to Visual Perception* (Boston: Houghton Mifflin, 1979).

4   Kurt Koffka, *Pnnciples of Gestalt Psychology* (New York: Harcourt, Brace & World, 1935), 7.

5   Koffka, *Principles of Gestalt Psychology*, 353.

The Meaning of Products

English sometimes also as "invitation character" or "valence." There is, however, an important difference between the demand character of the Gestaltist's object and the affordance as conceptualized by Gibson. For the Gestaltist, the demand character belongs to the phenomenal and behavioral, not to the physical and geographical, object. Koffka argues that an object, say a mail box, has its demand character only as long as the beholder needs to mail a letter.[6] On the contrary, Gibson maintains that an affordance is an invariant that is always there to be perceived. "The object offers what it does because it is what it is."[7]

Jakob von Uexküll, the precursor of ethology, described something similar to affordance in what he called the "counterability" (Gegenleistung) of manmade things:

> It is not without interest to start a stroll through the town if one remains conscious of a certain question while looking at things. Thus we want to ask which meaning objects striking the eye have and for whom do they have a meaning? We pass a tailor's shop; the garments exhibited are not only adapted to the forms of the human body, but change with the different activities of civic life which they serve.
>
> Next there is a watchmaker, exhibiting very different sorts of watches. The time of sun dials has long passed. Sunrise and sunset do not play a role in our civic life as they did formerly. Artificial illumination prolongs the day. And this little machine takes care of the regular distribution of our daily work dividing day and night into time spans of equal length by its course, whereas still with the Romans, depending on the seasons, either night or day had the longer hours. Thus we have corrected the course of the sun, originally the mistress of time and hour, according to our needs.
>
> We like to stop in front of the bookseller's display offering that object which is today most important for communication between human beings—the book. We know that between all these big and small covers there are words slumbering, which we can awake any time and which will tell us all about human life.
>
> Now comes a butcher's shop. There we see the meat of animals, serving as our nourishment, ready for further treatment. How few of the passers-by know that this meat is an artful apparatus of unequaled precision which endowed the animal with movement and warmth.
>
> A staircase of stone leads us to the terrace of a café where carefully trimmed trees afford shadow and well cultivated flowers give pleasure to our eye. We sit down on comfortable chairs and let the picture of passing carriages impress us, which roll by now pulled by horses now driven by motors.

6   Koffka, *Principles of Gestalt Psychology*, 354–55.

7   Gibson, *The Ecological Approach to Visual Perception*, 139.

Everything—indeed everything which we get to see is adapted to our human needs. The height of houses, of doors and windows can be reduced to the size of the human figure. The stair fits our gait and the banisters the height of our arms. Each single object is endowed with sense and form by some function of human life. We find all over an ability of man which the object sustains by its counter-ability. The chair serves seating, the stair climbing, the vehicle riding, etc. We can talk about something being a chair, a stair, a vehicle without misunderstanding, because it is the counterability of the human products which we really mean by the word which denotes the object. It is not the form of the chair, the vehicle, the house which is denoted by the word, but its counter-ability.

In the counter-ability lies the meaning of the object for our existence. This counter-ability is what the constructor of the vehicle has in mind, what the architect thinks of when designing the plan of the house, what the butcher thinks of who slaughters the ox, as also the writer writing the book, the watchmaker fabricating the watch. The gardener trimming the trees and planting the flowers prepares them for counter-ability. Everything surrounding us here in town has only its sense and meaning by its relationship to us humans.[8]

To demonstrate how similar the concept of counter-ability is to Gibson's term affordance, here is a passage he wrote 66 years after von Uexküll's text appeared: "Civilized people have altered the steep slopes of their habitat by building stairways so as to afford ascent and descent. What we call steps afford stepping, up or down, relative to the size of the person's legs. We are still capable of getting around in an arboreal layout of surfaces, tree branches, and we have ladders that afford this kind of locomotion, but most of us leave that to our children."[9]

As similar as the concepts of von Uexküll's counterability and Gibson's affordance may be, there is a difference between them in the role attributed to the object. For von Uexküll the object—he calls it *Gegengefuge* (counter-structure)—is only an episode in the function cycle (*Funkitionskreis*). This cycle starts with a counter-structure's perceptual mark (*Merkmal*) which is transformed into a perceptual sign (*Merkzeichen*) in the organism. Depending on the organism's need, the perceptual sign triggers a behavioral sign (*Wirkzeichen*) which in turn inflicts a behavioral mark (*Wirkmal*) onto the counter-structure. The function cycle ends because the behavioral mark cancels the perceptual mark, as von Uexküll puts it. It follows that depending on the needs of the organism, the same counter-structure may play quite different roles in the function cycle. For Gibson, these different roles would not depend on the

8 Jakob von Uexküll, *Tierwelt oder Tierseele*, 1913, quoted and translated from Thure von Uexküll, *Jakob von Uexküll, Kompositionslehre der Natur* (Frankfurt, Berlin, Wien: Ullstein, 1980), 249–250.

9 Gibson, *The Ecological Approach to Visual Perception*, 132.

need of the organism but on invariants in the makeup of the counter-structure, on an organism-environment fit.

Whatever the epistemological nuance in the status of the ecological object may be, there must be optical information available to the organism for perceiving counter-abilities or affordances. In fact, perceiving never has to do with value-free objects to which meaning is associated in a second phase. According to Gibson, at least, all ecological objects are full of meaning to begin with. Surfaces, their layouts, and the substances they delimit always exhibit affordances for someone. Affordances may be positive or negative. A stair invites stepping down by its small height, a cliff warns not to step down because of the abyss below its rim. The information specifying positive or negative affordance is always accompanied by information specifying the perceiving organism itself: its body, legs, hands, nose, and so forth. As mentioned above, we cannot perceive the environment without perceiving our self within it. This shows once more the Yin-and-Yang nature of the organism-environment relationship.

In special cases there may be misinformation issuing from certain objects such as large glass windows, which appear to birds as the medium to fly through. And many of us have in a hurry bumped our heads against a glass door mistaking it for an opening. Taking our cue from Gibson, let us observe: when Kofflka said that objects "tell us what to do with them," he forgot to mention that they may lie.

The semiotics of surfaces and their layouts
The syntactics of surfaces and their layouts

As proposed above, our habitat is best described by its medium, its substances, and the surfaces delimiting the substances. Hence the information on the affordances must be directly specified for the organism by surfaces and their layouts. Gibson provides a systematic nomenclature of different kinds of layouts. It results from the syntagmatic combination of the syntactic elements surface and medium. All such combinations may occur in both the natural and the manmade environments.

One such combination is the ground, referring to the terrestrial or a paved surface. The ground implies not only bordering with the medium above it but also the effect of gravity, a horizon, and the sky. If there were only the ground, the layout would consist of an *open environment*. But this condition is only realized in a flat desert. Generally, the environment is full of *convexities* and *concavities* and all kinds of natural or manmade "clutter." An *enclosure* is a layout of surfaces surrounding the medium. The totally enclosed medium is rarely realized, as, for example, in the case of an embryo. A *detached object* consists in a layout of surfaces entirely surrounded by the medium. Examples of detached objects are all moving animals, including humans, and vehicles, balloons, or airplanes. Most objects seem to be *attached*, that is, only partially surrounded by the medium. Most of them are attached to the ground. A *partial enclosure*, such as a concavity, a hole, or a cave, consists of a surface layout that partly encloses the medium. A *hollow object* is an (attached) object if viewed from the outside but an enclosure (partial) if considered from the inside. Examples are the snail shell, a hut, or a pitcher. A *sheet* consists of two surfaces that enclose a substance but are very close together in relation to their dimensions. A *fissure* is a layout of two parallel surfaces that are very close together in relation to their size and enclose the medium within a thin opening, like in a crack of a stone. A *place* is defined by Gibson as a location in the environment, a more or less extended surface or layout. Places have a name but no sharp boundaries. They can be located by inclusion into larger places (the fireplace in the living room of a house in Philadelphia). The habitat of animals and humans consists of places.

There are some more terms given by Gibson for surface layouts, but for our purposes the above catalog should suffice. These types of surface layouts are the signifiers of our environment; what they afford is the signified.

What surface layouts present as basic affordances: natural and manmade terrain layouts
As we have seen, there are natural and manmade surface layouts. They all present some basic positive or negative affordances. Natural *terrain layouts* either facilitate or prevent locomotion for animals and humans. Paths, that is, channels not cluttered by objects, afford the locomotion of pedestrians from one place to the other. Obstacles, barriers, water margins, and brinks are surface layouts exhibiting negative affordances with respect to locomotion. Slopes may or may not permit locomotion depending on their angle. But for millenniums, humans have been changing the natural terrain by constructing roads, stairways, and bridges, all artificial surface layouts, to facilitate locomotion. They have also constructed walls, fences, and other obstacles to prevent access to their enclosures.

Architecture as the design of places and shelters
Different *places* in the habitat of animals or humans have different positive and negative affordances. Some places serve as a refuge from predators, others, which are partial enclosures, as homes. There are places to hide. Hiding means to position the body in such a way that observers may not see it. Privacy in the design of housing means to provide opaque enclosing surfaces in order to prevent others from looking in. Curtains on windows let in light and permit seeing without being seen.

Since the atmospheric medium changes from warm to cold and from rain to snow, humans must have *shelters*. Originally they used caves, partial enclosures adapted to their size, but then they started constructing artificial shelters, so-called huts. Huts are hollow objects attached to the ground. They feature a *roof* affording protection from rain, snow, and sunlight. The *walls* protect from the wind. The *doorway* permits entry and exit.

The affordances of natural objects, tools, clothing, and display surfaces

Objects are of persisting substance with closed or nearly closed surfaces. They can be attached or detached. An attached object such as a tree branch, permits climbing, as does a ladder. A detached object may be carried, and if it is of an appropriate weight it affords throwing. Hollow objects can be used as containers. *Tools* are objects of different affordances and can be considered extensions of human limbs, especially of the hand. Similarly, clothing is a part of the human body while being worn.

There are at least five classes of surface layouts of manmade detached objects which constitute basic tools:

1 elongated objects afford pounding, raking, lifting, and piercing: clubs, hammers, rakes, levers, spears, needles, awls, etc.
2 sharp-edge objects afford cutting: knives, axes, etc.
3 elongated elastic objects afford binding and tying: fibers, threads, ropes, etc.
4 objects affording throwing: missiles, balls, slings, bows, etc.
5 objects to make traces with: chisels, brushes, etc.

Humans have developed *display surfaces* such as pictures which afford visual information. This information is "second hand" since it permits the beholder to see as a surrogate what the maker of the picture saw in the original.

A whole set of affordances typical for a given species can be called its ecological niche. Whereas the term habitat refers to the set of places where a species lives, the term niche means how it lives.

What surface layouts present as ritualized affordances: "ritualization" of affordances

The basic affordances mentioned thus far are not only valid for homo sapiens, but also for hominids and partially for higher animals. The homo sapien has transformed his relationship to the environment in such a way that "ritualized" affordances have been grafted onto the basic ones, accommodating different levels of ritualized behavior. Thus, forms of social life changed from hordes to families, family clans, and nations. Division of labor introduced professions and social classes of different prestige, primitive mythologies transformed into highly developed religions, and more recently technologies advanced drastically. These changes have had their repercussions on the meanings of buildings and objects. Today, buildings and design objects afford more than privacy and shelter or simple extension of the human body.

The social affordances of buildings

Division of labor has multiplied the types of buildings affording spaces and arrangements for groupings of people around different tasks. We now have a whole list of different names for different types of social affordances or meanings by which we identify different surface layouts. For instance, a church has a surface layout different from that of a factory; a high-rise apartment building's surface layout varies from that of a family house. Yet, we recognize the different affordances of their different surface layouts more or less directly.

In a recent pilot study, I showed adult subjects drawings and photographs of buildings of different social functions and asked them to identify their affordances. The drawings had been abstracted from the photographs; the first series featured only the contours of the buildings, the second series added the stories, the third series the windows. The fourth series was constituted by the photographs themselves. The four series thus provided a sequence from minimum to maximum information on the surface layout of the buildings. Each subject was given one series at a time, with two-week intervals between, starting with the minimum information and ending up with the photographs. The task was to identify the social affordance of the building (e.g., church, office, factory, etc.), to name the cues that helped the identification, and to estimate the degree of certainty experienced in making the identification. The results of the study are shown in table 1.

Table 1 shows that the number of different building functions (i.e., social affordances of buildings) named decreased and the degree of security increased significantly as detail about the surface layouts was increased. When detail was very scarce, the information on building size and height (verticality) and on the roof and additional features such as steeples and chimneys was used. But already with the addition of stories in the building picture windows were mentioned most frequently, the story outline being taken probably for an indication of (large) windows. Windows were most frequently mentioned at the stage when they were added to the building drawings. In the photographs such details as curtains or

Table 1

Different types of affordances named per total namings and degree of security

	coutours only	storeys added	windows added	photographs (texture added)
Different namings per total namings	0.347	0.343	0.284	0.215
Degree of security	3.703	3.949	4.225	4.737

symbols (cross, writings, etc.) were used to disambiguate the building's function.

The results of this study were used to design another investigation in which the subjects were asked to estimate the probability of encountering certain surface layout features they might see when confronted with buildings of different social affordances. The buildings were office, factory, church, school, high-rise apartments, and family house. The surface layout features were for the contours: building size (large vs. small), secondary building (present vs. absent), direction of building shape (horizontal vs. vertical), roof (flat vs. gabled); for the internal organization of the facade: stories (many vs. few), number of windows (large vs. small), window size (large vs. small), direction of window shape (horizontal vs. vertical). The results of the study are shown in table 2.

If the results shown in table 2 are put on a common scale, "phantom drawings" of the different building types may be made.

The conclusion of the two studies is that we identify the different social functions of buildings with a fairly high degree of accuracy if sufficient cues on the surface layout are present. Also, in the course of our environmental experience, we seem to have internalized "stereotypes" of these building types, which serve as "templates" for the recognition of building affordances.

Specialized affordance in tools

Division of labor has not only multiplied building types but also, by specialization, types of tools with different affordances. A look into an average tool box will show us that there are more tools than affordances because some tools offer multiple affordances (table 3).

Table 2

**Mean probability values in percent
for surface layout features of six building types**

	large	secondary building	horizontal	flat roof	many storeys	many windows	large windows	horizontal windows
Office	43	27	36	48	52	54	48	41
Factory	50	39	42	46	36	43	38	34
Church	45	57	44	14	16	35	44	23
School	47	32	43	40	40	53	51	42
Apartment	54	22	36	51	57	45	31	36
Family House	20	16	40	27	19	35	30	38

Table 3

	slide gage	rule	water-level	straightedge	square	compass	wooden bar	T-square	wire-brush	sandpaper	plane	file	rasp	chisel	ripping chisel	metal saw	saw	plate-shears	cutting knife	scissors	cutter	pincers	combination pliers	flat nose pliers	pipe-wrench	vise	clamp	monkey-wrench	box-spanner	screw driver	rubber hammer	hammer	mallet	punch mark	graver	screw drill	boring machine	scraper	brush
measuring	•	•	•	•	•	•	•																															•	
aligning			•		•																																		
directing			•	•			•	•																															
removing											•	•	•	•	•	•																						•	
planing										•	•	•	•																										
roughening										•	•		•																										
abrading											•																												
cleaning										•																													
notching														•	•																								
cutting																•	•	•	•	•	•	•	•																
pulling out																						•	•																
holding																							•	•	•	•			•	•									
bending																							•	•															
pressing																										•	•												
turning																									•			•	•	•									
driving in																															•	•	•						
pounding																																•							
marking				•																														•	•				
piercing																																			•	•	•		
laying on																																						•	•
spreading																																						•	•

Similar analyses can be carried out on other "object ecologies." For instance, we might analyze a great industrial fair as the "tool box of a nation" and a World's Fair as a "tool box of humankind."

How surface layouts present their affordances: denotative and connotative meanings of buildings and designed products

Thus far we have dealt with differences in affordances corresponding to differences in surface layouts. In other words, we talked about *what* different types of buildings or objects afford in terms of different functions. We call this type of "functional" meaning "denotative meaning." Now we consider the case where the functions of a building or design object remain constant but there are more or less pronounced changes in the surface layouts affording them. In other words, we talk now about how the same function can be implemented by different surface layouts. This topic is also known under the heading of "style" (in a broad sense, not as art historians use the term). We call this type of "stylistic" meaning "connotative meaning" because it represents variations in affective affordances. "Connotative meanings" result from the fact that every architectural or design problem can be solved in (many) different ways. The result may be socially functional in that this variety prevents uniformity. On the other hand, the variety of solutions to the same problem can be used in a dysfunctional way, as is the case where unnecessary distinctions between social classes are fostered by different kinds of designs for buildings and objects.

Connotative meanings in buildings

Students learn early in art history classes how different surface layouts afford the same function. For instance, the windows of

The Meaning of Products

Roman cathedrals have round arches, Gothic cathedrals have pointed ones.

Facades of buildings serving the same functions can be coded in terms of the elements they feature by overlaying a grid. Thus, we find out that facades of buildings built around the turn of this century feature more types of elements and their tokens in a heterogeneous distribution, whereas the facades of "modern" buildings are often laid out with fewer types of elements with their tokens in a more homogeneous distribution. I showed pictures of the two kinds of buildings to many people and asked them to rate their affective meaning.[10] The results of these studies are shown in table 4.

Affective reactions to different "styles" of surface layouts may undergo changes in the course of time. In a world of uncluttered facades, a few cluttered ones may afford more pleasure than in a world of cluttered ones. The same could be said about entire cities if the layout of medieval European cities is compared to the grid formula of American cities. In the last decade, we seem to be attending a change from uncluttered surface layouts to more cluttered ones.

Affective reactions to buildings and their facades seem to be deeply rooted in our human ecological scale. Since we are always bodily present in our perception of the built environment, tall buildings make us "feel small." It is for this reason that walking through a forest of high trees awakens the same feeling of awe as entering a cathedral. In this sense, David Berlyne's "collative" variables complexity, incongruity, puzzlingness, ambiguity, uncertainty, indistinctness, conflict, surprisingness, and novelty may reacquire actuality in a "New Ecological Esthetics."[11]

Other sources of affordances such as prestige and mythological reference may have to do with a more symbolic type of meaning. A "villa" imitating a Renaissance palace or a dome standing for the "vault of firmament" are examples of symbolic affordances of buildings.[12]

Connotative meanings in design objects

As is the case with surface layouts of buildings, design objects also have connotative meanings. As in architecture, the same or similar surface variables often may constitute the same or similar affective affordances for design products. In one experiment on door handles, I found that light alloy door handles of plain design were attributed the connotative meaning of simple, sober, clean, linear, slick, unobtrusive, modern, pleasant, economical, cheap, modest, and cold.[13]

In contrast, door handles of nonferrous metal with decorations afforded such connotations as old-fashioned, striking, ornamented, decorative, luxurious, playful, flourished, craftsmanlike, warm, and soft.

The affective connotations afforded by automobile bodies depended on size (big vs. small) and shape (predominance of round vs. angular contours),[14] as can be seen in table 5.

10   Martin Krampen, *Wahrnehmungs-und Anmutungs-dimensionen als Gestaltungsziele* (Berlin: Internationales Design Zentrum, 1976).

11   David E. Berlyne, *Conflict, Arousal and Curiosity* (New York: McGraw-Hill, 1960).

12   Mieczyslaw Wallis, *Arts and Signs* (Bloomington: Indiana University, 1975).

13   Krampen, *Wahrnehmungs-und Anmutungs-dimensionen als Gestaltgngsziele.*

14   Krampen, *Wahrnehmungs-und Anmutungs-dimensionen als Gestaltgungsziele.*

Table 4

Two different kinds of apartment buildings' facade surface layouts and their affective meanings

Surface layout	affective meanings
	pleasant
	friendly
	overdone
	diverse
presence of decoration	playful
heterogeneous	personal
distribution of elements	expressive
	natural
	fertile
	loose
	irregular
	unpleasant
	unfriendly
	sober
	monotonous
absence of decoration	serious
homogeneous	impersonal
distribution of elements	inexpressive
	technical
	sterile
	inflexible
	orderly

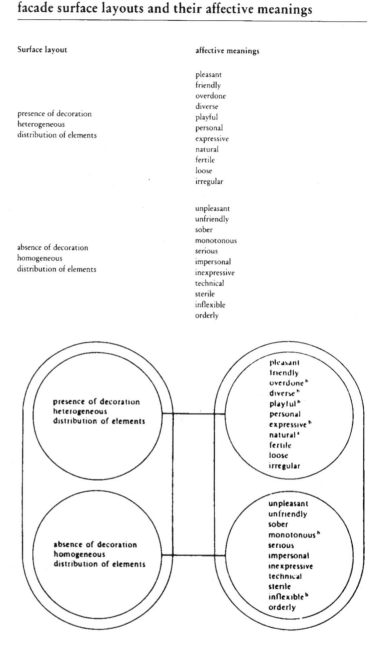

One affordance the differentiation of surface layouts of objects seems to have is, at least in Western society, prestige vs. nonprestige. Prestige is mostly conveyed by increase in size, greater angularity, and choice of more precious materials. But prestigious objects need not necessarily afford a sense of beauty. Often very small, more rounded facets of surface layouts afford the sense of beauty and preciousness, although not of power. Objects with a

Table 5

Four different car body designs and their effective meanings

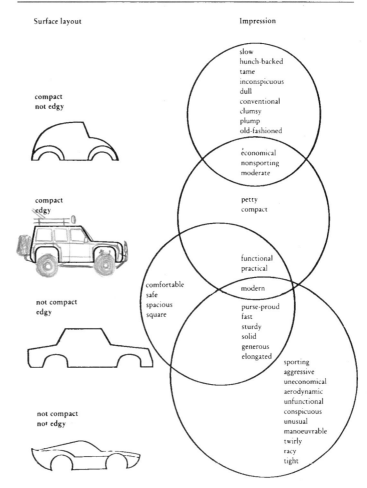

Surface layout

compact
not edgy

compact
edgy

not compact
edgy

not compact
not edgy

Impression

slow
hunch-backed
tame
inconspicuous
dull
conventional
clumsy
plump
old-fashioned

economical
nonsporting
moderate

petty
compact

functional
practical

modern

comfortable
safe
spacious
square

purse-proud
fast
sturdy
solid
generous
elongated

sporting
aggressive
uneconomical
aerodynamic
unfunctional
conspicuous
unusual
manoeuvrable
twirly
racy
tight

mythological sense, such as those used in religious ceremonies (e.g., crosier, mitre, tabernacle, etc.) achieve their strikingness by the use of gold and precious stones and materials. The esthetic affordance of design objects probably also has to do with such variables as complexity, incongruity, surprisingness, novelty, etc. which result from collating the object with our own scale of incongruity or our succession of experiences (surprisingness, novelty) in "scenes" of human-object reciprocity in which we also see the object together with parts of ourselves.

The context in which surface layouts present their affordances

Gregory Bateson drew attention to the fact that there is a straight connection between the phenomena of context and meanings.[15] Some semioticians go as far as to say that only the context can disambiguate the meaning of a sign. I draw attention now to the fact that buildings and objects often occur in functional contexts. Thus,

15 Gregory Bateson, *Steps to an Ecology of Mind* (San Francisco: Chandler Publishing Company, 1972).

Table 6

Matrix of semantic distances between different objects estimated on a seven-point scale (adapted from Moles 1972)

	cup	saucer	spoon	table	book	paper	decanter	chair	telephone	bread
cup	0									
saucer	1	0								
spoon	1	1	0							
table	2	2	2	0						
book	3	4	4	2	0					
paper	3	5	5	2	1	0				
decanter	3	2	3	2	2	4	0			
chair	4	5	6	1	2	4	5	0		
telephone	4	5	6	2	2	3	4	3	0	
bread	3	3	4	2	5	3	2	4	6	0

hotels cluster around railway stations or airports and cups occur together with saucers and plates. In fact, we might estimate the semantic distance between objects on a scale and obtain an ordering of object ecologies according to their functional conccurence (table 6).

Meaning is also connected to (functional) similarity. Objects having similar affordances can be grouped together under the same meaning. Thus, *dwelling* is afforded by apartment buildings, row housing, and family homes, and *containing* by most hollow objects forming a partial enclosure (e.g., pitchers, cups, decanters, etc.). Warehouse catalogs often provide these groupings for us and thus partake in the context of objects by providing their pictures and descriptions.

Differences between the semiotics of architecture and of industrial/product design

The meanings of buildings and objects follow the same rule insofar as functional and affective affordances emerge in a context in which we are always copresent.

There are obvious differences, however, between the two especially in the scale of their surface layouts. If one looks for a systematic foundation of this difference, the opposition between individual and collective seems to be one of the semantic roots.[16] The life of individuals, at least in modern Western cities, depends to a large extent on collective supply networks for traffic (streets), communication (telephones), energy (water, electricity, gas), sewage disposal, etc. Thus, the individual instance is constituted by the set of relationships a citizen maintains with objects where the individ-

16 A. J. Greimas, "Pour une sémiotique topologique," in *Sémiotique de l'espace* (Paris: Denoël/Gonthier, 1979).

The Meaning of Products

ual is the center of a network of relationships. The collective instance instead presents itself as a set of supply networks the terminals of which are constituted by individuals. Now it seems that architecture is more conditioned by the collective network, whereas objects of industrial/product design are more conditioned by architecture. In fact, architecture tends to enclose these objects which in turn appear to be enclosed by it most of the time. "Street furniture" and vehicles are an exception to this rule. Comparing architectural objects with those of industrial/product design, the opposition outside-inside seems to be a semantic indicator of their location. To use a metaphor: architecture and its surface layouts afford a stage for human action, objects, the requisites, and props.

As a consequence, the surface layouts of architecture are attached to the ground and are immobile, constituting the "fixed feature" environment; objects of industrial/product design are for the most part detached and mobile, forming the "semifixed feature" space.[17] Many of them are not only extensions of human limbs in the form of "tools" affording pounding, lifting, cutting, etc. but represent surrogates for entire human action programs—e.g., electric heaters substitute for the getting of wood and making a fire. This automatization has contributed to what has been called "desemantization" of our environment.[18] But after *desemantization* has taken its toll, *resemantization* may compensate for the loss of meaning. Thus, people having central heating in their house may also want a "real" fireplace.

Whereas we do not tend to touch the surface layout of architecture, industrial/product design objects are generally touched by our hands. This has consequences for the design of texture. In architectural surface layouts, texture plays only a visual role. In objects that are handled, texture must also afford pleasant tactile sensations.

Architecture is not operated upon in the true sense of the word. If doors or windows are opened, design objects such as handles come into play. In contrast, many design objects are operated upon. Therefore, an important role is played by the "interface" between the operator and the object. This is not the case in architecture.

All the aforementioned differences in affordance between architecture and industrial/product design objects condition a difference in scale: architecture is large and the objects are small in comparison with the human body. Confronting the built environment, parts of our body (or the bodies of others) enter into perception much smaller than the objects involved. When we face design objects, our own body (or that of others) is present in perception at an equal or larger scale. At this scale we often perceive our own hands manipulating things. Both perspectives are sometimes combined. Thus, in a Renaissance palace the portal is often very large and high in order to afford, for esthetic reasons, a sense of incongruity that makes us feel small and humble. At the same time we see a human-size "door in the door" designed to afford entrance.

17 Edward T. Hall, *The Hidden Dimension* (Garden City, NY: Doubleday, 1966).

18 Greimas, "Pour une sémiotique topologique."

Shaping Belief: The Role of Audience in Visual Communication
Ann C. Tyler

As the goal of all communication is "to induce in the audience some belief about the past..., the present..., or the future,"[1] audience considerations are integral components of the process of visual communication. During that process, the designer attempts to persuade the audience to adopt a belief demonstrated or suggested through the two-dimensional object. The purpose of this persuasion is to accomplish one of the following goals: to induce the audience to take some action; to educate the audience (persuade them to accept information or data); or to provide the audience with an experience of the display or exhibition of a value for approval or disapproval, values with which an audience may wish to identify or may wish to reject.[2] An exploration of the relationship between audience and communication goals will reveal how belief is shaped through design.

The relationship of the audience to the communication process is viewed in widely different ways. In one perspective, the object is seen as isolated as a formal esthetic expression, with the audience consequently, regarded as a spectator. For example, within design competitions, exhibitions, and publications, objects are often displayed with little or no commentary, with no discussion of communication goals. This presentation of design emphasizes the esthetic sensibility of the individual designer[3] and severs the object from its relationship with the intended audience.

Another view characterizes the audience as a passive reader in the communication process. The audience decodes or interprets a visual statement but is not an active participant in the formation of meaning. This view is evident in Hanno Ehses's "Representing Macbeth: A Case Study in Visual Rhetoric,"[4] in which the designer combines a variety of formal devices to construct different messages and the audience then interprets the message. Ehses's analysis is a grammatical model because it treats design as the construction of statements or visual sentences;[5] linguistic and pictorial content are joined like parts of speech to form the message. In "Representing Macbeth," "classifications of speech,"[6] such as "antithesis," "metaphor," and "metonymy,"[7] provide designers with a structure for generating a range of messages. The designer begins with the subject and then explores concepts or themes by applying the grammatical model to the subject. In this model, the message is examined in relation to the original subject and is clear or unclear, successful or unsuccessful. The audience either understands the message, finds

1   Richard Buchanan, "Declaration by Design: Rhetoric; Argument, and Demonstration in Design Practice," in *Design Discourse: History Theory Criticism*, ed., Victor Margolin (Chicago: The University of Chicago Press, 1989), 92.
2   All the goals occur to some degree in one design, but a particular goal is dominant
3   Buchanan, "Declaration by Design," 91.
4   Hanno H. J. Ehses, "Representing Macbeth: A Case Study in Visual Rhetoric," in *Design Discourse: History Theory Criticism*, ed., Victor Margolin (Chicago: The University of Chicago Press, 1989), 187–97.
5   Ehses, "Representing Macbeth,"193–94.
6   Ehses,"Representing Macbeth," 187–97.
7   Ehses,"Representing Macbeth,"189.

it confusing (the message is not a "true" or "correct" interpretation of the subject), or finds it unintelligible. The audience is viewed as involved in no deeper engagement than that of decoding references to the subject. A grammatical approach thus emphasizes the scientific over the esthetic aspects of design. In addition, since the audience brings nothing particular to the process, it is not particularized in any way; it is both a *nonspecific* and a passive audience.

Semiotics, a third and closely related view, recognizes the specificity of the audience. An audience holds or recognizes certain beliefs and reads messages based on these beliefs. In Roland Barthes's "Rhetoric of the Image,"[8] denotation and connotation distinguish the literal and symbolic messages within visual communication. The audience reads the literal message while also interpreting the signs which express the "iconic message."[9] The potential readings of these signs outside the communication device are multiple, but the interpretations are particularized within the design through their combination with other signs and the denoted messages.[10] The audience, with its cultural beliefs and understanding, is also involved in particularizing the symbolic (connoted) message[11] thereby becoming an active reader.

Yet another view, to be explored in depth here, is a rhetorical analysis of design.[12] Within a theory of rhetoric the audience is not characterized as a reader but as a dynamic participant in argument. In this rhetorical view, visual communication attempts to persuade a specific audience through argument as opposed to making a statement within a grammatical structure or conveying a message within the dynamics of semiotics. Designers utilize existing beliefs to induce new beliefs in the audience. It is the use of existing beliefs, as much as the attempt to induce new beliefs, that contributes to maintaing, questioning, or transforming social values through argument. Designers persuade an audience by referencing established or accepted values and attributing those values to the new subject.[13] The specific audience's experiences within society and its understanding of social attitudes are an essential aspect of argument and necessary to the communication goal.

The selection of examples of design within this essay, though not comprehensive, shows the use of devices and strategies to construct argument, the use of existing beliefs in argument as a strategy to induce new beliefs, and the role of the audience in accomplishing communication goals. The formal devices in each example are discussed in terms of the primary goal[14] of the design: to induce action, to educate, to create an experience.

Persuading the audience to act

Persuading an audience to attend an exhibit, travel to another country, or invest in a company is inducing that audience to take an action. In an attempt to persuade, the designer develops an argu-

8   Roland Barthes, "Rhetoric of the Image," in Semiotics: *An Introductory Anthology*, ed, Robert E. Innis (Bloomington Indiana University Press, 1985),192–205.

9   Barthes, "Rhetonc of the Image," 195.

10 Barthes, "Rhetoric of the Image," 199–201.

11 Barthes, "Rhetoric of the Image," 201–03.

12 In addition to Richard Buchanan's "Declaration by Design," see also Buchanan, "Wicked Problems in Design Thinking," *Design Issues*, 8/2 (Spring 1992) 11–12. A useful beginning point for understanding the rhetorical approach in general is Wayne C. Booth "The Rhetorical Stance," *Now Don't Try to Reason with Me: Essays and Ironies for a Credulous Age* (Chicago: The University of Chicago Press, 1970), 25–33. For a discussion of the relationship between grammar and rhetoric see Paul de Man, *Allegories of Reading: Figural Language in Rousseau, Nietzsche, Rilke, and Proust* (New Haven: Yale Universiy Press, 1979), 3–19.

13 Judith Williamson, *Decoding Advertisements: Ideology and Meaning in Advertising*, 4th ed (New York Marion Boyars Publishers Inc., 1983), 50–66.

14 A detailed exploration of forrnal devices is an important area of research, but is not within the goals of this paper.

ment within the two-dimensional space that defines and represents an audience's future experience. The argument becomes a promise: if one attends A, one will feel B; if one goes to C, one will see D; if one uses E, one will become F.

The goal of the first example *(figure 1)* is to persuade the audience to visit the New York Aquarium. The poster's argument, made through formal devices, defines the audience's future experience at the aquarium: if you go to the aquarium, you will have an emotional experience based on a friendly, intimate relationship with members of the animal kingdom. Intimacy between audience and mammal is created through scale. The mammal takes up most of the space, creating the appearance that it is close to the viewer. Personal contact is also suggested because the mammal appears to make eye contact with the audience. Standing in such close proximity to a large animal could be frightening rather than intimate, but any feeling of confrontation is avoided through the dreamy, soft quality of the image, the profile position of the mammal (it is not coming directly toward the viewer), and the friendly expression on its face (it appears to smile).

The formal devices suggest the nature of the aquarium experience by referencing and reinforcing beliefs regarding the relationship between individuals and nature—i.e., nature is friendly toward human beings and animals enjoy being the object of our attention. Although the word "aquarium" indicates confinement, the image defines it as vast, showing no cage or boundaries.

While the aquarium poster promises the audience an experience based on an emotional relationship with the subject, the PanAm travel posters *(figures 2 & 3)* offer a future experience predicated on distance and observation. The communication goal is to persuade the audience to travel to Bali or Japan. The posters argue that the audience will have an esthetic experience in these countries. The first poster, of Bali, is a rural scene of a terraced agricultural area and the second, of Japan, features a sunset and two figures in traditional clothing. Like the aquarium poster, both travel posters use monumental imagery. But the large-scale imagery in these travel posters, combined with other formal devices, makes a very different argument. The PanAm images are architectural in nature: the terraced land forms a contrasting figure/ground pattern; the two people standing with their backs to the audience become shapes against the sky. People and land become objects of beauty. Distanced from the scene through perspective and the lack of any reference back to the viewer, the audience thus remains "outside" a beautiful, tranquil scene. Landscape and people are frozen in time for the audience to view as they choose—as in a museum of artifacts. Both posters promise the audience an esthetic, *nonparticipatory* experience if they travel to these distant lands.

The travel posters have transformed these foreign countries and people into art, referencing a paradigm which says that art is to

The Meaning of Products

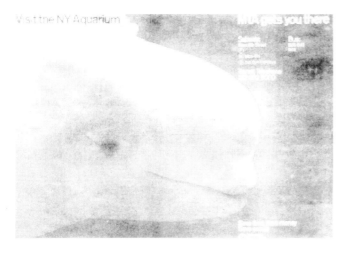

Figure 1
(NY Aquarium poster) Designed by Michael Bosniak and Howard York, Photograph by Russ Kinne. *Visit the NY Aquariium*. 1974. Offset lithograph, Printed in color, 42 × 59 1/2. Collection The Museum of Modern Art, New York. Poster Fund.

Figure 3
(Japan) Designed by Ivan Chermayeff, Thomas Geismar, and Bruce Blackburn. *Pan Am Japan*. 1972 Offset Lithograph, printed in color, 42 × 28". Collection, The Museum of Modern Art, New York. Gift of Pan American World Airways.

Figure 4
Caremark, Inc. 1985 annual report; Designed by Jim Berte, Robert Miles Runyan & Assoc.; Reproduced from *Graphic Design USA: 7*. Courtesy of the American Institute of Graphic Arts.

Figure 2
(Bali) Designed by Ivan Chermayeff, Thomas Geismar, and Bruce Blackburn. *Pan Am Bali*. 1972 Offset lithograph, printed in color, 42 × 28". Collection, The Museum of Modern Art, New York. Gift of Pan American World Airways.

Figure 5
Congaree Swamp brochure designed by Bruce Geyman ©1991 L. Chapman.

be observed, not experienced. The posters reinforce a belief that these cultures are static and removed from the audience's own experiences. This is achieved through formal devices that create the appearance of a nonparticipatory audience relationship. The audience appears in the role of observer, yet they do participate by bringing cultural beliefs about beauty and art to the argument.

The final example of design that persuades an audience to act is an annual report. The primary communication goal of annual reports is to persuade the audience either to invest or to maintain their investment in a company. Designers persuade the audience by making an argument that represents the company's philosophy, achievements, and financial solidity. The argument is often made through the company's employees or people using their services; in this way, the audience attributes the values embodied in these individuals with the institution they represent.

The Caremark Inc. 1985 Annual Report *(figure 4)* makes its argument through Dominick Petone, an individual benefiting from the company's services. The design argues that Mr. Petone, and therefore Caremark, has strong, moral values; he is hardworking, trustworthy, and straightforward. The dominant image is a photograph of a hardworking man in working-class clothing with his tools in the background. The audience knows he is hardworking because he is wearing a T-shirt, is slim, and appears to be serious in the workplace. The written text states that, though ill, Mr. Petone continues to work. From this information we can gather that work and self-sufficiency are important to him. He is also a rugged individualist: the lighting highlights and accentuates his facial features. He is portrayed as a role model, a hero. The portrait is isolated on the page as in an art catalogue; the borders around the photograph are the same proportions as in traditional art matting while the small serifed type of the written text reinforces the serious and classical image. Yet Dominick Petone is approachable: he makes direct eye contact with the audience, his gaze is open, not aggressive, and he gives the audience a "Mona Lisa" smile.

Although Mr. Petone is separated from the investor audience by his economic class, the audience identifies with him through the shared moral values of responsibility, honesty, and stability. These values are also intended to represent the institution and are shared by the image (Mr. Petone), the producer (Caremark), and the audience (investors). The beliefs represented by Dominick Petone are values that bind the culture, values that the audience recognizes and then attributes to Caremark.

Educating the audience

The second communication goal is to educate the audience or to persuade the audience to accept and interpret information. Information can be seen as valueless, as not reflecting a particular belief system. But all communication involves an interpretation of information,[15] an interpretation based on data, perspective, analysis, and

15   James W. Carey, *Communication as Culture: Essays on Media and Society* (Boston: Unwin Hyman, Inc. 1989),195.

The Meaning of Products

Figure 6
Angeles Corporation logo; Designed by Robert
Miles Runyan, Robert Miles Runyan & Assoc.

Figure 7
Screen Gems Inc. logo; Designed by Tom
Geismar, Chermayeff and Geismar, Courtesy of
Tom Geismar.

Figure 8
Seatrain Lines Inc. logo; Designed by Tom
Geismar, Chermayeff and Geismar, Courtesy of
Tom Geismar.

16 Logos are then applied to communication
    devices and those devices may have
    other primary goals, such as inducing the
    audience to buy a product.

judgment. Educational materials are no exception; information is interpreted and communicated according to the paradigms of academic communities. Educating the audience often includes making an argument that the information is "fact," that it is "true."

The map and guide to the Congaree Swamp *(figure 5)* is intended to educate the audience about the swamp's ecosystem. The argument suggests that nature has an inherent logical order and that the information provided is scientific, i.e., rational and factual. For information to appear factual, it must seem stable, unchangeable. Various formal devices such as detailed illustration techniques, minor changes in scale, and a lack of tension in margin and spacing mitigate against an emotive response by the audience, while a heightened sense of order is achieved through the clearly visible organizational grid system. The brochure is basically a diagram—codified information without expressive characteristics that might suggest individual authorship. Information, such as this, is presented as data and appears to be communicated through an omniscient voice. When the omniscient voice of science is used, the audience seems to be nonparticipatory. The audience is, apparently, only a reader. This dynamic is similar to that of the travel posters *(figures 2 & 3)*, but here the image lacks a sense of drama or emotion, eliminating the appearance of interpretation or perspective. In sum, the organization of facts in the Congaree Swamp brochure is an argument relying on a scientific paradigm. While learning about the swamp's ecosystem, the audience's belief in the rational order of the universe is also reinforced.

The goal of educating an audience also occurs within communication from the business community and through objects not generally classified as educational materials. Corporate and institutional logos are an example of design that attempts to educate.[16] The logo defines the company and persuades the audience that the qualities of the logo are also the qualities of the institution it represents. The audience includes both the company employees and those who come in contact with the company. Audience identification with the values of the organization serves the goals of management as well as those of public relations.

Simplified, geometric logos became the symbols of large corporations and dominated design in the 1960s and 1970s. These reductive icons were developed to represent the "modern" corporation as a large, anonymous entity driven by technology and the values attributed to science—rationality and objectivity. The icons reference science through formal devices such as diagrammatic imagery, an efficient use of line and shape, and an emphasis on positive and negative space *(figures 6, 7, 8)*. As in the swamp brochure *(figure 5)*, the elimination of individuality and emotion suggests an omniscient voice and the presentation of fact. Geometric simplification of form continues to be applied to logos, but the 1980s also saw the reintroduction of more formally complex shapes and "naive" representation. The icons began to take on some of the qualities of

Figure 10
CHIASSO logo by Jeff Barnes.

folk art imagery by referencing individual (handmade) characteristics. These new logos *(figures 9, 10)* reflect the same communication goal: educating the audience by defining the organization. Rather than referring to the values associated with science and distancing the audience, these logos communicate a more emotional relationship with the audience. The quotidian quality of the logos represents the company not as an anonymous institution but rather as an organization comprised of individuals like the audience. The audience's relationship to the organization is based on self-identification. Though not overtly participatory, an argument involving personal identification recognizes the audience's existence.

In the previous examples, existing beliefs are transferred to the subject to create new beliefs. In posters within an exhibition titled "Visual Perceptions," existing beliefs are replaced with new beliefs. The goal of the posters is to educate the audience regarding the stereotyping of African Americans within the print and broadcast media.[17] Several posters in the exhibition invoke stereotypical images and racist values and then refute those beliefs within the argument. Beliefs are not only a strategy of argument but the subject of the posters as well and so must be clearly visible to the audience.

"Triptych," a series of three posters in the exhibition, alters the audience's relationship with and interpretation of the information over time. The first interpretation is ambiguous and may lead to a stereotypical conclusion, while the information received later exposes that stereotype. For example, in the last poster of the series *(figure 11)*, the audience first sees a blurred figure of an African-American man running juxtaposed with the headline "CRIME." The photograph suggests anonymity through cropping, motion, and soft focus; this is a man portrayed without individual characteristics. The large type screams like a tabloid headline and a label. Both the image and headline are ambiguous in meaning. Did the man commit a crime? Was a crime committed against him? The audience can only read the small type after coming closer to the poster, after the opportunity to form a stereotype has presented itself. The small type, contrasting in size and detail, shifts the ambiguity and tells the audience how to interpret the poster. ". . . Seeing my color makes me a criminal. But what is my crime?" Through the text the man must now be seen as an individual trapped within the context of racial stereotyping. By making the audience aware of their participation in the argument, the poster challenges the audience to recognize and confront their own beliefs and assumptions as well as those of the media. The formal devices that divide the audience's interaction into two clearly defined segments are merely expressions of a deeper engagement by the audience. Through this device, it is revealed that the *audience* holds or understands the beliefs demonstrated in the argument and that the *audience* is attributing those beliefs to the subject.

17 Tibor Kalman, "I Don't Think of You as Black," *International Design* (vol. 18, no. 2, March/April 1991): 56–59.

The Meaning of Products

Figure 11
"Triptych"; Designed by Greg Grey.

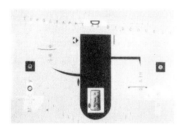

Figure 12
Typography as Discourse poster, designed by
Allen Hori; design directed by Katherine
McCoy; *the 100 Show: the twelfth annual of
the American Center for Design.*

Providing the audience with an experience through the display of values

Though all design creates some type of experience for the audience, experience is rarely the primary communication goal. If the goal of a design is experiential,[18] then it is often interpreted as a focus on the esthetic moment. Experience, is a display of values, however, and esthetics is simply one of any number of values. When an experience is the goal of an agent, the design displays or exhibits particular values for the audience to consider. The audience may identify with the values or they may condemn or reject the values.

A display of esthetic values can be seen in "Typography as Discourse" *(figure 12)*, a poster directed toward an audience of designers. Formal devices in the poster raise issues of the role of esthetics in typography and design. Because words are broken, displayed backwards, and read in different directions, the audience experiences the letters as shapes, patterns, and codes. Type becomes a symbol, not of language, but of an esthetic. In creating an experience for the audience, the poster argues a *particular* esthetic. Adherence to an esthetic is a cultural belief and this poster develops an argument for a certain esthetic, a specific cultural belief.

Experiencing *social* beliefs as a primary goal is demonstrated in the controversial series of ads produced by Benetton, the clothing manufacturer. The ads reproduce documentary photographs that reference values. These images, placed within an ambiguous context when used in an advertisement bearing the name of Benetton, are used without any explanatory or contextualizing text. The ads, which have included images of a death-bed scene of an AIDS patient, an overcrowded ship of Albanian refugees headed to Italy, and a newborn infant with umbilical cord, blood, and mucus,[19] create an experience for the audience through displays of social values.

It could be argued that the goal of these ads is to induce action, to induce the audience to buy clothing. In fact, the ads may result in an audience remembering Benetton and supporting the company if the audience identifies with the values the ads seem to imply. Or it may be argued that the goal of these ads is to educate, to induce in the audience an awareness of the issues and values referenced. But the ads do not interpret the beliefs referenced, so the argument does not attempt to persuade the audience of a particular belief. And so no particular belief is attributed to Benetton either to induce an action or to educate. The argument of these ads is a display of beliefs and the *role of the audience* within that argument is to experience the beliefs exhibited.

The formal devices within the Benetton ads define the audience's role and also suggest the audience's deeper engagement with the communication process. The quality of the photographs expresses their documentary origins. Some of the photographs have the harsh graininess of an enlarged snapshot, some express the

18   John Dewey, *Art as Experience* (New York: Capricorn Books, 1958).
19   Ingrid Sischy, "Advertising Taboos: Talking to Luciano Benetton and Oliviero Toscani," *Interview*, April 1992, 68–71.

immediacy of a captured moment, and all place the viewer as a voyeur in a private, emotional, or intimate scene. Audiences have become accustomed to this voyeuristic role in the context of the news media. By altering the context and placing the image where the audience expects to see a product, the audience becomes uncomfortably aware of its role as an active participant in the argument.

Shaping belief

The goal of visual communication is to persuade an audience to adopt a new belief. However, this necessitates a reference to existing beliefs through formal devices. In developing an argument, a designer does not have a choice of referencing beliefs or not referencing beliefs; the choice lies in what beliefs are referenced. In making this choice, existing beliefs will be affected (maintained, rejected, or transformed) and a new belief will be shaped. The designer, of course, cannot combine just any set of beliefs with a subject to reach the communication goal. Communication is directed toward a *specific* audience and that audience comes to the argument with *particular* cultural beliefs and understanding. The audience is a dynamic participant in the argument and the designer must discover the argument that will persuade a particular audience.

The range of argument achieved by varying the combination of formal devices seems limitless, and experimenting with formal devices within argument has been a major focus in graphic design. By examining the shaping of belief and the role of the audience in argument through a theory of rhetoric, what are some additional directions for investigation in design? Currently, there are many discussions concerning the responsibility of the designer in relation to the subject. What of the designer's responsibilities in referencing beliefs? And as an active participant in shaping belief, does the audience have a responsibility within the communication process? Are there avenues for exploring argument other than varying formal devices or varying the beliefs referenced? Are there communication goals not yet explored through visual communication? Questions of this sort may set a much needed new agenda for design inquiry.

Figure 13
Benetton Advertisement; Photo: Oliviero
Toscani for Benetton; Courtesy of Benettons.

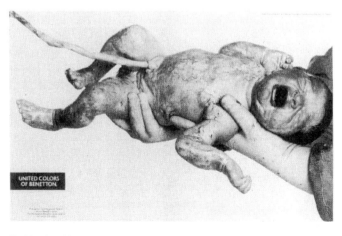

The Meaning of Products

The Power of Punctuation
Martin Solomon

Punctuation (pŭngk′chōō-ā shən) *n.* The use of standard marks and signs in writing and printing to separate works into sentences, clauses, and phrases in order to clarify meaning.

The American Heritage Dictionary

,	**COMMA**
;	**SEMICOLON**
:	**COLON**
.	**PERIOD**
—	**DASH OR EM DASH**
–	**DASH OR EN DASH**
~	**SWING DASH**
-	**HYPHEN**
?	**QUESTION MARK**
¿ ?	**QUESTION MARKS, SPANISH**
!	**EXCLAMATION POINT**
¡ !	**EXCLAMATION POINTS, SPANISH**
′	**ASPOSTROPHE**
( )	**PARENTHASIS**
[ ]	**BRACKETS**
‹ ›	**BRACKET ANGLE**
{ }	**BRACES**
" "	**QUOTATION MARKS**
' '	**DOUBLE & SINGLE**
...	**ELLIPSIS**

Figure 1

pp	(pianissimo)	– very soft
p	(piano)	– soft
mp	(mezzopiano)	– sort of soft
mf	(mezzoforte)	– sort of loud
f	(forte)	– loud
ff	(fortissimo)	– very loud

Figure 2

One of the first rules of grammar we learn is the proper use of punctuation marks. Their application abides by traditional standards, indicated in the style guides that dictate punctuation usage in formal texts. In general writing, however, most of us use punctuation in a more flexible manner. We omit, substitute, improvise, and alter many of the given rules. Application is determined by both tradition and the writer's personal style. Because of this casual treatment, punctuation is often taken for granted.

Most punctuation marks are composed to be seen but not heard. These subtle, often understated, devices are quite important, however, for they are the meter that determines the measure within the silent voice of typography *(figure 1)*. Punctuation directs tempo, pitch, volume, and the separation of words. Periods signify full stops. Commas slow the reader down. Question marks change pitch. Quotation marks indicate references.

Symbols in music perform comparable functions *(figure 2)*. During the performance of a piece of music, each conductor interprets the intensities and durations of these notations according to his or her own style. Similarly, designers can improvise upon the standards of punctuation.

Punctuation marks have tonal value just as letter forms do; they also have mass and energy, which may vary according to their structure. The various marks can be classified as major ? ! [], intermediate : ; " " () /, and minor - ' * in correspondence with their mass. Full-bodied punctuation marks, such as question marks and exclamation points, contain the definite characteristics of their type style. Intermediate and minor punctuation marks, although in keeping with their type style, correspond more closely with the typeface weight.

Punctuation marks vary widely from one type style to the next. A period, for example, is round in Futura, square in Helvetica, diamond shaped in Goudy, and oval in Ultra Bodoni *(figure 3)*.

Designers need not be confined to using only the punctuation included in a type font. They can utilize punctuation from other

Figure 3

Futura Light .
Helvetica Medium .
Goudy Old Style .
Ultra Bodoni .

fonts or Pi sorts. However, they must consider compatibility between type and punctuation *(figure 4).*

With punctuation marks designers can create illustrations without pictures. A single line of copy set in a light typeface contrasted with a bold, larger period creates a more dramatic stop than a period of conventional size and weight. Exaggerated quotation marks flanking a message offer another example of illustrative punctuation. The contrast in size and weight indicates to the reader, primarily through design rather than grammatical intent, that an important message is being presented *(figures 5 and 6).*

Figure 4
Cover design by Martin Solomon

Figure 5
From a poster designed by Martin Solomon

Figure 6

❝The player must know how to relieve
the soft with the loud and
how to apply each of these in its
proper place, for following the familiar
expression in painting, is called light and shade **❞**
Leopold Mozart

Asterisks function as visual movers, telling the reader to go to another location for a reference or definition *(figure 7)*. When this direction is coupled with the energies within the asterisk's geomet-

The Meaning of Products

ric design, a bold or enlarged asterisk becomes a strong statement. The area surrounding exaggerated punctuation marks should be supportive of the size and weight of these images. Exaggerated punctuation should not be used with all messages. The indiscrimi-

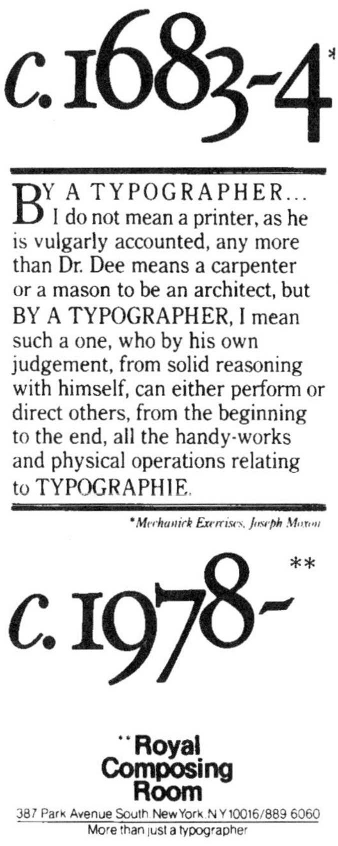

tī-päg-rə-fē

(the art of printing with type)

Royal Composing Room, inc. 387 Park Avenue South, New York, NY 10016 (212) 889.6060

Typograph(y?)

Art is simply a right method of doing things. The test of the artist does not lie in the will with which he goes to work, but in the excellence of work he produces.
THOMAS AQUINAS:
Summa Theologiae, LVII c. 1265

Royal Composing Room, inc.
387 Park Avenue South
New York, NY 10016
212 889.6060

nate display of punctuation for the sake of design turns these marks into devices unrelated to concept; punctuation used out of context can diminish the effect of a message *(figure 8)*.

A greater or more interesting arrangement within any typographical composition can be created through the positioning of punctuation. An example is the abbreviation of the word *number*. By aligning the lower case *o* with the top of the capital *N* and inserting a small horizontal dash or rule beneath it, letters and punctuation work in concert to form a design unit: N°. Although rules and underscores are not punctuation, they can be used to support or intensify characters or words. A period can replace the dash or rule, N°. This simple usage of supporting punctuation creates a personality that can be more effective in endorsing a theme than the commonly used *No.* configuration *(figure 9)*.

Punctuation marks need not be considered only in relation to texts in which they are an obvious part of the design. The sensitive application of punctuation in even the most commonplace unit

---

c. 1683-4 *

BY A TYPOGRAPHER... I do not mean a printer, as he is vulgarly accounted, any more than Dr. Dee means a carpenter or a mason to be an architect, but BY A TYPOGRAPHER, I mean such a one, who by his own judgement, from solid reasoning with himself, can either perform or direct others, from the beginning to the end, all the handy-works and physical operations relating to TYPOGRAPHIE.

*Mechanick Exercises, Joseph Moxon

c. 1978- **

Royal Composing Room
387 Park Avenue South New York, N Y 10016/889 6060
More than just a typographer

Figure 7
Poster designed by Martin Solomon

Figure 8
Advertisements designed by Martin Solomon

No. Nº Nº NO.

Figure 9

(212) 254-1177
(212) 254-1177
212 / 254-1177
212 254-1177
212 254·1177
212 254.1177

Figure 10

Figure 11

Figure 12

changes the entire feeling of a design. One frequent application in which punctuation is taken for granted is the telephone number *(figure 10)*. *Telephone numbers traditionally have been indicated by parentheses enclosing the area code and a hyphen separating the next three numbers from the last four: (212) 987-6543.* Punctuation marks such as parentheses and hyphens are designed to center on the x-height letters and, as a result, sit low in relation to lining numbers, which are designed to correspond to the height of uppercase letters. Adjusting the position of such punctuation marks can be done in the type specifications. This grouping of numbers can be simplified by omitting the parentheses and inserting a slash or a word space after the area code: *212 987-6543.* The grouping can further be changed by substituting a bullet for the hyphen: *212 987•6543.* Base aligning a period is a better option, because the powerful circular shape of a bullet is noncommittal to the area it occupies and is unrelated to type style and spacing. If preferred, a wide variety of devices such as ballot boxes, triangles, arrows, and dingbats can work better in concert with respective letter form shapes *(figure 11)*. An additional option is to omit all punctuation or punctuation marks: *212 987 6543.*

Designers must understand the subtleties involved in working with punctuation. These subtleties include refinements in spacing and position. Spacing refinements maintain the optical alignment and tonal value continuity of a typographical composition. Hanging minor weight punctuation partially outside a flush left and right pica measure, for example, will maintain optical column alignment *(figure 12)*. Hanging punctuation on centered lines maintains vertical optical consistency between lines *(figure 13)*.

"Formative art" is what matters most in our time, where the new means of production—the machine—has changed the whole social background of our life, depriving the old forms of their former vital expression. Only formative art can create new genuine expression. A new conception towards formative art is beginning to make itself felt. Today we insist upon the form of a thing following the function of that thing; upon its creator's desire for expression following the same direction as the organic building-up processes in nature and not running counter to that direction. We insist upon harmony again being achieved between intellect and desire.

Statement by Walter Gropius.

"Formative art" is what matters most in our time, where the new means of production—the machine—has changed the whole social background of our life, depriving the old forms of their former vital expression. Only formative art can create new genuine expression. A new conception towards formative art is beginning to make itself felt. Today we insist upon the form of a thing following the function of that thing, upon its creator's desire for expression following the same direction as the organic building-up processes in nature and not running counter to that direction. We insist upon harmony again being achieved between intellect and desire.

Ellipses set with too much space between the dots appear too light in tonal value in relation to the rest of the copy and therefore should be specified with no additional letter space between the dots. All of these refinements contribute to the totality of a compo-

The Meaning of Products

Typography: the art of printing.

Figure 13

sition by creating an harmonious interrelation between punctuation and words.

Punctuation is to typography what perspective is to painting. It introduces the illusion of visual and audible dimension, giving words vitality. Whether prominent or subtle, punctuation marks are the heartbeat of typography, moving words along in proper timing and with proper emphasis.

Design and Order in Everyday Life
Mihaly Csikszentmihalyi

Art and order

Since the time of Aristotle, a recurrent theme among thinkers has been the idea that art exists because it helps bring order to human experience. This notion still stubbornly survives, despite the fact that in recent times the arts have not been distinguished by a concern for maintaining harmony.

László Moholy-Nagy claimed (not so many years ago) that the goal of art is to form a "unified manifestation . . . a balance of the social, intellectual, and emotional experience; a synthesis of attitudes and opinions, fears and hopes."[1] Gyorgy Kepes thought that people of the twentieth century live in chaotic environments, are involved in chaotic relationships, and carry chaos at the core of their consciousness. The job of the artist, according to Kepes, is to reduce all this free-floating chaos by imposing order on the environment, and on our thoughts and feelings.[2] Psychologist Abraham Maslow expressed a similar idea when he claimed that art helps reconcile the conflict between ancient biological instincts and the artificial rules we have developed for organizing social life.[3] E. H. Gombrich restates this theme in its most complete form in his latest book on the psychology of design and decoration.[4]

But what does it actually mean to say that art helps bring order to experience? How does this mysterious process take place? As a psychologist I was dissatisfied with the vague and metaphorical accounts of how art affects the consciousness of the viewer. As a result, ten years ago my students and I conducted a study in which we interviewed a representative cross-section of families in the Chicago area, to find out how "normal" people responded to art objects and design qualities in their environment. We conducted the interviews in the respondents' homes, asking them such questions as: What kind of "art" objects did they have in their homes? How often did they notice such objects? What went on in their minds when they did respond?

Soon after we started interviewing, however, we realized that we were having difficulties. The people we talked to, even professional, educated persons, had very little to say about the subject. They were able to repeat a few impersonal clichés, but it was clear that art played a decidedly insignificant role in their lives. Although most homes contained a few paintings or sculptures, usually reproductions, these works were marginal to the owner's sense of psychological or spiritual well-being.

1 László Moholy-Nagy, *Vision in Motion* (Chicago: Paul Theobald, 1947), 28.

2 Gyorgy Kepes, *Education and Vision* (New York: Braziller, 1965).

3 Abraham Maslow, "Isomorphic Interrelations Between Knower & Known," *Sign, Image, Symbol*, Gyorgy Kepes, ed. (New York: Braziller, 1966), 134–43.

4 E. H. Gombrich, *The Sense of Order: A Study in the Psychology of Decorative Art* (Ithaca, NY: Cornell University, Press, 1979).

The Meaning of Products

There were, however, in every home, several artifacts to which the owners were strongly attached. These objects often lacked any discernible esthetic value, but they were charged with meanings that conveyed a sense of integrity and purpose to the lives of the owners. So instead of asking questions about artworks, we changed our tactic and asked what objects were special to each person, and why.[5] Eventually we interviewed 315 individuals in 82 families, observing the respondents for a few hours at a time with these objects in their homes.

The meanings of household objects

In one interview a woman showed us with pride a plastic statuette of the Venus de Milo. It was a tacky specimen, with thick seams and blurred features. With some hesitancy the interviewer asked the woman why the statue was so special to her? She answered with great enthusiasm that the statue had been given to her by a Tupperware regional sales manager as a prize for the quantity of merchandise she had sold. Whenever she looked at the Venus replica, she didn't see the cheap goddess, but an image of herself as a capable, successful businessperson.

In other cases, a woman pulled out an old Bible that she cherished as a symbol of family continuity; a man showed us a desk he had built, a piece of furniture which embodied his ideals of simplicity and economy; one boy showed us his stereo with which he could make "weird sounds" when he was depressed; while an old woman showed us the razor which her husband, who had been dead for eighteen years, had shaved with and which she still kept in the medicine cabinet. Finally, a successful lawyer took us to the basement where he unpacked a trombone he used to play in college. He explained that whenever he felt overwhelmed by his many responsibilities, he took refuge in the basement to blow on the old trombone.

In other words, we found that each home contained a symbolic ecology, a network of objects that referred to meanings that gave sense to the lives of those who dwelt there. Sometimes these meanings were conveyed by works of art. To be precise, of the 1,694 objects mentioned in the study, 136 or eight percent referred to the graphic arts (photography excluded), and 108 or six percent referred to sculpture, including the Venus de Milo replica. But to be effective in conveying meanings, the owner had to be personally involved with the artifact. It was not enough that the object had been created by someone else; to be significant, the owner had to enter into an active symbolic relationship with it.

A large majority of the 136 graphic works were homemade; they were often the work of children, relatives, or friends. Their value consisted in reminding the owner of important personal ties,

5   Mihaly Csikszentmihalyi and Eugene Rochberg-Halton, *The Meaning of Things: Domestic Symbols and the Self* (New York: Cambridge University Press, 1981).

of the qualities of the people who made them. In some instances, a picture was cherished because it reminded the owner of a particular place or an occasion, such as a Mexican landscape bought on a honeymoon. Rarely were the esthetic, formal, syntactic qualities of the object mentioned as a reason for liking it. Of the 537 reasons given for cherishing the 136 graphic works, only sixteen percent had anything to do with *how* the pictures looked. The objects were special because they: conveyed memories (sixteen percent), or referred to family members (seventeen percent), or to friends (thirteen percent). Formal qualities alone almost never made a picture valuable to its owner. On the relatively rare occasions in which a person was sensitive to the formal qualities of a painting or sculpture, the object was special because the owner recognized its esthetic value. By actively appreciating the object, the owner joins in the act of creation, and it is this participation, rather than the artist's creative effort, that makes the artifact important in his or her life.

Table 1 shows the ten types of household objects that were mentioned as special or important by the largest number of respondents.

Table 1[6]

Percentage of respondents who mentioned at least one special object in a given category.

Objects	Percentage
Furniture	36
Graphic art	26
Photographs	23
Books	22
Stereo	22
Musical instrument	22
Television sets	21
Sculpture	19
Plants	15
Plates	15

As the table shows, the most frequently mentioned special object in the home was some kind of furniture. Again, it was not the design quality of the piece that made it special, but what the person did with it, and what the interaction meant to the person. Because different people have different goals and do different things, the kinds of objects cherished and the reasons why they were special varied dramatically by age and sex.

The youngest generation of the families interviewed chose stereos, television sets, furniture, musical instruments, and their own beds, in that order. Their parents most often chose furniture, graphic arts, sculpture, books, and musical instruments; while their grandparents' chose photographs, furniture, books, television sets,

6   Csikszentmihalyi and Rochberg Halton,
     The Meaning of Things, 58.

and graphic arts. It was clear that the younger generations responded to the activity potential of the objects—to what they could do with them, while the older generations turned to things that evoked contemplation, or preserved the memories of events, experiences, and relationships.

For example, a teenage boy said that the kitchen table and chairs were among the most special objects in his home because they were very comfortable. He could also tilt the chairs and balance on them, hide under the table, or build a fortress with the entire set. "(W)ith another table, I couldn't play as good 'cause I love the feel of that table." A typical response from someone from the second generation was that of one woman who singled out a piece of furniture because of the memories it evoked about her friends, husband, or children: "I just associate that chair with sitting in it with my babies." For the older generation of respondents, objects often bridged relationships between several generations: "This chest was bought by my mother and father when they were married, about seventy years ago. . . . My mother painted it different colors, used it in the bedroom. When I got it my husband sanded it down to the natural wood. . . . I wouldn't part with it for anything. And I imagine the kids are going to want it, my daughter-in-law loves antiques."[7]

Responses also differed between genders, indicating that stereotyped sexual roles influence the way we perceive and respond to objects in the environment. Men, like many of the children we interviewed, preferred things that could be interacted with: television sets (ranked 2 in preference), stereos (3), musical instruments (5), sports equipment (7). Women responded more like the older generations of people interviewed and preferred objects of contemplation: photographs (2), graphic art (3), sculpture (4), books (5), plants (6). Women, more often than men, tended to see objects as special because they were mementoes of children or grandparents, or because they had been a gift or an heirloom. Approximately twenty-two percent of the women interviewed mentioned that special objects personified the qualities of another person, as opposed to only seven percent of the men.

These patterns, and many of the others that emerged from the data, suggest that (at least in our culture and in the present historical period) objects do not create order in the viewer's mind by embodying principles of visual order; they do so by helping the viewer struggle for the ordering of his or her own experience. A person finds meaning in objects that are plausible, concrete symbols of the foremost goals, the most salient actions and events in that person's life.

In the past, generally accepted symbols performed this function. Religious icons, patriotic lithographs, folk-art, for example, could represent the identity of the owner and his or her purpose in life. But today, widely shared cultural symbols have lost their power to create order. Each person, each family unit must discover a visual

7   Csikszentmihalyi and Rochberg-Halton, *The Meaning of Things*, 62.

language that will express what they most deeply care for.

Of the eighty-two families interviewed, some were enthusiastic about their home; parents and children loved the space and the atmosphere of the house in which they lived, and felt close to each other. In these homes each person mentioned things that reminded him or her of the other members of the family, or of events in which they had jointly participated. In the families where people were ambivalent about the home in which they lived, where conflict set family members against each other, such common symbols were mentioned less often.

If it is not the object that creates order in the viewer's consciousness, does it actually matter how the object looks? In other words, are there objective visual qualities that add up to "good design?"

In search of universal values: color and form

Artists and writers on art usually assume that some aspect of the visual stimulus will have a direct, immediate effect on the senses of the viewer, and that psychic harmony is created by means of such effects. Certain colors or shapes are universally pleasing, and it is by combining these formal elements that designers reach their audience.

Early psychological investigations supported the belief that some colors "belong" together, and that some forms are better suited than others to please the brain. These extrapolations from the findings of the natural sciences and mathematics were occasionally confirmed by laboratory experiments on visual perception, but turned out to have little explanatory value in real-life contexts.

The reasons for this failure are not difficult to understand. It is true that the light spectrum demonstrates regular relationships between abstract dimensions of color, such as hue, saturation, and brightness. It is also true that when we begin to think of color in this way we can generate categories of complementary or clashing colors. However, it does not follow that people perceive color according to the analytical rules developed by physical scientists.

In his delightful investigations among illiterate Uzbeks in the Soviet Union, Luria found that village women refused to combine colored skeins of wool into meaningful categories because they thought each was uniquely different from the other.[8] Instead of using abstract categories, such as "brown," they said that a particular piece of wool was the color of calf or pig dung; the color of decayed teeth, or the color of cotton in bloom. On the other hand, men from the same village called or named everything "blue," regardless of whether it was yellow or red.

In Western culture, colors are seen in terms of a rational analysis of the physical properties of light. Having learned these properties, one can't help but perceive colors in these terms. The names and relationships that physicists have bestowed on the light spectrum influence one's views. Harmony and conflict exist largely

8   A. R. Luria, *Cognitive Development* (Cambridge, MA: Harvard University Press, 1976).

(perhaps entirely?) for those who have learned a specific way of coding colors. For example, for the shepherds of Central Asia, color is rarely an abstract dimension. The quality of an object is inseparable from its concrete manifestation: the redness of the apple is not the same as the redness of fire or the feverish cheek of a child. When one uses categories, they are derived from the practice of everyday life: the Uzbek women, for instance, found in dung and flowers handy organizing principles of color.

The notion of a universal propensity for certain harmonious color combinations based on "unnatural" categories or on underlying neurological preferences does not seem tenable. True, it is possible to threaten a viewer's sense of order by distorting the accepted conventions of representation. Most people still do not accept the painting of a yellow sea, a green horse, or an entirely black canvas, but not because these colors are wrong in some absolute sense. The clash is not due to physiological or perceptual incompatibility. The sources of the conflict are entirely different and must be sought in the habits of symbolization that people in a given culture have acquired.

The same argument holds true for perception of spatial relationships. Since the time of Pythagoras and Aristotle, thinkers have been seeking harmony among lines and spaces—golden ratios, mystical quantities. More recently, Gestalt psychologists have asserted that certain figures were more "pregnant" than others, that they possessed stimulus qualities which were more pleasing to the nervous system. Esthetic preference was supposed to be based on the underlying stimulus qualities of a picture, which were reducible to simple geometric patterns.

Like the early color preference work, this approach assumed simple one-to-one relationships between abstract characteristics of the visual field and the way people perceive and interpret stimuli. In fact, it turns out that people do not necessarily perceive the visual configurations that Euclidian geometry made so popular. Basic patterns such as straight lines and right angles are easily isolated and recognized by people living in a "carpentered world," but those used to a more organic environment fail to perceive such "units" as separate from the rest of the perceptual context.[9]

Here, the research of Luria provides interesting insights.[10] In his Uzbek study he asked respondents to sort a number of geometrical designs, which in the Western world would immediately be classified as squares, circles, and triangles. The Uzbek peasants, however, were unable to see such "natural" similarities. For them a completed circle was a ring, whereas an incomplete circle was a moon, and hence two circles could not be sorted in the same pile. A triangle, however, resembled a *tumar* (a piece of traditional jewelry) therefore, it could be grouped with the circle as a ring.

It is not difficult to see that the categories which critics and psychologists have used to analyze esthetics reflect theories of

9 M. Segall, D. Campbell, and M. Herskovits, *The Influence of Culture on Visual Perception* (Indianapolis: Bobbs, Merrils, 1966).

10 Luria, *Cognitive Development.*

perception, not the actual process by which untutored viewers apprehend visual stimuli. The laws of perception are based on the properties of light, on the axioms of geometry, but might have little to do with the organization of the nervous system, and even less with the phenomenology of perception.

This applies also to some of the more recent psychological theories of esthetics, such as the one proposed by D. E. Berlyne.[11] Like most modern theorists, Berlyne's ideas are based on ancient ideas reinterpreted through current neurological models of the mind. In this case, Aristotle's axiom has been repeated by so many others that the pleasure of perception derives from balancing monotony and confusion.[12] According to Berlyne, a person is attracted to visual stimuli that produce an optimal arousal of the nervous system—stimuli that are neither extremely redundant nor entirely chaotic. Optimal arousal results from a design that has a basic pattern or order, but enough variation to require an active perceptual struggle on the part of the viewer to recognize and maintain the pattern.

Berlyne's model is an attractive one, and it is moderately useful in explaining simple esthetic choices. But as long as it remains a purely neurological theory it quickly runs into the same problems as the others reviewed so far, in that people do not necessarily perceive order and disorder objectively. For example, let us suppose that slide A contains a square pattern composed of twenty-five exact replications of a simple design. Slides B through F are the same, except that ten percent of the elements are randomly changed until slide G has no pattern. According to the optimal arousal theory, people would prefer some of the middle slides in the series; not A or B. which are too regular, nor F or G. which are too chaotic. In effect, this does not happen. One reason is that people do not perceive order and disorder in the designs the way their mathematical structure would seem to require. Some persons rate slide D as the most regular, for example, while others perceive F and G as the most regular, even though objectively it is clear that A is the most regular of all the slides.

There is no question that people can be easily trained to recognize which design is more orderly according to some objective criterion. In the laboratory, one learns readily to agree with whatever the experimenter wants you to see. But the fact remains that in real life people do not carry in their minds yardsticks for measuring abstract concepts of "order" or "disorder." What they see and what they prefer are not determined by objective characteristics of visual stlmuli.

The social construction of visual values

This does not mean, however, that how a thing looks has no bearing on how it affects the viewer. Visual qualities obviously have a lot to do with how we react to an object or an environment. But our reactions are not direct "natural" responses to color and form. They are

11   D. E. Berlyne, *Aesthetics and Psychobiology* (New York: Appleton-Century-Crofts, 1971).

12   Gombrich, *The Sense of Order*, 54.

The Meaning of Products

responses to meanings attached to configurations of color and form.

The extent to which a visual stimulus helps create order in consciousness does not depend on inherent objective characteristics of the object to trigger a programmed response from the brain. What happens instead is that some people in a given culture agree that straight lines (or curved lines) are the best way to represent universal order. If they are convincing enough, everybody will feel a greater sense of harmony when they see straight lines.

Visual values are created by social consensus, not by perceptual stimulation. Thus art criticism is essential for creating meaning, especially in periods of transition when the majority of people are confused about how they should be affected by visual stimuli. Art critics believe that they are discovering criteria by which they can reveal natural esthetic values. In reality they are constructing criteria of value which then become attached to visual elements.

When Vitruvius attacked the fanciful pictorial compositions ornamenting the walls of Roman palaces, he based his critique on the realistic premise that "such things neither are, nor can be, nor have been." Vitruvius and his modern followers believed that natural representation is intrinsically valid and any departure from it inevitably brings disorder or chaos. Order or disorder were seen as being inherent in the representation itself. In actuality, it was the theories and arguments of Vitruvius that linked order with realistic design, and disorder with surrealistic decoration. Romans who were unaware of Vitruvius's critique could have looked at the fanciest Pompeian fresco without a stirring of unease; while those who had heard of the new symbolic code might think: "This is degenerate art, full of falsehood that will destroy our civilization."

Without the consensus-building efforts of the art theorist or critic, each person would evaluate objects in terms of his or her private experiences. In each culture, however, public taste develops as visual qualities are eventually linked with values. The visual taste of an epoch is a subset of its world-view, related to the norms and values that regulate the rest of life. Like other values, visual values can be unanimous or contested, elite or popular, strong or vulnerable, depending on the integration of the culture.

The relativity of esthetic values does not mean that there cannot be "good" design. Good design is a visual statement that maximizes the life goals of the people in a given culture (or, more realistically, the goals of a certain subset of people in the culture) that draws on a shared symbolic expression for the ordering of such goals. If the system of symbols is relatively universal, then the design will also be judged good across time and cultures.

Public works of art gain symbolic power because they are admired by an elite. The average person meets the recognized art object with the respect due something awesome and expensive, but usually the experience leaves no permanent trace in consciousness.

On the other hand, an old china cup, a houseplant, a ring, or a family photograph has symbolic power if it produces a sense of order in the mind. This happens when the owner, in seeing the object, feels that: his or her desires are in harmony; his or her goals might be reached; the past and the future are related in a sensible way; that the people who are close to them are worthy of love and love them in return. Without such feelings, life is not worth living. The objects we surround ourselves with are the concrete symbols that convey these messages. The meaning of our private lives is built with these household objects.

The varying styles of visual expression, that which artists and critics debate endlessly, is part of the public image each culture fashions for itself. It provides abstract, general statements about the problems of a particular historical period. Therefore, the high arts help create order in the thoughts and feelings a given society has about itself. But these are often the thoughts and feelings of a small minority struggling to formulate its experience in terms of a public symbolic vocabulary. Most people create their own private set of references, singling out objects that will give order to what they have experienced.

The creation of private meaning is no less miraculous than the accomplishments of Rembrandt or Michelangelo. It is true that a great master is able to condense, in a given moment of historical time, the expressive striving of a great number of people. The artist's work brings together what many people want to say yet can't express. The creation of meaning in everyday life often uses trite symbols—kitsch rather than originality. Yet our lives are held together by the strands of meaning these worn forms convey.

Product Symbolism of Gandhi and Its Connection with Indian Mythology
S. Balaram

The importance of rhetoric in India

Mythology and symbolism have always played and do still play important roles in Indian life. Many Indians see their own culture as basically nonmaterialist and reliant more on spiritual than on physical values. Indians also like to distinguish their own approach, which gives preference to feelings, emotions, and inexplicable inner convictions, from the Western approach, which is predominantly analytical, intellectual, and logical. The Indian approach often expresses itself as seeing a symbol in everything. Symbols and meanings are so important that realism sometimes seems to be deliberately discarded. For outsiders, this Indian-culture emphasis on symbolism frequently is misread as "suspension of reason."

Most Indians do not question the outer form of a god with a thousand arms, four heads, an elephant head, or both male and female features. In the Indian context, the inner meaning behind an outer form is most important. This apparent neglect of realism in India has ancient roots and permeates much of contemporary culture. It can be recognized in virtually all art forms from the traditional performing arts to modern popular films.

For example, as part of a performance, Indian classical dance always has accompanying musicians positioned right next to the action. Moreover, the classical Sanskrit drama has a "Sutradhar" who from time to time intervenes with the presentation, talking directly to the audience by either interpreting or commenting on the action. Further, nearly all folk performances contain ritualistic elements, and performers wear exaggerated costumes, jewelry, and colors far removed from what one encounters in the reality of Indian everyday life. Such classical alienation devices are quite common in the other arts of modern India as well.

Probably the most widely accessible cultural form in modern India is its film. The immense success of song, dance, and melodrama presented in this genre is indebted to their deep roots in Indian mythology and popular culture. Indian audiences are not only familiar with their myths but easily can and do transcend beyond the surface reality presented to them into a different realm. As K. G. Subramanian says, "The mythology-filled Indian mind reduces everything to symbols of enormous tolerance and elasticity which persist through successive changes in religious ideas, magically transforming themselves becoming large in content and expansive."[1]

Popular Indian film continues to use traditional mythological images for virtually all of its heroes. Whether it is N. T. Rama Rao and M. G. Ramachandran of the south or Amitabh Bachchan of the north,[2] their roles essentially copy archetypal mythological heroes from which they differ only in emphasis. Although one may be identified with poor youth and the other with god, the movie roles all derive from near word-to-word translations of myths whose heroes perform the impossible with magical powers, destroy evil, and always win in the end. The immense popularity of Indian film heroes is evidence for the continuous power of Indian mythology in modern media expressions.

It is my contention that it is the mythology of a culture that generates artistic expressions and political discourse, including industrial forms which in turn reinterpret and materially support the psychological reality in which these mythological forms exist; and that an understanding of these symbolic relationships can in fundamental ways aid the design for contemporary needs. Unfortunately, modern artists and critics are often attracted to the surface appearance of these mythological forms, to their grammar and medium as opposed to their social roots. This superficiality is perpetuated by a simplistic and a historical semiotics that analyzes whole forms into separate signs and symbols at the neglect of references to the larger mythologies that underlie the stories of everyday life in India. A notable exception to this general neglect is the ingenious understanding and application of mythological symbolism by the late Mohandas Karamchand Gandhi, who led India's independence movement.

Figure 1
Gandhi at work in his typical dress and sitting posture.

1   K. G. Subramanian, *Moving Focus: Essays on Indian Art* (New Delhi: Lalit Kala Akademy, 1978).

2   These are names of popular film actors from major regions of India. Interestingly, N. T. Rama Rao and M. G. Ramachandran have used their screen image—Rama Rao as mythological god and Ramachandran as do-gooder—to become elected chief ministers of the states of Andhra Pradesh and Tamil Nadu, respectively. Amitabh Bachan, with the screen image of an angry young man (destroyer of the bad), is about to do the same.

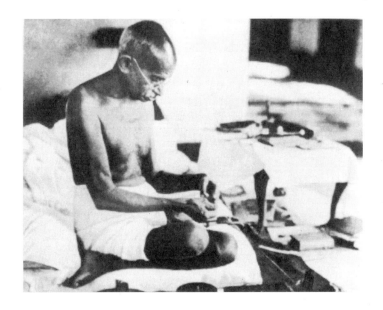

The Meaning of Products

This article[3] grew out of realizing the amazing presence of Indian mythology in nearly all contemporary popular-cultural expressions and is part of a larger effort at exploring mythology-based symbolism for use in industrial design. Here I am concerned with demonstrating what might now be called the product semantics used by Gandhi in effecting major sociopolitical changes in India. His symbolic use of artifacts was, of course, only part of his complex political strategy.

Indian mythology and Gandhi and Krishna as symbols

Gandhi lived his life as a well-publicized experiment. Not only did he use everything around him for its symbolic significance, but he ultimately became a symbol himself, a demigod, invested with more mythological meaning than he may have wanted to bear.

The enormous popular symbolic importance of Gandhi is demonstrated by the fact that in many Indian homes the pictures of Lord Krishna and Gandhi are hanging side by side. To gain a deeper understanding of how product semantics is embedded in Indian mythology and how the process of symbol creation works, it is useful to compare the life of Gandhi, a contemporary and real person who became a mythological figure, and that of Lord Krishna who is the most popular mythological figure of the Indian epics.

With this comparison, I hope to shed light on the differences in the communication strategies both figures actually and allegedly used, the meanings attributed to them, and the kinds of objects or symbols they created to sustain their symbolic roles. The similarities lie in their appeal to the Indian population with all its diversity — in the case of Gandhi, of communicating with hundreds of millions of illiterate people during a rather short period of time and persuading them to engage in political action or accept restraint.

According to the great epic *Mahabharata*, Krishna spread the doctrine of love while eventually effecting the great war between the Kauravas and Pandavas. Similarly, Gandhi adopted the doctrine of nonviolence (Ahimsa[4]) while actually leading the historical Indian fight for independence from Britain. The deceptively simple rhetorical devices used by Gandhi not only conveyed certain values but raised political awareness and successfully persuaded the Indian masses to adopt certain attitudes toward the economy and form a social movement whose magnitude is probably historically unprecedented. In terms of utility or economic viability these devices may not stand the test of time, but they very much resemble the persuasive strategies attributed to the mythological Krishna.

A political leader sitting down and working with a spinning wheel (Charkha) when civil war was blazing all over the country was paramount to Krishna singing the *Bhagavadgita* in the midst of the great Kurukshetra battle. The apparent paradox disappears, however, when one looks at these two behaviors in their nonphysi-

3 Part of this article was originally intended as a paper for ARTHAYA, a National Seminar on Visual Semantics in Bombay in 1987, but it was not presented.

4 The word "Ahimsa," meaning "nonviolence," was popularized by Gandhi.

Figure 2
A popular picture of Krishna, the Hindu mythological god.

5   Kusum Jaisingh, "Communication and
    Tradition in Revolutions: Gandhi and Mao
    as Mass Communicators," *Communicator*
    (October 1980): 37–43; "People against
    Charisma," *Communicator* (October
    1981): 20-25.

cal sense. Krishna used the battlefield as context to put forth the essence of Hindu philosophy, the doctrine of Karma (unattached duty). Likewise, Gandhi used the freedom fight as a context to put forth the doctrine of Ahimsa (nonviolence) and economic self-reliance. Working a spinning wheel suggested the importance of communal industry and independence from imports from Britain and brought Gandhi closer to ordinary people. Thus Gandhi's spinning wheel, a purely mechanical device, became a symbol through which he could communicate to large masses of people both the actions that needed to be taken and his personal philosophy.

Contrary to the prevailing belief in the West, Gandhi was not a charismatic leader, a superhuman hero.[5] He was made into one only after his death. All his life Gandhi was constantly in touch with common people and always tried to be identified with them by all his means—personal appearance, manner of speech, behavior, and the objects he associated himself with. His style of communication

The Meaning of Products

was not "top-down"—people at the top telling people at the bottom what to do; it was "bottom-sideways"—people at the bottom telling each other what to do. He even succeeded to some extent in an extraordinary "bottom-up" communication—people at the bottom telling people at the top what to do. Unquestionably, Gandhi's popularity with the masses is attributable largely to his use of symbols and rhetorical devices that have their origin in Indian mythology and popular culture.

Man in the image of God: comparative analysis

The communication devices used by Gandhi and Krishna can be analyzed in terms of objective, subjective, and self-identification symbols. Objective symbols concern the conscious application of communication devices toward desired ends. Subjective symbols concern the largely subconscious use of personal artifacts and related objects. Self-identification symbols refer to a communicator's identification with the messages, symbols, or artifacts he or she uses, whether intended or not. Identification lends credibility to intended (objective) messages and may determine their persuasive force. For instance, the author of a book on poverty may not want to show himself as a "fat millionaire" lest his message lack credibility.

Mythology is probably the most important cultural treasure of a people. It occupies the peoples' collective dreams, aspirations, and visions. It is stored in the form of rituals, symbols, and innumerable artifacts, which serve as constant reminders of cultural unity. Symbols that can be interpreted in terms of powerful mythologies can overcome the limits of conventional communications. Gandhi drew immense strength from myths, probably unconsciously, in persuading millions of illiterate people with whom conventional methods of communication would not have worked. A deeper understanding of successful uses of symbolism in mass movements would surely bring new insights in the area of communications (broadly defined) and help designers to "liberate" people with designs rather than alienate them from the environment. Ill-fitting shoes hurt the feet, ill-fitting chairs constrain the body, ill-fitting messages retard the mind; while well-fitting shoes protect the feet and feel good, well-fitting chairs comfort the body, well-fitting messages stimulate the mind, thus causing liberation. Designed objects can provide physical support and enable people to do what they cannot do otherwise; but it is their symbolic qualities, their largely mythological meanings, that can liberate people from psychological depression, from social oppression, and add a spiritual dimension that is individually invigorating and culturally creative.

Gandhi surrounded himself with objects of deep mythological meanings. His behavior inspired many to take a path leading toward their own liberation. Although far from being a professional designer he often initiated and inspired new designs that would communicate the possibility of liberation and support this direction.

Table 1

Correspondences between Gandhi's and Krishna's Symbolisms

GANDHI	KRISHNA
General Aspects	
Temporal placement: contemporary.	Temporal placement: ancient.
Existence: real.	Existence: puranic.
Made later into a mythological hero	Mythological hero.
Title: Mahatma—the great soul.	Title: Paramatma—the super soul.
Noncharismatic: In spite of great achievements, always asserted, "What I was able to do anybody can."	Noncharismatic: In spite of divine powers, Bhagavata purana emphasizes his simple village life.
Principal leader in freedom struggle but held no high position in office.	Principal leader in Mahabharata war but held no high position.
Promoted "nonviolence as a way for peace."	Promoted "love" as a way to reach salvation.
Toward the end disappointed at the fights among his people; died unnatural death.	Toward the end disappointed at the fights among his people; died unnatural death.
Objective Symbols	
White cap adopted to create unique identity and to signify Gandhian principles and human dignity.	Peacock feather adopted to create unique identity and to signify natural beauty.
Khadi: hand-spun and handwoven cloth, the wearing of which is possible to all levels of people and which signifies self-reliance and a common identity across all classes.	Hari-Naam: vertical mark on the forehead, the wearing of which is possible to all levels of people and which signifies acceptance of vaishnav principles and identity with other vaishnavs.
Spinning wheel (Charkha): signifying the act of self-reliance. Metaphorical identity with Dharm Chakra. Also a tool of self-employment that brings self-reliance and self-respect.	Discus (Sudarshan Chakra): signifying the act of dynamic psychic force. Also a tool in destroying evil for establishing Dharma (social justice). Also flute: simple local product standing for self-reliance
"Ram Dhun" songs and prayers as means to bring people together for common action.	Songs and dance as means to bring people together for common action.
Evolved "Satyagraha" as unique way of opening the eyes of others whenever reason failed.	Showed "Vishwarupa" as unique way of opening the eyes of others whenever reason failed.
Subjective Symbols	
Dress: white linen cloth signifying purity, simpleness and identity with poor masses.	Dress: yellow cloth (Pithambara) signifying auspiciousness and prosperity to all.
Thin lean body (due to often-observed fasts) identifying with hungry millions.	Blue body: signifying infinity; also metaphorical reminder of rain cloud which is important for an agricultural country.
Often seen with children and cattle signifying compassion toward the weak and helpless; also the importance of cattle in Indian agricultural communities. Called "Bapuji," the father.	Often seen with cattle, cowherds, etc. signifying compassion toward the weak; also the importance of cattle in Indian agricultural communities. Called "Gopala," the cowherd.
Self-Identifcation Symbols	
Identified with masses though born in high society.	Identified with masses (mostly cowherds) though born in high society.
Pronounced: "World is my family."	Pronounced: "I am the Universe."
Emphasized actions, continuous experimenting, said "My life is my message."	Emphasized deeds rather than things and preached "philosophy of action" (Karmayoga).

The Meaning of Products

To this end he demonstrated extraordinary ingenuity in using the immense symbolic significance of ordinary tools, simple clothes, and community development in an agricultural country that was and still is mostly illiterate. Gandhi's semantic ideas, however, have their origins in ancient Indian mythologies that were and still are at the core of Indian culture.

Roots of Indian product semantics

In the west, product semantics is often referred to as a new discipline of an old and unconscious practice.[6] This characterization does not apply to India, where the beginnings of product semantics are as ancient as the Vedas. The Indian Vedic texts and the later Puranas contain several references to the use of physical implements for their symbolic significance. This is not to deny that religion in the West makes heavy use of symbolism as well and can hardly be explained without it. I suggest, however, that the semantics of artifacts probably never was codified in a manner comparable to the Vedas; and because the major religions in the West are comparatively recent, their religious meanings probably never governed the entire spectrum of things in everyday life and never penetrated the whole Western culture down to the fairy tales and popular heroes of ordinary village folk. Not only are the Hindu gods invested with symbolism, as I said above, but so is every article associated with them: the objects they carry in their hands (Ayudhas), their mounts (Vahanas), their dress (Vastras), their special jewelry (Alankaras), and all the other symbolic forms. These are all delineated with vital and sometimes complex symbolic meanings. The powerful product semantics in India governs the use of objects not only in religious rituals but also in daily life, not just in the forgotten past but also in the living presence.

Take a mundane industrial product like a bangle, which every Indian woman wears. It is a decorative object, insignificant in its function, size, and cost—the cheapest item of jewelry compared to any other jewelry an Indian woman might wear. However, it had and continues to have the utmost semantic significance. It is so strong, that in villages a woman dare not be seen without bangles unless she is widowed. While the form remains the same, differences in material, color, texture, and finish speak of vastly different meanings. In Gujarat, a red-painted ivory bangle with gold lining is auspicious and indicates the bridal status of the woman wearing it. A glass bangle of any color is the sign of a married woman. Plain metal bangles devoid of any color or elaborate pattern indicate that the wearer is a widow. Even such simple products are governed by a complex semantics whose grammar every Indian readily understands. Such a language speaks clearer and louder and expresses human relations and social status more efficiently than words ever can.

6   Klaus Krippendorff and Reinhart Butter, "Product Semantics: Exploring the Symbolic Qualities of Form," *Innovation* 3/2 (1984): 4–8.

Product semantics of Gandhi: a holistic approach

Gandhi's semantic use of objects was simultaneously multivarious and integrative in nature.[7] Although for the convenience of analysis one can categorize his methods and devices separately, they cannot be fully understood in isolation. They played parts in Gandhi's many-pronged strategy together with numerous symbolic actions such as writing, making speeches, reciting prayers, and engaging in fasts; his personal identification with particular problems was also significant. Most important were the contexts he carefully chose.

As is the case with the mythological Krishna, Gandhi sought a composite approach to life. He used different levels and various kinds of semantic strategies for purposes that were only superficially different; they were holistically related to his main goal. These strategies complemented each other and achieved a synergistic effect. In this way, "freeing India from British rule" must be seen not as a separate aim but connected to the removal of untouchability, to praying together, to spinning every day, and to many other symbolic events.

The power of semantics over function

Arms have always played a decisive role in social-political revolutions and wars. Even nonmilitary artifacts have greatly aided such events. Hitler, for instance, exploited Porsche's development of the Volkswagen (people's car) for political ends. But products such as arms, cars, and so forth are always thought to be used primarily for their functional qualities. It is Gandhi who started using industrial products mainly for their extraordinary symbolic qualities.[8]

The important products employed by Gandhi were:

- **Charkha:** The traditional spinning wheel. Many times modified by Gandhi, it developed into a compact portable Charkha for his use in traveling.
- **Gandhi Cap:** The white cloth cap worn traditionally by Gujarati people.
- **Khadi cloth:** Hand-spun and hand-woven cloth Gandhi and his followers always used as their apparel.
- **The half-Dhoti:** A lower garment worn by lower-caste Hindu men. Gandhi made this his permanent attire.
- **The Gandhi Chappals:** Traditional Indian slippers. Gandhi not only simplified the design but stitched them himself.
- **The mud house:** Home to most villagers. Gandhi adopted it for his own needs.
- **The staff:** A simple ordinary stick Gandhi used for walking.
- **The watch:** Large, pocket size watch. Since Gandhi had no pockets, he hung it above his Dhoti.
- **The glasses:** Simple, round glasses without decorative embellishments.

Gandhi advocated that his followers use the first three items. Using the other products himself, he made sure that others

7   Mohandas Karamchand Gandhi, *An Autobiography or the Story of My Experiments with Truth* (Ahmedabad: Navjeevan Publishing Co., 1976).

8   I hasten to add here that Gandhi was not the only one to use products for their symbolic significance, but the emphasis he placed on these qualities and the conscious and consistent application of symbolic notions has been, I dare say, rare and exemplary.

The Meaning of Products

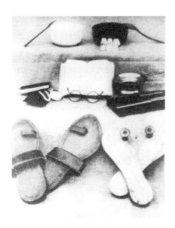

Figure 3
The products used by Gandhi.

would see how he handled them. In insisting on wearing or using these articles all the time he recognized the importance of the "totalness" of a multidimensional message; communication does not happen through isolated strategies. As a public figure, being constantly watched, everything he did contributed semantically to his holistic message. He himself declared, "My life is my message." Thus he went far beyond Marshall McLuhan's "the medium is the message." He foretold a simple and basic truth which scholars in semiotics, communication, and cognition became aware of only later.

Product territories

There are some commonalities in all the artifacts with which Gandhi identified himself. They were all products of everyday use to people at the bottom of Indian society. The people were thoroughly familiar with them and their sociocultural histories and understood, perhaps unconsciously, their role in mythology. One could say they all were archetypal manifestations of poor Indians' belongings. They were simple, mundane, and humble and created a strong sense of identification and belongingness. For the Indian masses these were "our very own" basic symbols of being. A third-class train compartment in which Gandhi preferred to travel is something which ordinary people at the bottom experience and, therefore, is theirs. Had Gandhi traveled in a first-class compartment or by airplane it would have been something most people never experienced and could not relate to, a luxury they do not have direct experience with. Therefore, it would not be theirs.

All of us could be said to be at home in different territories of products according to our experience or familiarity with them. Those using the same products share a common territory. The territorial imperative of product semantics suggests that people who live in the same product territory more readily accept each other's messages than those belonging to different territories. This imperative implies that people by themselves don't just talk to each other. The symbolic qualities of the material things they associate with always speak with them.

A major reason why many political leaders who followed Gandhi's ideology but not his symbolic strategies could not reach the Indian people as much as Gandhi did is explainable in these terms. The late Prime Minister Nehru, for example, was loved by the people for his sincere work to advance the country but he was never considered part of them. He always made attempts to socialize, mix, meet, dances and play with ordinary people, and these symbolic gestures won him the people's goodwill and indeed media headlines; but the products he used put him into a territory far above the majority of Indians. The beautiful Shervani and coat with its delicate red rose and the palatial building—all these sent a strong message: "He is a nawab[9] with a Gandhi Cap."

9 "Nawab" is an Urdu word for "prince," but with metaphorical connotations of luxurious living for which the Moghul princes were famous.

Present Indian politicians, including the current prime minister, now use another method. Whenever they visit a different state (India is so vast that almost every state has its indigenous culture and often houses several languages), they dress like the local farmer (India also is an agricultural country) when addressing the people. It probably helps in making the audience feel somewhat more comfortable and adds color to the meeting, but because people know that after the event these politicians change into their usually rich dress, get into an expensive car, and fly off by a special airplane, their message can hardly be taken as sincere.

Fighting armed with symbols

As I said above, Gandhi considered artifacts not only as tools but as symbols of action as well. Tools may not be available to all, but symbols can be made out of virtually anything by everyone and motivate their effective use. Guns are neither easily accessible nor affordable by everybody, but such ordinary things as Khadi cloth, a Gandhi Cap, or a spinning wheel are both. Guns also require users to be trained, while all Gandhian implements are usable with few skills. Gandhi chose products and related actions everyone could have access to and use, no matter how lacking he or she was in skills, education, and economic resources. Each could participate and act according to his or her own level and contribute toward the cause of "social and political freedom." Gandhi did not fight the British in their own terms but managed to pitch symbols against guns and succeeded in "disarming" the colonial power to the amazement of the British and perhaps the whole world.

Coherence of product symbolism

While preaching nonviolence, self-reliance, and certain communal qualities, Gandhi adopted a style that, as I showed above, is symbolic of simple living. The simple Gandhi Chappals, the watch, the pencil, the postcard, a small desk, his insistence on walking while others used a car, his traveling in third-class compartments, his manner of sitting in public meetings, etc. made his message coherent and consistent with prevailing mythologies. The conscious choice of these products and practices indicate their application as objective symbols to support his basic message.

The importance of the credibility Gandhi achieved through the choice of coherent symbols usually is underestimated. I feel coherence is of the essence in any communication and also for industrial design. Even after a message has reached its target, communication may not have taken place. If a product is bought by or given to potential users, it may not make a difference in their practice. It is only its coherence with other objects in the same territory, with the life-style of potential users, and with the mythology everyone—designers, users, beneficiaries, bystanders—is familiar with that renders it credible, acceptable, and usable with personal engagement.

Continuous transformations

Continued identification leads to immense involvement between communicator and communication, and it is almost inevitable that in this process the communicator and his or her message become an indistinguishable unity.

I already quoted Gandhi as saying, "My life is my message." A well-known Indian poet and scholar, Professor Umashankar Joshi, who personally knew Gandhi, mentioned to me that Gandhi's way was *not* communication but communion. His deep involvement in the subject made Gandhi *one with it.*

Before asking people to fast, Gandhi fasted himself. Before asking others to remove untouchability from the lowest caste, Gandhi lived with untouchables. He refused special treatment in jail. And so on. This was exemplary for any action Gandhi asked of others. His advice was, "Before you transform others, you should transform yourself."

This is again found in Indian mythology, which insists on a special relationship or bond between the actor and action. In many ancient rituals, persons conducting them become possessed and therefore indistinguishable from the act performed by them. Ancient Indian estheticians were aware of this transformation and prescribed strict codes to this effect for the artist to achieve Rasa Siddhi (the attainment of emotion). In Kuchipudi *Bhagavata Mela* dance drama, for example, the man playing the part of Lord Narasimha (though his part is very brief) has to be on fast and perform Puja[10] before coming on stage. According to Hindu mythology, Narasimha is one of the ten incarnations (Dasavatara) of Lord Vishnu, who appears before his devotee Prahlada as a man-lion. He kills his adversary the demon king Hiranya Kashipu by tearing him apart. This is a very popular dance item among Kuchipudi performers. Once an actor, who played the role of Narasimha, so completely identified himself with his role that he actually tore the Hiranya Kashipu player apart, on stage!

There is further evidence for this phenomenon of identification between actor and action. Heinrich Zimmer writes, "According to Hindu theory, it [the mind] is constantly transforming itself into the shapes of the objects of which it becomes aware. Its subtle substance assumes the forms and colors of everything offered to it by the senses, imagination, memory, and emotion."[11] Accordingly, icons in Hindu temples are not images symbolizing god; they are not called "Pratima," suggesting the likeness of a deity, but they are called "Murti," a Sanskrit word for embodiment and manifestation, a transformation of god himself or herself.[12]

For designers to be convincing they too have to become involved with the object of their design, become one with it or indistinguishable from it. Only then can they expect to produce artifacts that are meaningful in the sense of reflecting the very mythology that guides users and is part of any designer's psychological reality as well.

10 "Puja" means "worship, done traditionally to invoke god."

11 Heinrich Zimmer, *Philosophies of India* (Princeton: Princeton University Press 1985), 284–85.

12 Diana L. Eck, *Dorshan: Seeing the Divine Image in India* (Chambersburg, PA: Anima Books, 1985).

Product meanings in two-way interaction

According to the above, all designed products take on the image of their creator at the time they are born. The Nakashima chair and the Le Corbusier building are good examples of individual styles, of the marks left by their designers. When such artifacts are subsequently used, they not only gradually acquire the character of their users but also influence and give some of their character to those users in return. Thus, designer, artifact, and user influence each other in two-way interaction and become one with the emergent symbolic qualities or meanings that the product subsequently manifests. I recall the American film *Witness* in which the old man tells the child not to touch the gun because it sends out evil vibes. Indian product semantics does not consider this a superstition but a psychological truth. It is a common observation that individuals' mentalities and behaviors change drastically after they get a telephone in their homes. The telephone acquires a meaning through its use and affects its user in return. Similarly, a man's mental condition and behavior will be markedly different when he has in his pocket a gun, a million dollars in cash, or a rubbing stone. All emerge as powerful symbols in users' lives.

The interaction between designer, user, and product is also demonstrable with the products originally used and promoted by Gandhi. The cloth cap, for example, was chosen by Gandhi as an accepted, common-man's symbol of dignity. This cap was a mundane and traditional product, and it is therefore difficult to say through whom its meaning was acquired, or whether it had a particular designer's style at all. However, at the beginning of the Gandhian movement it meant dignity. After Gandhi adopted and promoted it, it slowly took on all the values that Gandhi stood for: Ahimsa, self-sacrifice, patriotism, equality, and so on. This traditional Gujarati cap came to be known as the Gandhi Cap and became the main symbol for Gandhiism.

After Gandhi's death, the Gandhian values started eroding, but his so-called followers kept wearing the Gandhi Cap, not so much because it stood for his values but to take political advantage of the Gandhian image. They initially succeeded. But soon their true intentions surfaced, and the resulting interaction gave a new meaning to the Gandhi Cap. In popular movies, theater, literature, etc., the Gandhi Cap now is the symbol of hypocritical and deceitful politicians.

Gandhi in his lifetime seemed to have been very much aware of this two-way interaction between product and user. He took great care in maintaining compatibility between what the objects he was using meant for others and the personality he sought to project. He was also much concerned with how the objects in his immediate environment would influence him as a person and therefore surrounded himself with artifacts whose symbolic qualities would enable him to realize the values he preferred. The mud hut, the postcard, the half-Dhoti, and the staff not only stood for but also

The Meaning of Products

Figure 4
Gandhi in his typical attire with one of his followers behind him wearing a Gandhi Cap.

influenced him toward the principles he laid down for himself; for him these artifacts also stood as a symbol for his people.

The limitation of linguistic and graphic communications

Existing means of linguistic and graphic communications have severe limitation. They entirely depend for their effectiveness on the user's verbal and visual literacy. In large sections of the world where such literacy is lacking, the linguistic and graphic forms are meaningful only to the educated and quite incomprehensible otherwise. One of the best ways to communicate with or design useful artifacts for such people is to learn from and adopt their own mythology, their own meaning system, their own semantics as expressed through the artifacts they experience and handle daily. Not only does this guarantee an immediacy of understanding and natural involvement, it also reflects the fact that artifacts of everyday life always express themselves through more than one sense. Products can not only be seen but can also be touched, heard, felt, tasted—and, above all, used. Multi-sensory experiences provide the basis for whole gestalts, and cross-sensory meanings provide richer experiences than could be conveyed by either talk or sight alone. In his essay on the "Necessity of Temples," Gandhi once wrote, "somehow or other, we [the people of India] want something which we can touch, something which we can see, something before which we can kneel down."[13] This attests to Gandhi's awareness of the power of multi-sensory product semantics over mono-sensory forms of educated communication.

Action and the "product"

If products are classified as either end products, intermediary products or tools, Gandhi used all three types for purposes of communication: the Gandhi Cap, an end product; the Khadi, an intermediary product; the Charkha, a tool. Gandhi was not satisfied with projecting the first two as concrete and accessible symbols of self-reliance. He also wanted to emphasize the "process of making," and presumably therefore developed the spinning wheel into a full-fledged symbol of production and insisted on spinning with it. His public meetings always made spinning a regular (symbolic) activity and gave it an important role in his own daily schedule. Spinning was only one method through which the need for action was expressed. The Salt Satyagraha, which shook the powerful British, was another essentially symbolic act toward self-determination and independence.

The importance of visual metaphors

Gandhi also made conscious use of the symbolic power of metaphors. For him, the Charkha was not a mere tool that could be afforded and used by millions of people. Its mechanically transparent appearance became a simple-to-understand icon of the complex principles of self-reliance, active employment, and productivity. But through its resemblance to other valued symbols, as metaphor, it

13 R. S. Nathan, *Symbolism in Hinduism* (Bombay: Central Chinmarya Mission Trust, 1983).

had even greater significance. It resembled the Dharma Chakra, the wheel of righteous action, which has a long and deep sociocultural history. Gandhi realized the great metaphorical impact of this wheel; therefore, he and his followers adopted it as the main icon on the Indian flag. The wheel is loaded with deep rooted meanings: the universal law of motion, the cycle of life, death and rebirth, the universe as seen with the inner light of illumination, the concept of continuous change, the Buddhist Wheel of Law, and so on. The Chakra is the most frequently found image in Hindu culture. Between these aniconic and iconic meanings, the Chakra also best represented the transition from tradition to modernity that Gandhi strove for and sought to represent.

When Gandhi wanted to increase the mechanical efficiency of the Charkha, Morris Friedman designed an eight-spindle spinning wheel which increased productivity many times. Yet, Gandhi rejected this design saying that it looked complex to people and hence would not be accepted by them. It shows Gandhi's concern with the persuasive force of a product's metaphorical quality as a semantic dimension more vital than its technical performance.[14]

As a practicing Indian designer for nearly 20 years, I know of numerous examples of product failures due to ignorance of the persuasive aspect of their forms. Functionally, esthetically, and economically excellent solutions are insufficient to gain acceptance and use. The improved bullock cart with pneumatic tires is still not accepted by Indian farmers. Fishermen refused to live in the concrete buildings given free to them in place of their huts. In a recent case, even educated air hostesses refused to wear the more functional aprons because of the unacceptable meanings they conveyed. These rejections are not to be explained by sheer surface preferences but by the people's metaphorical grounding in the familiar and sacred.

Appearance is not esthetics alone
The appearance of an object is not to be confused with mere esthetics. It too goes much deeper. Its chief determinant is its semantics. Since "meaning is in the mind of the beholder," whoever wants to render something understandable must either communicate with and educate that beholder's mind or make use of myths already existing, beliefs already held, or meanings already familiar to the mind of that beholder. Gandhi attempted both these methods.

Several enlightened political leaders of modern India now engage designers to make their meeting places, the podium, and objects on it visually attractive on site as well as on TV. Designers usually accomplish this by hiding ugly wires and microphones, selecting elegant furniture, tablecloths, etc. But what meanings do such places then project for the masses of poor people who are expected to attend? To them the semantics of political meeting places is clear, and their reading is straightforward and simple:

14 Suchitra Balasubramanian, *Gandhi's Way: A Study of Communication as if People Mattered* (Ahmedabad: Diploma Project, National Institute of Design, 1987). I was a guide to this graduate diploma project, and many of my ideas on Gandhi's methods of communication crystallized in discussions with this student.

"Beauty is covering ugliness." "Beauty is expensive and not affordable by us." In contrast, Gandhi's Charkha suggested: "This is our spinning wheel. It gives us strength against weapons. Its use is easy, and practicing it is all that our historical fight needs." The indigenous Charkha does not mystify its purpose like the beautifully designed podium now does.

The meaning of surface: forms, colors, and textures

The surface qualities of products, such as their forms, colors, and textures, are widely recognized concerns of product semantics. Gandhi used predominantly white and natural color in the materials chosen for his artifacts. He wore and advised his followers to wear white. His walking stick was an ordinary one, without adornments. His eyeglasses consisted of simple circular lenses with a thin metal frame. The mud huts in Indian villages are usually decorated with beautiful drawings, patterns, and even colors. Gandhi carefully avoided these on his own mud houses. While he wanted his hut to signify the village hut, the avoidance of surface treatment not only on his mud houses but also on the Charkha and the Chappal made all his products less locally identifiable and brought them closer to their archetypal meanings, meanings that were easily understandable by most Indians, without distraction by ornamentation. The semantic attributes of all his products are now described in terms of simplicity, austerity, economy, and minimalist attitudes, but deep inside always was the nonmaterialism of the Indian sages.

Gandhi's Chappals and the Bauhaus

As I described earlier, meanings of objects arise and change in interaction among designers, artifacts, and social circumstances. Aware of the inevitability of such changes, Gandhi chose the products he promoted largely for their potential to convey archetypal meanings, and through his actions he very much assumed that they would acquire them. The Khadi he used was initially a poor man's cloth, reflecting economic status. Under Gandhi's leadership, white Khadi became a symbol of the freedom fighters, irrespective of their economic level. It became a political symbol of widely shared significance.

We have noted that when Gandhi chose his mud houses and carefully redesigned the Charkha and the Chappal, he eliminated all decorations, carvings, and traditional adornments, simplified their form, and reduced their appearance to their essentials. Surprisingly, his frequent advice "omit the unimportant" is quite consistent with several European design philosophies such as the tradition of the Ulm School of Design and perhaps even of the Bauhaus. But Gandhi's aim was not a formalist one; it was largely socially motivated. The omission of unnecessary ornamentation discourages social differentiation and can and did indeed symbolically support the tremendous integrative force his India needed. These choices reveal his unprecedented awareness of the social and political dynamics of product meanings and their mythological connections. I do not quite know whether the minimalism and universalism of Ulm was similarly motivated. However, the situation of Germany at that time and Ulm's self-declared objective to aid the physical, esthetic, and social reconstruction in postwar Europe suggests an at least unconscious use of product semantics there as well.

Contexts change meanings

Clearly, the product meanings I examined here belonged to Gandhi's own times and arose in a particular sociocultural and political context of use. Today, this context has changed and so have the meanings of the surviving artifacts.

With the advent of cheaper, more durable, and easier to maintain synthetic cloth, Khadi became costly. With the freedom fight won, its victory also quenched its spirit. The rich elite, who could continue to afford buying and maintaining Khadi as a product, started using it in order to distinguish themselves socially from those who could not. Today, wearing Khadi is a mark of socioeconomic status. With this change in context, the very product that once was a symbol of equality is now a symbol of its opposite, a means to differentiate the rich from the still poor and largely illiterate masses. I already mentioned the change in meaning of the Gandhi Cap from a unifying symbol of members of the liberation movement to the symbol of corrupt politicians.

The Charkha also changed its meaning drastically. As machines took over its functions of spinning, people no longer used it in communal settings, and its earlier symbolic value eroded. Miniature models of Charkhas started appearing as drawing room showpieces. Its wheel is still incorporated in the Indian flag, but it is also used in promotional material. Thus, the Charkha changed from an active working symbol to a passive decorative element of other products.

Concluding remarks

This article started by saying that product meanings are the more persuasive the more they materially support and can in turn be interpreted in terms of the powerful mythologies of the especially rich culture of India. I have tried to demonstrate that these meanings arise in interaction with their social contexts of use, particularly including designers, users, and other artifacts in the same product territory. Perhaps the lesson to be learned from Gandhi's symbolic strategies is that successful artifacts symbolically mediate between the relatively stable mythological heritage of a culture and the relatively fast-changing socioeconomic contexts of their everyday use. Without the symbolic reference to mythology, product meanings become entirely dependent on their variable context and hence semantically and motivationally unstable. Without the expressive connection to their contemporary contexts of use or functions, traditional product meanings easily become mere decorative reminders of a no-longer living past. While alive, Gandhi managed to maintain and revitalize the powerful mediation process involving himself as well as the products whose symbolic qualities he helped shape thereby. It is this symbolic mediation process between mythology and everyday life that product semantics must inform.

Many Indians consider Buddha, who lived only 1,500 years ago, already one of the incarnations of Lord Vishnu.[15] Whether Gandhi will one day be treated as one or be forgotten is not as important as to learn from the exemplary way he acted in concert with powerful mythologies, shaped the symbolic qualities of several products, and thereby persuaded people to participate in a movement—a movement unprecedented for modern times, not just against an imperial power but to simultaneously liberate themselves. I maintain that the material products of a culture can never be regarded as user-independent in function or separately understandable entities. They acquire meanings in use, become integrated in everyone's whole life experiences, and interact with the mythology from which they derive their symbolic strength. They collectively participate in and carry forward the message of what that culture is about. I hope and suggest to incorporate such remarkable Gandhian insights into a product semantics for design.

---

15 Indian mythology has many gods, but Hindus believe that these are but different manifestations of one ultimate god.

The Gift
Clive Dilnot

We are forgetting how to give presents. Violation of the exchange principle has something nonsensical and implausible about it.... [Today] even the private giving of presents has degenerated to a social function exercised with rational bad grace, careful adherence to the prescribed budget, skeptical appraisal of the other and the least possible effort. Real giving had its joy in imagining the joy of the receiver. It means choosing, expending time, going out of one's way, thinking of the other as a subject: the opposite of distraction. Just this hardly anyone is now able to do. At best they give what they would have liked themselves, only a few degrees worse. The decay of giving is mirrored in the distressing invention of gift-articles, based on the assumption that one does not know what to give because one really does not want to.

Theodor Adorno,
Minima Moralia: Reflections on Damaged Life (1944)

1. A paradox of gift giving, often alluded to, is that when conducted as obligation, it is profoundly depressive. There is something wrong here. After all, the act of giving, if we disengage it from Christmas and its horrors, should be a positive thing. The gift ought to be that which, when proffered by the giver, induces a double joy—that of the receiver in the object, and that of the giver at the receiver's joy. Neither of these joys is inconsiderable. It is worth analyzing them because they tell us something about how things work for us and, therefore, something about the character of design activity.

Ideally the receiver of the gift obtains a double joy. First, and most obviously, there is a joy in the thing itself, the object received. The proper gift gives happiness because it matches perfectly one moment of the receiver's needs and desires. Sometimes it even helps receivers discover and satisfy desires they did not know they had. Second, the gift gives joy because the successful gift affirms a positive relationship between giver and receiver. It is concrete or evident proof that the giver knows, and has understood, recognized, affirmed, and sought to concretely meet the other's most intimate needs and desires. Moreover, the receiver finds additional joy in being the subject of the imaginative work undertaken by the giver in securing and giving this gift. The successful gift proves to us that our relationship to the giver is more than merely formal or nominal.

For the giver, the joy is perhaps more subtle, but nonetheless

A considerably edited version of this article was published in my "Design & Ideas" column in *I-D/International Design* (November-December, 1992).

The Meaning of Products

significant. It is a joy, first and foremost, in pleasing others, in getting to know their tastes, interests, and character, in recognizing and accepting their needs and desires (even if contrary to our own). But it is also a pleasure in successfully finding a material thing that successfully concretizes these desires—that gives receivers "exactly what they wanted."

Note that the gift is not just the thing itself. If the nature of the object or product that we proffer is essential, it is, nonetheless, not all we give. What the giver gives besides the gift-object is recognition—which both Lacan and Hegel recognized as the fundamental human desire, which we crave above all else.

2. Needless to say, this complex potential joy of the gift is not what the word calls to mind when we think of Christmas or of bridal showers, birthdays, and all the other occasions when someone, somewhere is formally expecting to receive a "gift" from us and we are obligated to provide one. The transformation of an act that should be based on love and free will into one based on social and economic obligation ensures that resentment dominates the relation.

In this context, what should be the easiest thing—to give joy to others we know—becomes almost impossible. Separated from close empathic relation to the other (especially perhaps from members of our own family), we really have no idea what the other wants.

In any case, resentment is economically induced. While the gift relation obligates us to spend money (and to know that the price of things is always known to the receiver), the double meanness of our economy—which fetishizes scarcity and constantly tells us that we lack everything, yet obligates us to buy and to feel belittled if we cannot spend to excess—makes us resent "squandering" precious financial resources. Is it surprising then, as Adorno intimates, that instead of joy, bad conscience (and a sense of disappointment in ourselves) dominates the act of giving?

3. The bad grace that the *obligated* gift relationship so often induces finds its counterpart in the objects which are invented to service its requirements.

The invention of the gift-article—the *bête noire* of industrial designers—is a result both of the logical economic exploitation of the enforced gift relation (why look a gift horse in the mouth?) and of creating an "answer" (for the would-be gift buyer) to the "problem" of the true gift. The gift-article as substitute for a genuine gift becomes an object made to carry a superficial connotation of a "personal" relationship, and is almost wholly unrelated to either its buyers or receivers. As Adorno reasons, the gift-article exists indeed only to fill in the absence caused by the fact that "one does not know what to give because one really does not want to."

Not only does the gift-article, almost by definition, exclude those moments of joy referred to earlier, but the thing itself, the gift, takes on a peculiar condition when it is given under these circumstances. When it is not prosaic and relentlessly practical (e.g., the list of items the middle-class bride and groom make available at Bloomingdales in order that one can help them furnish a home with fondue sets and a fake onyx bathroom set) the gift-article is an excessive and useless item—indeed, it is like a simulacrum, a thing which is almost not a thing (as with the "gift book," for example, which is a book that is very nearly not a book).

But this is consistent with how the gift-article is intended to work. Just as the gift book is not intended to be read but merely given, transactionally, as a sign of expenditure, so the first principle of the gift-article as a whole is to signify for both receiver and giver a certain "wasteful expenditure" (by the giver, for the receiver). But this expenditure is nominal, not substantive: the gift-article is simply the sign of "money spent."

In some ways we may think this scarcely matters. But while the small gift-article is often used precisely to signify or mark a relationship to the other (the gift as a token of friendship, a sign of caring), a generalized culture of gift-articles marks the existence of a formal but not a substantial relationship to the other. Because most of our relationships are now of this order, the gift-article is paradoxically their perfect representation. (Proof of this last point is that we would never buy those we love a "gift-article": only real and substantive things will do for those with whom we have a real and substantive relationship.)

That the gift-article is only a sign of a thing and that it marks only a formal and not a substantive relationship is consistent too with how "gifts" work in public exchanges. The White House and Buckingham Palace are both stuffed with the bad taste of a thousand such empty "relationships." All of this explains, also, the natural obloquy we feel for the "gift" object (and the contempt we feel for the culture of Hallmark and other purveyors of the gift culture—including those extraordinary minions whose exalted job it is to be corporate gift buyers)!

It also explains why we feel that the gift culture lies at the opposite end of designing and making from professional industrial design. The gift-article seems to possess few, if any, of the restorative, recuperative, or transformative powers that real things can have for us.

4. Any idea that reflection on gifts and giving is marginal to the professional concerns of object makers is quite wrong. Neither the seeming peculiarity of the gift-article—neither its triviality, nor the fact that it seems to include, as a category, almost wholly nonuseful things—as if it were a quantum of the useless which marked the superfluity of the gift process itself; nor again the (nominal) work that gifts perform and their almost "decorative" or representational condition, nor even the "femininity" of gift giving rules out the gift-article as a mirror to the conditions of designing things today.

The Meaning of Products

On the contrary. In the condition of the gift-article and the obloquy into which the very idea of "the gift" has fallen lie some important truths about our relations to things and objects.

In the first place, the gift-article is a perfect exemplum of the diminished affect and valence of things and products in general characteristic of many industrial products. The state to which the gift-article is reduced mimics the generalized loss of a real relation to the subject which we find over and over again in the usual run of contemporary (sign-)products.

Even the contemporary use of narrative or semantic models of product meaning echoes in a way what is already known well in gift shops, namely, that gift articles sell themselves largely on the basis of visible associations. Hence, the product too can be seen as a substitute, an item whose rationale for existence many times has no greater logic than that of the gift commodity.

It is instructive in this respect to re-read Adorno's critical comments on giving and the gift. They could well stand in part as a descriptive critique of the basis of some of the worst forms of product development: a process also summed up in his sentence that in giving, the resentful givers "at best [give] what they would have liked themselves, only a few degrees worse." In other words, looked at carefully, the gift-article is not the other to the professional product design but its twin: the image of what, in actuality, the designed object often is more nearly like.

5. However, if the gift-article is a kind of mirror to the alienating product, the more positive side of this parallel is that the quantum of joy lying in the gift relation is there to be potentially opened in *any* everyday relation between a product and a user. This argument would imply that the act of giving—in the wide positive and reciprocal sense I sketched above—is more integral than we might think both to the work of design and to making in general, and to the art of being human.

Adorno points out that the gift relationship, in its positive aspects, is inescapable. Even those "who no longer give are still in need of giving. In them wither the irreplaceable faculties which cannot flourish in the isolated cell of pure inwardness, but only in live contact with the warmth of things. A chill descends on all they do, the kind word that remains unspoken, the consideration unexercised. This chill finally recoils on those from whom it emanates. Every undistorted relationship, perhaps indeed the conciliation that is part of organic life itself, is a gift. He who through consequential logic becomes incapable of it, makes himself a thing and freezes."

To put it another way, where the ability to understand the worth of the outer gift—"the warmth of the object"—is lost, so too is inner life. The gift keeps open the passage between inner and outer life. Without it both moments disintegrate.

We can begin to make sense of these claims by seeing how the notion of the true gift, and model of gift giving, offers a different way of conceptualizing how it is that, at best, objects work for a user from those tacitly accepted. Economic theory, for example, from which design practice draws a number of its axioms without always understanding that it does so, stresses the functioning of goods either in terms of commodity exchange (where the object has almost ceased to be a substantive thing) or in terms of how goods function for the isolated and monadic individual subject in terms of material welfare and comfort on the one hand, consumption, possession, and display on the other.

What is notable here is that these essentially *possessive* models of the object put so dominant a stress on the acquisition and deployment of objects by the individual subject that we find it almost impossible to conceive of a different relationship to things and to the other. Thus, even if goods are also sometimes seen in an inter-individual context, as elements in an information system, for example (say as markers of categories, most obviously of status),[1] the stress is always on their use by the individual subject, never on how the objects work *between* two subjects.

Yet, why do we make things *for another's use* at all? Is there not, at the core of our impulse to make things, something closer to the ideal gift relationship? To put it another way, is not the work of the designer, at its best, nearer to the impulse that motivates the gift giver who gives out of love than to the huckster who provides the market with another "substitute" object? And is this not because objects work not only possessively, for the individual subject who owns them, but also *dialogically*, that is, between subjects, working at once to aid subjects materially in how they live but working also as a means of establishing concrete relations with the other?

That this offers a picture of making or of the working of objects which is unfamiliar to us today is not because of inherent limitations in the conditions of making and designing but of the real distortions placed into the relationships between subjects and objects. To free ourselves from these—insofar as this is possible within a commodity-driven economy and a performance-driven technology—is to need to rethink the possible basis of the interactions of subjects and things.

6. Of course, we make things in order to meet material needs (and, in our society, in order to produce goods to exchange at a profit). But we can also see the design and making of things as having the purpose of transforming the external world from one which claims indifference to human fate to one which acknowledges human sentience and the conditions of how we are, as humans, in the world. In other words, it is objects that give us a human world.

This idea rapidly leads to two more. First, we make things not only in order to make things as such (things in themselves), but

1   On goods as an information system, see Mary Douglas and Baron Isherwood, *The World of Goods* (Harmondsworth: Penguin, 1976).

The Meaning of Products

to make a world that is a particular kind of world in which we can be particular kinds of human beings (for how we can be as human beings is dependent, in large part, on the kinds of human worlds we can make). Second, we make things not simply for *them*selves but for *our*selves, and for the use of another. If this point is "obvious" its implications are not.

To make *for us* means that making is undertaken to create a world that acknowledges, knows, and recognizes us, and in that knowing seeks also to alleviate some of the severe limitations (physical, physiological, psychological) that we have as human beings. (We invent computers to make up for deficiencies in our abilities to mentally process information. We invent more mundane—but not less significant—things to defray our more physiological limitations: clothes to keep us warm, shelters to protect us, products to aid our lives.)

But this means that to make and to design something is to create something whose end is not in itself but is rather "in" the subject *for whom* the object is made (whether that subject is individualized, or is ourselves, collectively, as a whole). On this argument, then, the object is never autonomous, never just "for itself." It is, in fact—as Elaine Scarry puts it in the important essay which forms the last chapter of her book, *The Body in Pain*—always "only a fulcrum or lever across which the force of creation moves back onto the human site and remakes its makers. "[2]

7. This changes, or should change, how we think about the object. Relativized in importance by the fact that it has its ends outside of itself (in the other for whom it is made, and to whom essentially it is *given*), the object is simultaneously raised in significance in terms of the work that it performs *for us*. Objects (help) make us. Making (and designing) are moments of making (and designing) ourselves.

The object is not denied in this process. On the contrary, it is substitutive, but in a wholly, different, and opposite and more beneficial sense than in the case of the gift-article. The object is the substitute for ourselves in the special sense that things work to provide us artificially with what nature "neglected" to bestow on us. But the object is not for all that disconnected from us. Things have their origins, by and large, not only in almost physiological projection from our bodily conditions (as we can read a chair as a mimetic projection and externalization of the spine) but also as a projection, even more fundamentally, of our awareness of the conditions of our sentient existence as a whole.

Thus, a chair, for example, can best be understood as a counterfactual projection about the problem of body weight and the pain of standing—as sentient and physiological "awareness materialized into a freestanding design." As Scarry points out, only when the chair acts as though it itself knew the pain of standing, or as though it were itself aware of the actualities and complexities of our sense

2   Elaine Scarry, *The Body in Pain* (New York: Oxford University Press, 1985), 307. Scarry's book is essential reading for anyone interested in these issues.

of "embodied aliveness" and the needs and demands that this produces, will it truly accommodate our requirements.

Scarry gives another, rather beautiful, example of this process when she notes that a lightbulb is not merely a physical object. Rather, it is one which

> Transforms the human being from a creature who would spend approximately a third of each day groping in the dark, to one who sees simply by wishing to see: its impossibly fragile, milky-white globe curved protectively around an even more fragile, upright-then-folding filament of wire is the materialization of neither retina, nor pupil, nor day-seeing, nor night-seeing; it is the materialization of a counter-factual perception about the dependence of human sight on the rhythm of the earth's rotation; no wonder it is in its form so beautiful.[3]

The beauty of this passage might obscure its conceptual import. What Scarry is offering us here is a creative redescription of the work of the object (one surely fertile for rethinking product categories and the work of things). The basis of this redescription is a transformation of how things are thought: not as "dead" possessions or signs or markers but as "live gifts" working, at base, "for" us, and working in their "circulation" between and among us to establish a circle of making and self-making.

The lightbulb, so thought, is a remarkable object, *even if we do not recognize this as such*. As the actualization of a series of felt perceptions about our human condition, each analogically rendered into the various moments of its design, the lightbulb (or any similar object) *is* the bringing of these perceptions to real consciousness for us. Only as such can these perceptions truly become evident in the world, and only as such can the sense we have, for example, of the limitations, frailties, needs, and requirements of ourselves as psychically, physically, and physiologically determined beings, find a necessary echo in the reparative and extensive forms of the things we deal with. So put, we can understand objects as a crucial point of exchange, or a vital switch point or mediator between embodied consciousness, that is, the sense of ourselves, and, in actuality, the indifferent world.

To look at things in this way is not just a romantic affectation. It is rather a means of trying to strip away the crudescence that commodity production has interposed between the real work of things and our understanding and consciousness of what it is they do. What is being proposed here is two-fold. First, objects embody a perception about our condition and work to alleviate the problems that this truth about ourselves causes us. This means that objects fundamentally "wish us well." But second, this means that the object, no matter what its mundanity, is like a collective gift: it is issued for all of us, and its function or work is giftlike in that its form embodies recognition of our concrete needs and desires. It is,

---

3 Scarry, *The Body in Pain*, 292.

to adapt what I said earlier, concrete proof that the giver—in this case the designer-maker—knows, and has understood, recognized, affirmed, and sought to concretely meet our most intimate and human needs and desires.

Thus, far from standing over us, or against us, objects are, in Scarry's argument, models of beneficence, a gift that we humans give to each other—indeed, the most ethical of gifts.

8. It is worth exploring this point a little further. One way of thinking about this relation between the gift and the ethics of objects is to see the ideal gift relation, *as it is embodied in the object*, as the opposite of a relation of obligation. Now, to say that the gift relation is at best not a relation of obligation—or at least not directly so—is significant. Anthropological, psychoanalytical, and philosophical explorations of the gift concur that obligation (and its subtle and not-so-subtle manipulation) is the point where questions of power enter into the process of gift giving. Obligation is how the gift is "worked" to create systems of deference and inter-implication (to bind the other into a particular structure of reciprocity).

But the object-as-gift, in the sense we are developing it here, largely negates this condition. Obligation enters the gift structure because the gift is given as a moment of establishing personal or collective relations of power, deference, and obligation. The gift is here in effect a sign or an agent (even allegorically) of these relations. But the object—and especially the mundane object, the every-day product—is not "given" in this way.

To be sure, as a moment, or the agent, the vehicle of capital, the object as commodity, establishes (or helps establish and keep in place, and continually renew) capitalist social relations. The commodity is a condition of existence of capital. But even as a commodity the very impersonality of the relations involved in the market negates the personalized relations of the gift as such. The object as commodity implicates one in capitalism: yet, in its alienation the object, and we its purchasers, users, and consumers, are peculiarly freed, that is, freed of the "personalized" obligations of gift giving.

To put it another way, although the object-as-gift is clearly subject to considerable distortion as a commodity—although all the Marxian strictures on the commodity and alienation apply with ever renewed force to the object in our culture—still the structure of object purchase and use, in its very disengagement from personalized relations, may paradoxically work to enable the object to work for us as a "free" gift—that is, as a gift without obligation.[4]

The object-as-gift, then, in the form of its giving to the other—not as a gift exactly, but as "something given" without expectation of like-reciprocity—may slip the system of obligation. But this also means, inasmuch as obligation is at the same time the structure of morality, that to slip "obligation" in the first sense is also to escape obligation in the second, moral sense. The object-as-gift, then, "escapes" morality.

4   Though of course there is no "free lunch," the obligation vis-á-vis the capitalist commodity is participation in the wage-labor/market system. But it is in the freeing of personal senses of obligation that capitalism speaks to the desire to escape from the limits implied by personalized obligation.

Does this mean that the object, then, lies outside of morality altogether? This is certainly one apparent implication of this argument. Translated back into the terms of capitalism and the commodity, it is not difficult to see the ways in which it is easy to maintain this disconnection. It has become, indeed, an axiom of contemporary thinking that this is so.

But it is possible to read this argument in quite another way. To say that the object-as-gift does not participate in a structure of obligation and does not therefore participate in morality, is to say that the object is therefore freed to construe genuinely ethical relations. Indeed, it is to say that it is precisely by negating the structure of morality-obligation that it allows the ethical and the imminent to come into view.

That this suggests an opposition between morality and ethics, and the replacement of the one by the other, is interestingly congruent with developments in contemporary ethical thought. This shift, which is fundamentally a shift from thinking ethical relations under the rubric and limits of morality to a more genuinely ethical concern with imminent relations between subjects,[5] is also based on a movement from a notion of ethical relations thought or understood as an obligation imposed from without[6]—morality as an abstract law which determines an ideal "ought" for practice (whether as a moral ought or as an autonomous, and yet morally justified, ideal)—to a stress on the understanding of the concrete implications, for the other, of the consequences of an action.

This distinction is of more than semantic or merely philosophical import. It signals a different orientation, a different way of standing to the problem. Deleuze, speaking of Spinoza, puts it in a way that emphasizes both of these points: "Ethics, which is to say a *typology of imminent modes of existence*, replaces Morality, *which always refers existence to transcendent values*."[7]

This distinction, between an abstract law and "a more properly ethical conception of the relationship to the Other," is essential, the more so because, conceptually at least, we still remain under the sway of the force of the moral ambition. So dominant indeed is this model that it both encourages a countervailing stance—the denial of morality, the "freeing" of design and technique or technology in its autonomy from the confines of moral law (a recurring ideal expressed in architecture and design since the early nineteenth century)—and makes it difficult to free the notion of the ethical from the occlusions, suspicions, and obloquoy which an emphasis on morality induces.[8]

Where this comes back to the object is that in turning from the abstract law imposed from without ("form follows function") to an exploration of "imminent modes of existence" of things and subjects, one is not turning away from the processes of designing and making but toward them. It is imminence, not abstraction, that describes the intimate involvement with the thing and its configuration that characterizes the design

5   In formulating this contrast I have drawn on a number of recent essays on ethics, notably Drucilla Cornell, *The Philosophy of the Limit* (New York: Routledge, 1992); Seyla Benhabib, "The Generalized and Concrete Other," in *Feminism As Critique: Essays on the Politics of Gender in Later-Capitalist Societies*, ed. Seyla Benhabib and Drucilla Cornell (Minneapolis: University of Minnesota Press, 1987); John Rajchman, *Truth and Eros: Foucault, Lacan and the Question of Ethics* (New York: Routledge, 1991); Bernard Williams, *Ethics and the Limits of Philosophy* (Cambridge: Harvard University Press, 1985); Richard Rorty, *Contingency, Irony, Solidarity* (New York: Cambridge University Press, 1989).

6   "Morality designates any attempt to spell out how one determines a right way to behave, behavioral norms which, once determined, can be translated into a system of rules." Cornell, *Philosophy of the Limit* ,13.

7   Gilles Deleuze, *Spinoza: Practical Philosophy*, trans. Robert Hurley (San Francisco: City Lights, 1988), 23 (my emphasis).

8   The textual instance, from the conservative side, nasty though it is, is David Watkin's splendid essay *Morality and Architecture* (Oxford: Clarendon Press, 1978). With gross exaggeration and distortion, Watkin registers acute disapproval of attempts to weld modern architecture to moral rightness.

9   Marcel Mauss, *The Gift: Forms and Functions of Exchange in Archaic Societies* (New York: Norton, 1967).

The Meaning of Products

attempt at establishing both a configurational and a psychological "fit" between a thing and the subjects who will make use of that thing.

This brings us back to the gift—which is, also, of course, the opening of a relation of imminence. Marcel Mauss made it clear in his classic essay on the gift[9] that gift exchange is inherently a multi-valent phenomenon—"one whose transactions are at once economic, juridical, moral, esthetic, religious, and mythological." To put it another way, we can say that the gift (in the full sense of the term) not only establishes concrete relations with the other, it opens up those relations to other kinds of exchange. Thus, far from limiting relations, the gift expands relations.

It is the same with the object-as-gift. The mundane object-as gift-object passes both among and between people. Moreover, it renews itself with use (only placed in a museum is it an aberration). And again, once used it is let go—in order that, freed of some of the material problems of sentience, we can move on to other "more human" activities. As we have said, even the apparent "impersonality" of the relationship involved here is significant because it frees the relations involved between ourselves and things of negative personal relations. What this means in turn is that we are not embedded with and by things. All of this is the opposite to "consumption" in the economic sense. The gift-object is a positive circularity, an agent of (subtle) reciprocity, which could also be understood, at once literally and analogically, as a "reservoir of available life."[10]

9. That objects are potentially gifts in this last sense of the term we can also understand if we remember that one common denominator to all notions of the gift, even perhaps the most debased, is that the recipient of the gift is just that, a recipient. The receiver cannot buy the gift, nor even acquire it by an act of will. As Lewis Hyde reports in his interesting essay, *The Gift: Imagination and the Erotic Life of Property*,[11] gifts are bestowed, not bought. The purchaser can buy the object, but the moment "within" the object, which is giftlike in the positive sense referred to at the beginning of this essay, is supplementary to the object as commodity (which is again why the gift-article, which attempts to bind commodity and gift, fails). In other words, this moment of the "gift" cannot be bought. Insofar as it inheres in the object, it is the work or consequence not of the purchaser but the maker and designer.

To put it another way, we can say that, in effect, all commodities, all products, are subject to an act of choice as to whether they may potentially function as a true gift. This implies that the difference between "gift-objects" and products is not a difference of types of object, but of the *conditions of things* (which includes the conditions of how we receive and understand things to be). Most, if not all, gift-articles are not gifts in this sense. Equally, most mundane objects contain (or may potentially contain) a moment of the "gift" in the second, better, sense of the term.

10 Mauss, *The Gift*, 26–27.
11 Lewis Hyde, *The Gift: Imagination and the Erotic Life of Property* (New York: Vintage, 1979).

But insofar as products can contain this giftlike quality, it is because this moment is given to, or is bestowed on, the object by the designer/maker. The gift the designer/maker offers here is not inconsiderable. But it is less directly material than it is perceptual. As with Scarry's lightbulb, which offers itself as the "materialization of a counter-factual perception about the dependence of human sight on the rhythm of the earth's rotation," *it is the quantum of the designer's creative apperception of the conditions of human subjectivity, together with his or her ability to translate and embody this apperception into the form of the object and to offer it again to the potential user, that marks the designer/maker's "gift" to the user.*

10. This "other" (the user) to whom the product-as-gift is offered is not that of the "other" considered as an abstracted economic unit or as a statistical moment. This is a substantial concrete human other, an other who is thought of (whether explicitly or not) in something of the terms that Adorno has the real giver thinking of the receiver when he reminds us, in the quotation we began with, that "real giving ha[s] its joy in imagining the joy of the receiver. It means choosing, expending time, going out of one's way, thinking of the other *as a subject:* the opposite of distraction."

This formulation of the other who one designs and makes for, *as a concrete other*, a real imagined recipient, has echoes to the recent reformulation of ideas of the subject both in ethics in general (where the stress is on the "other" considered not as a generalized abstract other—a subject in the formal sense of the term—but substantively)[12] and in feminist theory.

Seyla Benhabib, in her much-quoted essay,[13] has recently characterized the shifts in thinking involved here as the shift from a model of the generalized (abstract) other to the standpoint of the *concrete other*. This shift involves a move from the model of the subject as an abstract rational consciousness, disembodied and disembedded, possessing formal rights and requiring the legal and political recognition of their formal equality as subjects,[14] to a standpoint on the other which, in her terms, requires us to view all subjects as "individual[s] with a concrete history, identity, and affective-emotional constitution," to "comprehend the needs of the other, his or her motivations, what s/he searches for, and s/he desires."

This is a standpoint of mutuality, of "equity and complementary reciprocity" and is based on the idea that "each of us is entitled to expect and assume from the other forms of behavior through which the other feels recognized and confirmed as concrete, individual beings with specific needs and capacities."[15]

These formulations are doubly significant in this context. First, they announce in general a decisive turn in ethical theory: a turn away from (abstracted) morality toward a more concrete and substantial concern with ethical relations between subjects. Second, and of massive relevance to design, the model of the subject devel-

12 In ethical theory, it is the relation to the other that is often said to be the counter to idealism. This is a point Jacques Lacan notes in regard to Freud; see his *Encore* (Paris: Seuil, 1975), 58. It was noted earlier and more extensively by Simone de Beauvoir, *Pyrrhus and Cinéas* (Paris: Gallimard, 1927). On de Beauvoir, see chapter 3 of Sonia Kruks, *Situation and Human Existence: Freedom, Subjectivity & Society* (New York: Unwin Hyman, 1990).

13 Benhabib, "The Generalized and Concrete Other."

14 But *not* necessarily any recognition of their substantive rights, for example. The difference between formal and substantive rights is essential here. The force of moral and legal theory in the modern period has been to establish the formal (i.e., the abstract political and economic) right of the possessive individual. The weakness of this moral (and legal and political) theory is that formal rights are not connected to substantive rights. Thus, for example, one may have a formal right to a vote, or to possess property, but no substantive right (e.g., to a job, to free or decent health care, to an education, to adequate shelter). We are so used to thinking in terms of formal (or procedural) rights and so unused to terms of substantive rights, that we have only very inadequate ways of trying to deal with a person's substantive rights. The political problem, in the wide sense, in the coming decades will be to establish substantive rights and to balance these with what has been achieved through the development of abstract formal rights.

15 Benhabib, "The Generalized and Concrete Other," 87.

oped here is far more congruent with a designer's instinctive understanding of the actualities of the subjects he or she designs for than the older model of the "abstract generalized other."

The latter, the nominal subject of law, science, and indeed of all thought in the modern period, has always been problematic for design. Modernism's worst moments came when it embraced too closely and too slavishly this model, to take one example. Although the model of the abstract other formally recognizes the other as a being who has "concrete needs, desires and effects," in practice this essentially disembodied and disembedded schema gave us a conception of the subject whose "embodiedness" was all too easily rationalized and reduced—say, to a set of ergonomic criteria.

The model of the "concrete other" by contrast, though itself not without problems, is congruent with our being able to think of subjects as embodied and effective in qualitative, concrete terms. In other words, it lets us think of subjects as, indeed at best, a product designer will think of the potential user. This is also, of course, how the giver thinks of the receiver. The giver begins from a desire to give. But that desire becomes real only when the giver moves to the imaginative apprehension of the other's needs and desires.

But once the giver does so move, the process of choosing the gift/designing the object becomes a double process of confirmation and affirmation. The act of thinking of the other in this way confirms and affirms both the relationship with the other and our own work. To put it in subject terms: as I anticipate the other's enjoyment and use of my object, and as I concretize those anticipations in an object that I choose/create, then I get the immediate pleasure and consciousness of having satisfied a real human need through this creative work.

In a more abstract sense I receive the pleasure of understanding that I (the giver) through my gift/object will be experienced by you (the receiver/user) as an augmentation of, and even as a necessary part of, yourself. Thus, as Marx puts it in an early commentary, in some rather beautiful sentences: In this process "I would know myself to be confirmed in your thought as well as in your love. I would know that I had created through my life expression immediately yours as well. Thus in my individual activity I would know my true essence, my human, common essence is contained and realized. Our production would be so many mirrors, in which our essence would be mutually illuminated."[16]

This seems a suitable ambition for what the making of things might once again become, if the moment of the gift-object (rather than the gift-article) were to become the chief analogy by which we could define the character of the things we make.

16 The quotation comes from some notes by Marx on James Mill in the *Notebooks*, Appended to the *Pariser Manuskripte*. They are not published in the English translations. This version comes from Seyla Benhabib, *Critique, Norm & Utopia: A Study of the Foundations of Critical Theory* (New York: Columbia University Press, 1986), 63–64.

On the Essential Contexts of Artifacts or on the Proposition that "Design Is Making Sense (of Things)"[1]
Klaus Krippendorff

Introduction

The etymology of *design* goes back to the Latin *de* + *signare* and means making something, distinguishing it by a sign, giving it significance, designating its relation to other things, owners, users, or gods. Based on this original meaning, one could say: design is making sense (of things).

Design is making sense (of things)

The phrase is conveniently ambiguous. It could be read as "design is a sense creating activity" that can claim perception, experience, and, perhaps, esthetics as its fundamental concern and this idea is quite intentional. Or it can be regarded as meaning that "the products of design are to be understandable or meaningful to someone" and that this interpretation is even more desirable. The phrase *of things* is in parentheses to cast doubt on a third interpretation that "design is concerned with the subjective meanings of 'objectively existing' objects." The parentheses suggest that we cannot talk about things that make no sense at all, that the recognition of something as a thing is already a sense-derived distinction, and that the division of the world into a subjective and an objective realm is therefore quite untenable.

However, *making sense* always entails a bit of a paradox between the aim of *making* something new and different from what was there before, and the desire to have it make *sense*, to be recognizable and understandable. The former calls for innovation, while the latter calls for the reproduction of historical continuities. In the past, sense was provided by alchemy, mythology, and theology. Now we speak less globally of a symbolic ordering that is constitutive of cognition, culture, and reality. Somehow, the word *design* has not remained in this creative state of paradox, but has shifted to one side. Its current meaning amplifies the aspect of *making* or, more specifically, of applying a technical-functional rationality to the material world at the expense of the *sense* that was to be achieved thereby. Perhaps, the pendulum has swung too far. Perhaps, technology has moved too fast for culture to keep up with it. Whatever the explanation, the current concern with product semantics is noth-

1 Part of this work was supported by the design firm RichardsonSmith, Worthington, Ohio, and Ohio State University, Columbus, while on sabbatical leave in 1986–87 from the University of Pennsylvania, Philadelphia.

The Meaning of Products

ing other than a reaction to the missing *sense* modern industrial products make or a deliberate effort to recapture this lost territory for design.

Product semantics

Elsewhere, we introduced *product semantics as a study of the symbolic qualities of man-made forms in the cognitive and social contexts of their use and the application of the knowledge gained to objects of industrial design.*[2] By this definition, product semantics is not a style, program, or movement. Rather, it is a concern for the sense artifacts make to users, for how technical objects are symbolically embedded in the fabric of society, and what contributions they thereby make to the autopoiesis of culture.[3] The definition recognizes formally what in the past good designers may have done intuitively but without a conceptual and linguistic repertoire to talk about it. Designers who are aware of product semantics may work quite differently from those who are not. They articulate different aims and criteria and tackle different design problems. The illustrations provided in this issue by practitioners speak for themselves.

Product semantics should not be confused with *ergonomics*, which is almost entirely committed to the aforementioned technical rationality of optimizing systems performance. The experiential fact that people voluntarily accept considerable inconveniences to drive the car of their dreams, live with furniture they like, or wear clothes for which they are admired, suggests that other than technical criteria dominate everyday life and individual well-being.

Product semantics is also far from being a mere marketing tool. Although it has contributed to economic success,[4] the celebration of wholeness, the concern with how material artifacts connect people to each other, the respect for mythology and archetypes that are rooted deep in the collective unconscious, and the interest in an ecology of symbols and mind go beyond industry's immediate concern with production and consumption.

Product semantics should not be tied to traditional semiotics either. The symbolic qualities or the meanings objects may have to different users easily escape traditional semiotic conceptions[5] insofar as they locate meanings either in the objective referents of signs (naive referential theory), in the imputed relation between signs and what they are intended to stand for or represent (referential theory proper), or in the somewhat more objectively describable form, nature, or features of sign vehicles (physicalistic theory). Such conceptions have been made explicit in the indissoluble triad of semiotics. The version in figure 1 is taken from Charles Sanders Pierce, who defined a sign as "something which stands to somebody for something in some respect or capacity."[6]

Although these referential notions must be overcome here, to be fair, traditional semiotic approaches are not entirely without merit for industrial design. However, I see only two valid applica-

2   Klaus Krippendorff and Reinhart Butter, "Product Semantics: Exploring the Symbolic Qualities of Form," *Innovation* 3, 2 (1984): 4–9.

3   The idea of *autopoiesis*, the process of self-production, has its origin in biology and was introduced in Humberto R. Maturana and Francisco G. Varela, *Autopoiesis and Cognition*, Boston Studies in Philosophy of Science (Boston: Reidel, 1980). It is considered as a defining process of living systems and is contrasted there with *allopoiesis*, the process of producing something materially different from what produced it, including reproduction. The original authors are somewhat hesitant to apply the notion of autopoiesis to social systems. However, a culture as a whole certainly produces itself continuously and in the same physical space. The role of machines in cultural autopoiesis is explored in Dorion Sagan and Lynn Margulis, "Gaia and the Evolution of Machines," *Whole Earth Review* 55 (Summer 1987):15–21. Alain Touraine's *The Self-Production of Society* (Chicago: University of Chicago Press, 1977) assumes a sociological perspective of autopoiesis.

4   See Robert I. Blaich's experiences with product semantics at Philips Corporate Design, presented to the National Conference of the Industrial Designers Society of America on "Forms of Design," (Evanston: Northwestern University, August 7–10,1986). A similar report is included in this issue.

5   Krippendorff and Butter, "Product Semantics," cited above, and Klaus Krippendorff, *Überr den Zeichen- und Symbolcharacter von Gegenständen: Versuch zu einer Zeichentheorie für die Programmierung, von Productformen in Sozialen Kommunikationsstrukturen,* Diplom Thesis (Ülm: Hochschule für Gestaltung, 1961).

6   Charles Sanders Pierce, *Collected Papers* (Cambridge: Harvard University Press, 1931–1953), 228.

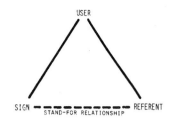

Figure 1

tions. The first sheds light on the use of linguistic expressions (for example, printed user's instructions and labels) and nonlinguistic graphic/acoustic/olfactory signs (whether as symbols, icons, or indexes), all of which stand for something other than themselves (for example, for contents, internal states, options of functions, and movements available). The second concerns itself with how information from outside an artifact is processed and perceptively exhibited (for example, through TV monitors, loud speakers, information displays, and scales of measurement) to users who interpret what they see as covarying with distant or otherwise unnoticeable events. Neither of these applications *of* semiotics is my primary concern nor do I believe these to be central to industrial design.

A suitable starting point for product semantics is the experiential fact that people surround themselves with objects that make sense to them, they can identify as to what they are, when, how, for what, and in which context they may be used. Such objects can hardly be viewed as substitutes for something else, as traditional semiotics may have it, but they do reveal, communicate, or present *themselves* in the experiences of people. This is true for the whole spectrum of everyday things, from industrially produced consumer products to highly individualized works of art. To be of use to someone, things must be capable of this kind of presentation.

The self-reference this presentation implies does not fit into the semiotic triad, however. And for semiotics to exorcise self-reference from analysis because of its lack of fit and thus to impose other referential notions, instead, encourages both a way of interpreting the world and a particular design practice. The latter particularly encourages products that either appear different from what they are (are made in the image of something else, hide their operation behind unrelated facades, deceive users with fake symbolisms) or are covered with linguistic instructions and graphics. I am convinced that this kind of semiotization of material culture alienates people from participation in the real world and has always been a mark of bad styling. Although product semantics is not committed to any style, good or bad, we should not simply dismiss semiotic ideas for their limitations, but rather avoid semiotics' epistemological traps.

Sense-making

When presenting everyday artifacts, such as furniture items, vehicles, tools, office equipment, and so forth, to ordinary people and asking them what they see, the range of responses is extraordinary. Very few responses occur in semiotic categories of *what the object resembles, represents, signifies, points to, and is about.* Most are concerned with *what the object is, indicated by its name; what it is made for, what it does; how its parts are connected and work together; who typically uses it and in which situations, what others would say about it or about its use; what it is made of and by what processes; who designed it, who made it, who sold it; how its*

The Meaning of Products

operational principles differ from the usual; relative size, appearance, work-manship, durability, price, how it effects the environment; and how efficient its use is; and so forth.

When respondents are more familiar with objects or are presented with very personal items, additionally they relate to these in the following additional terms: *who gave it to them; how it was acquired; of whom it reminds them; in which circumstances it figured prominently; how much care, service, repair, or even affection it consumed; how well it fits with other possessions; how enjoyable its presence is; how it feels; and how close it is to the user's definition of him/herself.*

The list reflects what Ulrich Neisser[7] observed after many experiments of this sort: people do not perceive pure forms, unrelated objects, or things as such but as *meanings*. The distinction between what an object is and what that object *means* to somebody may not be demonstrable as far as perceptual data are concerned.

The above answers suggest that *objects are always seen in a context* (of other things, situations, and users, including the observing self). Responding by saying what something is for puts that something into the context of an intended use. Responding by anticipating what others would think about its user puts that object into a social context that includes other people. Even naming what is seen puts the named in the context of language use.

The context into which people place the object they see is cognitively constructed, whether recognized, anticipated, or wholly imaginary. Seeing something in a store as a chair requires imagining its use at home or in an office, a context that may or may not be realized in practice. Estimating its durability requires constructing from past experiences contexts of misuse or extreme stress.

Meaning is a cognitively constructed relationship. It selectively connects features of an object and features of its (real environment or imagined) *context into a coherent unity.* The reasons for such relationships are numerous. Engineers and ergonomists have almost exclusively settled on functions, measurable, causal connections that are manifest in the push and pull of controlled physical forces. Although functional accounts (including semiotically informed "stand-for" relationships) are undoubtedly meaningful to some, ordinary people also employ many noncausal relationships, such as similarities, contrasts, family belongingness, associations, synchronicities, harmonies, or social conventions, to relate objects to their environments. The perception of how something fits into a cognitively constructed context has no causal base, however.

What something is (the totality of what it means) *to someone corresponds to the sum total of its imaginable contexts.* A knife has all kinds of uses; cutting is merely the most prominent one. Prying open a box, tightening a screw, scraping paint from a surface, cleaning dirty fingernails are as imaginable as picking a pickle from a pickle jar. In the context of manufacturing, a knife is a cost. In the context of sales, a knife has an exchange value. In the context of a hold-up, a

7   Ulrich Neisser, *Cognition and Reality* (San Francisco: Freeman, 1976).

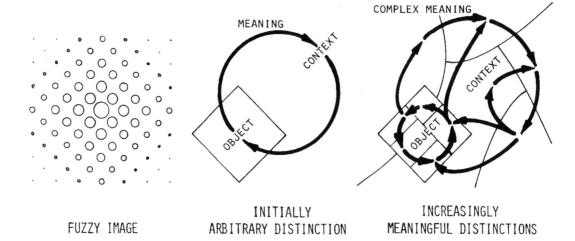

FUZZY IMAGE

INITIALLY
ARBITRARY DISTINCTION

INCREASINGLY
MEANINGFUL DISTINCTIONS

Figure 2

knife may constitute a significant threat. All possible contexts define what a knife is to people capable of using their imagination.

I am furthermore suggesting the following: *Making sense is a circular cognitive process that may start with some initially incomprehensible sensation, which then proceeds to imagining hypothetical contexts for it and goes around a hermeneutic circle during which features are distinguished—in both contexts and what is to be made sense of—and meanings are constructed until this process has converged to a suffeiently coherent understanding.* Explorations of something new and the "aha" experiences of having understood the idea respectively exemplifies the circular process of sense-making and its product. In perception, such processes may take little time, but the fact that the same stimulus may give rise to different responses in different situations by different people demonstrates the importance of individual cognitive contributions over those present in the "objective stimulus." A user's sense-making process is graphically depicted in figure 2.

The Harris Comic of figure 3 illustrates on two levels what the somewhat abstract figure 2 is intended to show. The left frame ignores the fine lines and shows a configuration that affords not much more than that it is distinct from its context. The center frame

Figure 3

The Meaning of Products

makes more sense: two people are facing each other, but this isn't funny. The addition of the quotation is what enables the reader to integrate all the components into a meaningful whole. Moreover, the comic is based on changing the expected context of a recipe, that is, cooking, to that of home improvement, in which what the recipe informs receives a totally unexpected meaning.

Form and meaning contextualized
What is true for ordinary people ought to be true for professional designers as well, for both are equipped with the same cognitive apparatus. I am therefore suggesting that the *forms* designers create—in German, industrial designers are called "form-givers"—result from nothing other than a professional, as opposed to ordinary, sense-making. Form and meaning are intricately related, however, and their relationship is a fundamental concern of product semantics. Something must have form to be seen but must make sense to be understood and used. Form entails a description (of something), *without* reference to an observer or user (for example, see geometry,[8] physics, and objectivist esthetics, which need no reference to the person applying them). In contrast, meaning always requires reference to someone's (self or other) cognitive processes. Accordingly, the designer's "form" is the designer's way of objectifying and, hence, disowning their own meaning in the process of making sense for others. How this relationship comes about is depicted in figure 4.

When one thinks of measurable performance characteristics, function has the same objective status as form. The slogan "form follows function" thus implies abstracting the ordinary (scientifically naive, nonengineering-trained) user out of the equation and discarding the meanings that users construct and see. The increasingly appealing suggestion that form may not follow *function* but *meaning*, brings the user back into the picture and strongly suggests that designers need to discuss not only the contexts in which their forms are used, but also how these forms are made sense of or what they mean to someone other than themselves. No one can presume that form (the designer's objectified meaning) and (the user's) meaning are the same; hence, the need for product semantics to study how they relate. The consequent prescription, adopted by semantically informed designers "form follows meaning," is intended to reflect on this relationship which essentially is a relationship between designer's and user's or client's cognition. Such a prescription is an empty slogan, however, unless it is clear how a man-made form (artifact) is conceived and how its meanings can be understood.

The circular process of constructing meaningful relations between objects and contexts and the somewhat pragmatical distinction between form and meaning suggest that overlapping principles are operating here. Developing a single theory of meaning applicable to all design situations may not be possible though.

8   Helga and Hans-Jürgen Lannoch make the point that geometry cannot account for an individual user's point of view and, thus, is incapable of describing the meanings that spatial forms may acquire in human communication. Their proposal is to construct, instead, a different notion of space associated with natural language called a *semantic space*, which explicitly includes human perceptions and attributions of meanings. Helga Lannoch and Hans-Jürgen Lannoch, "Toward a Semantic Notion of Space." *Design Issues*, V, 2 (Spring 1989), 40–50.

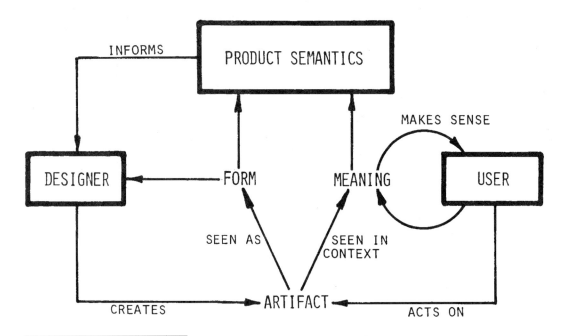

Figure 4

Just as in linguistics, where several longstanding controversies concerning conceptions of meaning have been resolved by pursuing in parallel several incompatible theories of meaning,[9] it seems plausible that product semantics may also have to settle on several parallel theories.

The following text outlines four essentially different contexts in which objects may mean in different ways. These four contexts should provide fertile concepts from which powerful theories of meaning for industrial designers may grow:

- *operational context,* in which people are seen as interacting with artifacts in use
- *sociolinguistic context,* in which people are seen as communicating with each other about particular artifacts, their uses and users, and thereby co-constructing realities of which objects become constitutive parts
- *context of genesis,* in which designers, producers, distributors, users, and others are seen as participating in creating and consuming artifacts and as differentially contributing to the technical organization of culture and material entropy
- *ecological context,* in which populations of artifacts are seen as interacting with one another and contributing to the autopoiesis (self-production) of technology and culture

Operational Context

Operational experiences with things are most common in everyday life. Artifacts—from cups to cars and furniture to complex computer systems—are handled all the time. Unfortunately, people and organizations are often included in this category of objects as well. Although

9   See Gilbert H. Harman, "Three Levels of Meanings," in Danny D. Steinberg and Leon A. Jacobowitz, *Semantics* (London: Cambridge University Press, 1971): 60–75.

designers are intent to create forms that are *self-evident*—that is, *immediately identifiable for what they are, obviously clear as to how they can be manipulated,* and *motivate the user to interact with them*—practice suggests that artifacts often end up meaning something quite different from what was intended. A designer may conceive a car as a means for transportation but provide, instead, the material basis of social status changes, commitments to a factory tradition, affectionate gifts among friends, and something to do on weekends for someone else. Within limits, any designed form may mean different things, and they can become wholly different objects for different users.

An operational theory of meaning should explain how forms constrain the sense users make of things in their environment. There usually is give and take in sense-making processes. Distinctions are drawn, relationships are hypothesized, and both are confirmed or selectively dismissed after acting on their consequences.[10] Meanings are therefore not entirely invariant either; they are acquired and learned, they change with use, expanding or contracting, all depending on the inventiveness of the user, the affordances seen in a form, and the linguistic, cultural context in which this sense-making takes place.

Despite the range of possible meanings designers consider, a limited set of variables or semantic dimensions, as Lannoch and Lannoch call them,[11] describe most operational meanings of objects—*identities; qualities; orientations; locations; affordances states, dispositions, and logic; motivations; and redundancies.*

The notion of a cognitive model, with which users approach, explore, or interact with what designers consider a form is central to all of these dimensions. With semantic considerations in mind, designers may not start with the functions that a product is to perform, but with the cognitive models that users have at their disposal, can construct from available metaphors or metonyms or easily acquire through practice. If there is any intentionality in design, its forms should fit or be interpretable in terms of the cognitive models that lead to their safe and socially desired use.

Identities

Individuals typically approach the partitions in their environment with identity questions in mind. They may ask themselves what kind something is and which name applies. Thereafter, people may have associations or expectations which come to play, representing a set of behavioral "programs." The identity of a form usually serves as a key or directive to a more detailed examination.

Identities may be defined by the following characteristics of an object:
- *shape* (whole appearance)
- typical *pattern or organization* (the logic by which parts are connected)
- identifying features (which it has or does not have)

10 Klaus Krippendorff, "An Epistemological Foundation for Communication," *Journal of Communication* 34, 3 (1984): 21–36.

11 Hans-Jürgen Lannoch, "How to Move from Geometric to Semantic Space," *Innovations* 3, 2 (1984): 20–22. Helga Lannoch and Hans-Jürgen Lannoch, "Vom geometrischen zum semantischen Raum," *Form* 118 (1987):12–17.

- characteristic *behavior* (how it interacts with other things and users)

Shapes, patterns of organization, features, and behaviors are some of the vehicles through which designers can invoke the perception of identities.

A distinction can also be drawn between identities that are cognitively skeletal and present "deep structures," the "gist"[12] or "wesen"[13] of something as opposed to those that rely on considerable detail, surface appearances, or elaborate meanings.

Qualities

Recent research into categorization, particularly by Rosch,[14] has shown that the classification of what something is or does relies not so much on formal resemblances, or distinctions among sets of objects as on cognitively constructed ideal types (unfortunately also called prototypes). People assert qualitative differences to these types. These qualities are often expressed by adjectival constructions—fast cars, high-tech bicycles, black tulips, sleek performances—and can therefore also be called *attributes*. The attribution of qualities tends to create subordinate categories, and their absence reveals the name of the ideal type of a category, often expressible by simple nouns. Differences between a chair and a high chair, a book and a children's book, or a store and a grocery store show the differences between basic categories and subordinate categories. Athavankar[15] lists several examples (modified and extended here):

Subordinate category	Source of the specific attribute
baby shoes	user
sport shirt	attitude
evening dress	occasions
five-star hotel	social class/price
Shaker furniture	region and craft
baroque church	style
high-tech watch	technology
steam engine	source of energy
high-speed train	speed dimension
circular table	shape

12 John Rheinfrank, personal communication 1986, and in various informal presentations.

13 Jochen Gros, "Das zunehmende Bedürfnis nach Form," *Form* 107 (1984): 11–25.

14 Eleanor Rosch, "Principles of Categorization," in Eleanor Rosch and Barbara B. Lloyd, eds. *Cognition and Categorization* (New York: Wiley, 1978): 27–48.

15 Uday A. Athavankar, "Web of Images Within." ARTHAYA, *Proceedings of a Conference on Visual Semantics* (Bombay: Indian Institute of Technology, Industrial Design Center, January 20–22,1987). This paper also includes an excellent overview of categorization (Rosch, *Cognition and Categorization*) from a design perspective. A modified version is included in *Design Issues*, V, 2 (Spring 1989).

Superficially, such attributes may seem to divide a genus into the species of Aristotelian definitions, but, according to the research referred to above, they are more appropriately thought of as indicating distances or differences between any member of a category and its most central exemplar; the ideal, or prototype. Below dimensions, characters, and features are distinguished and the latter is subdivided into parts, properties, and configurations, all of which may be used to explain the semantic differences in qualities.

Dimensions are always present in a particular form and indicate variable extents. Physical objects have volumes, masses, temperatures, speeds, colors, textures, and shapes, for example. Chairs are more or less comfortable to sit on, and the dimension of comfort is an inalienable part of the definition of chair, just as a ball has variable amounts of bounciness and a letter has variable amounts of information. (Note that the dimension of amount of information is not part of the conception of a ball and letters cannot bounce.)

Features may or may not be present in a particular form and, thus, do not enter the definition of its ideal type. Telephones may or may not have a redial button and therefore differ in *parts*. The canard-type airplane differs from a conventional airplane in its *configuration* of wings and rudders. Both are airplanes proper. Gases and fluids, for example, differ in certain *properties* that can be conceived of as different responses to particular actions including the reflection of light, or whether they can be breathed, placed into an open container, etc. Parts, configurations, and properties are all optional to the definition of a form said to have them.

Characters are symbolic analogues to features in that they require semantic (dual) interpretations. For example, a column may have the property of supporting a certain load but may appear too fragile to be trusted for this purpose. Butter's truck interiors[16] have the characters of "high-tech," "low-tech," "contemporary," "functional," and "futuristic," respectively. Characters qualify objects as adjectives qualify nouns.

Orientations

Users describe the forms of objects rarely in terms of three-dimensional geometry or by reference to the physical forces holding them together, but in relation to their own body, vision, or motion. Except perhaps for a perfect sphere, most objects have "faces" that under normal conditions face their user. For example, the screen and the important controls of a television set are "in front." The remainders are sides, top, bottom, or back. Rarely does anyone confuse such obvious orientations. There also is an inside and an outside. There are directional pointers in the shape of a gun, for example. Movements are described toward or away from a user. Underlying many orientations are metaphors of interpersonal communication: the front of a person faces the front of another and so is the front of an object defined to face its user. Other orientations are derived from viewing something from a distance, the preferred view being the one that provides the most relevant information.

Locations

Objects may have not only orientations relative to a user but also locations in a space constituted by other things. A picture may be kept inside a box, lay on the floor, or hang on the wall, framed or not. In right-side driving countries, the driver's seat is on the left side

16   See Reinhart Butter, "Putting Theory into Practice," *Design Issues*, V, 2 (Spring 1989), 51–57.

of the car. A kitchen appliance may be either stored on a shelf or sit on a working surface, perhaps together with required containers and supplies. A bicycle wheel may be either detached or mounted, and so forth. True, locations are sometimes expressible in geometric terms, but the examples express locations in reference to a semantical space and relative to other objects in a user's environments.

Affordances

Affordances, a term taken from Gibson,[17] denotes all possible behaviors (form) that confirm what a user expects the object to do (meaning). A chair should afford support of a user's weight. A telephone should afford talking beyond the range of voice. Note that *chair* and *telephone* and their affordances refer to cognitive models or constructions that users identify as things of a particular kind, not to what they "objectively" are. Whatever an artifact's form, if it is capable of performing according to a particular user model, it can be said to afford it. If it frustrates such a model, it does not. Forms may mislead a user regarding affordances, suggest capabilities that are not there (errors of commission), or hide what can be afforded (errors of omission). Errors of omission are not so bad because inventing a new use for a well-known product is always possible and concealing how something could be handled from particular user groups may sometimes be desirable, for example, making it difficult for children to open a medicine bottle. However, our current consumer-oriented society is especially prone to errors of commission: promising something valuable that experiences do not quite bear out. Examples range from sophisticated looking, high-tech, electronic equipment, with many controls and indicators that are largely decorative, to plastic house plants with variable fragrances.

Designing with affordances in mind starts not with a specification of functions but with perceivable dimensions, characters, and features that feed into the range of readily available cognitive models, including linguistic metaphors and metonyms facilitating their onsite construction. Self-evidence, the efficient and instantaneous semantic indication of what something is, is an example of the "correct" presentation of a product's affordances to its user.

In analyzing how affordances are expressed, the tendency is to distinguish between *manual inputs*, the features that afford touch, movement, manipulation, and programming; *visual orientations*, the features enabling users to coordinate their actions with those of the artifact; and *responses in context*, the experiential effects of manipulations of the environment ultimately controlling *users' perceptions* and either supporting or disconfirming the cognitive model in mind.

States, dispositions, and logic

Even the most simple artifact can be thought as being in one of several *states:* a door is open or closed, a cup is full or empty, an engine is running or is off. Such near binary state systems can be

17 James J. Gibson, *Reason for Realism,* edited by Edward Reed and Rebecca Jones (Hillsdale, NJ: Erlbaum, 1982). Gibson uses the term *affordance* in a more objectivist or naive realist sense, suggesting that objects possess these capabilities for users to simply "pick up" or see. As one cannot possibly list all affordances of something without reference to someone, I am instead suggesting to start out with that someone's cognitive models, including motivations and situational determinants, according to which expectations are formed and affordances are seen.

described by propositional logic whose expressions are either true or false. The usefulness of such descriptions suggests that man-made forms have more to do with logic, language, and mind than with physical continua, including geometry. After all, people describe what they do in language, they communicate with others about what they wish to accomplish, and it is therefore no surprise that artifacts are designed according to an *operational logic* that makes sense. People seek to understand the world in these logical terms as well.

What makes artifacts complex is the multitude of states they may assume at different times and the multivalued nature of the logic needed to describe their operation. However, unlike engineers who must be aware of all details of a complex system, designers must realize that users bring simplified cognitive models (homomorphisms) to bear on such systems and link experiences from other semantic domains by metaphor to enrich the cognitive models of what goes on within them. Naturally, in such simplified user models, anthropomorphisms often reign supreme. Thus, programming becomes a kind of teaching and states are seen as *dispositions,* that is, as a readiness to act in a certain direction. Behavior sequences are interpreted in terms of purposes, and whole systems, as having a will of their own, including psychopathologies, being either user-friendly (cooperative) or hostile (frustrating user expectations).

Indications of an object's states and logic need to afford users' conceptions, however different these conceptions may be from those of their inventors. In the extreme, the difference between engineering and scientific models (forms) and user's models (for constructing meanings) may be reflected in the difference between how the inside and outside appear respectively. In practice, different models may call for a *layered semantics* that enables users to penetrate through the simplest and, literally, surface appearance to deeper and deeper levels of understanding. The Xerox photocopying machine designed at RichardsonSmith is a good example. The surface can be handled with desk-top metaphors for paperwork. Opening it allows users to see paperflows and enables them to fix simple processing errors. Further penetration is reserved for qualified repair persons and the final layer for engineers.

Motivations

The notion of a value system posits values as unalterably fixed dispositions or as socially shared superindividual purposes, either of which are assumed to provide invariant motivations of individual behavior. This view denies the variety of individual cognitive constructions that users engage when interacting with their environment. Such a position is untenable. Instead, I conceive motivations as arising with the exploration of the opportunities objects afford users in particular contexts. Rheinfrank, et al.[18] distinguish between extrinsic and intrinsic motivation.

18   John Rheinfrank and the Exploratory Design Laboratory at RichardsonSmith, Worthington, Ohio, have used this distinction repeatedly in work for various clients. Also see John Rheinfrank, "A Conceptual Framework for Designing User Interaction into Products," *Innovation* 3, 2 (1984): 28–32.

Extrinsic motivation derives from using something as a means to an end. The desirability of this end then motivates the means' use. Forms that promise the achievement of something desirable are attractive for this very reason, whereas forms that do not express such expectations cannot possibly provide a basis for instrumental use. This simple fact establishes the dependency of extrinsic motivation on recognizing instrumental opportunities in a form and, thereby, the primacy of semantics over axiology.[19]

Intrinsic motivation stems from using something for its own sake, from interactive involvement regardless of possible gains. Whereas extrinsic motivation is always explained by reference to some product, result, or something outside of it, intrinsic motivation is uniquely rooted in the process of interaction. It stays within the confines of a circular cognitive process, for example, within the rules of an engaging game, and suggests an esthetics of process rather than of form.

Perhaps the crucial difference between extrinsic and intrinsic motivation is that they refer to two different cognitive paradigms, the instrumental and the symbolic. In the instrumental mode of thinking everything is directed toward and justified in terms of a goal—a problem to be solved, an obstacle to be removed, or desirable conditions to be optimized—whereby the artifacts affording such purposes have no value in themselves. In industrial design, this motivation unquestionably underlies industrial production, marketing, and advertising and is embedded in traditional functionalism. In the symbolic mode of thinking, everything seems directed to achieve balance: a sense of integrity, coherence, harmony, or wholeness of divergent parts, a sense of self-realization in interaction with others, a sense of oneness with the environment. Extrinsic and intrinsic motivations are not mutually exclusive, however. For example, a competitive game may simultaneously motivate by the prospect of winning and by being humanly engaging, regardless of outcome. Artifacts that cannot provide either kind of motivation are not usable in any sense and, hence, of little concern to product semantics.

Redundancies

Industrial production creates large numbers of identical forms that must be usable by and understandable to many very different users. One way of supporting this kind of production is to promote a uniform understanding; another is to build redundancy into the operational meanings of products. The former was the aim of functionalism; the latter is more in line with product semantics, and it recognizes that individuals differ markedly in how they construct and approach their world. People have sensory preferences: some are visually oriented, others tend to rely more on tactile, acoustic, or verbal information. People bring amazingly different cognitive models to a situation and develop different interaction and learning

19 *Axiology* is the scientific study of values and aims at a logic of objective value judgments as if values had nothing to do with the way people construct their worlds or their artifacts and communicate with each other through them. I am supposing here that individuals are more autonomous in their world constructions and preferences than an axiology might grant.

The Meaning of Products

styles. People have different cultural histories that emphasize reliance on some clues over others or favor different paths of exploration. Unless designed for very homogeneous populations, industrial products must afford these differences, allowing visual, tactile, acoustical, and verbal indicators or clues to different interpretations of forms to exist side by side. This parallelism of expression may either be redundant, consistently supporting the same operational meanings in diverse populations of users and thereby increase motivation, or it may lead to contradictions and paradoxes, cause confusion, and, thereby, decrease motivation by either removing the fun inherent in smooth and competent interaction (which could provide intrinsic motivation) or increasing the possibilities of errors (which reduces extrinsic motivation). Esthetics has always been associated with redundancy[20] and the operational theory of meaning extends this to all levels of users' involvement with artifacts and, ultimately, with themselves.

Sociolinguistic Context

Solitary use of everyday things is rare. We worry about what to wear to a party, consider the appropriateness of a gift, have opinions about someone's taste, imitate our idols' patterns of consumption, and talk about all of this to friends. These examples involve bystanders, critics, judges, or interested parties to which users relate. These need be neither real nor present, however. When acquiring a product, for example, buyers usually think of other individuals, both recognizable when seen and wholly imaginary, who serve as references for their decisions and are consulted in the buyer's mind. "What would my mother say about my wearing this dress?" is the kind of question to which an approving answer may have to be found in order to feel comfortable wearing it. Although such a discourse may take place entirely inside a user's mind and between hypothetical people, it matches in importance what people talk about in fact. Discussion of everyday things takes place in language and subjects the things talked about to social definitions and meanings. In this context, *objects participate in human communication and support linguistically mediated social practices.*

Figure 5

20 Gregory Bateson, *Naven* (Stanford: Stanford University Press, 1958), and *Gregory Bateson, Steps to an Ecology of Mind* (New York: Ballentine, 1972).

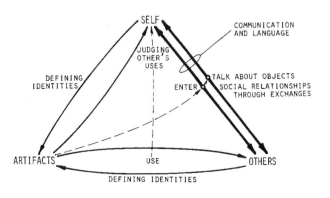

In the absence of in-depth literature about this context, I will elaborate four sociolinguistic uses of artifacts and comment briefly on their implications for design:

- expressions of *user identities*
- signs of *social differentiation and integration*
- *content of communication*
- material support for *social relationships*

This context could be viewed by means of the triangle in figure 5 involving the self, others, and material artifacts among which a variety of relationships and their dynamics are at issue.

User identities

When it comes to showing who they are or want to be, people seem to totally abandon utilitarian criteria or at best assign them a subordinate role. This is obvious with jewelry and fashion, for which technical considerations are minimal, indeed; however, even in highly technical domains of decision making people often abandon technical criteria as well. For example, driving below 55 miles per hour, a Porsche drives as well as a Honda Civic or a VW Rabbit. Worse, a Porsche offers less space, incurs far higher maintenance costs, and is more likely to be stolen, but it gives its owner a special flair, a sporty, wealthy, "yuppie" identity few other cars can provide. These attributes make the difference, not the technical data published and discussed in the salesroom.

Designers are not free from identity considerations either. Designers who are unaware of product semantics may professionally advocate the most radical functional perspectives while surrounding themselves with demonstrably beautiful things, ordinary objects cast into elegant shapes, expensive designs by famous firms or architects. This is exemplified by Gerrit Rietveld's chair, which neglects all comfort for its exquisite geometric style. Indeed, people and even entire countries, are willing to carry considerable burdens, inconveniences, and expenses just to be special, which often means surrounding themselves with objects aimed at defining their identity, for themselves to feel good about and for others to recognize.

The criteria that govern choices of this kind show little resemblance with those of problem solving or representational uses. Means and ends are indistinguishable here, and objects and what they mean become one. The criteria are based more on gestalt considerations and are concerned chiefly with how users weave their own identity into the symbolic fabric of society. The way people relate to their homes may serve as an example here. Based on Jungian notions, Cooper[21] shows a home as the place where individuals feel in the center of their own self-constructed universe, at which point their identity becomes indistinguishable with the things chosen to symbolize it. Users then are in a part-whole (metonymic) relationship with the complex of objects surrounding

21 Clare Cooper, "The House as Symbol of Self," in N. M. Prohansky, W. H. Ittelson, and L. G. Rivlin, eds. *Environmental Psychology, People and their Physical Settings* (New York: Holt, Rinehart or Winston, 1976): 435–48.

The Meaning of Products

them. (This relationship contrasts sharply with the means-end relationships of operational use.)

Social differentiation and integration

People want to be different but never so different that they no longer resemble others in some respect. A user's identity is but one extreme by which the self is distinguished from all others. By the above premise, individualization can never be total. The feeling of belonging to or being part of larger social entities, classes, professional groups, or religious denominations is, again, mediated largely through the deliberate use of particular objects. With the emphasis on similarities, Csikszentmihalyi and Rochberg-Halton[22] point out that such objects become *symbols of integration*. That many established designers drive BMWs, that architects are connoisseurs in fine restaurants, that "yuppies" live with chromed steel furniture, and so forth are slightly exaggerated examples of ways to express belongingness, shared attitudes, or common privileges.

However, marking belongingness to one group entails excluding belongingness to others. For objects to serve as symbols of integration, they must also draw distinctions between those who can afford, are able to, or are entitled to their use and those who are not so privileged. Thus, they function as *symbols of differentiation* as well. Things that are rare, expensive, or difficult to have access to or use are particularly suited to play this dual social role, and the extent to which industrial products must serve this function limits their mass production. For this reason, one cannot get everyone to wear the same clothes, live in identical apartments, or drive the same kind of car.

The delicate dialectic between differentiation and integration has often been overshadowed by status conceptions. Indeed, the process of differentiation and integration is rarely neutral and most cultures seem to rank people according to the power, respect, envy, or privileges they command. Only the artifacts chosen to support these inequalities vary. However, status is not a linear scale. There are status conflicts, incompatibilities, and shifts, and designers must recognize the social dynamics their products may initiate; for example, when objects designed for use in one group employ symbols of integration for another, or when high-status symbols are made easily accessible to low-status groups. Therefore, industrial interests to produce greater numbers of identical products can easily conflict with social needs for symbols of differentiation, integration, and status. Designers can respond by providing ways of individualizing, customizing, or altogether losing this social motivation for consumption or use.

Content of communication

Objects also provide important topics of conversations, and, by so doing, acquire meanings that are in fundamental ways different from operational use. Things are distinguished, named, and classified through language. Thus, objects that are not clearly distin-

22 Mihaly Csikszentmihalyi and Eugene Rochberg-Halton, *The Meaning of Things: Domestic Symbols and the Self* (Cambridge: Cambridge University Press, 1981).

guishable linguistically are also often confused in practice. For example, the generalization of the word *Jeep* to all rugged-looking four-wheel-drive vehicles bothers American Motors, as seen in its advertising. It is in language that things are joked about, criticized, or praised. Products that can easily be made fun of rarely succeed. There is a legend of examples where jokes and funny names prevented products from widespread use. The official name for Volkswagen's rugged utility and hunting vehicle, Thing, for example, cannot easily be incorporated into linguistic discourse. "I am driving a Thing" makes many people wonder what is meant, whereas substituting the word *Jeep* or *Thunderbird* for it would not. The car never became popular, probably for sociolinguistic rather than functional reasons. It is also in language that objects are admitted into specific social practices. The distinction among wine glasses, and between them and other types of glasses, follows conventions negotiated in language and usage (which glass for which occasion) and is socially evaluated and judged.

Inasmuch as criteria for evaluating and judging objects are formulated in language and negotiated in communication among people, including users, forms may have to be designed in view of the categories and distinctions drawn by the speakers of language. Designers often seek to fuse two well-known technologies into a new device that cannot be easily recognized and talked about for its neither-quality. The language used by consumers often differs from the language used by designers, who must fit their designs into commonly available categories or cause enormous advertising costs to gain acceptance. Linguistic categories are also subject to their own dynamics. The transformation of portable radios into tape-playing "ghetto blasters" (boxes) shows how social definitions change and how particular groups can appropriate objects as symbols of their own.

Finally, language provides the research medium into users' cognitive models, motivations, and meanings. Charles Osgood's semantic differential,[23] to use a well-known example, calls for rating products by scales, whose end points are marked by polar opposites, for example, fast/slow, expensive/cheap, active/passive, attractive/repulsive, and, thus, involve objects in simple adjectival constructions. Protocol analysis,[24] on the other hand, maps how users describe themselves as interacting with objects. Either result is rooted in language and cannot be separated from respondents' linguistic use of objects in communication with others. When a truck cabin is said to be compact, sturdy, functional, comfortable, and so forth, this description may say more about the linguistic use of the words *truck cabin* than about truck cabins. Research methods in product semantics that use verbal instructions, stimuli, or responses are therefore also methods of establishing the sociolinguistic meanings into which designers have to fit their products. All efforts to establish design languages[25] attempt to make sense of objects by verbally putting them in the context of conversations.

23 Charles E. Osgood, George J. Suci, and Percy H. Tannenbaum, *The Measurement of Meaning* (Urbana: University of Illinois Press, 1967).

24 K. Anders Ericsson and Herbert A. Simon, *Protocol Analysis: Verbal Report as Data* (Cambridge: MIT Press, 1984).

25 For example, Richard Fisher and Gerda Mikosch, *Grundlagen einer Theorie der Produktsprache* (Offenbach: Hochschule für Gestalung, 1984); Toenis Kaeo and Julius Lengart, et al., *Productgestalt* (München: Siemens AG, undated).

Social relationships

Objects also play an important role in establishing, maintaining, or changing social relationships. This role is a necessary consequence of transferring the ownership of material entities among people and of the meanings objects thereby acquire. After repeatedly purchasing from the same merchant, a buyer may become a favorite customer, which entails a special relationship of trust that both buyer and seller recognize and seek to cultivate. In other words, consumer products must not only look worth their cost to the consumer at the point of sale, because this exchange is based on and feeds relationships of trust, products may have to be designed with this affordance in mind. Gifts, as another category of exchange of goods, provide a more interpersonal example. Although a gift is always thought to be of benefit to a receiver and affordable by a donor, it necessarily introduces some asymmetry into an existing social relationship. Receiving a gift not only requires that the receiver express some gratitude to the donor, but also imparts an unspoken obligation to reciprocate in the future. Similarly, symbols such as wedding bands are not merely signs of married persons but constant reminders of the special relationship between two people and the church or state that invests its power in protecting this relationship. (The word *symbol* comes from the ancient Greek tradition of two parting friends breaking a coin into two halves that each carries in the hope that this will bring them together again.) Industrial products, bribes, loaned or borrowed objects, gifts, and symbols are all involved in mediating social relationships, which designers may accidentally ignore and disable or deliberately honor and support.

Context of Genesis

Artifacts are not only instrumental to users (operational context) and constitutive of social realities (sociolinguistic context), but they are also created, produced, marketed, consumed, retired, or recycled, and experiences with them inform a subsequent generation of artifacts. This process forms a grand cycle, oversimplifyingly called the production-consumption cycle, which knits designers, engineers, producers, suppliers, distributors, advertisers, salespersons, consumers, users, waste managers, applied scientists, researchers, and regulatory agencies into an ongoing process of technological autopoiesis.[26] These participants have a stake in maintaining this process and can therefore be called stakeholders. Simplified and with the designers' part too exaggerated, this cycle is depicted in figure 6.

Design students learn and practitioners frequently repeat the misconception that industrial designers *create* industrial products for mass consumption. This conception lacks awareness of the differential roles other stakeholders play and unduly emphasizes tangible products over the process of generating them. Designers usually are involved with two kinds of activities, and successful

26 Sagan and Margulis, *Whole Earth Review* cited above.

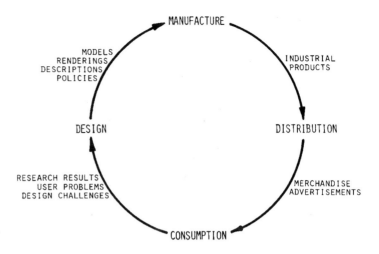

MANUFACTURE

MODELS
RENDERINGS
DESCRIPTIONS
POLICIES

INDUSTRIAL
PRODUCTS

DESIGN

DISTRIBUTION

RESEARCH RESULTS
USER PROBLEMS
DESIGN CHALLENGES

MERCHANDISE
ADVERTISEMENTS

CONSUMPTION

Figure 6

designers engage both well. First, designers create highly individualized *patterns* in the form of drawings, sketches, models, descriptions of possible uses, specifications (of materials and production processes needed to enable others to realize their ideas as rendered), corporate strategies, and advertising campaigns. The materiality in which these patterns are embodied is irrelevant or secondary to the information they carry and the sense they make to others. Within the semiotic framework, designers create representations or descriptions of things; but because these creations are things themselves, I prefer to view them as information or manifestations of patterns in transition.

Second, designers must convince others to get involved or their creations (pattern) rarely bear fruit. In fact, most designers spend the greater portion of their time developing presentations, selling their ideas, and communicating with clients. Some designers claim that 80 percent of their time is presentation, 10 percent is administration, and 10 percent is searching for solutions. In convincing others, designers do tailor their patterns, like messages, to what clients want, are willing to accept, and are able to use (produce and pass on). With speech-act theory, one could say that designers are above all communicators and the patterns they produce must have some *perlocutionary force*[27] for other stakeholders to be attracted to and influenced by them.

Thus, in the context of genesis, *artifacts can best be seen informationally, as temporarily frozen manifestations of pattern.* The ideas in the designer's mind becomes frozen in the form of drawings. Drawings are used by engineers to develop production schedules. Production schedules enable marketers to settle on distribution plans and advertising strategies. These attract potential users to acquire or consume the products. Industrial concerns usually stop here, but the process of transforming patterns into different materialities continues. Research on the patterns of interaction between

27 John L. Austin, *How to do Things with Words* (New York: Oxford University Press, 1962).

The Meaning of Products

products and users feeds back to and informs designers and producers. Users apply industrial products to their individual environments (an issue discussed in the section on ecological context), and all artifacts are ultimately retired, recycled, or decomposed and collectively influence the physical environment in unintended and barely understood ways. Problems recognized in the subsequent environment provide the fertile ground motivating new ideas. New ideas are but combinations, reorganizations, or modifications of patterns already in existence. Thus, the production of artifacts neither has a natural target nor terminates with an end user: *it continuously feeds on itself.*

In the context of genesis, artifacts—and natural objects could be included here as well—are always in transition. They are the products of one process *and* the inputs to others, semantically carrying their own history into the future. They are like messages in circuit, as Gregory Bateson[28] has taught, being continuously created, articulated, interpreted, and translated into other messages that collectively produce the very technology that produced them. The stakeholders in this process are then best described as communicators of organized matter that make a difference in their lives.

The context of genesis affords several laws. Stated in factual terms, the most important law reads as follows: *The existence of any artifact is living proof of the viability of all of its genetically preceding manifestations.* Obviously, an idea that is unthinkable cannot be sketched. Something indescribable (something that cannot be expressed in words, drawn on paper, or otherwise communicated) to a producer cannot be built. A product that is unknown to potential users cannot be sold. The law boldly suggests that the chain of a pattern's transformation cannot be broken. Nothing comes from nowhere. The nonviability of any one manifestation in this chain can become the reason for a pattern to become extinct.

Stated prescriptively, the law could read: *Patterns should be designed to survive all the successive transformation into manifestations (artifacts) that are necessary to ultimately support themselves.* Thus, in the context of genesis, the unit of design concerns is not a consumer product but the circular process through which those patterns may travel that enable a particular behavior to evolve. If artifacts are to carry their own history into the future, they must be equipped with the semantics to do so.

For designers to take responsibility for this circular process the following requirements must be satisfied:
- *Addressing the network*
- *Comprehensibility*
- *Resource availability*
- *Costs and benefits*
- *Adaptability*
- *Entropy and pollution*

28 Bateson, *Steps to an Ecology of Mind* cited above.

Addressing the network

Ideas might not find their way through the complex network of a production-consumption cycle by themselves, unless they bear the addresses to the intended stakeholders. Indeed, many great ideas have been wasted by falling into the wrong hands or arriving at their destination at inappropriate times. In addition, and unlike mail, which bears just one address, designers are not the only ones who have clients. Clients have clients too. It follows that patterns must be designed to travel by efficient paths through a whole circular chain of stakeholders. Each manifestation must then include the addresses to the remainder of the intended path. The histories of artifacts may become lost but what gives them direction should not.

One mode of addressing used by designers employs symbolism, which some receivers find attractive and seek out for themselves when needed. Advertisers think that way, but only about buyers. Another mode uses a language that only the intended stakeholders know how to interpret. Drugs tend to be described in vocabulary only qualified doctors understand for fear they might get into the wrong hands. During the product development phase, successful design firms often involve as many stakeholders as possible in a process that includes reaching consensus on who does what, when, and how. Advertisements are naturally placed in magazines that reach desired consumers. The exclusion of children's access to medicine bottles was already mentioned. Ecologists have convincingly argued—though not in these words—that addressing should extend beyond marketing concerns to where retired products can be recycled or may be disposed of without causing environmental destruction.

Comprehensibility

Stakeholders cannot be expected to proceed with anything that does not make sense to them. To render intelligible what might otherwise appear nonsense is difficult. Even though designers might complain about the gory taste of engineers or about the culturally irresponsible opportunism of sales personnel, rarely does one group have what the other lacks. Difficulties in communication are usually rooted in different professional histories, experiences, conceptions, and interests. To overcome these calls for agreement on a language capable of expressing patterns in forms that afford the stakeholders different cognitive models, refer to individually different experiences, and appeal to different values.

Functionalism in engineering, ergonomics, and marketing provided such a bridge in the past, but it did not embrace the social and cultural domains. Product semantics is an example of a developing framework by which designers can communicate about their previously inexpressible sensitivities, cultural responsibilities, and user concerns at the same time. It promises knowledge about how people make sense of their physical environment, presents methodologies and replicable tests for the design of human interfaces in a variety of contexts, and provides a platform for consensus about the concepts used. This framework is applicable not only to the stage of consumption, but to all stakeholders involved in the flow of pattern.

There are no perfect tests for whether an artifact works other than that its underlying pattern has succeeded in making sense to the stakeholders throughout a complete production-consumption cycle. Comprehensibility is a requirement for transmission of pattern (information) and a significant bottleneck for genesis.

Resource availability

For a pattern to be realized or implemented requires that stakeholders command adequate resources. There is no sense in proposing technologies of unknown availability, products for consumers who do not exist, or distribution mechanisms whose costs are inestimable. Recognizing the availability of adequate resources requires a level of understanding that goes one step beyond comprehensibility by involving the physical processes that designs or patterns need to inform.

For designers, this step implies explicitness as to how a pattern may be implemented, acted upon, or used and which physical conditions are required to succeed in this endeavor. Successful design firms not only present their ideas, but also bring potential producers, suppliers, banks, market researchers, user groups, and so forth together, inform their clients where adequate resources are available or how available resources may be utilized. In this respect, designers resemble technology managers rather than applied artists who produce their own works. In the absence of such efforts, designers are likely to be conservative of familiar practices, parochial in scope, or fail.

Costs and benefits

Within the production-consumption cycle, motivation tends to be unevenly distributed. For consumers, the time between paying for a product and experiencing the benefits of its use is short and the margin of profit (benefits minus costs) tends to be small. Marketing and advertising seek to ensure that a product's form prominently expresses its benefits. In comparison, yields from investments in research and product development are large but typically arrive with considerable delay. It follows that producers have greater investments in the circular process than consumers, leaving little for recyclers and waste managers.

Whereas consumer benefits of a product can be expressed in that product's form, a major design problem in the context of genesis is to sustain the producer's expectations of benefits to the point of actual yield. Research and product development commitments usually follow from high expectations of benefits derived from convincing presentations by designers, supportive profitability analyses, and market research results. However, the initial enthusiasm erodes as development and production costs accumulate, unless this enthusiasm is continuously fed or nourished. It requires designers either to be part of the process or to communicate with their designs something that sustains this motivation at least to the point of actual yields.

Adaptability

Traditional machines, such as scissors, steam engines, bridges, and automobiles, serve just a few anticipated functions, forcing users to adapt. Designs for these products are equally fixed. This situation is changing through the invention of adaptive systems and user-programmable computers and the extension of design activities into social systems. The creation of production-consumption cycles represents the most sophisticated example. Such systems can have a life of their own, adapting to their own environments, learning from users, changing their behavior, growing and developing into product niches, and protecting themselves from misuse. They can also generate additional artifacts and be self-maintaining.

Since the advent of cybernetics, intelligent systems are no longer unusual. Human interfaces with such systems call for a product semantics quite different from simple and relatively fixed form-meaning relationships of traditional design applications. Intelligent systems are similar to behavioral chameleons, and their appearance should explain whether (and how) they grow like crystals or computer networks, learn like mice in a maze or generate novel responses from given rules.

Three directions for such a semantics are currently explored. One is the design of computer interfaces by means of screens and controls expressing the opportunities and tools necessary to make them do whatever users desire, their range of affordances being virtually inexhaustible. A second is the design of components that enable users to assemble a nearly unimaginably large variety of applications, each corresponding to individualized needs. A third is the design of corporate strategies that are generative of a coherent line of products which are responsive to changing situations, new technological developments, and different user demands. These directions conceive patterns as language-like facilities—user-adapted programming concepts, combinatorial grammars, and generative design languages—whose particular "expressions" are always merely one of many and within that language possible forms whose particular realization escapes its designers' exclusive control.

Entropy and pollution

In the context of genesis, the communication of symbols, messages, and artifacts and the transformation of patterns they inform drive the flow of energy and matter in a production consumption cycle. Two laws, simplified but of considerable generality, are relevant here:

energy used = work + reusable energy + entropy

raw material = organized matter + recyclable waste + pollution

The first equation restates the first two basic laws of thermo-dynamics. The second is the material analog of thermodynamics in which pollution is a dispersion of matter that is impossible or too costly to reverse and that represents maximally disorganized matter. Figure 7 depicts the application of these distinctions to any one stakeholder's work. What is true for individuals or groups also applies to whole systems. All production of organized matter or artifacts requires work but irreversibly increases entropy and pollu-tion. Only the rate at which these measures of decay increase differ from product to product. Globally, entropy makes available levels of energy increasingly useless, and pollution makes available raw material increasingly costly. According to these laws, the physical production of things makes that production increasingly impossible.

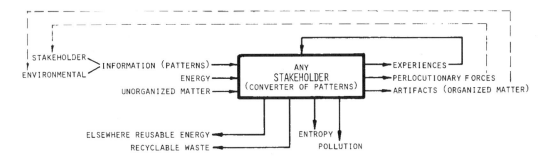

Figure 7

Designers should be especially aware of and responsible for the global effects of their creative efforts. From the point of view of a responsible product semantics, inventing and pursuing symbolic strategies that slow down the inevitable processes of decay are important. This may be accomplished by designing industrial products that can be produced in an energy-efficient manner, can adapt to users' sense-making needs, can direct their own recycling, and can protect other species of artifacts from needless decay. This is the most general recommendation of a product semantics in the context of genesis.

The Ecological Context

Ecological concerns are usually articulated in terms of preserving the natural environment of some time ago. Although these concerns have some merit, they must include the artifacts people live with as well. Hence, I take ecology as a framework for exploring how the interaction among different kinds of artifacts make sense.

The idea of ecology comes from biology, where it is defined as the interaction of *populations of species* and is applied largely to plants and animals. It is attractive as a model for four reasons:

First, each population of species is regarded as living in its own environment to which it responds and by which it organizes itself into its very own categories (Uexküll's *Merkwelt*). The envi-ronment that a population affects (Uexküll's *Wirkwelt*) may only partly overlap with the former but may be "seen" or responded to by some other population (at least of human observers).[29]

Second, populations of species are thought to interact through such partially overlapping environments, without presumption that one "understands" the nature of the other, and the larger ecology is described as a network of such interactions. There is also no assumption of wholeness, no hierarchy, no master plan, no overriding purpose, and no central authority, even though some species are clearly more dominant than others. So conceived, an ecology is a distributed, heterarchical, and dynamic system.

Third, relationships between populations of species, whether they are cooperative, competitive, symbiotic, or parasitic, emerge in interaction or are "negotiated," so to speak, without some outsider unilaterally imposing them. There is no central ruler, only participants who may assert their will in their own environment of others. An ecology is not democratic, egalitarian, or just, but is responsive to every population.

Fourth, ecological systems seek balances or converge toward some equilibrium, at which point populations keep each other in check, maintain varieties of species, and ensure efficient use of limited resources. Gregory Bateson,[30] among others, described such an equilibrating tendency as distributed wisdom.

As Kenneth Boulding[31] points out, there are many species of artifacts, perhaps even more than biological species now existing. Items described in an unabridged Sears catalog are probably more numerous than biological species listed in a high school text on biology, and this catalog is far from being representative of the products available worldwide. Species of artifacts also cover greater ranges than biological species do. They range wider in size: skyscrapers are larger than elephants, artificial molecules are smaller than amoebas. They range wider in complexity: computer chips have more memory than lower animals, not to speak of stock markets that even humans cannot comprehend, and they can function much longer than any living organism, as museums can testify. Human beings can be considered artifacts to the extent they are social beings, speak a common language, assume social roles, conform to behavioral conventions, and are, in these respects, replaceable. Organizations are artifacts as well, created by humans, interacting with one another in particular environments containing various resources, markets, stakeholders, and regulatory agencies. The implications for product semantics of placing artifacts in ecological contexts are enormous and call for a whole book. However, only three aspects of particular interest to design are discussed here: *competition*, *cultural complexes*, and *autopoiesis*.

Competition

In linguistics, in discourse analysis, in particular, differences in meanings of words are recognized by differences in the linguistic environments in which they can or do occur. Accordingly, words

29 Jocob von Uexküll, "Band X, Abhandlungen zur theoretischen Biologie und ihrer Geschichte, sowie zure Philosophie der Organischen Naturwissenschaften," in *Bedeutungslebre* (Leipzig: Johann Ambrosious Barth, 1940) Uexküll develops a general theory of species-specific construction of meanings and environments that can provide a conceptual framework for accounting for the interaction among species in an ecology. It is consistent with my approach to semantics. In the absence of a translation, his *Theoretical Biology* (London: Paul Trench & Trubner, 1926) contains the rudiments of his approach.

30 Bateson, *Steps to an Ecology of Mind* cited above.

31 Kenneth Boulding, *Ecodynamics* (Beverly Hills: Sage, 1978).

The Meaning of Products

are synonymous if they are freely substituted for each other in the same text. So, the word *early*, as in the phrase "he came early," is usually substituted with *too soon*, making them synonymous, whereas *prematurely* can only occasionally substitute for *early*, the difference in context being the formality or informality of speech. The very same way of thinking about meaning applies to artifacts that might also be substituted for each other and, thereby, compete with each other for available positions. Cars substituted for horse-drawn carriages and depleted their numbers. Electronic messages and telefaxes are largely substitutes for written letters, save for the electronic environment needed, and are likely to reduce the use of postal services. Substitution is rarely perfect, however. Just as horses have found a niche in sports and pleasure that cars cannot easily penetrate, so has the telephone reduced letter writing but may not drive it to extinction.

Cars do not look like horses, but early cars very much resembled horse-drawn carriages, probably facilitating substitution, just as personal computers now look very much like typewriters and television sets, which they challenge. The form of these products is what directs whether they fit into contexts in which they compete with existing products and succeed or disappear as a consequence of the interaction they support. Designers must understand the dynamics of meaning that ecological interaction entails; they must create forms that survive such interaction, that are sufficiently similar to competing forms, and that are sufficiently distinct to make a difference.

Cultural complexes
Competing artifacts interact so that an increase in the numbers of one decreases the numbers of the other. In contrast, cooperating artifacts develop a variety of dependencies that support their respective population sizes. There are dominance relationships in which one population enables the other to increase in size, but the latter's decline will influence the former only minimally. Batteries dominate flashlights, but there are so many other uses for batteries that a decline in the flashlight population does not significantly influence the battery population. There are supportive-dependency relationships in which one population of artifacts, sometimes called secondary gadgets, support but are existentially dependent on the use of primary artifacts. Software is related to computers in this manner. Software has enhanced computer use tremendously, but computers existed before software was marketed on a large scale. Among the various dependencies that emerge are those governed by taste, style, and family belongingness. While chairs always cooperate with tables as lightbulbs do with books, beyond these family resemblances, items of similar style are attracted to each other forming mutually supportive wholes. However, there may also be parasitism and predation in which competition and cooperation is not mutual, just as in a biological ecology.

The point of this argument is that dependencies that develop among interacting populations of artifacts grow into *cultural complexes*, which consist of many different artifacts whose cooperative forms of interaction have become so stable that they could be considered composite forms or systems in their own right. The car complex is such an example. It consists of drivers, car dealers, automobile manufacturers, streets, municipal transportation departments, gasoline stations, oil producers, all of which cooperate with each other in keeping cars running and themselves in place. (I am ignoring here competition within any one category which does not change the system.) This complex has threatened public transportation, such as trains, buses, and the railroad; invaded the postal service; and put its stamp on the architecture of cities, all of which are cultural complexes of their own.

Newly designed artifacts rarely simply replace old designs. They seek and encourage the emergence of somewhat different environments, initiate shifts within their cultural complexes, cause chain reactions throughout the larger ecology, and, therefore, need to withstand the self-protective responses by those affected. The omission of chrome on American cars made whole factories obsolete. The initial success of cars with the new aerodynamic look forced many other manufacturers to rethink and find new forms. In an ecology with artifacts, the meanings of objects are always interacting and in flux. Changing one form may have enormous consequences for others.

Autopoiesis and conclusion

Ecologies with artifacts, including the cultural complexes outlined above, do not work without human participation. People design things, people direct production, and people put artifacts in their places. Without the collective use of symbolic strategies *for* local assembly and guidance, technology cannot behave as a self-productive or autopoietic system and would therefore decay.[32] True, designers can work within the functional tradition, with its linear logic of achieving terminal ends and a semantics of "stand for" if not "make-believe" relations to reality. Its exclusive emphasis on allopoiesis—the production of something other than itself—makes a functional perspective inherently limiting, unable to conceptualize meanings that develop from circular interactions within an ecology of artifacts and unable to participate in creating symbolic strategies that make autopoiesis happen.

I have argued that, in the operational context, cognitive models held by human individuals locally guide the assembly of artifacts into individually meaningful wholes and that this takes place in each individual's environment as cognized.[33] This applies to individual users of artifacts as well as to designers. The context of genesis provides designers with cognitive models to create things. Both models realize that *form follows meaning*, which is shorthand for

32 Sagan and Margulis, *Whole Earth Review* cited above.

33 For the distinction between cognized and operational models of reality, see Roy A. Rappaport, "Sanctity and Adaptation," *The CoEvolution Quarterly* (1974): 58–8, and his *Pigs for the Ancestors: Ritual in the Ecology of a New Guinea People* (New Haven: Yale University Press, 1978).

The Meaning of Products

saying symbolic strategies, not physics, govern the collective use and assembly of artifacts into cultural systems.[34]

Mythology probably is the most important and unconsciously embracing governing structure in an ecology of artifacts. A culture can hardly be conceived without myths, and its vitality derives directly from them. In some cultures, mythology is codified in ritual performances and stories of supernatural beings and gods. These gods perform deeds of immense power and interact with each other and humans through artifacts. In other cultures, notably in the industrialized West, mythology has become more hidden, unconscious, and implicit in superstitious beliefs and repetitive cultural practices, but it occasionally surfaces through powerful tragedies, movies, literature, and science fiction, as well as major inventions that guide and occupy generations of people, designers, producers, and users alike. Mythologies give coherence to cultural complexes beyond individual understanding by legitimizing its components, assigning them to perform meaningful roles and directing them to interact with each other. Design strategies that go against mythology go against the ancient ecological wisdom that has been cumulatively acquired during centuries of human social experiences; these design strategies are likely to fail in the ecological interactions they have to withstand. Although largely unconscious, artifacts always mediate symbolically between the deep-rooted mythologies distributed in a culture and the material contexts of everyday life.[35] With the support of powerful mythologies, artifacts can gain considerable ecological strength; denying this connection, whether by ignorance or by preference for a functionalism that cannot cope with meanings, produces an inhumane technology.

I have argued that, in the ecological context, cognitive spaces of different participants need not be the same for interaction to take place. Indeed, designers and consumers cannot be presumed to see the world with the same eyes much less so do computers, streets, forests, and grass. In any ecology, none of its participants—properly including animals and plants—can possibly understand the whole system of which they are part. Every participant is limited by his, her, or its own cognitive models and by their largely unconscious access to prevailing mythologies. Understanding an ecology is therefore necessarily partial. Superindividual wholes always are mythological indeed. Mythology in language bridges different cognitive spaces and serves as a medium for negotiating distinctions, differences, and typicalities and for coordinating the use of individual symbolic strategies. Designers are but one kind of participant in the ecological process, and the patterns they set in motion could travel over such bridges but never without involving the larger system of which they are a part. The designers of symbolic strategies for artifacts may claim to reign supreme in this ecology, but they cannot escape the hidden governance of collectively shared

34 This is also stressed in Uexküll's work, *Bedeutungslehre* cited above.

35 See S. Balaram's analysis of Mahatma Gandhi's use of artifacts. S. Balaram, "Product Symbolism of Gandhi and Its Connections with Indian Mythology," in this volume.

archetypes and mythologies whose meanings must be respected, grasped, tapped, and drifted with.

None of the four contexts of artifacts or the four constructions for the theory and practice of product semantics exists entirely outside someone's mind. They are suggested here as four principle types of cognitive models for designers to create forms that make sense for others. Thus conceived, product semantics is a radical proposal for *an ecology of designers' minds*. Its concepts of meaning enable designers to communicate through the designed world with other fellow human beings and to participate responsibly in an ecology that is, at least in part, their own creation. The properly self-referential nature of this kind of product semantics correlates with the cultural autopoiesis it viably informs (figure 8).

Figure 8

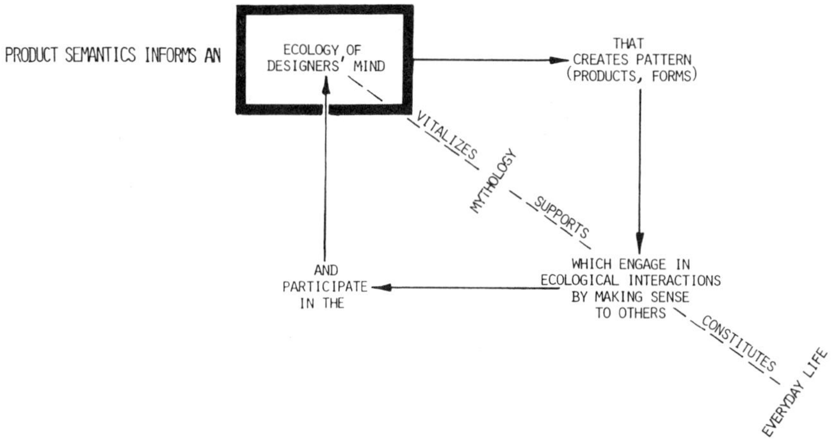

PRODUCT SEMANTICS INFORMS AN — ECOLOGY OF DESIGNERS' MIND — THAT CREATES PATTERN (PRODUCTS, FORMS) — WHICH ENGAGE IN ECOLOGICAL INTERACTIONS BY MAKING SENSE TO OTHERS — CONSTITUTES EVERYDAY LIFE — AND PARTICIPATE IN THE — VITALIZES — MYTHOLOGY — SUPPORTS

Section III

Design and Culture

Design, Development, Culture, and Cultural Legacies in Asia
Rajeshwari Ghose

The very idea of writing on contemporary or "modern" design issues pertaining to any country or civilization seems to evolve around two methodological assumptions. The first assumption is that there exists something called *design* as ontological equipment. If not, at least a belief that design exists as a full-fledged discipline in quite the same way as economics, sociology, or history exist, distinct from the specifics of disciplines such as current monetary policy of the People's Republic of China, analyses of football hooliganism in Britain, or the causes of World War I. This broad rubric then could accommodate architectural, industrial, communications, and fashion/garment design, woven together as it were by a common methodological thread. Constituted thus, it could form the basis of teaching curricula.

The second assumption is that nation states have identifiable cultural, socioeconomic, and esthetic aspirations and predictable patterns of lifestyle, which despite all their variegated heterogeneities, exhibit at least a certain identifiable common cultural substance and provide the necessary *tabula rasa* on which modern design may be projected.

When these general assumptions are applied to Asian design, new problems emerge. Despite dissensions, the contemporary mainstream concept of design in the West is in some vague manner connected with new sources of energy, technological breakthroughs, mass production, minute specializations, and global quest for markets. It is perceived as a visible tool of both commerce and industry, carrying with it other legacies of nineteenth and early twentieth century ideals, for example, that design could act as a leveler of society through more equitable accessibility to mass-produced goods as well as introduce a sense of clean, rational, impersonal order. This sense of rational order is a direct descendant of the Enlightenment ideology, which in Weberian terms produced the Western brand of capitalistic transformation of society. There were, no doubt, several variants to this historic Western model, but underlying it all were two central principles: The first was that modernization, of which design was but a tool, was *endogenous,* that society was capable of transforming itself from within, and where there was inadequate endogenous impetus, such as in Germany, the state would become a central agent in the transformation of society. The second principle was that this modernism would be based on rationalism and thus certain kinds of particularist esthetics, value systems, contexts and

Many of the issues discussed in this paper were raised in an international conference, Design and Development in South and Southeast Asia, held in Hong Kong, December 5–8, 1988. References to papers and oral discussions held at this conference appear in the footnotes under the abbreviated form DDSSEA. Proceedings of the conference were published as *Design and Development in South and Southeast Asia*, ed. Rajeshwari Ghose (Hong Kong: Centre for Asian Studies/University of Hong Kong, 1990).

cultures, religion, and rites and rituals would be universally applicable and all embracing: "from the sofa cushion to urban planning."[1]

At present, most Asians see First World technology and consumerism as handmaidens of design and harbingers of modernity. They hope to implant this combination on their soils and achieve comparable results. Perceived in such a manner, Asian design issues become closely interwoven with issues involving technology/design transfers from the First World, as well as problems associated with adapting new or changing technology to diverse economic, social, cultural, and political conditions. The issues then revolve around the current Third World realities of being "Late Comers" and often lead to self denigration at being slow learners. This, in turn, is then expressed in terms of frustrations at poor quality and high prices, stagnation, particularly in the field of industrial design, and as K. M. Munshi, an industrial designer from India, sums up: "while the rest of the world was changing fast, large Indian Industry remained stagnant. . . . Product innovation was a far cry. Lack of quality bothered neither the buyer nor the seller."[2] This situation was exacerbated by "protection," captive markets, import substitution, and a whole range of developmental policies. Munshi continues that it was only in the mid-1960s that "design was recognized as one of the factors which could help exports." Seen from this point of view, the difficulties of writing Asian design history and discussing Asian design issues become obvious. How does one separate it from technology/design transfers, foreign aid, foreign trade and investment, International Patents Acts, government policies of import substitutions and export orientations, from, above all, the whole idea of development? Is there an Asian design history at all apart from the histories of all these with a few case studies of either successful or unsuccessful adaptations of First World design? How else does one write design history, how else does one approach design? Surely, to quote the following expression often heard in countries of Asia: "Design is an ancient activity even though a modern profession." What then is the link between the activity and the profession? The quintessence of contemporary design issues in Asia lies in the asking of these questions, in the provoking of new debates. Discourses on design are so overpowered by dominant First World methodologies that we must wait quite awhile for new approaches to evolve and be cogently articulated. Until then, Asian design issues will find mention under a small section, sometimes tellingly entitled "Anti Design."[3] True, in India, for example, a number of very successful adaptations have been made, particularly in the field of consumer goods. This applies especially to kitchen utensils and electrical gadgets, and some innovative designs like an oxygenator and solar rice cooker are still waiting to find local sponsors.

However, extreme caution must be taken in the use of such a blanket term as *Asian design*, for "Asia is One," was a myth that had

1   This oft-repeated phrase which now appears in its many variants, is believed to have been coined by the architect Hermann Muthesius. See Joan Campbell, *The German Werkbund* (Princeton, NJ: Princeton University Press, 1978),1.

2   K. M. Munshi, "Dynamics of Design and Technology: An Indian Overview" in DDSSEA.

3   Penny Sparke, *Culture and Design in the Twentieth Century* (Winchester, MA: Allen & Unwin, 1986), particularly page 198.

Design and Culture

very little credibility even at the time it was being propounded and that died soon after Japan's defeat in World War II. Japan, with its elevated status as a First World power, and the "Four Little Dragons," with their newest apellation as the newly industrialized countries of Asia or the NICs for short[4] operate under different paradigms and constraints and are heirs to different historical legacies from the larger countries of South and Southeast Asia. In the early phases of the colonial era, Orientalists usually divided this huge continent into two vast cultural belts: Indic and Sinic, with a vague understanding that all the land in between was Indo-China. Economists now speak in a neo-Weberian manner of the common heritage of "secular" or "vulgar" Confucianism, which has contributed to a Sinic brand of capitalism. Until recently, China was excluded from this vast and eminently successful belt composed of Japan, South Korea, Hong Kong, Taiwan, and Singapore. It is, however, in the opinion of some economists, at the point of being admitted as the big dragon into this comity of nations with the recent adoption of market socialism. Most developing countries of Asia have begun to perceive design in the contemporary First World model as an agent of capturing markets in an increasingly competitive world. Hence, *product differentiation is* the buzz word.

Two statements in the official Japanese publication *Japan Focus* (January 1989) summarize this approach. The first: "Today the technological level of manufactures has become standardized. . . . Thus, in order to provide products with individuality, the trend toward placing importance on design is strengthening more than ever before." The second: "The trend toward utilization of foreign designers by Japanese makers has become increasingly active since the end of the 1970s. To foreign designers, perhaps the *short life cycle of Japanese products* (italics added) compared to those of the West, with even such items as cars undergoing frequent model changes, makes the Japanese market particularly attractive."

This article lays no claim to address the complexities of the macro Asian design scene, but will limit itself to just a few of the crucial issues in the lesser developed countries (LDCs) of Asia, particularly those issues pertaining to India.

In the 1960s in India, a few men of vision set up a modern design education center based on broad humanistic principles. The designer Charles Eames, one of the founders of the National Institute of Design in Ahmedabad, India, hoped that it be "concerned with quality and the ultimate values of the human environment."

The Ahmedabad Declaration on Industrial Design for Development, promulgated in January 1979, stated in clear terms the role of design in a developing society. It called for (1) understanding the values of one's society and then defining a quality of life within its parameters; (2) seeking local answers for local needs by using local materials and skills, while making use of advanced science and technology; and (3) creating new values, addressing

4   Recently, the term has been changed into NIE, Newly Industrialized Economies, to accommodate Hong Kong, which will in 1997 be a part of the People's Republic of China. The "Four Dragons" are South Korea, Hong Kong, Taiwan, and Singapore. Japan was often referred to as the Big Dragon, but recently, the term has been associated with China more to indicate its huge potential. Peter Burger is believed to have been the first to use the term "vulgar Confucianism" to signify Confucianism and its value system, when operating under a free-market economy. It refers to values such as obedience, hierarchy, thrift, hard work, This-world-ism, group mentality, and so forth, as the kind of qualities that made the Sinic brand of capitalism possible.

priority needs, and preserving plural identities. The document recommended several ways in which these ideas could be put into practice. The recommendations included consciousness raising exercises, establishment of well-planned design institutions, dissemination of knowledge, and the inculcation of new values throughout the country. This was a manifesto of appropriate design for the developing world. Ten years later, the same plea is made by Chee Peng Lim.[5] Asoke Chatterjee, an educationist from India, commenting on the practical application of these ideologies, stated in unambiguous terms: "Yet, the original inspiration for bringing design to this land (India) . . . remains virtually untouched. Basic needs . . . are outside the designer's purview, challenging the conscience of this young profession and its ancient inheritance."[6] The questions posed are, therefore, centered around educational ideals and pragmatic realities and are inextricably woven around theories and policies of development—will the benefits trickle down? Must the emphasis be on acquiring the necessary sophisticated skills and experience in operating on that more international sector, or must the relevance or irrelevance of a design skill be constantly tested and contested?

Beginning with the 1970s, according to S. Balaram, another industrial designer from India, the design profession began to gain respectability in the country but not necessarily entirely in the manner envisaged by the Ahmedabad Declaration. A small number of professional designers, numbering 600 in all, found themselves in great demand, with many of them absorbed in the more glamorous types of activities, leading to Balaram's wry remark that, in the 1970s, the "designer star" was born.[7] This glamour image was promoted primarily by the wealthy, private consumer sector, where design acquired a snob value and sometimes snugly fitted in with traditional aspirations of ostentation associated with oriental courtly life. The image of ostentation at the extreme end of the economic and cultural spectrum, now appears in the super affluent circles in the form of "megamarriages," where high technology, affluence, and fantasy provide a strange combination in which professional design help is sought to create the desired ambience. Computer-aided design and laser technology are used to inscribe on the blue firmament two hearts being pierced by a common arrow, with the names of the bride and groom dutifully inserted. Such extravaganzas are being planned, at the time of writing, for the opening of the French National Festival in Bombay, which will introduce more technological gimmicks to a very receptive audience. This festival is a French response to the Indian National Festivals, which, in their attempt to create a favorable impression of India abroad, contribute to a high-society profile for the design profession. These events are highly jazzed-up occasions that provide individual designers with opportunities to obtain lucrative national and international contracts and add a certain quality of glamour. This is, however, a mixed blessing. In the Philippines, this flamboyant image was a part

5   Chee Peng Lim, "Appropriate and Inappropriate Transfers of Technology" in DDSSEA.
6   Asoke Chatterjee, "Design in India: An Experience in Education" in DDSSEA.
7   S. Balaram, "Decision Making by the Indian Government and Its Impact on Design" in DDSSEA.

Design and Culture

of the "Imelda Cult," fostered by the former First Lady's form of patronage of art and design.

There are major variants to this design approach and to the range of the spectrum from country to country and between sectors within each country in Asia. But there is an underlying unity marked by heavy reliance on imported models. Shou Zhi Wang, a design historian from Guangzhou, categorically states, "China had no modern design education until the late 1970s. Design education has been formed mainly in Western countries. Without an international design education structure and curriculum, China has no way to develop its own structure and curriculum."[8] Competition, an open-market economy, and export drives are seen as the necessary stimulants for design activity. The NIC model is far too overpowering and the temptations to imitate Hong Kong far too strong in motivating China in its drive toward modernity to enable any thought-provoking debates to emerge just as yet. Whether the NIC model can at all be replicated, given the dramatic changes in the geopolitical and geoeconomic situations and vast differences in cultural specifics, and what precisely is to be learned from this model are still baffling the developmentalists.[9] The design schools in China are meanwhile gearing themselves to capitalizing on their cheap labor factor and on imitating Western design, as a part of the export drive. Fashion magazines are coming of age in China and The Central Academy of Arts and Design, Beijing, has launched its first issue of a magazine, entitled *Design*. The magazine is in Chinese but with a table of contents in English. This publication will, in all likelihood, be the first of the tidal wave of information on First World design, and to resist being swept away by powerful tidal waves is difficult, particularly after an era of parched isolation. The essential question is whether this approach to design is a necessary corollary to the forms of development planned, particularly in the wake of the failure of state capitalism.

If design is viewed from this perspective, and very few cogent alternative "ways of seeing," to use an expression of John Berger, have emerged, then the Proton Sagas and the Marutis, et al., are simply appendixes in the histories of Western/Japanese design, at best, and footnotes, at worst. Their issues are closely tied with open-market economy, competition, global markets, and so on, which are issues vital for survival but, nevertheless, in too embryonic a stage as far as design is concerned for tomes to be written. This early stage of development is a contributing factor to the absence of books on Asian design (other than Japanese) or even a good design magazine. There is just not the confidence yet to write one nor is there a consensus as to what exactly is this alternative way of perceiving design, even though there is a growing feeling among a minority that there exists, or certainly ought to exist, another way of approaching the whole subject. Design issues in Asia, I feel, have to be perceived in the context of this slowly emerg-

8 Shou Zhi Wang, "The Internationalization of Design Education: A Chinese Experience" in DDSSEA.

9 A number of works have appeared on this subject. I refer the readers to two short articles on the subject: Amartya Sen, "Public Sanction and Quality of Life in Developing Countries, in *Oxford Bulletin of Economics and Statistics* (November 1981), 287–319. Richard Robison, "Structure of Power and Developmental Strategies in Southeast Asia: Policy Conflict in a Changing World Economy" in DDSSEA.

ing "new ways of seeing" and in all the open-ended questions that are being asked. Although some questions raised are only of regional relevance, others are global and form the part of a worldwide concern on the manner in which development is taking place.

If design is perceived as an ancient activity that has gone on for several centuries rather than as a brand new profession, then our whole perception of what constitutes Asian design begins to change and, thenceforth, issues pertaining to Asian design assume different forms. The transition from seeing things in terms of continuity to seeing things in terms of discontinuity marks the principal break between traditional design and modern design.

Colonialism and the erratic pace of postindependence industrialization have caused considerable dislocation in countries such as India. The designer's main task in these countries is to operate at the levels of protohistoric continuities and chaotic discontinuities and to introduce a sense of order into this highly fragmented environment. The design profession must cope with both endogenous and exogenous agents of transformation. This situation possibly accounts for the operation of dual forces: a very great capacity for integration and modernization and very powerful mechanisms of exclusion and marginalization. Designers who wish to address the issues of the marginalized majority must start a brand new learning process and attune themselves to different socioeconomic realities and cultural behavior patterns. There exists no common vocabulary between the integrated and the marginalized.

The present-day dynamic blend of pragmatic functionalism and ideological *mass* consumerism is very new in Asia. It is a part of a new evangelical post-War/post-Colonial capitalism, a creed that was introduced in much of Asia at about the same time that the concept of development was becoming a much debated issue. Modern design schools were set up to cope with the massive import substitution that followed on the wake of independence. These were quite distinct from the nineteenth century art or industrial arts, or art and industry schools that were established in different centers of the British Empire in India.

The rise of these industrial arts schools and the nineteenth-century polemics involved in the setting up of these schools not only form an interesting chapter in the Arts and Crafts movement in the British colonies overseas, but throw light on some of the legacies of industrial design in India. In the Industrial Arts Exhibition in London in 1851, the Indian pavilion attracted enormous attention and the whole collection of East India Company exhibits were bought for a new British museum to provide "the highest instructional value to students in design." The expressed hope was that by exposure to the suggestiveness of some of these Asian design elements the "vulgarities in art manufactures . . . of England . . . may be corrected."[10] This not only confirms the existence of design traditions in India, but also and much more important, throws light

10 Mahrukh Tarapor, "Art Education in Imperial India: The Indian Schools of Art" in *Changing South Asia: City and Culture*, Kenneth Ballhatchet and David Taylor, eds. (Published for the Centre of South Asian Studies, University of London, 1984), 92.

on the manner in which oriental design was perceived by members of the Arts and Crafts school who were the main connoisseurs of these exhibits. On the advice of people such as William Morris, the decision to establish arts and industries schools in India was made. Soon, however, the changes in the forms of patronage, coupled with the long, drawn-out arguments between the Occidentalists and Orientalists, totally altered the aims of design education in India. Both British and Occidental Indians believed that what ought to be taught in these schools should be Western nineteenth-century academic art and crafts useful for the needs of the Public Works Department. Schools were set up in new, big colonial towns, which had no tradition of crafts. Not surprising, the early students were rejects from the formal institutions of learning.[11] The new forms of buildings and lifestyles required draftsmen and workers who could adequately carry out instructions based on designs provided from Britain, and soon the colleges of art and industry became culturally arid and produced mechanistic, soulless objects.

The poor quality of crafts exhibited just 20 years later in the 1871 exhibition dramatically revealed the damage done by this system of design education. The so-called crafts as part of the great tradition slowly withered away but continued to survive as rural subsistence modes of production. Both the systems of patronage and the social categories under which they operated were transformed, not by predominantly endogenous forces born of economic intellectual and industrial transformations, but mainly by exogenous factors and at an immense speed. The transformations were also very sectoral, both in the groups of people they affected and in the areas of activities they touched upon. This sectoral aspect made the holistic claim of an all-embracing design philosophy from "sofa cushion to urban planning" untenable, for the key characteristic of these transformations were fragmentation. The new students of design were not drawn from the ancient craft sector but from the modern educational system, and traditional crafts as sources of inspiration often had to be relearned.

The new design schools were inheritors of a new tradition. This was the age of Bauhausian ideologies being transplanted into the Indian soil by teachers trained in the eminent design schools of Europe. It was also broadly the age of Le Corbusier's Chandigarh and Nehru's vision of a new India, decolonized, modern, and international, poised for an industrial takeoff. These were symptomatic of the new age in Asia. This new age was marked by the hope and conviction that by the right mix of technology and capital input and by the right degree of government intervention, the country could take a giant step from medieval, feudal, and colonial inequality to enlightened democracy and a more equitable distribution of wealth while establishing a rational, secular sense of order. The change was to be accomplished by administrative fiats and large doses of government intervention to offset the inadequacy of endogenous forces of change.

11 Mahrukh Tarapor, "Art Education in Imperial India: The Indian Schools of Art."

No wonder then that neither of the terms *design* nor *development* have natural equivalents in most of the Asian linguistic traditions, for they carry with them all the ideological underpinnings of First World associations, aspirations, and debates. This realization and, more recently, the deep dissatisfaction that has followed this realization, both from an ideological/cultural as well as a pragmatic point of view, has led to some very serious soul searching among the thinking designers of Asia in recent years.

On the pragmatic plane, this soul searching was prompted by the recognition of two sad home truths. First, post-war political independence failed to generate for most of the Third World countries of Asia national, international, or structural independence. Second, the unbalanced growth within the Asian nation states has generated a kind of maldevelopment, creating a "twin nation" syndrome in which a low-growth, near subsistence-level majority economy coexists with a high-growth, minority elite sector. The latter is marked by a sharp rise in expendable incomes, thereby fueling a consumer boom. Both of these are forms of dependency, that is, internal and external, and both have led to insecurity, imbalance, unequal exchange, and finally exploitation. The means and goals of development have become enmeshed in a structure based on *consumption patterns and propensity to consume,* often at the cost of deprivation and drainage of the other social strata, especially the bottom quarter.

Some Asian LDCs, such as India, have not yet been able to produce a coherent, consistent, grassroot-oriented development approach and model. "There is talk of a self-reliant model on the one hand and imitation of the Western maldevelopment model on the other hand."[12] The First World's models of development are consumption-demand-creative and, hence, consumerist, labor saving and, therefore, capital and technology intensive, and, finally, overdeveloping." The designers, caught in this schizophrenia of developmental models are expected to be sensitive to and operate at disparate levels of ethnic specificity and economic disparity and come to grips with grassroot problem solving. This task is so mind boggling that much of the design discourse often degenerates into verbal platitudes, at worst, and sporadic conscience easing exercises, at best. For example, even the most talented and well-meaning architects and designers have been accused of having a double personality—on the one hand, the international-conference image, upholding appropriate and innovative technology/design, and, on the other, the hard-core reality of the upper-crust client's need of imitating First World lifestyles. Even if the cynics are right, the discourse is at least bringing certain issues to the forefront; repeated verbalization must rub off, and several new projects are being designed with local sensibilities in mind. Design education curricula are planned with long-term objectives in mind, and the young designers trained in these institutes should look for models to suit

12   Amalendu Guha, "An Alternative Self Reliant Development, Why and How: South Asia in the Global Perspective" in *Changing South Asia: Development and Welfare,* Kenneth Ballhatchet and David Taylor, eds. (Centre for South Asian Studies, University of London, 1984).

Design and Culture

specific needs. The resumés of design students looking for jobs show increasingly well-designed lists of projects undertaken to solve problems of basic needs. This observation is not made in a purely cynical vein, for role ideals are at least being provided, even if they are not always easy to transform into tangible realities. There is an idealistic element in the learning process.

Imported solutions to local problems have proved unworkable in many cases, either because of cost or the total alienation of the solution from the reality of the problem, or a combination of both. Low-cost housing has proven too expensive to benefit those for whose benefit it was originally planned, has failed to take into consideration the socioeconomic and psychological requirements of the targeted occupants, or, simply, has made a mockery of what the programs were supposed to stand for. A classic example of the last phenomenon is the creation of Islamabad as the Islamic capital of Pakistan which has as much of the essence of Islam in its architecture and town planning as a supermarket complex in downtown Boston.

This search for an appropriate cultural model and apprehension at the loss of cultural identity was effectively voiced by Lee Kwan Yew, Singapore's Prime Minister, when he expressed the fear that Singaporeans would become the flotsam and jetsam of Western mass culture floating on Asian waters. Cultural and economic divides (and their related issues) form a part of the problem for designers in their quest for a "modern" and "national" visual identity.

This "common cultural substance" that makes nations consisting vaguely of national ideas and products is in most countries of Asia, in a queer manner, in a state of becoming and a state of being at the same time.[13] This process of cultural transformation and of constant attempts at defining and redefining culture in a self-conscious manner is part of the existentialist anxiety of the newly emerging or newly decolonized states of Asia, be it of American-dominated Philippines or British-dominated South Asia.

With decolonization and the achievement of independence, this interest in restating one's culture has received an official definition. Language, national history, archeological monuments, folk arts and crafts, classical music, dance, and drama have become symbols of modern national identities, alongside the national emblems, Five Year Plans, parliamentary institutions, and atomic installations. The definition is selective and creative. A traditional culture, notably that of large countries such as India, is too vast and variegated to be displayed adequately in Republic Day parades, and not all cultural traits are regarded as suitable for display. It is thought best for some to wither away in provincial obscurity.

Those cultures that become active visible symbols of the officially sponsored "unity in diversity" ideology undergo a tremendous change by the very nature of their new roles. Tribes that are expected to perform a fertility rite dance every time a state dignitary arrives or that are exported as parts of National Festivals

13   See Milton Singer, ed., *Traditional India: Structure and Change* (Philadelphia, American Folklore Society, 1959). Preface and Introduction by Milton Singer.

acquire a certain self-consciousness and a new kind of fossilization. Quite often, a living culture with a primordialist identity uses this identity as an instrument to acquire economic resources, regional autonomy, and political power. When these expectations are not met, the claim to be the only "sons of the soil" is voiced and all others are boycotted as aliens. How much of cultural pluralism? What aspects of culture? What kind of identity? The nation state, by its very existence, is expected to act as an agent of change in integrating the whole country by suppressing active primordialist loyalties and, yet, promoting cultural awareness as a source of creativity. As an agent of modernization, it is expected to absorb imported technology and create the right infrastructure for these exogenous forces to be adopted and indigenized. What form will a centrally patronized plural culture adopt? What visual means of cultural identity should the mass media portray? Regional? National? Mixed? In what proportions?

Here too designers have the dual task of documenting and understanding ethnicity and regional cultures, for understanding them is the essential first step to evolving a medium of visual communication and restoring local confidence in an age when traditional institutions are crumbling fast and benefits of industrialization are yet to trickle down. Documenting hitherto undocumented and little-understood material has become one of the main educational tasks of the enlightened design schools of Asia. The National Institute of Design in Ahmedabad, India, for example, has accumulated vast amounts of information on the lifestyles and socioeconomic conditions of people living in several regional belts. To be involved in the task of helping local craftsmen improve their tools of operation or introduce them to elements of modern design, the introducer must know what they know, where their talents lie, and under what social and market forces they operate. This basic information is unavailable as mainstream secondary education provides very little provision for understanding conditions near the home of the students, and institutions of knowledge particularly in English medium schools cater to students who have little understanding of majority culture. The inculcation of sensitivity to local environments and empathy with people working under conditions outside parameters of middle class urban existence is one of the tasks that design educators believe is imperative. Despite all attempts and in spite of winning design awards, the communication media in India still remain remote from the common man or woman. Evidence is seen in a recent set of award-winning posters for contraceptives done as part of the social marketing of a birth control program—the faces of an affluent, beaming family of three adorn the posters. The unappreciated reality in the cases of the underprivileged is that having a large family often means more chances of economic survival as children are hired out from the ages of six and seven to act as factory, agricultural, or domestic labor.

Design and Culture

One cannot help feeling a certain sense of *deja vu,* of going back to the turn of the century when the full impact of the first wave of Western ideas and technological power was first felt. At that time, the intellectuals sought answers either in wholesale Westernization or in returning to their native roots. The Asian response to the first wave of Western ideas and technology produced the Alisjahbanas and the Kemal Ataturks, the Nehrus and the Gandhis, the U Nus and the Ho Chi Minhs. There are, however, major differences. The West represented to the educated Asian a pool of ideas: the Protestant work ethic and utilitarian liberalism, scientific rationalism and philosophic positivism, socialist romanticism and Marxist radicalism, and above all, self-righteous nationalism, operating ironically enough within the framework of unacceptable colonialism. Above all, it stood for an ordered, planned environment, both physical and cultural, ideologically neat and physically sanitary. The West then was a source of inspiration for Asian thinkers, even as they were plotting the overthrow of Western rule, and Western thought trickled down to the masses after going through several sieves and filters.

The present-day second wave of Westernism or, more strictly speaking, "First Worldism" (for Japan is a great trendsetter) is vastly different. It consists of a mass consumer-oriented movement that has reached remote village societies. National VCRs and Sony Trinitron TVs have become household aspirations, resulting from unprecedented advances in information technology. So the average new "Westernizer" in Asia has a new faith in a kind of acquisitive individualistic hedonism, expressed on a large scale. This holds that what gives the individual maximum material pleasure is the moral good and that the most ideal form of pleasure is to be defined in terms of the acquisition, possession, and consumption of material objects. Traditionally, this philosophy was meant only for the feudal lords; currently, it is the part of mass expectations and, without proper distributive policies and operating under conditions where only a few of the traditional checks are still valid, it could become an overwhelmingly destructive force.

This trend is buttressed by two factors that have come into play during the past decade. Asian labor is being exported to other countries. In 1986, for example, 15 million Indians were living abroad In the remote hills of Hunza, Pakistan, many have returned after working in West Germany, where, thanks to the efforts of the Aga Khan, short-term contracts are worked out for the Hunzakites. Pakistanis have for long been drawn to the oil rich Middle East. Apart from this personal contact, exposure to foreign education and foreign media has exerted a tremendous influence on the consumption patterns of the elite minority sector within these countries. This exposure coincides with a period of new and vigorous consumerism in the West and a virtual explosion in all forms of the entertainment media.

The third wave of First World thought is concerned with ecology and quality of life. This prompted the New Year issue of

Time magazine to nominate the planet Earth as the planet of the year, with the caption "Endangered Earth" instead of the usual "Man of the Year." Such fears are understood only by a small minority worldwide and by even a smaller minority in the developing countries. The argument often heard from industrialists and manufacturers and even from the general populace is that ecological considerations are the luxuries of the developed world. The race for development must go on and the only rules that are known to have succeeded in the past are the ones that the First World, after its own success is assured, has finally begun to question. Concerned people, visual communicators included, are trying to raise the consciousness of those around them to these vital issues.

Meanwhile, the dominant economic elites in these countries, totaling a vast number even if they are a small percent of the total population of the Asian LDCs, constitute a market that is *qualitatively* clearly differentiated from the majority subsistence sector and their demands are different not only in degrees but also in kind. For example, just 18 percent of India's 21,000 publications are in English, but they account for more than half of all the money spent on printed advertising. Industrial goods, private cards, office furniture, and anything to do with slightly sophisticated technology is advertised only in English. The reason is because the top 10 percent of the professional and modern business sector alone constitute the market and this afffluent intelligentsia is English educated. Anyway, most advertisement designers and copywriters would be too completely divorced from the native Indian sector to be able to produce a decent advertisement exercise in any of the vernacular languages. The recruiting policies of advertising firms only accentuates this phenomenon, as their copywriters are mainly drawn from the English speaking sectors, who can spot the international trends.

Thus, restatements of culture are now receiving urgent attention from totally different quarters and for completely different reasons. What is similar about first wave and second wave responses to external stimuli, however, is the concern of intellectuals with issues of culture. There is also a great deal of skepticism associated with this self-conscious designing of culture. Thus, Doreen Fernandes, who is actively involved with the Aquino Government's decisions regarding cultural policy, expresses deep concern about what she calls "the giant inferiority complex" of the colonial mind, which makes a Filipino "dress, sing, dance American" and where the American dream is inextricably woven with images of "Dynasty," "Miami Vice," and "L.A. Law."[14] The Alliance of Artists is clamoring for a rejuvenation of national culture and asking the Aquino Government to form a Ministry of Culture. On the other hand, there are people such as Alfred Yuson, poet and novelist, who disdainfully dismiss attempts at Filipinization of culture as just "another bromide, like democratization." The key question is the definition of what constitutes a Filipino culture and

14   Doreen Fernandes, "Mass Culture and
      Cultural Policy: The Philippine
      Experience" in DDSSEA.

this is crucial to the visual form that it will take in the years to come—will it be subsumed under mass American culture or will its designers, architects, and artists give it a new value system?

Modernization in most Asian countries is seen as a willed mobilization of forces by the state. In most of these countries, the government is not only a major client—a buyer of products and services—but also the agent of change, and, hence, designers in Asia feel that they have to lobby their respective governments to introduce national design policies that will dovetail with developmental policies, thereby making design an agent of the visual manifestation of the ideologies of development. Thus, if the fundamental aim of the developmentalist is to provide national confidence and self-reliance and bring in some sense of equity, visible symbols of this confidence and self-reliance will have to be shown not only in the styles of architecture adopted, but also in the materials and processes adopted, the manner of advertising undertaken, the styles of clothing exhibited, the nature of products manufactured, and the skill in converting modern imported technology into products distinctive for the specific needs of the people. In an economically and culturally splintered society, this overall cohesive planning for "the common good," as the utilitarians would have phrased it, is not an easy task. Nonetheless, there is an intense awareness of and a desire to foster autonomous and indigenous development among designers and developmentalists.

The British architect, Lawrie Baker, often called "the only Indian Architect," advocates mud buildings, not only as the only solution to the one family, one home idea in India, but also from the point of view of the amount of energy involved in producing the material. He concedes that for mud buildings to be acceptable, the right status associations would have to be provided; acceptance should start with the upper middle class, the moneyed people, even the Prime Minister living in mud houses. ASTRA (Application of Science and Technology for Rural Areas) has built a whole complex of school buildings using compressed earth blocks in the southern Indian city of Bangalore for the children of the Indian Institute of Science staff members. This complex seems to work very well and to withstand all the pressures of school children's *joi de vivre!*

Such an approach to design is a part of a historical legacy of India, a continuation of the Gandhian ideology, and owes its origins to the days of the *swadeshi* (literally, an adjective meaning "of one's own country" and denoting objects locally produced with indigenous material and local skills) movement, which combined economic realism with the political power struggle against British colonialism. This Gandhian ethos pervaded the Indian environment in the form of the handloom, homespun cloth, the *khadi,* the low Indian stool, the vernacular dwelling, the village handcrafted slippers, and a whole lifestyle, attitudes, and values that were inculcated with the sole purpose of giving Indians a sense of confidence and cultural dignity in an age of foreign domination. Gandhi had an almost uncanny intuition of investing objects with a meaning. Following partly on this model, Balaram advocates a Maoist operational tactic of evolving a system of "barefoot designers,"[15] who could serve the craft sector desperately in need not only of design input but also of design management, with all its ancillaries such as marketing, legal aid, etc. Another talented designer, Dasarath Patel, denounces the present system of arranging production and distribution of goods as a new form of colonialism operating within the country, the exploitation of the village by the city and the expropriation of the profit by the middleman. Such designers see their role as "mediators," "appropriating technology from a structure that is inaccessible to the common man" and see the answer in providing the village craftsmen the necessary confidence to create objects that will have local relevance. They see themselves as advisors on the choice of materials and processes within the reach of the impoverished craftsmen and as rejuvenators of the vernacular skill and understanding. They see design activity as a team activity, a participatory activity, and as closely related to raising the social awareness and self-confidence of people.

Thus, as Balaram points out, use of CAD/CAM for designing a more effective basic sickle or a bullock cart in India should not be seen as an anachronism but as a necessary and innovative use of technology for a society operating under two widely disparate levels.[16] Again, graphic designers should address the problems of the uneducated washerman whose own traditional methods of identifying clients' washing is severely being put to trial by the complexities of urban life. Projects such as these undertaken by the design students, even if done only during the idealistic school days when they are removed from the harsher realities of job hunting, reflect attempts at redefining design and placing it within a more complex social and political paradigm.

Designers are beginning to redefine their role in the context of the search for self-confidence, the need to face local problems, and the readiness to come up with dignified, relevant, and esthetically pleasing solutions. There are few stories of success to serve as inspiration for others to follow.

The emphasis keeps shifting from cultural identity as a source of confidence and self-awareness and, hence, self-enrichment to the simple practical cry that imported design solutions are not functional. Yasmeen Lari summarizes the plight of the Karachi slum dweller, who, when rehoused in a modern block of flats, had just one simple query of the developer and the urban/architectural planner: Where shall I house the chickens? Chickens were not luxury pets but a life-sustaining subsidiary source of income for the family. Balaram pointed out the case of the fishermen in Madras, who, when they were rehoused in modern high-rise apartments, rented their low-cost housing and moved back to the slums on the

15 S. Balaram, "Decision Making by the Indian Government and its impact on Design."

16 S. Balaram, "Decision Making by the Indian Government and its impact on Design."

Design and Culture

beach.[17] The old slums have a well-developed social structure and provided the necessary security to its inhabitants in times of need. The self-contained flat systems could be effectively operated only by the slightly more affluent, with access to other infrastructural benefits. Pakistan and some states in India have not realized the cost-effectiveness of upgrading informal settlements rather than resorting to slum clearance.

On the one hand, while Singapore is exporting its construction skills all over Asia and putting up multistoried structures in China and even in Brunei,[18] Sri Lanka is restricting the heights of buildings to four stories. As Nimal De Silva, the architect conservationist from Colombo pointed out, apart from the issue of retaining a cultural identity in the built environment, the LDCs working with less-efficient provisions for putting out fires and usually poorer maintenance standards could hardly cope with the safety hazards posed by multistoried blocks.[19] When a high-rise building becomes either a status symbol of modernity or a product of the excessive greed of land speculators, the solution has to be sought on the basis of the local conditions. The designers realize that the modern International Style cannot be a standardized method of solving problems. The Lawrie Bakers and the Ishwarbhai Patels[20] and the Yantra Vidyalaya are all the inheritors of the philosophy of alternative design and the basic needs approach to development, which had its heyday in the West in the 1970s.[21]

Furthermore, there is quite another dimension of design in the LDCs of Asia. The faith that design will, in conjunction with modern marketing and management practices, also evolve products for both the sophisticated markets at home and the international markets. In short, design and development is a quest for non-standardized answers in an age of standardization, where the faith in standardization, be it of specifications for a product or culture, is seen as a simple, economic, and efficient answer. Economies of scale and the globalization of markets in addition to making a lot of economic sense, provide the necessary teleological arguments for those who subscribe to the convergence theory of industrial development. Much of the polemics concerning design and development in Asia is centered around this inherent tension between the local and the global, both in the material and cultural sense. At one end of the design spectrum are those who believe that the Asian countries can and will achieve First World standards of living if only the right technological mix can be worked out and the right degree of patience and the necessary amount of time required for the trickle-down effect to take place can be achieved. At the other end of the spectrum are those who believe in the Center-Periphery modalities, view development and underdevelopment as corollaries of each other, and consider the built-in unequal relations between the center and periphery as a structural barrier to economic development.

17 S. Balaram, "Decision Making by the Indian Government and its impact on Design."

18 Lam Lai Sing, "Construction Services for Export: Policy and Prospects of Singapore's New Industry" in DDSSEA.

19 Nimal De Silva, "Cultural Identity in Sri Lankan Architecture" in DDSSEA.

20 Ishwarbhai Patel started designing cheap, sanitary latrines for the economically deprived sectors, and his humble, individual efforts led to the establishment of Safai Vidyalaya in Ahmedabad, which has undertaken a crusade against the uncivilized conditions under which the untouchables have to work in India as toilet cleaners. More than one and a half million toilets have been built under the auspices of this institute.

21 There are several cases one could cite as examples of design for need, but on the whole, it still remains a much neglected area. Recently, government-sponsored programs for the design of waterpumps in villages, the eradication of illiteracy, the improvement of health and hygiene, and other programs have been launched, and attempts are being made to introduce a coordinated drive in which designers work with a team of people from other disciplines.

The rise of the NICs has strengthened the first school who advocate a strong export-oriented drive. Egged on by the NICs model and by IMF and World Bank recommendations, there is a great impetus for producing both traditional and nontraditional goods for the export market. Whether the NIC model is replicable as mentioned earlier, is an ever present debate.

Designers caught in these debates have experimented with different approaches. Rajiv Sethi, a Delhi-based designer, felt that by combining Indian craft skill with design input from the West and by cashing in on the international reputation of designers such as Mario Bellini and Ettore Sottsass and others, an international market can be created that would provide modern hand crafted objects.[22] The experiment met with only very limited success and aroused a heated debate. There are other designers, such as Laila Tyabji and a whole group of people who have formed themselves into a pressure group called the Dastakar, who believe that craft must have a steady market to survive and that exposing the part-time craftsmen from the villages to the vagaries of the international markets would be dangerous without sacrificing quality and the security and solidarity of the craftsmen's regular native clientele. Their objective is to make crafts a part of everyday living. Laila Tyabji works on maintaining a steady flow of excellent quality workmanship in embroidered and appliqued cloth, while members of such groups as INTACH are trying to revive a whole traditional patronage network for crafts, so that the revived cottage industries could be sustained by a slow but predictable growth in the market. They believe in restoring historic monuments, not simply as museum pieces but as means of reviving a way of life that could incorporate labor intensive and low-capital industries. These are a few examples of nongovernmental sectors in operation. The design input is to help the craftsmen to understand the market, and the designers often have to decide how much and in what manner traditional designs should be preserved, altered, or abandoned to suit modern demands. Designers also try to introduce design-related marketing principles to the vernacular craft sector. The question remains: Are they trying to turn the clock back? Their answer is that at this moment in the socioeconomic life of India, such revivals are endogenous agents of social transformation and an indigenous solution to rapid social and economic dislocation.

The thinking design world as the thinking world of the developmentalist is thick with ominous question marks "as menacing as incipient schizophrenia." This is paraphrasing Misha Black and his comments were applied to the world of Western design, where he saw the schizophrenia manifesting itself in the miasma of developmental doubts, of obsolescence and transience of products, of wastage because of unnecessary duplication and the cosy comfort of a welcoming mass market. All this appears on an exaggerated canvas on the Asian scene. The size of the population, the rate of

22 This experiment, called the "Golden Eye," was done with the help of Cooper Hewitt Museum, New York, and the Handicrafts and Handlooms Corporation of India Ltd., New Delhi, and was coordinated by the Golden Eye Studio. They invited eleven of the world's leading architects and designers to visit India to discover craft traditions that could be used to serve modern needs. Sir Hugh Casson, Mario Bellini, Frei Otto, Jack Lenor Larsen, Bernard Rudofsky, Mary McFadden, Charles Moore, Ettore Sottsass, Hans Hollein, Ivan Chermayeff, and Milton Glaser collaborated with each other in the group exhibition.

inequality, the speed with which industrialization is taking place, the scale at which ecological damage is going on and seen as an inevitable price of progress, the enormity of the cleavage between the haves and have nots, and the accelerated speed of cultural differences between sections of the community inhabiting the same nation state are projecting issues on such a large scale that as Carl Aubock, the Viennese designer emphatically stated, "we need to dream of a new vision" for we are closer to a colossal revolution of a scale we have never before witnessed.[23]

---

23 Carl Aubock, "Industrial Design and
    Technology Dependence" in DDSSEA.

A Geography of Power:
Design History and Marginality
Tony Fry

Design history is understood here as various and competing explanatory models of design. As with other emergent and established forms of institutionalized knowledge and practice, it exists in and produces conditions of marginality. The aim of this paper is to explore such conditions in the context of the rise of design history in Australia. To engage in such an exploration productively, a complex geography must be put in place and traversed. There are two elements of this exercise: one is an exposition, in general terms, of what is meant by marginality; the other, an acknowledgment of how the notion of geography being put into play is marked by the spatial, the social, the historical, and the economic, as expressed in and by relations of exchange.

Marginality has most commonly been configured in a binary model in which it is the "other" of centrality. Two ways of viewing this configuration dominate. One poses marginality on the geographic edge of a metropolitan center, in either national or international terms. The second view has, as its basis, power, rather than location. Being on the edge of centers of political or economic power thus becomes defined as powerlessness, irrespective of physical distance from any center of power. In many ways, Australia has had a history of marginality to the dominant forces that have shaped the world economic and cultural order, both in political and economic terms.

Another way of thinking about marginality must also be acknowledged here. In this additional formulation, marginality is a condition of isolation, inbetweenness, and ineffectuality. This model depends upon a unified center, thus no simple binary relation can be imposed. The "other" of marginality in such a schema is a network, a system of circulation, or a community of knowledge that can function in concentrated or dispersed forms. Being on the edge, therefore, is not identified so much by an exercise of mapping as by an appeal to other means. Here, the second element, based on relations of exchange, comes into play.

Exchange, as the expression of the economic, always requires a material or a symbolic object, an agency, and a plurality of social actors. It can be predicated upon an economic or a cultural transference. Either way, for exchange to take place, it has to be driven by a particular dynamic (desire, need, greed, communication, and so on). The elements implicated in exchange always exist in some kind of relation to each other. Hence, their disposition can be conceptualized as a geography. Marginality in this context is being on the edge or outside of the relations of exchange, no matter where they are located, on what scale they might be, or who or what is powering the activity. In none of the ways that marginality has been considered here is a value being loaded on to it—it is not viewed as either good or bad. This is not to say that it is not read through such polarities of assessment.

First, my comments aim to extend my own contribution to the design history debate, which has involved, among others, Clive Dilnot, Cheryl Buckley, and Victor Margolin.[1] Without reciting the details of what has already been written, concerns with the character and function of design history will be picked up and sometimes cut across. Second, writing from Australia means that my statements are variously formed in a location on the geographic margins of the discipline and its objects. Australia is on the edge of the "developed" world. What has happened here in design terms—apart from the design of a few icons of place (especially Sydney Harbour Bridge and the Opera House) and a few products that have been mythologized (the stump-jump plough and the Victor mower, for example)—is largely unknown beyond its shores.[2] Internationally, Australia has, as yet, no significance in any of the currently recognized paradigms of the historical study of design or its literature.

Several areas of historical and theoretical inquiry are now beginning to recognize the importance of understanding the circumstances surrounding the production of knowledges of design, seen as readable appearances, objects, processes, and practices. Within design studies, for instance, there is a modest but growing concern with its methods, including gender specificity, a major marker of the protodiscipline's developments.[3] What a critical view Mom Australia delivers is a consciousness of just how flawed is the universal model of knowledge and history upon which the assumptions of the history of design rests. This comment holds true for both interesting and insightful work and impoverished, reductive genres.

1 Tony Fry, "Design History: A Debate?" *Block* 5 (1981):14-18, and *Design History Australia* (Sydney: Hale and Iremonger, 1988); Clive Dilnot, "The State of Design History, Part I: Mapping the Field," *Design Issues*, Vol. 1, No. 1 (Spring 1984): 4-23 and "Part II," *Design Issues*, Vol. 1, No. 2 (Fall 1904): 3-20; Cheryl Buckley, "Made in Patriarchy: Toward a Feminist Analysis of Women and Design," *Design Issues*, Vol. 111, No. 2 (1986): 3-14; and Victor Margolin, "A Decade of Design History in the United States 1977-1988," *Journal of Design History*, Vol. 1, No. I (1988): 51-72.

2 The stump-jump plough (1875, a plough that jumps the obstacles it hits) figures in the history of technological adaptation to local conditions. It tells a story of local innovation, which is familiar during the conquest of the land in eighteenth- and nineteenth-century colonial societies. The Victor mower (a motor-driven rotary mower), invented just after World War II in Australia, is an example of a functionally well-designed product that has been mythologized in a number of ways.

3 See, for example, the special issue on design of *Feminist Art News*, Vol . 2, No. 3, (December 1985).

The "manmade" designed world, constituted as recovered history, not only puts women on and in the margins, as an historical agency, but also puts all peoples in this position—other than those who populate the few nations at the center of the rise of metropolitan capitalism.

The issues raised by the investigation of gender formation and social factors undercut the theories of knowledge upon which almost all histories stand. For example, the exposure of phallocentric assumptions reduces to fiction historical accounts that claim to be empirically grounded within a rational framework of ruling historical fact.[4] So, too, do the critiques offered by the nonuniversal accounts negate and challenge the foundational knowledges of many areas of history, including design history. Here, then, two variants of marginality intertwine as produced, and sometimes contested, material conditions of existence of those people either rendered silent or who can only speak as an echo of, or in the tones permitted by, the dominant voice. The power and the sound of a dominant theory of knowledge, as embedded in common asstlmptions, is, of course, found on many margins as the local expression of the universal (hence, reference is made to the "echo," a voice characterized by Frantz Fanon as white words out of black mouths).[5]

The above-mentioned issues, which have been set in the context of Australia and the creation of design studies from an Australian perspective, can be grounded in a more concrete manner, by working through the following agenda:

- An outlining of universal accounts that are conceptualized as Eurocentric, ethnocentric, and logocentric
- Reflections upon design history, modernity, and colonization
- A reading from Australia—another kind of narrative, another kind of voice (one which is the resonance of an echo)

A cyclopean project: consideration one, first take
Two eyes become one. The cyclopoid labored to cast thunderbolts for Zeus. Thus, the myth of a singular locus of knowing is forged out of the crucible of (en)cyclopaedic knowledge. Let me explain—rationality has an irrational history. The history of Western culture, to tread a well-trodden track, cannot be separated from the establishment of the sited seats of knowledge in canonized texts, thinkers, and institutions. The West, as cultural, economic, and political complexity, constituted by a diversity of agencies, not only set out on an aggressive project of geopolitical global conquest over several centuries, but it also moved inward to inhabit the inner worlds of models of thought and knowing. It impurely occupied the mental spaces of imagination, rationalization, and representation. The world became dominated as much by classification, its order of naming, as by physical occupation and the imposition of form. Western culture, as unified cultural difference, synthesized and

4 For a discussion of phallocentrism, history, and theory, see Carole Pateman and Elisabeth Gross, *Feminist Challenges, Social and Political Theory* (Sydney: Allen and Unwin, 1986).

5 Frantz Fanon, *The Wretched of the Earth* (Harmondsworth: Penguin, 1976).

Design and Culture

articulated the social subjects' movement between inside (mental) and outside (material) existence. Such binary divisions, which are myriad, are at the very heart of the Enlightenment tradition upon which Western thought stands. These models of structuring knowledge provided the means for the Enlightenment is attainment as the intellectual motor of modernity. Latterly, these divisions, as the building blocks of rationality, have been specified as the target of major theoretical and critical concern.[6]

While the West almost, but never quite fully, conquered the world, the universal naturalization of its methods of cognition, especially in the discourses of science, produced a geographically noncentralized authority, which ordered other knowledges as subordinate and of lesser explanatory power. This history cannot be separated from the history of colonization as the latter slipped from an objective of an imperial nation state to a subjective state of mind. Modernity, seen as the rise and materialization of Enlightenment thought, drove the process of modernization and its condition. Modern life evidences the dynamic expression of knowing the world and its manufacture as the forms of mental and physical fabrication—all by design. Logocentrism arrived ontologically (that is, as the being of a mind-set), figured in various epistemologies as a lived-by rational irrational knowledge (phallocentricism and Eurocentricism themselves negate rationality).[7] Logocentrism became the sovereign taken-for-granted mode of thought for a "full certain knowledge of a place in the world."[8]

What resides at the core of the tightly packed philosophical observation above is that logocentrism is a foundational condition of the ethnocentric bias of Western thought. And that the intellectual culture of Eurocentric rationality has a history of domination, ordering all knowledge through the frame of its own cognito. At best, such an ethnocentrality has created hierarchies of knowledge in which the thought of the "other" culture is subordinate and constituted within the identified classificatory systems of Western rationality. At worst, ethnocentrism has led to ethnocide—the total destruction of the culture of the "other."[9]

Design history has not been as much in the wings of this philosophical history as it might seem. The fact that design history is almost exclusively located in those nations economically formed in the paradigm of Western capitalism (Japan included) not only centers development but, more significant, it obscures the effects of design as a social and economic agency. Three observations follow:

- Design history, its objects and historiography, is but one of a myriad of histories that have been Eurocentrically constituted.
- Design history, while implicated in the inquiries into the nature of modernism, has failed to recognize the formation and place of design in the rise and extension of modernity. This failure negates the operation of design as a generative medium in the formation of the modern social subject

6 What I have done here is allude to one of the major debates of the late twentieth century which runs across a vast intellectual terrain (Barthes, Baudrillard, Foucault, Deleuze and Guattari, Lyotard, Rorty, Habermas, Irigaray, Kristeva, Derrida, Weber, White, and Virilio are some of the producers and proper names used as markers and authority in this debate). The debate has been one of the main preoccupations of a number of significant journals (for example, *New German Critique, Telos, New Left Review, Theory, Culture and Society,* and *October*). Much of what has been written has sought to establish, question, critique, or displace the rise of postmodernism/ postmodernity. Such has been the backdrop to Lawrence Cahoone, *The Dilemma of Modernity* (Albany: State University of New York, 1988); Jurgen Habermas, *The Philosophical Discourse of Modernity* (Cambridge, MA: MIT Press, 1988); Eugene Rochberg-Halton, *Meaning and Modernity* (Chicago: University of Chicago Press, 1986); and David Frisby, *Fragments of Modernity* (Cambridge: Polity Press, 1987). Likewise, a revitalized interest in earlier enquiries into modernity has been driven by the postmodern context—the work of Adorno, Bataille, Benjamin, Kracauer, and Nietzsche have been especially significant.

7 The turning back of Western-generated epistemologies against themselves is interestingly discussed by Zygmunt Bauman, in "Is There a Postmodern Sociology," *Theory, Culture and Society,* Vol. 5, No. 2 (1988): 217–37.

8 Elisabeth Gross, "Derrida and the Limits of Philosophy," *Thesis Eleven,* No. 14 (1986): 2643.

9 For an exposition of the important concept of ethnocide, see Pierre Clastres, "On Ethnocide," *Art and Text,* No. 28 (1988): 5058.

through the globalization of the practices of the capitalist means of production, modes of consumption, and cultures extended into inner and outer worlds as the effects of commodities, processes, and appearances.

- Design history has been complicit in the maintenance of the Second and Third World as almost silent and as having a "lack" of history. In this and other ways, the consequences of industrial culture have been omitted from Its purview.

These observations reinforce and move forward the linking of the abstract and the concr'ete content of my agenda. They will be discussed below through the linking of modernity and colonization, an essential couplet in the nature of Australian history.

Every map has its margins: observation one, continued: take two
The stated and implied crisis of authority, which has characterized a good deal of postmodern theory, has largely rendered the exercise of "mapping the field" a dysfunctional exercise, or at least a very problematic one. Without a digression into this debate, pointing out that such mapping projects are always fabricated from an illusory structural position of observation and writing is worthwhile.[10] All maps center a point of origin, they are mono-and logocentrically archetypical (they view from the single I/eye). Although maps may serve useful heuristic functions, they inscribe a power of author(ity) that always has to be challenged. Where one stands to point, speak, write, or draw is always a locus of power within that being described. Maps start from a specific position, hence their reference to origin. They cannot be drawn from a disengaged distance. Every plan—that is, every map—is drawn from an elevated point of view that is reached by an ascent from the ground, literal or metaphorical. Maps are strategic; they prefigure discovery rather than record it.[11]

If you are reading this text somewhere in North America or Europe, then I write from a place on the margins of *your* map, whether you place me where I am, in Sydney, Australia, or somewhere on the edge of *your* current preoccupations with design history. There are no "classic" or "timeless" design typeforms here in Australia of which anyone anywhere else is going to take much notice. Talking up the local product is a flawed exercise in self-deception that obstructs development rather than enables it. The history of the visual arts in Australia, with its constant drive for global recognition, continually demonstrates this. Likewise, Australia has no major designer heroes of international standing, no outstanding design institutions (commercial or educational), and no pathfinding avant-garde groups that have grown out of nonmetro-politan sources. There are no degrees in design history here, only a few courses within other programs. Thus, there are only a few students who would contemplate becoming specialists in the area.

10 Such a notion of the problematic of the overview is inseparable from the crisis of the intellectual; see, for example, Jim Merod, *The Political Responsibility of the Critic* (Ithaca, NY: Cornell University Press, 1987).

11 The issue of maps and mapping is dealth with interestingly by Paul Foss, "Theatrum Nondum Cognitorum," *Foreign Bodies Papers—Local Consumption*, Series 1 (1981): 15–38.

Design and Culture

None of this is to say that interest in design and its history is not burgeoning, for, with prompting, interest is slowly developing. The situation suffers from a mix of imitation and an absence of ortho-dox design history preoccupations, yet there are also very significant opportunities. In particular, Australia has been historically consti-tuted by the process and forces of import as a diverse and nuanced range of social appearances. This can be regarded as a materialized *bricolage* formed from eclectic patterns of objects of immigration and appropriation, drawn from the forms of a modern world elsewhere.

What can be frequently found in Australia is a fallout and modification of that which was originally created for other circum-stances. Australia is the land of the simulacrum, a place of original copies and unplaceable familiarity. In this vast, underpopulated, and often environmentally harsh country, there are 16 million people scattered across historical time, from the preindustrial to the postindustrial age. Equally, major divisions of distance create spatial isolates—pockets of urban development within which there are many divisions of unevenness. The rule of geography is absolute in this land, colonized so as to become the invisible outpost of the *designed* instruments of British imperial penal discipline and punish-ment.[12] Dislocation is an internal and external condition, of long-term and short-term existence, and of this history.

Dislocation is inseparable from marginality as a state of mind. Such a lived condition has a consciousness or repression of yearning as its foundation. A key part of this yearning is the knowl-edge/feeling that what is wanted can never be. Desire, on the other hand, can be momentarily sated—the whole seduction of consump-tion depends upon the continual remaking of this moment. Conversely, the nonrealization of yearning, in all its vast array of forms, delivers nothing but a deepening bitterness and resentment. The yearning of the marginalized, regardless of geographic location, generates a tradition of wishing for tradition and belonging. As a perpetual condition of being, it creates partly a culture of despair, no matter what signs of pleasure and frivolity appear on the social surface. All of this, for Australia, is grounded in the passage across time in the despair of the gulag as experienced by convict and jailer alike in their mutual exile in the vast space of the continent.

Design, however, conceptualized, is but one object in passage across the global and local geography which becomes deposited in fragments—signs, products, processes, practices, and environments of the late-modern world. These fragments arrive as manufactured forms, or as prefigurations of local production, via what Edward Said calls "the traffic in texts."[13] The limited scale and concentration of the means of distribution contribute to the uneven-ness of modern Australia, a small nation with a lot of land that is hinged between the First and Third Worlds.

Implied in this quick characterization of the Australian condition is an opportunity for a new approach to design history,

12 Robert Hughes, *The Fatal Shore* (London: Pan Books, 1987).

13 A traffic of arrivals, lateness and losses—see Edward Said, *The World, The Text and The Critic* (London: Faber and Faber, 1984)—Said explores the relations of textual production, power, theory, and the geography of cultural domination in several essays in this book; see, especially, pages 32–53 and 226–247.

where work in Australia has the capacity to lead development as it creates its own nonuniversal model. This model itself increases the scope of concerns of the protodiscipline. Taking marginality as its key focus of inquiry, this' approach offers an opportunity to research and write a history of design on the margins. Such an undertaking is inseparable from and a potentially valuable contribution to increasing knowledges of modernity and latemodernity. This way of thinking about modernity is specifically in terms of the process of transfer and transformation of the material fabric of one social text, from one culture of place to another across time and space. Here social text implies the total reading surface of the appearances of a society, be they cultural or economic.

Advocating an approach from the margins returns me to arguments about the necessity of refusing design history as a discrete discipline.[14] At the same time, it advances the claims of the possible usefulness of the area of study. Such usefulness can be addressed in a number of ways—my own characterization is close to Zygmunt Bauman's proposals for a sociology of postmodernity, as a "sociology of the consumer society."[15] Here I am making a broad interpretation of sociology as an arena of disciplinary convergences and dialogues rather than yet another discipline in crisis.[16] The appeal of such a sociology is that it does not invite a division between cultural and economic inquiry. Thus, it could advance the paradigms of knowledge set running by studies of material culture (limited by attachments to economic anthropology) and cultural studies (limited by attachments to culturalism, a relative autonomy of the cultural sphere). One major proviso—a sociology of consumer society is not simply an investigation of consumption. Rather, drawing on but extending Bauman's argument, it is an inquiry of the dialectical relation of "seduction and repression" across the geography of the latemodern world. Acknowledging internal local, national, and international divisions in which marginality is created is essential in this schema.

The designed production of commodified pleasure and mechanisms of its control are inseparable in the past, present, and future of the Enlightenment ideas by which the drive to rationalize the modern world generates increased nonrationality. What this means is evident across a range of institutionalized forms. The relationship among science, education, industry, products, and museums is one such example. The logic of scientific education, product research and development, and the presentation of the narratives of the history of science, in printed texts and museums, are all grounded in the idea of progress. This idea of progress is at the very core of the Enlightenment. Within the orbit of this logic, overcoming encountered problems that stand before the path to progress is accomplished by technologically determinist methods. The consequences of this applied history are familiar: problems are often outside the general terms of agreed-upon human need and,

14   Fry, "Design History: A Debate?", 14–18.
15   Bauman, "Is There a Postmodern Sociology?, 235
16   One of the key characterizations of the crisis of sociology was the influential text by Alvin Gouldner, *The Coming Crisis of Western Sociology* (New York: Basic Books, 1970).

frequently, for every problem solved, many new ones are generated. Of course, science itself is not to blame for this situation. Rather it is what and who directs science and why—as well as the way science becomes an object of faith. From this perspective we can consider again commodified pleasure through, for instance, the relationship between science and television—a product delivered by rationality but one that generates many effects which cannot be identified or understood by rationalist models.

No longer can the discourses of rationality be called upon uncritically, because, as already stated, these knowledges are Eurocentrically grounded and have shown historically that they can deliver regress as much as progress. What can be said of design history can be said of most disciplines: if they reject an inquiry of marginality, they simply continue to contribute to producing marginality in all its forms and on all levels. The history of modernity—its objects, its subjects—is a history that also figures the regress of progress, although it is not yet widely read or written this way. Design history, in this context, is not only too discrete; it is also too clean and celebratory. We need to gain a far better understanding of how design is articulated in the mess of history. Beware of neat narratives.

Modern part players on the field of modernity: observation two
A number of comments already made must be reiterated and expanded. To begin with, applying the discussion of modernity to modernism is worthwhile, not least because of the way the latter is reductively figured in design history[17] Modernism, as the collective term applied to encompass the multiple moments and projects of the attempt to create the high culture of modernity, was neither stable nor always coherent across its nineteenth- and twentieth-century history. Modernism should be viewed against modernity as

Figure 2
Mac Robertson exports chocolates to England 1924 (author's collection).

17 See, for example, Dilnot, "The State of Design History, Part 1,"17–19.

the economic, political, and cultural structure of the modern world, viewable as a means of production and consumption, the state and its agencies, and everyday life and its institutions. Modernity has its own culture: mass culture. Modernism is thus posed against that which it appropriated in order to reinvigorate itself—mass culture constituted as popular culture.[18]

From the above framing of modernism, contemporary cultures can view the utopian ambitions of the European avant-gardes to either produce, represent, and become the culture of the new at the turn of the century as a very different formation from, for example, the faltering faith in progress that underscored the degeneration of the high culture of modernity into the formalism of modernism in post-World War II USA. The horrors of two world wars, the consequences of fascism upon European culture, the lasting effects of the atomic clouds over Nagasaki and Hiroshima, and the loss of idealism in the promise of science and technology, along with the vast expansion of the culture industries, not only transformed a Eurocentric perception of its own humanity (or lack of it), but also changed many of the aims and agencies of modernist culture.

Modernism, as the high culture of the culture of modernity, has become increasingly defined against the designed world of the sign economy of popular culture. In this economy, style and taste drive both demand and promotion. Such was and is the terrain of the First World sign war—the conflicts of style. Notwithstanding the attempts of modernism to appropriate and to be loaded onto the imagery of mass-produced commodities, popular culture and the commodity sphere won the conflict with art. Art as aura or spirit is now dead. In spite of a seamless stream of inflated rhetoric by a universal rear guard, clinging hopelessly to traditional or avant-garde culture as either a redemptive force or a fetishized hiding place from a cruel world, there is *nothing but* the culture industries, with art being *nothing more* than the commodity form of a micro or macro niche market. Such developments mirror and are part of the actions of modernity as a global order. This can be seen as the pluralization of capitalism as a co-existent spectrum of old and new modernities and the continued growth of consumer society across ideological difference.

The form of contemporary modernity as consumer society (de facto and desired) is readable as a social text, that is, as the designed world and the semantic structure of its forms, functions, and mediated appearances. The designer in such a context has to be named and interrogated not as creative subject but as deployed laborer, as expression of the corporation and commodity. (Where is the design history of this shift?—still looking for true meaning, the *real* object, the DNA of design?)

Marginality, from subject to nation, manifests itself as an almost complete inability to shape the world. The geography of this moment in the frame of neocolonialism was, and still is, a heightened

18 For a full exposition of these ideas, see Tony Fry, *Old Worlds, No Images* (Sydney: Hale and Iremonger, 1989).

Design and Culture

colonization of the imagination; common desires for centeredness extend across massive divisions of difference in wealth, status, class, race, sexuality, age, culture, and geolocation. Singular universal dreams of design worlds (modern "lifestyle") contradict, and certainly do not unify, great unevenness, difference, and ideological division in this late modern world. They do, however, bring differences to an imagined space of sameness of consumption, which acts normatively as a reference point of measured proximity to the modern.

It is worth replaying the drift of these general observations through the Australian context. The modern world for Australia has not been an evolutionary development based on the rise and continual remaking of capitalist modalities and the passage of the social theory, formed in the Enlightenment, into the creation of nation states and industrial society. Similar to many other postcolonial societies, Australia was first constituted by imposition. The slow progression to self-determination, in conditions of dependency, was bonded to models of the modern drawn from elsewhere—especially Britain and, later, the USA. Modernity was thus not a driving historical condition of transforming social and economic conditions and their cultural consequences. Rather, it was a regime of signs—the arrived appearances of the modern world of metropolitan capitalism. Such signs were nodal connectors, they stood for absent totalities, systems, and ensembles. The representative singular substituted for the integrated plural; for example, one modern product, factory, or industry acted as the representative of modern production and consumption per se.

Even from a limited characterization, we can see that design served quite a different sign function within colonial society and its movement to semiindependent nationhood via the process of modernization. Objects, such as imported machinery and manufactured goods, and images, such as imported illustrated publications, acted to create a typology that registered the look and operation of a modern world. The condition of modernity was an eclectic assemblage of typeforms of the representative modernity. Design, even prior to the management of a design profession, intervened to undercut the formation of modern Australia as discordant *bricolage*. Appropriation was organized but not within a systematic plan. There was neither total chaos nor directed order but a pragmatic falling together of fragments. The disparate arrival of Ford and Fordism is one contained example of this history.

The first Ford car was brought to Australia in 1904. Commercial importing began in 1909 with the Model T. As sales increased, an ad hoc system of distribution became locally established. Because of corrupt and profiteering practices that grew up around this network, the Ford company refused to trade with it and set up its own local administrative and distribution system instead. Ford Australia was formed in 1925. Fordism, however, as an industrial system of mass production based on the in-line assembly of

Figure 3
The Ford Motor Company arrives—an assembly building under construction at the plant in Geelong Victoria, 1925 (Ford Archive).

19   Tony Fry, *Design History Australia*
     (Sydney: Hale and Iremonger, 1988), 114;
     and Geoff Easdown, *Ford: A History of
     the Ford Motor Company in Australia*
     (Sydney: Golden Press, 1987).

20   Antonio Gramsci, "Americanism and
     Fordism," *Selections from the Prison
     Notebooks*, edited and translated by
     Quintin Hoare and Geoffrey Nowell Smith
     (London: Lawrence and Wishart, 1971),
     277318. Gramsci's seminal essay is
     significant here not simply because of its
     early acknowledgment and theorization
     of the relation between an economic
     modality and a cultural order but also
     because the conjuncture being interro-
     gated (divisions in Italy) is formed by
     uneven development. Marginality and
     modernity were key concerns of
     Gramsci's analysis, which was contempo-
     rary with Ford's arrival in Italy (roughly
     the same time as Ford arrived in
     Australia). For a description of the new
     labor process, see Andrew Sayer, "New
     Developments in Manufacturing: The
     Justin-time System," *Capital and Class*,
     Vol. 30 (1986): 43-72.

interchangeable parts, arrived in Australia a year earlier. A Sydney-based manufacturer of compressors introduced such a method to its factory in 1924. Ford's own plant, in Geelong, Victoria, built in less than 12 months, began manufacturing and assembly in 1925.[19] Product design and advertised image (the symbolic forms) were drawn from the USA. Here, then, was a mixture of appropriation and imposition, order, disunity, and disorder, *and* the object (the car, its system of production and distribution, and its symbolic form) as a sign of modernity. All of this adds up to one example of a local sign of a particular conjuncture and paradigm of modernity—"Americanism and Fordism" in Australia.[20]

The kind of structural condition that I have outlined suggests that a modern post-neocolonial nation like Australia is dependent, as is often the case, not just on the geospatially diffuse metropolitan capitalisms, which do not reduce to clear or singular centers, but also on the local modalities of metropolitan modernity. Design, then, is configured in relations of dependence, with the local designer, whether individual or corporation, as one of the key mediators gatekeeping the induction of the elsewhere. The history to unfold here, then, is of the knowing or unknowing sign management of *bricolage*. The delay in the establishment of an infrastructure of modernity was also a crucial factor—mass production did not really arrive in Australia until the 1950s and even then it could not be fully established because of the limited scale of the nation's home market, which was the focus of national economic policy. The late arrival and the underdevelopment of both design education and the design profession are inseparable from this history. What has only just begun to be realized by a few technologically literate members of the national economic community is that new development in labor processes *could* liberate Australian manufacturing from the limits of market scale. But Australia's problems include declining local manufacturing; foreign ownership masking assembly as manufac-

Figure 4
The Australian-designed GM Holden—the car
Detroit did not want (Holden Archive).

ture; gaining highvolume capital investment; and a small "mass" home market linked to the underdevelopment of export-led economic expansion. The new labor processes, especially the just-in-time system and its incorporation of FMS (flexible manufacturing systems), have the ability to produce difference in volume. The very structure of manufacturing is changing as are the service/culture/ information industries. The history of the past is thus not fully determinate of the history of the future, in both general economic and cultural terms and specifically in relation to design and marginality.

A story similar to the one of modernity can be told of modernism(s). Its twentieth-century signs first arrived in Australia in the 1920s and 1930s, before a local modernity was secured. The diversity of the projects of the European modernists and their grounding in the concerns and conditions of metropolitan modernity were unknown, overlooked, or filtered out—often by the processes of mediation via Britain. The guardians of British culture neutralized and diluted the avant-garde objectives of the variants of European modernism as they were represented to British society and its tastemakers. Although Britain was not the sole source of

Figure 5
The car Detroit did want—the F. J. Holden is launched in 1948 by Prime Minister Ben Chifly as "Australia's own car" (Holden Archive).

cultural forms for Australia, it was dominant and in modernism's transposition to here, it again screened out the vanguardist dimension of the avant-garde projects.[21] The consequence of the double mediation was a contentless and stylistic, periodized modernism—a modernism stripped of everything save exterior appearance. Thereafter, in disadvantaged local hands, it further degenerated into a deformed reflection of unconvincing simulation.

The first coming of modernism centered on Sydney; the second, in the 1940s, on Melbourne (the two cities, incidentally, are a two-days' drive from one another). The later modernism was a very different configuration from the earlier one. The war gave artists a heightened sense of marginality; the condition was felt in new ways. Australia was not only on the edge of the action but it was a point of external view upon the thought disintegration of the center. Fascism seemingly was destroying European culture; thus, the margin's feeling of placement was disoriented by witnessing this scene, while, at the same time, the center arrived on its shores clad in khaki, a weapon in one hand, nylons in another. The response was complex. A variety of local hybridized modernisms were assembled via raids upon expressionism, surrealism, and social realism, the strongest synthesis being an expressionist/ social realist axis. This new visual culture wasmobilized against an older colonial conservative landscape tradition. Of course, all of this was happening at a moment of change in the nature of Australian nationalism. The focus upon a center shifted from Britain, bathed in the after life of the Empire's dimming star, to the rising star of North America.

Every nation believes in a need to claim the uniqueness of its culture as proof of its identity. On this basis there has been an enormous cultural and economic investment in Australian modernism. Its emptiness has been inscribed and reinscribed with national meaning, through the agency of the art market and art history joining in the common hegemonic objective. What matters in this collaborative context is not agreement, value judgments, or quality but visibility, noise, and exchange value. The degree of "critical" attention and the market price is what directs the reading of the work, rather than its qualities.

Marginal modernity is built upon appropriation. In addition, its economy is sign driven (as word and image), by more than the sign relations described but ahso because desire is produced by the circulation of directly or indirectly imported signs. What such a history of marginality throws into question is a good deal of the conceptual geometry of postmodern theory in its various guises. What this means is that although postmodern theory has been variously conceptualized, it has almost always been so thought with a Eurocentric model. Appropriation and decenteredness Uameson, et al.) and the political economy of the sign (Baudrillard) are longstanding features of Australian modernity—its nonmodernity and postmodernity are, in fact, inseparable.[22] Because Australia has

21   Australia, art, and the preoccupation with national identity is the basis for the forthcoming book by Anne-Marie Willis, *Illusions of Identity: The Art of Nation* (Sydney: Hale and Iremonger, 1989).

22   Frederic Jameson, "Postmodernism or the Cultural Logic of Late Capitalism," *New Left Review* 146 (July–August 1984): 53–92, is one representative text; Jean Baudrillard, *For a Critique of the Political Economy of the Sign* (St. Louis: Telos Press, 1981) is another.

23   Meaghan Morris, "Jetsam," *D'un Autre Continent: la rêve et le rêel* (Paris: Musée National d'Art Moderne, 1983). This is one of the most significant of the texts that address Australia in this way.

Design and Culture

never been other than a culture of appropriated fragments and difference, postmodernism, at least as a rhetoric, was taken up here with vigor.[23] What has received less attention, as a feature of this historical postmodern condition, is the longstanding presence of the sign driven economy—the sign as it prefigures production.

Design history—sending signals here and there: observation three

I am writing for myself, as a reification of a moment of knowing. I am writing for design history, which, as I have argued, needs to question further the nature of the discipline as it is and might be. At the same time, what I have stated is also a communication (via the direct line and the echo) to some of the members of the Australian design community.

What I have outlined in this article travels two ways—away from the margins and toward them. Meaning will alter with geography. Consider these summary points below, for more is at stake than the development of a discipline and its academic recognition:

a. Design history on and in the margins [the "other" story and (her)story of (his)story] is a different kind of history.

b. A nonuniversal design history is not simply an additional or supplemental approach within a plurality of positions. Rather, it is a fundamental challenge to the nature and authority of the current Eurocentric models of history writing. It will not be based on the same agenda, objects, rhetoric, or concerns.

c. Design is implicated in the history of colonialism and neocolonialism. It has been used (which is not to claim ordered directional function) to prefigure the made nature of the social world we occupy as an environment and as an imaginary.

d. The potential of design history is not as a discipline in and for itself (although holding such disciplinary space can be institutionally strategic). Rather, it can play a major role as a means to interrogate the social text within an organic relation to a sociology of consumption. This is to say it can and should provide useful and critical transformitory knowledges.

e. Design history has the potential to illuminate the history of modernity and late-modernity in its metropolitan and marginal forms.

f. We cannot have a reductive theory of design's totality or its specific sign functions if we are to understand its multiple forms. In the geography of design, where meaning shifts by movement and conjuncture, there is no essence outside of a Egocentric view.

g. Australia has little to offer design history as currently constituted. It has a considerable amount to offer a design history that might be.

A postscript

I have taken liberties with the notion of geography. It has been used as a concept of the disposition of mind, matter, and space upon a material, geophysical, and cultural terrain. This is acknowledged and if blame is to be apportioned, let it be directed at the late Michel Foucault: "Geography acted as the support, the condition of possibility for the passage between a series of factors I tried to relate."[24]

Figure 6
Local signs.

24   Michel Foucault, "Questions on Geography," *Power/Knowledge,* ed. Colin Gordon (London: Harvester Press, 1980), 77

The Development
of Modern Japanese Design:
A Personal Account
Takuo Hirano

During the past forty years Japan has gone from being a country in which there were no designers, much less design education, to one where currently there are large numbers of designers and myriad design education opportunities. To chronicle my career in design and design education in Japan, albeit a personal account, therefore, is to document the growth and expansion of these related activities in Japan, as well. This growth in design has been considerable, and although basic issues and areas of concern must still be resolved, heightened corporate, commercial, and public awareness of the function of design now exists, which is an encouraging indication that designers can, indeed, play a greater role in enhancing the quality of life.

Education and early career
My interest in creating things as a youngster led to my enrollment in the Tokyo National University of Fine Arts and Music in 1953, where I majored in crafts. During my third year, I entered a vase in a competitive exhibition. My delight turned to frustration and then to anger upon discovering that visitors were not allowed to touch or handle the displayed objects. If prospective users could not touch an object in which they were interested, how then could they decide whether or not to procure it? I strongly believed that works of art were meant to be appreciated and used. I therefore embarked on a project to hand produce well-designed ashtrays; at the time only crudely made, functional and overpriced ashtrays were available. After many long hours of work I began thinking about machine production, not only to alleviate my own labor but to lower the cost to the consumer.

I share this vignette because the experience led me to consult my academic advisor prior to graduation about remaining in school to pursue studies in technology. After listening patiently to my reasons, my professor recommended that I enter the Ministry of International Trade and Industry (MITI) and seek assignment to its patent office. I followed his advice and became a patent application examiner. For two years I was absorbed in studying a wide range of applications, not only to fulfill my responsibilities but to quench my thirst for information about technological advances.

I digress here to note that these were the years following the end of World War II when Japan was still war ravaged and strewn with rubble. Gradually, using salvaged lathes and presses, and tin cans and bottles discarded by the United States military forces, Japanese manufacturing started up again with the production of toy cups, saucers, and pans. By 1953, Japanese goods were competing with European-made products in the American market to the extent that moves to suppress imports from Japan were being made. Many imitation goods, particularly cigarette lighters, toys, tableware, and other such products were being used in daily life. These Japanese goods were cheap but poorly made, and the paints used in manufacturing some of them were highly toxic.

About the same time, the Japanese government vigorously promoted industry's use of designers but there were none. No institutions of higher learning, including my alma mater, offered courses in industrial design. At best, sculptors and painters engaged in industrial design as a hobby. Troubled by this situation, the government established a study-abroad program specifically aimed at training industrial designers. But burdened with tremendous debts, Japan could only afford to send four persons abroad per year. To further hasten the educational process, the government also requested that four-year programs of study be shortened to one-year. The schools abroad agreed and it was under this scheme that I, as a member of the second group sent overseas, departed for Los Angeles.

At the Art Center School (currently the Art Center College of Design) both day and evening courses awaited me. Needless to say, the program was extremely strenuous and I was frequently perplexed and surprised. For example, soon after my arrival, my first project was to redesign a hand mixer. In retrospect it may seem foolish, but at the time I did not have the faintest idea what a hand mixer was, where it was used, or for what purpose. Despite the problems of adaptation, however, there was great stimulus in finding new things that made sense, so although always challenged, I was never bored or dissatisfied. Using high-quality American, British, and German art supplies and taking courses not available in Japan, including basic design, human engineering, plastic and metal materials, I completed the four-year course in approximately one year.

Upon my return to Japan, I was shocked and disappointed by the belated development of Japanese industry. As an MITI bureaucrat I was given teaching and consulting responsibilities, in addition to my administrative duties. I was assigned to teach what I had learned in the United States at the Tokyo National University of Fine Arts and Music, the Women's College of Fine Arts, and the Kanazawa University of Fine Arts and Crafts. I was also given the task of advising firms in western Japan about the design of products for export to the United States and, perhaps more important, of educating these companies about new approaches to design.

In due course, Japan moved from exporting imitations to freshly designed products. No doubt, governmental encouragement

Design and Culture

of newly designed products was appropriate at the time, but over the years a shift from traditional habits, forms, and measurements has also resulted. The gradual distancing of Japanese products from classical modes of production and the need to adapt to new systems and cultural patterns are some of the prime concerns today.

The design education that I offered at the three universities mentioned above was appraised highly and attended by faculty and students from other institutions, as well. Some classroom space was provided by MITI for additional evening sessions but soon that arrangement proved insufficient. Other facilities were procured and a new school, Our Design School, was founded. The faculty was comprised of persons who had studied in Germany, Italy, and the United States. Thirty percent of the students were already employed as designers by manufacturers, the remaining seventy percent were students enrolled at other universities. What began as a volunteer effort soon developed into a thriving learning center. To generate funds to pay the teachers, I established a design office staffed by myself and three students. We provided manufacturers with designs for the actual production of goods and thereby earned a sufficient income to remunerate the teachers. During this period, in 1960, I resigned from my full-time position at MITI to concentrate on design and design education.

In 1965, Our Design School closed. By that time, design education opportunities were available in universities and within companies, at least in the Tokyo metropolitan area. Furthermore, graduates of the school were teaching in various places. Our Design School had served as the training site for the first pool of design educators

Teaching and design education

During the subsequent years, I have concentrated on teaching design and design management and have devoted time to serving on government councils. In 1965, I began a three-year teaching assignment at the Kyoto City University of Arts, where I taught basic design. That opportunity later proved to be the first step in building a bridge to new design in western Japan. My current affiliation with Tama Art University, a top tier art institution, began in 1970. There I introduced a new pedagogical approach in which a student and faculty member together select a subject or theme, search for an ambiguous or unknown problem, and work toward a resolution. This teaching method is effective and an appropriate venue for strengthening the student-teacher relationship which, in turn, improves the quality of education. Since 1978, I have also taught at the Tokyo Institute of Technology, a national university renowned for its excellence in the natural and applied sciences. When I first began teaching industrial design there, only 15 students enrolled in my class. Currently, I have more than 200 students. I like to think that the importance of design has taken root, even in this bastion of science and technology.

Traditionally, education in Japan, as in other Asian countries, is based on a one-on-one relationship between student and teacher in which the student observes and then imitates the teacher. The traditional arts of calligraphy, classical dance, flower arrangement, painting, and the tea ceremony follow this learning mode. It is believed that long years of practicing established patterns lead to high levels of accomplishment. Of course, some students of these arts do create something new with their own imaginations, but they are few.

When the more efficient, European model of education was introduced to Japan in the 1850s, it was quickly and enthusiastically accepted but with minimal understanding of its basic tenets. Focus was placed on the structure, organization, and methodology rather than on the underlying philosophy. As I view the current educational scene, I find that little has changed and wonder if this is simply a reflection of the traditional Japanese way of thinking. This has been true in my own experience: when I have introduced new and different teaching methods, others have been quick to assimilate the structure and methodology but few have understood the philosophy, the basic design spirit.

Among my students, unfortunately, more than a few graduates are convinced that they have learned and understood design but few truly comprehend the fundamentals. In my introductory design courses, for example, I cover paper structure in a laboratory session. Most students simply follow the models made by previous students rather than creating new models. They do not recognize the relevance of folding a single sheet of paper in half, the way it is strengthened perpendicularly along the folded side, making it stronger than before and not so easily destroyed. This fundamental exercise is applicable to paper packaging and automobile design, of course, but most students only perceive the exercise per se, not the link to more complex forms of design. Fault lies not only with the student but with teachers as well, for too often both fail to recognize the basic elements.

Another fundamental aspect of design that I integrate into teaching is working with clients. At least half of a designer's time is spent meeting and working with everyone from the company president to the machinists who finally assemble the product. If a designer is not only to convince decision makers about new design ideas but to promote full understanding, which leads to total commitment and effective followup, then working with people will take an inordinate amount of time. Without the recognition and comprehension of this designer role, I see little chance for even the best design to be realized.

Design practice

Having to earn enough money to pay the teachers at Our Design School led to the establishment of my own design firm, which I continue to head. It has grown considerably since its early days and now has 70 specialist designers, based in Tokyo and Chicago. To maintain a focus on underlying principles rather than the practice of skills, the organizational emphasis is on design management. The central core of our management style is conceptual design. Organized around it are the design specialties which enhance and reinforce the management core. No barriers between the architectural, interior, product, communication, and packaging design functions exist. The precise role of each function and its relationship to the others depends on the project in question. This emphasis on the core design management function enables the specialists to work to their fullest potential on any given project within a framework of overall management direction and, at the same time, to provide feedback to the design management core. Thus, our firm is organized organically capable of adapting to new challenges and opportunities, rather than rigidly by an inhibiting structure with hierarchical and lateral lines of responsibility and communication.

We design across a broad spectrum, from single products to whole systems, including the design or redesign of entire corporate structures. In each case, we initially assess the entire organization and focus on the operational, communication, and decision-making processes. Neither the size nor the nature of the company with which we deal alters our approach. Our team for such projects usually numbers between two and five designers and relationships with clients vary from four to more than twenty-five years. Even though the number of our clients increases and we maintain relationships with a growing number of firms, we find it unnecessary to increase staff because as both our expertise and our clients' understanding develop, long consultations are not required. Shorter but higher quality sessions with key personnel result in effective design management.

Our commitment, in every case, is to reconcile and creatively synthesize three important demands, all of which are necessary to maintain the high standards of design: the ultimate satisfaction of users' needs and expectations; the designers' concepts and aspirations; and the producer's commercial and economic plans and limitations.

Professional activities

In addition to my work in education and professional practice, I also continue to engage in numerous activities related to promoting and improving the understanding of design among manufacturers and the general public. For example, I currently serve on MITI's Export Inspection and Design Promotion Council and as a judge of G-Mark products. Both activities indicate that the Japanese government both supports and promotes design excellence and recognizes that design is an essential component of commercial success. The G-Mark system, with its "Good Design Products Section" under the jurisdiction of MITI and organized by the Japan Industrial Design

Promotion Organization, was established in 1957. At the time, imitation goods were rampant and the Japanese government was eager to build public awareness of well-designed products. More than thirty years later, research indicates that fifty percent of the general public knows of and recognizes the G-Mark seal placed on selected products. Designers of these products are given recognition within their firms for their accomplishment and are usually promoted. In addition, sales personnel find that promoting products with G-Mark seals is easier. Since 1984, in a major extension of the scheme, non-Japanese products have also been awarded G-Marks and introduced to the Japanese public. Indications are that this system is contributing to an increase in imports to Japan.

Basic approach

As a teacher, practitioner, or participant in professional activities, my basic approach is the same, to be dynamic and allow for adaptation to varying circumstances. The learning creative-developmental process can be represented as a spiral. Viewed from the top, a spiral is a moving circle, constantly expanding in scope. Viewed from the side, upward movement is evident, representing the addition of experience and understanding. As the upward circular movement of the spiral is repeated, potential energy is gradually added and increased. If we were to work on or study a given object, we would only have an elementary understanding, represented by the bottom of the spiral. But as our competence increased, our approach would be better represented by the top of the spiral. For example, most students in junior high read some Shakespeare. In senior high school they read more, and in college they may take courses devoted solely to Shakespeare. The literature under study remains the same, but as general knowledge and experience increases, students are able to read and interpret Shakespeare from new perspectives.

Designers must undergo the same developmental process. It is often said that it is important for design work to move beyond the commonplace to something new. This is a simple generalization. Human ability or capacity is essentially innate, so the creation of new ideas is largely dependent on the processes undergone and the capacity for expression that is added along the way. This process of idea development is an integral part of the European approach to education that I have added to my own spiral perspective. However, the spiral concept applies to Easterners and Westerners alike for it reflects the basic human instinct for learning, creation, and development. Moreover, it relates not only to individuals, but also to small groups and larger organizations, such as corporations.

The spiral does not extend outward or upward at a uniform pace. Because it is not evident that humans evolve at regular intervals, the key to encouraging learning is to help identify points of change. At any point, development may be accelerated. Conceptually, a jump of three steps in one revolution of the spiral can

Design and Culture

occur along with an expansion of the radii. Moreover, by drawing on the energy of the upward moving spiral and encouraging the expression of beauty and the student's own energy, discovery, and creation, the fundamental principles of education are fostered. I have attempted to facilitate and enhance this learning-creative process by providing opportunities in which I work with students not only in the usual laboratory settings but also in corporate settings, working on projects for clients. Initially, companies were reluctant to cooperate. However, as student designs were reviewed and highly appraised, firms became enthusiastic and invited students to give presentations. The learning-creative process is enhanced and magnified as students help resolve real issues and they gain firsthand experience in working with clients.

The experiment in university-business linkage has been successful at Tama Art University and will soon be introduced to other universities. However, many problems in the teaching of design remain. Faculty in Japan are granted life-long employment, similar to tenure in the United States, but without the rigorous process of peer review. With a comfortable work environment that does not require or demand serious creative work or self-assessment, most faculty lose their sense of intellectual and professional tension. The students, in turn, become easy going and carefree. Although design technologies are mastered, they are simply repeated and little creative work emerges. From this perspective, the state of design education in Japan is dismal.

The evolution of design in modern Japan

Although I have concentrated on my personal experiences, I do not wish to neglect a broader pattern of evolution and the significant periods in contemporary Japanese history that bear a direct relation to design. The period from 1950 to 1954 was the "age of existence," a time when materials were simply insufficient. Beginning in the mid-1950s, however, Japan concentrated on increasing production of similarly styled products for the next decade. Everything from steel desks to automobiles to clothing looked the same, regardless of the manufacturer. It was the "age of mass-production" during which basic cost performance was incorporated and developed.

The following years brought concerns about lower costs, durability, and excellence in function, and a small consumer demand for differences in design and ambience began to grow. Japan had entered an "age of quality differentiation." The 1970s brought another shift. Consumers began setting their own criteria for acquiring products. People began to recognize the merits of various products and to make deliberate decisions for themselves rather than following general preferences. Someone might choose to purchase a bicycle not only for transportation but for exercise, as well. Someone else living in a beautiful home might decide to acquire not only an audio system but an extraordinary audio system. Not only did discrimination increase during these years but so did the purchasing power of consumers.

This trend continued through the 1980s, the "age of assertion." With economic and social progress, the majority of the population set aside feudalistic ways of suppressing their own wishes for the sake of the country" and began asserting themselves, seeking products—accessories—that fit their individual needs and desires.

Future trends

The 1990s, no doubt, will be the "age of the spirit," for people are now beginning to develop individualistic life-styles. They seek enjoyment in creating environments pleasing to themselves. Furthermore, the scope of what individuals perceive as their environment is widening, from immediate living quarters to a broader milieu. As a result, small quantities of a great variety of products will be sought rather than standardized, mass-produced goods.

How is Japan responding to this future trend? Although technically refined robots are being developed, which are capable of new forms of manufacturing organization, large manufacturers are slow to modify their physical plants. They continue to rely on market research first learned in the United States at roughly the same time design was introduced to Japan. If research using similar techniques is used to survey the same markets about like products, then, naturally near uniform results will be obtained. If these results are conveyed to company planners and designers, then it is highly likely that similar products will be manufactured. Here too, the concept of the spiral, with its emphasis on change and adaptation, is relevant. Given the changing nature of the Japanese market and its growing preference for a wider range of products, the best manufacturers will respond to the increasingly personalized and therefore highly delineated markets and produce a great variety of goods. Short-sighted firms that fail to adapt will be in danger of going bankrupt.

Until the present, designers have been closer to manufacturers than to consumers. Designers must alter this relationship by becoming closer to consumers and less dependent on the leadership and demands of manufacturers. If they are committed to lessening the designer-abetted pollution that menaces the world, to meeting the needs and desires of consumers, and to integrating design excellence into commercial and cultural life, then designers must develop interactive relationships with both users and producers.

Line
A Cheng

Figure 1
"Landscape in a Rosy Light." Wang Yuan Qi. Ming Dynasty, 1713.

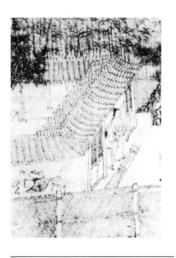

Figure 2
Detail from "Ode on the Red Cliff." Qiao Zhong Chang. Song Dynasty, twelfth century.

Many people who are familiar with Chinese painting would probably object to the idea that its primary characteristic lies in the use of line. Instead, some might reasonably suggest that it lies in the handling of full and empty space. The Chinese describe the two qualities of space in this way: "So sparse that a horse could go through, so dense that a needle would not fit." In contrast to their Western counterparts, classical Chinese paintings often present large areas of empty space.

Others might suggest that the most important feature of Chinese painting lies in the use of multiple rather than single-point perspective (*figures 1 and 2*). In "Notes from the Dream River," Shen Kuo (1031–1095 A.D.) particularly emphasized the role of multiple perspective in painting. Writing during the North Sung Dynasty, he said that if the normal perspective is used to draw a house, representing what is farther away as smaller, then the near corner of the roof will seem to jut upward in an awkward manner. The use of multiple perspective is vividly demonstrated in the famous horizontal scroll painting from the same period, "Scene from the Clear River in a Time of Peace," by Zhang Ze Duan. Several feet long, this scroll presents various street scenes, houses, bridges, wagons, and boats. To appreciate the work, viewers must keep in mind the changing perspective for each object and scene as they move from one end of the scroll to the other.

Multiple perspective allowed the painter great freedom in handling materials, but it did not mean that one could be careless. There is a story about a painter who borrowed the long "Clear River" scroll and made a copy. He kept the original for himself and returned his copied version to the owner. The exchange was soon discovered, however, and the evidence was striking: in one section the copyist had painted a sparrow standing on two lines of tile on a roof. A truly skilled painter would never have made the mistake of confusing two lines of perspective in rendering an object even so small as a sparrow. Multiple perspective is not a mistake in Chinese painting; it is common sense, just like knowing the size of a sparrow.

The human body also may be presented through multiple perspectives. For example, the individuals in figure 3 are displayed in such a way that their bodies seem distorted and misshapen. Some scholars think that the purpose of painting the human figure in this way is to illustrate anatomical structure. However, a presentation in this manner maintains a consistency and harmony between the human figure and the surrounding objects—in this case, the differ-

Figure 3
Detail from the inner lid of a porcelain teacup.
Qing Dynasty, nineteenth century.

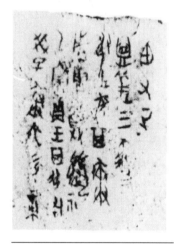

Figure 4
Jiaquwen. Chou Dynasty, c. 1100 B.C.

ent segments of the wooden bathtub. Multiple perspective suggests an esthetic principle concerning the way objects may be presented in relation to what is nearby. Interestingly, after the invention of the camera, which seemed to confirm the primacy of normal single-point perspective, the further development of the telephoto lens had the same effect as multiple perspective: whatever is farther away appears as large as what is near, requiring that the lines of each object be interpreted with a different sense of perspective. In fact, multiple perspective seems to emphasize the importance of line within the object, while single-point perspective reduces line to a function of the single point of focus.

Based on such considerations, one can argue that a special concern for line is the essential feature of art and design in China.

The importance of line for the Chinese is evident quite early in the development of their culture, but this alone is not unique among the cultures of the world. Line was an important feature of early Egyptian and Aegean cultures, as well. In Aegean culture, however, line seems to have been gradually taken over by the plane and the sphere. As a result, the perception of the sphere comes to dictate the position of line. In China, the fate of line is different: it remained an independent element, and its handling later matured into the highest form of creation.

The reason for the importance of line, I believe, is the unique development of writing in China. Because of the large number of theories devoted to the use of the brush, some have argued that the brush itself is the major factor in line creation. However, the perception of line—a distinctive Chinese conception of line—has actually been the major factor in creative art and design. The instrument is doubtless important, but the brush itself has limitations and cannot account for the exploration of line in other areas of art, such as architecture.

Most scholars agree that *jiaguwen*, the inscriptions on bones and tortoise shells of the Shang Dynasty, is the earliest form of written language in China possessing both phonetic and semantic functions (*figure 4*). The main function of line in such writing is organizational only: line transforms separate marks into a system of veins, an organic whole, and a meaningful character or word. Of course, some archaeologists think that the written language in this period also has different forms, and they use the slight differences to sketch a chronological development of Chinese writing.

With the emergence of *jinwen*, or seal characters, the function of line begins to change (*figures 5 and 6*). In lishu or official script (*figure 7*), line performs an organizational function but also begins to have a distinctive creative meaning of its own, taking on deeper esthetic quality. In fact, different styles developed within the same general mode of writing. Later scripts, such as *kaishu*, or regular script (*figure 8*); *xingshu*, or running hand script; and *caoshu*, or cursive hand script (*figure 9*), have evolved over two thousand

Design and Culture

years, with the result that line has reached a peak of creative expression in Chinese calligraphy. Many of these styles are regarded as paradigms in the modern world. People learning the art of calligraphy still copy them in their beginning lessons.

Figure 5
Small seal characters. Chou Dynasty, seventh century B.C.
Figure 6
Large seal characters. First century, B.C.
Figure 7
Lishu. Rubbing from a stone tablet. Han Dynasty, c. 150 A.D.
Figure 8
Kaishu. From *Notes on the Altar of Ma Gu (Ma Gu Xian Tan Ji).* Yan Zhen Qing. Tang Dynasty, 772 A.D.

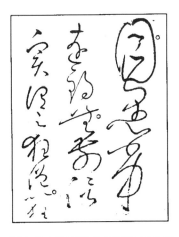

Figure 9
Caoshu. From *Introspective Notes (Zi Xu Tie).* Huai Su. Tang Dynasty, 777 A.D.

In Chinese, *shufa* literally means the rules of writing.

Metaphorically, however, it means the art of writing. Unlike other languages of the world (with the possible exception of the Arabic language within Islamic culture), the transformation or elevation of calligraphy into a high art form is a unique phenomenon of Chinese culture. The fact that *jiaguwen* and *jinwen* allowed different forms of writing for the same character (*figure 10*) is perhaps the main cause of the artistic development of Chinese calligraphy. Thus, although the emperor Chin Shi Huang (221 B.C.) ordered the use of the large seal characters as the standardized form of Chinese characters, one of the most important developments of Chinese art had already occurred: *shufa* had established the fundamental principle of line for Chinese painting. This is the reason that Chinese artists often say "writing and painting share the same origin." This expression is often thought to refer to the pictographic quality of Chinese characters. Instead, the expression actually refers to the principle of line creation shared by writing and painting.

Students' sketches and notes from Li Liu Fang's painting classes at the end of the fourteenth century were collected and edited into the famous book, *Painting Records from the Mustard Garden.* Regarded as the encyclopedia of Chinese painting techniques, it is in fact a book about how paintings are composed primarily from creative uses of line. Huang Bin Hong (1865-1955) is regarded as one of the most innovative painters in the Chinese tradition, known for his methods and techniques of *wenrenhua* (intellectual painting). His student, Wang Buo Min. collected his teacher's theories and notes and published *Notes on Painting by Huang Bin Hong.* Even a casual glance at the notes about the theory

Figure 10
Different ways of writing the word *eyebrow* in *jiaquwen* (right) and *jinwen* (left).

Figure 11
From *Notes on Painting* by Huang Bin Hong.

of lines in painting (*figure 11*) reveals that Huang is actually talking just as much about writing (that is, *shufa*) as about painting.

The following diagram illustrates the development of line in classical Chinese painting.

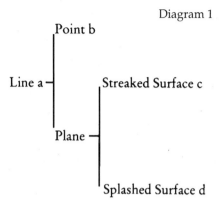

Diagram 1

Point b

Line a

Streaked Surface c

Plane

Splashed Surface d

a. No perpendicular line can go on forever without turning back. All lines eventually come to an end. The emphasis is on control and organization. Line, therefore, is not a concept but a concrete object.
b. A point is the constricted form of a line. It is controlled with the same principle as the line. Therefore, like *shufa*, a point has direction.
c. A streaked surface is an expansion of line created by the side of the brush. The nature of the streaked surface is not to create shadows but to create veins like the grain of wood.
d. A splashed surface is a further development of the streaked surface. Pouring ink onto paper creates a surface. Then, the surface is controlled by the brush.

Such an approach to line as the principle of Chinese art and design brings a deeper understanding of many aspects of Chinese culture. For example, some scholars recently have argued that Chinese painting after the fifteenth century, especially the *wenrenhua*, or intellectual painting, becomes progressively more abstract. From the principle of line, however, one would say just the opposite. Classical Chinese painting is inherently concrete, and the precision and control of concrete imagery perhaps reaches its highest point in the *wenrenhua*.

This view is further supported by the materials and techniques used in painting. The instrument—the brush—is made of soft lamb or rabbit hair (in the Qing Dynasty some brushes were made from a chicken feather). The ink, black or colored, is water soluble. The paper, *xuanzhi*, or rice paper, is highly permeable: after one stroke of the brush, nothing can be changed. In other words, all of the instruments and materials are non-formative: they are extremely sensitive to the artist's touch. In fact, these materials

Design and Culture

immediately reflect the artist's state of mind; they are the result of a sensitive mind's demand and choice. If one uses a soft brush with water-soluble ink on highly permeable rice paper, any change in the artist's mind can affect the marks on the paper. An artist must be quite sensitive or exceptionally intuitive before judging and controlling the movement of the brush. The movement of a line accurately reflects the artist's psychological changes. Line is the concrete image of the artist's mind, almost like the line produced by an electroencephalograph. Thus, one can say that the lines of Chinese calligraphy and painting are not concepts but *concrete objects*.

Painting on rice paper is a process of *exposure*. From the first stroke to the last, the whole process of one's control and handling is immediately exposed. Therefore, Chinese art is almost cruel in the demand for maturity that it places on artists. In the West, oil painting hides the process. Only the result is seen, not its beginning or its development. The impressionists began to reveal something of the process of painting in their works, and Cézanne often shows his beginnings. Perhaps this explains why so many Chinese painters like modern Western abstract painting: the process of art often is exposed with great candor. Western artists became aware of the touch of the brush, which led them in many new directions. The contact between the brush and canvas in modern painting can be enchanting.

From a Chinese perspective, recognition of the nature of line in the West perhaps truly began with modern painting. The lines of Matisse's works seem to have their own independent meaning. Though Mondrian was opposed to the cursive line in his mature work, he actually investigated the quality or quantitative meaning of abstract line. Kandinsky treated abstract line from a psychological point of view and in terms of the needs of the inner self. From a Chinese perspective, Kandinsky's exploration of line set a foundation for a renewed understanding of plane and sphere in the West—an important contributing factor for the theory of design developed in the Bauhaus. The importance of line in China is perhaps comparable to the development of linguistics in the West. Western linguistics has contributed to the understanding that language can be independent of the referential function and possessed of its own internal meanings. This is essentially the way line in art and design has always been understood in Chinese culture.

The importance of line is reflected in one traditional way of appreciating Chinese paintings—a technique that most people consider clumsy but that contains a portion of truth. A person would judge the quality of a painting by looking at details through a small cylinder, perhaps a piece of bamboo. By looking through the small aperture, one could tell whether the painting as a whole was good or bad, without knowing whether the subject was a mountain or a house. The method was simple, but the user was serious. He or she focused precisely on the quality of line and judged the painting accordingly. From experience, such a person knew that whoever

Figure 12
"Bamboo in Ink" Li Shan (1656–1762). Qing Dynasty.

Figure 13
Painted earthenware. Yongjing, Gansu. Second–third millennium B.C.

Figure 14
Receptacle (Yu type). Shang Dynasty, c. twelfth–fourteenth centuries B.C.

could draw a line well could paint the whole picture well. The essence of Chinese *shufa* and painting (especially *wenrenhua*) lies not in *what* one paints but in *how* one paints it. The subject matter of Chinese paintings is always limited and endlessly repeated: mountains, water, bamboo, rocks, and so forth. The repetition of the subject, perhaps like Cézanne's apple, makes the subject itself unimportant. What is important is the quality of line. Subject matter is only an excuse for the creation of an expressive line. Line is the common element and the joining power between a painting and the calligraphy that is placed on the painting (*figure 12*).

We can now turn to other areas of Chinese art, tracing out the roots of design thinking in terms of the principle of line.

The proper beginning point is the confluence of decoration, painting, writing, and religion in early China. The richness of expressive line is evident, for example, in the painted decoration of pottery from the second and third millennium B.C. (*figure 13*). In bronzes from the twelfth and fourteenth centuries B.C., contemporary with *jiaguwen* and *jinwen*, the conception of the structure of the decorative pattern has, to some degree, the feeling of painting, and it is completed through a painterlike handling of line (*figure 14*).

According to Harvard anthropologist K. C. Chang, from the time of *jiaguwen*, words took on special importance in divination and fortune-telling. Chang delivered an important series of lectures on early archeological discoveries in China at Beijing University in 1984. Though Chang raised many questions about the origin of Chinese words, he stressed the idea that the use of words in early Chinese civilization is intimately related to religious ritual. In his book, *The Bronze Age in China*, particularly in the chapter entitled "Animal Figures on Bronze from the Shang Zhou Dynasty," Chang demonstrates that the drawings must have functioned to help shaman priests communicate between man and God, heaven and earth.

I would further Chang's idea by suggesting that the enchantment with line in Chinese art is closely related to the spirit of early shamanism in Chinese culture. For example, Chinese artists and calligraphers emphasize the importance of grinding the black stone that produces ink, finding in this ritual a way to cleanse the mind before writing. Indeed, some believe that the best time for writing is after drinking, when the mind is most exhilarated. This was the favorite way of writing for the monk Huai Su, a famous artist of the Tang Dynasty. Many other artists share the same belief. Such preparations before writing or painting are, I believe, residual traces from early shamanism.

The development of sculpture and the representation of human and divine figures show another facet of expressive line in Chinese culture. The Chinese are known for their worship of ancestors, but ancestors and gods were never given forms or images in early China. Perhaps after the emperor Ching Shih Huang unified China (c. 221 B.C.), he also influenced the creation of unified images of ances-

Design and Culture

Figure 15
Stone carving. Han Dynasty, first century B.C.

tors. In any case, during the Han Dynasty (c. 200 B.C.), images of the mythic ancestors Fu Xi (male) and Nu Wa (female) began to appear, represented with the body of a human and the tail of a snake.

The development of the human image as a religious idol in China was influenced by Buddhism. Buddhism came to China from India at approximately the same time as the formation of Taoism. Though Taoism was, to some extent, a continuation of early shamanism—and in shamanism there was no worship of idols—the Taoists did, indeed, represent gods with a human image. Perhaps this was Taoism's way of competing with Buddhism. In any case, the development of mature Chinese religious sculpture took place within the context and under the influence of Buddhism. However, at least one branch of Chinese Zen, *Chan zong*, deliberately sought to eliminate the idols associated with Buddhism. Because Buddha is a pluralistic ideal, a concept of "everything and nothing" it was argued that Buddha should not be restricted to a single image. Perhaps in the same way that *Chan zong* and other forms of Zen modified Buddhism for the Chinese, the Chinese use of expressive line modified the representation of Buddhism's idols.

The sequence of development can be traced through four illustrations. The first is a common stone carving of unidentified human figures from the first century B.C., showing the way in which line is the primary means of creation (*figure 15*). Note the rich texturing of fluid, powerful lines and the lack of three-dimensional depth in each figure. The second example, in contrast, is a Buddhist sculpture from India (c. fifth century A.D.) (*figure 16*). Delicate lines are evident, but they are not the main form of creation. The beauty of this work rests in the form of the body, which the lines serve. The third example is a Chinese Buddhist sculpture from the sixth century A.D. (*figure 17*). The folded cloth is represented by a simple line that is consistent with the stone surface at the Buddha's back. Buddhism had already existed in China for several hundred years,

Figure 16
Buddha. Mathura, India, fifth century A.D.
Figure 17
Buddha. North Wei Dynasty, sixth century A.D.
Figure 18
Buddha. Sui Dynasty, sixth century A.D.

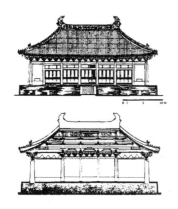

Figure 19
Chinese architecture. Yuan Dynasty, thirteenth
century A.D.

but Chinese artists were still "immature" in sculpting the body. They expressed themselves primarily through the richness of lines texturing the figures and the background. Finally, the last example, a late sixth-century sculpture of Buddha, shows the development of expressive line to its extreme, covering the veiled body with mountains, trees, houses, men, and other narrative elements (*figure 18*). The techniques used in figure 18 are almost the same as those used in figure 15.

Architecture poses special problems within Chinese culture, though it is important for understanding the history of design in terms of product and activity. Architects in ancient China, for example, did not have the same status as their counterparts in the West. No architect was regarded as highly in China as Michelangelo was in the West during the Renaissance. Moreover, architecture was not regarded as part of the liberal arts by Chinese intellectuals.

Few books about architecture remain from the past, although two are notable: *Laws and Rules for Architecture* [*Ying Zao Fa Shi*], by Li Jie from the North Song Dynasty (1100 A.D.) and *Heavenly Crafts to Create Things* [*Tian Gong Kai Wu*], by Song Ying Xing from the Ming Dynasty (1637). These books seem to cover almost every facet of *design* associated with buildings except how to *design* architecture—perhaps because so much of architecture was ruled by rigid tradition. For example, yellow was a color that could only be used by the emperor. If the builders of a temple wanted to use yellow tiles for its roof, they had to obtain special permission directly from the emperor. *Laws and Rules for Architecture* recorded, as its title suggests, rules for buildings appropriate to different social classes as well as detailed rules for the individual features of certain types of buildings. Therefore, having any other type of architectural design or, indeed, having creative architects and designers at all was nearly impossible.

Many researchers ask why Chinese architecture was almost always made of wood. Emperors continued to use wood for their palaces, even though each new dynasty usually burned the buildings of the previous dynasty. Were the emperors, all of whom wanted to rule forever, unaware that stone is harder to destroy? There was no shortage of stone materials, for the huge tombs were made of stone. Yet the coffin, the enclosure closest to the body, was always made of wood. The use of wood seems to be another residual trace of shamanism. In the ancient practices of shamanism, wooden instruments were used in ceremonies to communicate between heaven and earth. Indeed, wood functioned in a manner similar to *jiaguwen* and bronze, as a medium for divine communication. To burn the buildings of the previous dynasty meant to destroy the connection that that dynasty had between heaven and earth and, hence, to ensure divine blessing and protection for the new dynasty.

Though rules prescribed most features of architecture, leaving little room for creative development, richness and profusion of

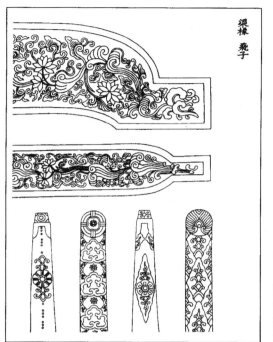

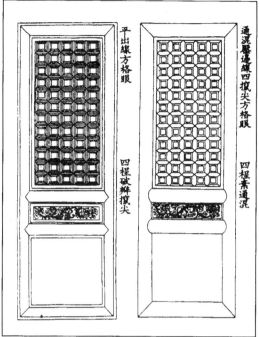

Figure 20
A common gate design appropriate for officials above the sixth level.
From *Laws and Rules of Architecture*.

Figure 21
Interior doors with "Square eyes" patterns. From *Laws and Rules of Architecture*.

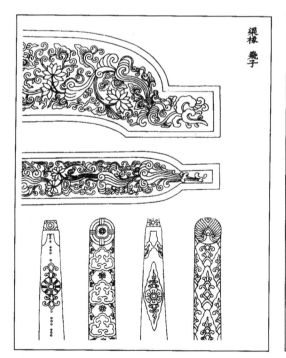

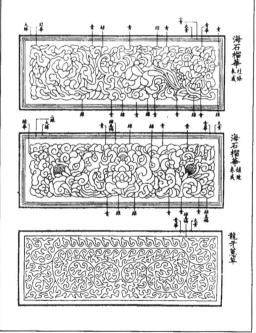

Figure 22
Decorated roof beams and pillars. From *Laws and Rules of Architecture*.

Figure 23
Floral patterns for use on base of columns, etc. From *Laws and Rules of Archictecture*.

line was still the dominant effect (*figure 19*). Figures 20, 21, 22, and 23 illustrate the quality of line in various architectural design details from *Laws and Rules of Architecture*. Not many buildings remain from before the Sung Dynasty (c. 1000 A.D.), but one can examine Japanese architecture for a further sense of the characteristic use of line in classical Chinese architecture (*figure 24*). The only remaining avenue for creative exploration of architectural design in China was in the area of landscape. Landscape architecture allowed artists to utilize new design ideas, and it reached a high level of expressive power through the esthetic principle of coordinated cursive lines.

Architecture provides some insight into the design of Chinese furniture. The structure of furniture is regarded as essentially that of architecture: furniture is small architecture, or architecture is large furniture. Low tables and beds were the earliest furniture, because people would usually kneel, sit, or lie on the floor when alone or in social gatherings. Desks and chairs began to appear in the fifth century A.D., but furniture design did not reach maturity until the Ming Dynasty (fourteenth century). "Ming furniture" has become virtually a generic term for all Chinese furniture. Aside from fulfilling a practical function, the distinctive feature of Ming furniture is its handling of line. Comparing an example of Ming furniture (*figure 25*) with the earlier example of Yuan architecture (*figure 19*), one notes the gentle upward curve of the chair back and the building roof. Similarly, the supporting structure under the surface of the table echoes the prominent curves of the building and is comparable to the beam of the roof or the arch of a doorway or gate. The strong, clean vertical lines of the chair and table legs are comparable to the simple columns of the building. Finally, the structural braces at the base of each chair resemble the slightly elevated foundation or porch of the building. All these features are distinctive of Chinese furniture design, and they all reflect the characteristic Chinese concern for line.

I conclude this discussion with a few comments on what may seem to be a minor art form but which is actually rich and powerful in spontaneously capturing the spirit of line, which lies at the heart of Chinese culture: the folk art of paper cutting. Perhaps paper cutting is a special case, because its nature relies on the *connection* of lines (*figure 26*). Farmers are very particular about expressing the trace marks of their scissors. They pay attention to the essential quality of the instrument and to the esthetic relation between material and line. Folk artists who are engaged in paper cutting tend to look down on artists who are engaged in paper *carving*. They believe that lines carved out of paper by means of a knife are slick, smooth, and, therefore, powerless. There is a surprising similarity between the expressive power of the two faces in figure 26 and many of the human forms in Picasso's paintings, particularly in terms of perspective.

Figure 24
Interior view, Japanese architecture.

Figure 25
Table and chairs. Ming Dynasty, fourteenth century A.D.

Figure 26
Examples of the Chinese folk art of paper
cutting. Shan Xi. Contemporary.

The Chinese concept of perspective is in reality a concept of
the nature of line. Every part of the line has its own perspective and
is an independent whole. Yet, every part is also a *continuation* of a
larger whole. Every part extends and contributes to the pluralism of
that larger whole. Chinese artists, generation after generation,
immerse themselves in this continuation. Through continuous
creation of their own parts and wholes, they achieve contentment
and happiness.

Translated by Barbara Shen and Richard Buchanan

Untimely Opinions
(An Attempt to Reflect on Design)
Gert Selle

Panorama 1988

The new Ford Opel from VW has had its premiere. The International Design Center (IDZ) Berlin moved to the Kudamm. The Design Council prints paper. Everywhere, design is exhibited and discussed. Now is the moment to turn the telescope around in order to reduce the topic to its real dimensions. Perhaps at present (of course empirical data are lacking) a few lifestyle-dependent user groups are more design-conscious (whatever that means) and inquire about more dainty or bizarre goods than previously. Perhaps the international competition for a renationalization of form, urged along on more stylistic planes, will again make distinctions possible so that German export art of a Kiefer or a Baselitz might follow a wave of "German design." (Equivalent big names don't come to mind.)

Since the 1960s, a few proverbs about the design *problematic* may have become current or developments may have so intensified that design must be discussed anew. But the network of economic, technological, and ecological conditions and oppositions in design is no theme for the present, no more than is the flood of design and advertising. The basic problematic of design has been overwhelmed by secondary considerations. Design seems incontestably to be expressive, economically relevant, and worthy of promotion. It is again being discovered as a political and cultural factor, as it formerly was in the Second Republic. That the instrument design is finally achieving liberty and could have a promising future to look forward to would have never occurred to this author without having glanced at exhibitions, catalogs, television broadcasts, and text-productions from newly invigorated design institutions. This skepticism is based on design's esthetic and ideological connections with the project of Modernism and with the discharge of tasks of representation of a no-longer depictable efficiency of high technology. What can be perceived behind the confusion of voices, behind the cultural activity, and "design politics"?

The product landscape has become more colorful—similar to a coffeepot, which is reminiscent of a distorted pyramid from a magical souvenir shop. The culture industry has focused on design; the media already are pushing design's bid to be considered entertainment. Only design festivals—at which spectacular exhibits will be burned as fireworks—are missing. In metropolitan centers, design-cum-architecture has become the leading medium of representation of a dubious urbanity. No wonder the institutions that must manage the socially highly regarded discipline hurry to do so; already, even the smaller cities unconditionally want their own design institutes. Yet there is no cultural or social scientific study of design, no investigation of the questions of esthetic ecology, anthropology of applications, or psychology of usage. The fundamental principles of design management remain unknown; a hermeneutics of industrial culture is unwanted. This is a humiliating lack (grave to Germany's neighbor France, for instance). The other lack is banal. It consists of the fact that the new colorfulness of the product landscape only conceals, with difficulty, the gaps in customary design efforts. As long as I trip over the vacuum cleaner, or get caught in the cord, or some other hasty and annoying occurrence hinders the housework, things cannot be good with normal design. This act means that, in spite of the idle chatter about design and in spite of the wealth of designed products, there is neither an analytically grounded knowledge vis-à-vis the phenomenon, nor can the concrete object about which so much fuss is being made be found in a condition that justifies all the discussion about it.

Behind this chatter is the awareness that the less design's boundaries can be broadened, the grander must be the figures that serve to legitimate the new freedom of form and cultural propositions through which design will be displayed. I must consider this unbroken and incomplete design awareness to be the result of a self-affirming process of delusion. That the new ideological thrust that is embraced with so much enthusiasm should be tied to motives arising from the current culture is a fact I cannot go into here. I certainly confess to being alarmed by this development.

On the other hand, the new product landscape leaves me cold. As long as I am not at close quarters with it, it does not bother me. As with most users, I utilize these things with the appropriate inattentiveness, as long as they are not esthetically aggressive or technically at fault. My Volkswagen example is of Philistine unobtrusiveness. It becomes a burden only when it will not run because work is needed on the clipped tube for the benzine-pressure line. I kick my Rowenta vacuum cleaner if the cord gets twisted behind me or it stops. That goes for the Miele machine too.[1] When someone wants to tell me about advances in design, I can only laugh. Moreover, the cultural brakes have been applied firmly. The brouhaha about style as nourishment does not help. What most people, as paying customers, understand by design is located in the labyrinth of discount furniture chains, development markets, or in the Quelle catalog.[2] That which is in exhibitions, on television, or in the advertising print media gives design the effect of unreality, such as a hothouse of desires from which an exotic little plant sometimes strays into mass-produced design. There, it serves the mixture of shortlived fashionable trends, which draw their forms from the oblique "Insider-High Culture," which, for its part, makes low-level

1   Rowenta and Miele are producers of electric household articles.
2   Quelle is the largest mail order catalog in West Germany.

loans. To pursue the path of form, the history of translucence would be worthy of investigation, as on the whole, the thicket of mobile and prosperous user cultures and interpretative models would be more exciting to show than the sight of the cramped designer searching for the next inspiration. The absurdity of antiquarians is in no way inferior to that of the most modernistic of the moderns. Current design has an emphatic *petit bourgeois* quality, particularly where this quality should be avoided at all costs. In addition, design is a middle-class problem, the little esthetic Social Darwinism of yuppies.

The current juxtaposed beauties and absurdities can become familiar. They do not hurt; tolerating the situation is possible. Insofar as I can keep things at a distance, I can scarcely perceive them—as is true for most people with or without an awareness of design. I could almost refer to a kind of collapse of my design perceptions and understanding and interest in design. There are grounds for this discouraging experience that can be grasped very quickly. First, design is inevitable. Second, design seems incorrigible. Third, design is a fallout product of industrial history. There is no escaping it. You can only neutralize it like nitrate or acid rain. Design is housed in stores or homes until its final destination in a museum or trash pile. The unexamined consequences of the management of designed products settles into habit and consciousness. A fundamental property of what is experienced never alters. Something can always be discovered about the state of a society and its cultural self-consciousness through types of phenomena and user patterns or "inner views" of products. Their place and bearings in the realm of industrial history can always be measured. And the deficits, surplus adaptations, and secret goals of this culture can always be found in these things. (The economic functions of design are clear from the first.)

That is, the possibility exists to question, in a much wider sense, the image of the state of objective culture (including the esthetics arising from design) according to the intellectual style and tendential development of the culture of the world's leading industrial nations. The magnitude of the forms of things should not be understood only as indicators of the conditions of the economic esthetic, but much more as indicators of the self-evidence of our industrial culture, which has neither a politically corrigible nor even a poetically maneuverable dynamic in the formation of cultural subjects. Yet to ask what stands invisible behind the forms in terms of the history of efficiency, the already experienced and still vital, is not of immediate interest in West Germany. The Greens have never once grasped that all the chatter about culture is a pretext to all the more easily avoid the matter. The Resource Culture (of which design and its history are parts) has long presented a process of exploitation and subjugation similar to what is found in nature.

Because there is an inner and an outer culture, as well as an inner and an outer human nature, what design must do with this inner and outer nature and with the executed forms of cultivation

Design and Culture

belong to fundamental questions of knowledge and politics. As always, design is the stage and, at the same time, a play within a play that historically is acted on it. The plot is being unfolded constantly in design, with the use of tools and objects as props. The actors on this stage, the prompters, their patrons, and their audience think that they certainly know the roles in this play, but whether they guess what they are playing or what is playing with them seems yet again highly uncertain. The activities surrounding design, that encircle all these questions, allow the impression to arise that design is the invention of designers and their apologists, just as some definitions of health or illness can be considered the invention of doctors and medical institutions. There are forms of activity that are self-legitimating. This fact gives rise to the suspicion that the new enterprise developing from design institutions bypasses the promotional measures of industries relevant to design, which formerly provided and upgraded their own expertise. Design has been in West Germany, unlike the DDR, an industrial sector institution, for a long time. Those to whom this new enterprise is addressed are not the producers or suppliers of design but, rather, the users. Manufacturers and designers have long known from their own perspectives what the situation is. Relying upon producer education, as in the era of the founding of the Werkbund, is no longer possible.

Industry must not change because of the swings in taste of the often disobedient and inattentive consumer who is usually denounced as obedient and docile. He or she drives a VW-Passat[3] (or a cheaper car from Japan), with coarse-fibered upholstery, and often enough looks like designers on television, who act as their own representatives. The immobility of the great user-masses is the "scandal" that continually keeps the legitimizing machinery of design institutions in motion. The "work of enlightenment" can succeed here. What kind of "enlightenment" is seen not only in the cryptic insider-texts, but also in the selection of new sites. Design counseling, with its own place in the Frankfurt fairgrounds, is not only symbolically closer to bank towers, but also resides in the very center of commerce. The International Design Center (IDZ) took lodging in the midst of the tourist section of Berlin, "the cultural capital of Europe," that it so much wanted to be near, but never suspected that this was the role that was drafted for it. What kind of innovation is this, which again sets afloat partially moth-balled conditions borrowed by German design institutions from post-war history?

A close view

For weeks I've been playing with an Olivetti tabletop calculator (Divisumma 18) that Mario Bellini designed in 1972, something unusual took place that had not occurred to me until now. It was not the insight that forms are convertible worldwide. Virtually any design school graduate has control over the methodical and esthetic instruments needed to solve similar problems. It was not even the

---

3   VW-Passat is a well-known middle-class
     car in Europe.

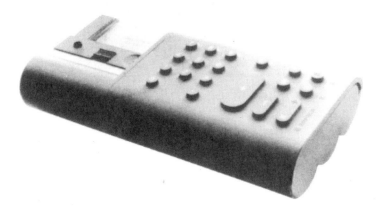

consideration of how obvious these forms are for many users. It was, rather, the unexpected discovery of the pleasure created by touching the thing. I understand nothing about electrical equipment; this calculator was not even working. I played around with it and found, to my surprise, that handling the thing was not bound to its function, that it was free from any goals. The instrument had tangible weight, plasticity, and an extraordinary haptic quality, which functioned sensually with no hidden agenda but merely as a material body that "serves" playfully. Is it an object for esthetic pleasure, freed from all the goals of necessity? A person can feel it, stroke it, lift it, weigh it, even compose on it; for it is also a musical instrument. I recall the slight pressure of sensitive, warm skin on tangible, rubber-covered keys and buttons, which offered a slight resistance; then the apparatus made a delayed and attractive clicking noise, without causing any dismay and which was similar to the spontaneous pressure that produces playful rhythmic patterns on a percussion instrument. And I remember how increasingly amazed I was by the forgotten process of approach and negotiation between the machine and my hand.

Of course, I was aware of the degree of sensual persuasive power that an empathetic designer can use. I had not yet encountered such evidence of this as here with Bellini. Time was needed to grasp what had been performed on my own flesh and senses and how this came about through a 1972 design. An example of the best design was before my eyes, the design of a seductive unity of person and machine, sensuality and playfulness, beauty of form and aptness of function. A sort of fusion dream, the staging of this dream as reality and, at the same time, the most treacherous delusion. The process of sensual persuasion in its unobtrusiveness, urgency, triviality, and even its absurdity seemed the point of departure for this phenomenon. Some cross between a teddy bear (transitional object), sculpture, and tool with completely incidental application, it strikes me as a harmless, fascinating fusion. The charming shape of the object seems to remove the objective distance between the technical tool and the hand touching it, allowing the contradiction between organic and inorganic to vanish, denying the fundamental opposition between

Design and Culture

subject and object, which previously had left each "hard" functional form unreconciled before the evidence of perception, whether intentionally or not. Classical functionalism had never concealed this break and, therefore, was finally unacceptable.

Today it is beginning to dawn on me that this contradiction can be given up not only as a theme from esthetics, but also from technological culture. Perhaps the boundaries between equipment and organisms have long ago been removed in an anthropologically effective sense so that the inner nature of humans is no longer in conflict with alien external functions, but is already socialized and cultivated—through design among other things—allowing this fusion to succeed without further ado. What good are the ridiculous juggling tricks and clumsy camaraderie of ordinary design measured against such a masterly achievement as this esthetic crossing of frontiers? I feel somewhat surprised and ill-at-ease after playing with Frau Divisumma. Am I already an industrially overdetermined, techno-erotically trained being who has forcibly subjugated all his needs and desires to his judgment and rationality? If there has long existed a collective unconscious, what is there that agrees with the modern organized techno-aesthete devoted to the mastery of nature that has long since put down roots in the design myth? It would be a myth of delusion, false reconciliation, the bursting of extrasensory limits seemed to be erected once and for all. Or, more positively, a myth of the benevolent control of technique and of productive rationality. I know that there is more to perceiving things than designers or interpreters assume, and these things reflect in their forms the relations that we unconsciously hold to them.

The proposal therefore, is to make visible to perception and thought that which is considered invisible in design so as to understand it. This seems to be a fundamental question of understanding design and its self-image, but it is omitted or skirted in the current discussion of design in the industrial culture. There is, as the above example shows, perhaps a palpable dividing line between collection and keeping some distance, being overwhelmed and forming a judgment, beyond which only lightness, beauty, and liberation, not fear, regret, or the tatters of deliberation, are to be felt. Experiences of this fusion do not replace mental reservations just because the capitalist interests of exploitation have merged with mild structuralism, as was claimed by the economics-influenced criticism of the late 1960s, but because a widespread and cultural sense of the unity of subject and object has arisen. Where the limits of the esthetic-ludic have been removed, the New Age postindustrial reconciliation of humanity, nature, technology, and culture, and of everything with everything has already dawned.

In design history, there are threshold-objects, that is, plans that make epochal phenotypica ruptures occur with exemplary clarity. Bellini's object seems to fit another category, one of various examples, that chance raided from a mass of similar forms. Yet, it is an example of extending definite perspectives on the breakdown of resistance; the nonviolent adaptation; and the removal of barriers between bodies and machines, spirit and technology, nature and civilization. The exemplay recognition (or supposition), based on my playful addiction to the Muse Divisumma, that can arise is that, in fulfilling design goals, a product can tilt into unintentional deception concerning the character and consequences of the now so lightly attached object relations. As the perfect design principle is fulfilled, its dialectic comes to light: a beautiful form means unity of function and form and, at the same time, allows all afflictions of industrial reality to vanish. Such perfect, cuddly objects are therefore dangerous. Yet, shall I not make an apology for my vacuum cleaner? The narcissistic offenses that workers have always experienced from the functionally "hard" environment and the "cold" tools—this lack of a supple, tender response to their need for acknowledgment of the extrafunctional subjectivity of experience—these failures were and are unobtrusive *aides-memoires*. A 1930s typewriter, a 1960s hydraulic press, a cabin of a contemporary crane, or any obsolete design of modern functionalism demonstrates the objectivity that human beings effectively face. To a certain point, industrial history is that of the machine as the more or less clumsy functional extension of the weary hand. Increasing machine-intelligence has in no way made human intelligence, much less the hands, obsolete. Meanwhile, the paleontologist, not the designer, reflects on the consequences of this. No longer being able to "think" with the hands, in the opinion of André Leroi-Gourhan, means the loss of a portion of normal, that is, phylogenetically based, mental abilities.[4] The current phase is a transitional stage in which the mass of workers have a claw with five "finger" appendages that they operate by pressing buttons. Now farmers plow with tractors in the fields. In heated cabins, with power steering and tape decks, the soil is just a surface as the distance to the work performed in this surface increases. For the subsidized large-scale enterprise of EG-excess production, eventually, there will be a system of electronically operated sewage disposal that will empty into the canals without anyone pushing a button. Then the picture of tractors with their kegs on the horizon blasting music will be history. This kind of development can scarcely be halted, because it follows its own dynamic of industrial rationality. Yet, as design is allowing every trace of this rationality and its "hardness" to vanish, the perception of the process that was once mediated through the senses is disappearing. The sensual pleasure that can be enjoyed in "grasping" instruments and in ludic intercourse with them can be seen as an intentional, large-scale regression. Not the recourse to historical forms, but the recourse to a functionally antiquated sensuality and to a preoccupied sensual consciousness is the dubious achievement of the so-called moderns. This recourse began in

4   André Leroi-Gourhan, *Hand und Wort: Die Evolution von Technic, Sprache und Kunst* (Frankfurt Suhrkamp, 1980), 319.

industrial design long before Bellini, and the powers that act upon human nature and are behind the rationality of ergonomics and the loveliness of beautiful forms must be questioned.

A question of position

If looking into the distance has revealed a panorama that can be tolerated with the proper inattentiveness, the glance at close range can show the exaggerated and the frightening that results from the magnification of insignificant but charming details. I would resolutely defend myself against this sight. For even with the naked eye, how one can see a flood of design encourages a questionable attempt to make all areas of life esthetically pleasing and, not least, the world of work is easy to see; this change is attempted under the pretext of humanization, beautification, and civilization of the machine and as the expression of cultural consciousness. Whether the flood of design is promoted under the viewpoint of liberal free enterprise or a socialistic planned economy makes no difference. The result is the same. Only the ideological interpretations differ.

A skeptical close inspection shows that design can very well distract one from the culture and its work as well as from nature, whose subject matter it claims to represent, under the pretext of being a cultural end itself. The motifs of concealing function and concealing functional relations by form are as old as industrial culture. The confusion has recently achieved a new characteristic since the identity of function and form as the moral of design has been abandoned for free symbolism. In this respect, Bellini's calculator is already an outmoded example. It must be so big and heavy because it assumes so complex a function. Today, an instrument that is efficient at the expense of being oversized is similar to a child's piggy bank, whose size, volume, and weight have no relation to its content, but which offers every freedom of form, even for whimsical attitudes.

The question of the miniaturization of function together with the heightening of efficiency with the freedom for all formal design possibilities currently stands at the heart of professional concerns. How this view widens the design horizons! It ever more clearly shows that everything possible is allowed now and that everything allowed is possible. Any functional organism can present itself in any dress, sometimes covered, sometimes exposed, sometimes excessive, sometimes ironic, sometimes playful. Apparently, these possibilities are an invaluable achievement. The distinction from 1888, when the original historical industry began to blossom, is that at that time there were agreements about the esthetic and culturally appropriate that are lacking today. For example, obscuring the technological unleashing of the esthetic and concealing the practical fabrication of the ornamental was convenient. A caveat, however, dictated that the mechanical, in its naked obscenity, remain secretly recognizable. Similar to the suppressed sexuality of human nature, which could be used effectively only in concealment, everyone knew from experience that it was there. Experience avoids what is in technology today. People can play with technology like computer freaks but can no longer sensually envision what is in the instruments and what happens behind their frames.

Where the As-If, the ludic value of the machine world, meets at the area of modest disguise, the self-delusion of industrial subjects has another quality. At present, there are things in design that are so formed they are corporeally and objectively palpable, even though this palpability is currently highly rationalized. Things no longer produce any realm of meaning from their functionality, or any symbolic aura; they no longer stink of the volcanic forge. This new sterility allows a place for every sort of whim or symbolism, but not for reverence. Design functions under the principle of collective camouflage to the thunderous applause of everyone who will neither pursue any endeavor nor simply dream and play. Basically, what has always taken place in the design-intensive. industries continues to happen, and no one wants to talk about it. Long ago, Evelyn Waugh did so in a clear-sighted manner concerning the American way of death. In the funeral industry, people die in beauty and are cosmetically decorated beyond all truth.

When the profound insecurities concealed behind the usual esthetic hurly-burly are considered, the new preoccupation with design can be regarded as merely a part of a monstrous machinery of repression, which has discovered the esthetic as the last exploitable raw material. The esthetic pushes itself through every fissure, spreads out, fills the consciousness, cushions us against the pressures of modernization, and is at the service of every expectation for compensation. Esthetic experience is uncoupled from authentic experience and knowledge, leaving only uncommitted play behind. That experience can be had with objects that have become opaque, but only if one is fiendishly attentive. If scrupulous, then oneself and design cannot be trusted fully. Location decisions are implied, which neither the producers nor their distributors, neither the interested design institutions nor the newly duped users of design, can impose on themselves. Such decisions were notoriously neglected questions in West Germany, which has a political culture that strings together the problems of rationality, unemployment, the modernization of the workplace, and all its social and cultural effects. That design is and must be an instrument and expression of political culture obviously does not occur to any cultural politician or design functionary. This, in a land that since the 1960s has been modern to an unheard of degree! What could Germany achieve in comparison to the First Republic of a stinking rich nation! Instead, there is a worldwide design that is splashing around on the swell of industrial history. We're swimming in it and asking why. Every design politics that does not ask this question is

Design and Culture

redundant. What is going to happen will happen regardless—economically, ecologically, esthetically, culturally, irresistibly and, therefore, with no need for promotion. But how gladly would I have a useful vacuum cleaner? Then I could think in peace while doing the housework. Or then, would my last resistance to bow to design principle be vanquished?

Translated from the German by John Cullars

The Idea of Comfort
Tomás Maldonado

It is certainly difficult to imagine any discussion of the quality of life that is not, at the same time, a discussion on the "livability" of our surroundings. But this "livability" cannot be proposed (and still less attained) in all contexts in the same way. For example, in a social reality in which human beings are forced to struggle for the most elementary survival, in a reality in which hunger, deprivation, illness, violence, and physical and moral compulsion on individuals, in fact, rule, the program of "livability" is identified with efforts to change such a reality. There are, however, other contexts that are not characterized (at least not to a major degree) by indigence and repression. In these other contexts, "livability" has a very different meaning: practically, it means the services that a particular ambient reality can provide in terms of convenience, ease, or habitability. In short, comfort.[1]

But if we are to deal with the idea of comfort, some preliminary clarifications are needed, because although the idea of "livability" may appear relatively simple, all things considered, the idea of comfort is much more complex. Comfort is a modern idea. Before the Industrial Revolution, the need (or expectation) for comfort—in the sense indicated above of convenience, ease, and habitability—was the privilege of the few. But the progressive diffusion of comfort to the masses was not accidental. There is no doubt that it has played, from the beginning, a fundamental role in the task of controlling the social fabric of the nascent capitalist society.

We may say, then, that, in its most hidden recesses, comfort is a scheme for social control. But we must not push this statement to the point of repudiating comfort in the global sense. That would be a typical interpretative abuse that leads to a simplistic, reductive distortion. Whether we like it or not, we must admit that comfort (at least in some of its manifestations) includes *also* elements of substantial advantage to the daily life of humanity.[2]

One may consider comfort as one of the factors contributing to the process of modernization. But how is comfort functionally a part of the process of modernization? It is a question of knowing, in summary, why the process of modernization manifests itself mainly in the qualitative and quantitative increase in the services that produce comfort. The answer isn't easy for the simple reason that comfort doesn't always come in the same way, but follows a dynamic that continually changes terms relating to supply and demand. It should be remembered that comfort, beyond a given critical threshold, can be transformed—as happens often enough—

This essay is a translation from Tomás Maldonado's book, *Il Futuro della Modernita* (Milan: Feltrinelli, 1987).

1   Although the term is obviously derived from the English *comfort* and this, in turn, from the French *confort*, its true derivation is from late Latin *confortare* derived from *com-fortis*, to render strong and, by extension, to alleviate pain or fatigue.

2   S. Kracauer recognized in his friend E. Bloch the rare intellectual merit of knowing how to enjoy the circus as a circus before denouncing it as an industrial enterprise. (Letter of S. K to E. B., 7.8.1967, in E Bloch, *Briefe 1903 bis 1975*, vol. I (Frankfurt am Main: Suhrkamp, 1985), 399.

into the source of new hardships and sufferings. In short, comfort can flow into a negation of comfort. One thinks, for example, of the perverse collateral effects (pollution, traffic congestion, etc.) that the automobile has produced.[3]

Such subtle considerations, however important, must not lead us to undervalue (and still less ignore) the fact that there exists an undoubted relation of reciprocal dependency between the dynamic of modernization and the diffusion of comfort. There are "areas" in which this connection of reciprocal dependency is fully revealed: the city, habitations, the work place. In particular, the home considered as a microcosm perfectly exemplifies the relation between modernization and comfort.

It has already been pointed out that the concept of comfort may be understood as a device for social control. Concerning the domestic sphere, we note that it deals with a very special discipline. In this specific case, in fact, comfort is seen as a procedure with a compensatory function, that is, a procedure seeking to restore—as much physically as psychologically—the energies consumed in the hostile external world of work. With standards more or less formalized, more or less explicit, comfort serves to structure daily life, to ritualize conduct, especially the attitudes and postures of the body in relation to furniture and objects intended for domestic use. It may well be noted that comfort expresses, better than any other cultural contrivance, the "techniques of the body"[4] appropriate to modern bourgeois society.

But comfort, in so much as it regiments daily life, also contributes indirectly to disciplining the family, radically transforming it, to facilitate its becoming nuclear or its modernization. Comfort, giving emphasis to the sense of the pleasure of private life, ratifies the central position of the home as the place for social activity and contributes to the formation and consolidation of the modern nuclear family. In summary, comfort is the new model for life proposed by the bourgeoisie; it is the new lifestyle. This hypothesis is fully confirmed by recent studies of the process that constitutes the "modern (nuclear) family,"[5] particularly those that dwell on the microcosmic influences of such a process. There is, in fact, no doubt that the new familial order at first appears narrowly tied to changes in the habitational space. It is sufficient to remember the structural changes in lodgings that came about during the transitional period between the traditional family and the modern family. From an open living space of fluid, imprecise, fugitive confines, typical of the environmental context of the traditional family, it passed, with the birth of the nuclear family, to a closed space, articulated in a system of rigidly fixed functions.[6]

And the purpose is clear: to block the excessive instability of the family, to shelter it from external intrusions, anchoring it to a precise location, tying it then to an *interior*. But creating an interior, enclosing a space, isn't enough. It is equally necessary that the new

3 T. Maldonado, "L'automobile: merce regina," in *Avanguardia e razionalita* (Turin: Einaudi, 1974). Another argument in defense of the automobile is the assertion that it assures a high degree of personal mobility. On the ideal plane, this should mean the democratization of mobility, the absolute freedom of everyone to travel anywhere. In reality, however, as has been shown in the last few years, possible mobility is in conflict with probable mobility. Theoretically we can use the automobile to travel, but increasing traffic congestion is such that the practical probability of traveling by car becomes ever more illusory.

4 M. Mauss, "Les techniques du corps," in *Sociologie et anthropologie* (1934) (Paris: Presses Universitaires de France, 1950), 363. As to what concerns the present disciplinary role of comfort in a particular habitational context (the living room), see the excellent and now classic empirical investigation of A. Silbermann, *Vom Wohnen der Deutschen* (Cologne: Westdeutscher Verlag, 1963).

5 On this topic, see E. Shorter, *The Making of the Modern Family* (New York: Basic Books, 1975); L. Stone, *The Family, Sex and Marriage in England 1500–1800* (London: Weidenfeld and Nicholson, 1977); and Emmanuel Le Roy Ladurie, *Montalliou* (New York: Braziller, 1978).

6 The "sociofugal" role of domestic isolation is denounced by B. Disraeli in *Sybil, or the Two Nations* (1845) (London: Oxford University Press, 1975).

space, due to its particular structure, be capable of promoting a new ideal of domestic life. In its emergent phase, the bourgeoisie, aware of this requirement, rushed to define the form and content of its ideal life: a life centered on privacy, on "the atmosphere of privacy." Yet bourgeois privacy is not defined solely in terms of intimacy. It certainly recalls the traditional spiritual values of private life, of values realized as the fruits of interiority. But at the same time, the dream (for it is a dream) of bourgeois privacy is based on a close regulation of material things. In practice, as Bachelard says, it is a *rêverie de l'intimité materielle*[7] (a reverie of material intimacy).

If one is very attentive, the question of privacy is seen to touch directly on the theme of comfort as a means of discipline. At this point further observations come to mind. There is no doubt that privacy appears, in many ways, conditioned by the ideology of comfort, but there is also another ideology that has a strict relation to it: the ideology of hygiene. One thing is certain: privacy without comfort and hygiene is vanishing. But what do comfort and hygiene have in common that, when missing, diminishes the quality of privacy? The answer is simple: order.[8] Comfort and hygiene are indicators of order. Moreover, they are suppliers of order.

In this vision, comfort could appear as a restrictive design that does not allow opportunity for the diversification of individual actions.[9] On the contrary, a new sensibility begins to make itself felt as an essential part of this design; in other words, a subtle, progressive change in sensibility, modes of being, preferences, and, at the same time, a modification of the collective and individual imagination is shaped. In respect to this, one speaks of the birth of a diverse sensibility (and sensuality) connected to the new procedures of personal cleanliness, to new means of relaxation, to the use of new artifacts: "Bourgeois things are the vehicles for the bourgeois sensibility."[10] Not by chance, with all the transformations this indicates, occurs equally "the destruction of the body" in favor of the formation of the "person." Progressively, though slowly, these changes become widespread, introducing themselves by way of the middle classes, ultimately to become a model for the less moneyed classes as well. "Perhaps the most obvious new reality with which middle class families can compete with one another," notes Peter Gay, "is what I would call the democratization of comfort."[11]

Now it is necessary to consider *the technology of the quotidian*, or the union of the technical and the practical that is at the heart of domestic material culture.[12] Even if we forget the very obvious fact that beyond a more or less rigid articulation of functional divisions (dining room, living room, bedroom, kitchen, bath, etc.), the living space is also a material regimen, an arrangement of movable and immovable objects (equipment and utensils for the making and saving of food, for the care and assistance of children, for hygiene and cleanliness; installations for the control of temperature; gadgets for recreation and communication; furniture; household goods; etc).

7 G. Bachelard, *La terre et les rêveries du repos* (Paris: Librairie J. Corti, 1948). Also important in this book is the stimulating chapter IV, "The Natal House and the Dream-Like House."

8 Concerning this, see M. Douglas, *Purity and Danger* (London: Routledge and Kegan Paul, 1967). See X. Rubert De Ventos, *Ensayos sobre el desorden* (Barcelona Kairos,1976).

9 The risk in excessively ideological use of such categories as hygiene, comfort, and order are well laid out by M. Roncayolo, *Propos d'étape.*

10 P. Gay, *Education of the Senses*, vol. I (New York: Oxford University Press, 1984). See in regard to this, J. H. Hagstrum, *Sex and Sensibility* (Chicago: University of Chicago Press, 1980).

11 P. Gay, *op. cit.*, 438

12 On questions of domestic material culture, see the stimulating essay by G. Martinotti, "L'informatica domestica," in A. Ruberti, ed. *Tecnologia domani* (Bari: Laterza, 1985). Critically adapting Giedion's celebrated work on the contemporary development of domestic technology, Martinotti proposes some very original interpretations on the past and future of electrical household appliances. See T. Maldonado and E. Wahl, *Grundsatzuntersuchung uber Haushaltgerate* (Ulm: Hochschule für Gestaltung, 1966).

Daily domestic life is, to a great extent, a continuous putting on of such a regimen with such a regulation.

These themes are certainly not new. Many scholars—archaeologists, ethnologists, sociologists, and historians of the family, technology, industry, and architecture—have made and continue to make important contributions to this area of research. An attempt not yet fully realized is the effort to integrate these bits of specialist knowledge into a complex vision of domestic material culture with particular reference to late capitalist society.

This is surely a difficult task, and I make no pretense of confronting it. On this subject, I only wish to indicate some aspects concerning the technology of the quotidian, particularly those that can aid us in better perceiving the nature of structural (and supportive) elements of such a material culture, in strict relation to the process of modernization. Let's begin with a first statement: the technology of the quotidian is not today, and never has been, neutral. It actually belongs to that type of device for social control that Joseph, following Foucault, has called "tactics and disciplinary figures for the home."[13]

Now we must ask ourselves how and when the tactics and figures that govern our daily domestic culture are going to emerge, that is, the control mechanisms that aid in structuring, and in the final analysis, stabilizing daily life in capitalist society; how and when, in other words, the system of values and norms that today is at the heart of all modern ways of considering useful objects, of prefiguring behavior, of articulating living areas will burst into the surge of history.

The answers to these questions can be sought in Victorian England. In fact, it is in that country—and in that particular historical moment—that one can verify the decisive turn in the constitutive process of tactics and figures mentioned above. After the devastating social impact of the first phase of industrialism, there surfaced in England an ever greater anxiety over the effects that such an impact could have in the long run on the reproduction of the work force. Remember that the panorama presents more alarming aspects: the drastic reduction in the average length of life; the elevated rate of infant mortality; the imposing increase in the number of abandoned or neglected children and elderly people, vagabonds, beggars; the propagation of epidemics through poor nutrition, promiscuity, and the absolute lack of domestic hygiene; the ever greater diffusion of the exploitation of women and children in the market place; and the spreading phenomenon of alcoholism, prostitution, and juvenile crime.

Confronting this dramatic state of things, already described in his time by Engels,[14] the dominant class responded with the introduction of some strategies to contain these phenomena. It created more varied relief institutions: homes for children and the elderly, almshouses for beggars, asylums for the "mentally ill"; it put into

13 I. Joseph, "Tactiques et figures disciplinaires," in I. Joseph and Ph. Fritsch, *Disciplines à domicile: L'édification de la famille*, in *Recherches* 28 (November 1977):29–208. See G. Heller, *"Propre en ordre": Habitation et vie domestique 1050–1930: l'exemple vaudois* (Lausanne. Edition d'En-Bas, 1979). On the "disciplinary" role of material domestic culture, with particular emphasis on women, see the pioneer contribution by B. Taut, *Die neue Wohnung: Die Frau als Schöpferin* (Leipzig: Klinkhardt und Biermann, 1924).

14 F. Engels, *La situazione della classe operai in Inghilterra* (1845) (Roma: Editori Riuniti, 1973). See J. H. Treble, *Urban Poverty in Britain 1830–1914* (London: Methuen, 1979) and M. J. Daunton, *House and Home in the Victorian City* (London: Edward Arnold, 1983).

operation a vast number of hygienic-sanitary measures in the districts and dwellings of the masses (the opening of wide streets, canalization, drains, etc.); it enacted laws relative to the length of the work day and to hygiene and security in the work place. In sum, capitalism, even if involuntarily, made concessions. As Engels said, "Big business, in its external aspects, is moralizing."[15]

Many tactics and disciplinary figures of the Victorian era, in particular those "within the domicile," seem initially strongly conditioned (or even determined) by the new typical-ideal construction, the ideology of comfort. The endeavors of those years, tending to guide the reconstitutive process of the working class family, can be identified with the attempt to set up, even justify, a model of material domestic culture. Such a model would have to, on the ideal plane, mediate between a rich and a poor culture; to promote a descending acculturation, a transfer of values from the upper to the lower classes. Not by chance, all of the grand projects to rationalize the working class home anticipated the maintenance within the small quarters of the same activities—and thus of the same distributive typologies—anticipated for upper middle class homes. Even if forms, qualities, and dimensions were "proportional" to the needs of proletarians, this transfer of habitational models also included the transfer of those categories of privacy, hygiene, and comfort that had already been acquired by the higher echelons of society. The fact that contributed the most to the success of such a project was precisely the ideology of comfort.[16]

As I've already observed, the ideology of comfort appears closely involved with at least two parallel categories: hygiene and order. Given their independent nature, it is very difficult to sketch a straightforward history of them, defining priority and derivations. We can, nevertheless, designate the central moments and the determining passages of their evolution. In the outline briefly sketched above of the historical phase immediately following the initial impact of industrialism, large-scale strategies are mentioned that were used to confront some grave problems connected with the urbanization of great population masses—schemes that have been called strategies for containment. Among these, the most significant operations are those connected with urban infrastructures. Hygienic preoccupations that were being pursued since the late eighteenth century, accompanied by the results of medical research and of scientific discoveries in chemistry, produced a radical change in living conditions in the great urban centers.

Disinfectants and deodorants, sewers and paved streets, the elimination of noxious gases in urban areas, safe water related to problems of the supply and distribution of drinking water, sources of illumination—these are all qualifying moments of such a transformation. At the same time, a specialist literature began to address the themes of public hygiene, the functional city, medical aspects of epidemics and social ills, including social morality. The binomials hygiene-morality,

15 F. Engles, Preface to 1892 editio, *La situazione...*

16 On the role of the ideology of comfort in the Victorian period, see F. Beguin, "Les machineries anglaises due comfort," in the Victorian period, see F. Beguin, "Les machineries anglaises du comfort," in *L'haleine des faubourgs in Recherches* 29 (December 1977): 155–86. See also J. Lavater, *The Age of Opitmism* (London: Weidenfeld and Nicholson, 1966) and J. and F. Fourastie, *Histoire du confort* (Paris: Presses Universitaires de France, 1973). One must furthermore recommend the now classic study of S. Giedion, *Mechanization Takes Command* (New York: Oxford University Press, 1948).

Design and Culture

cleanliness-dignity, physical health-mental health began to take an impressive form, first applied to the system of public, social, and urban hygiene, then gradually transferred to the system of domestic hygiene. A clean city is also a combination of clean houses. City and house are then an intimate part of the same system of hygiene.

It must not be forgotten, moreover, that there were also technological and productive conditions that allowed for the affirmation of a new domestic organization. An industrial system developed that was quickly able to furnish equipment for lighting, heating, the distribution of water, mass-produced furniture, and chemically produced cleansing products. In a kind of reciprocal conditioning, living spaces and the new household appliances began to constitute what would be the model for urban middle-class habitations.

Equipment for hygiene condition the dislocation of living spaces and redefine their use and function, even when the new order and composition of the family is in consideration. The appearance of the bathroom as a locale specifically used for personal hygiene became possible due to running water, heating, and the furnishing of "sanitary" equipment. At the same time, the bathroom modified the relationship of human beings to their own bodies and to all their physiological functions: the elimination of wastes became private activities. Thus there came into being one of the central pivot points for modesty and privacy unknown to earlier social norms.

Beyond any hygienic preoccupations, an increasingly emphatic intolerance for unpleasant odors—or those that were deemed unpleasant to the new sensibility—led to the enclosing of spaces that had traditionally been left open. Obviously this process also applied to other living areas besides the bathrooms.[17]

The kitchen underwent a radical transformation following its progressive reduction in size and the loss of its role as the central living space within the home. Equally decisive were modifications in the techniques of preparation and preserving of food, facilitated by the new equipment. Thus arises the process of rationalization of "the kitchen space" that, more than others, has been a theme for dispute and research. It suffices to mention the attempt to apply the principles of Taylorism to work in the kitchen by designing furniture and devices to ease the accomplishment of domestic activities.

The process of mechanization, standardization, and rationalization of the kitchen area, in fact, sanctions its functional specialization, the atrophy of its role as the vital and metaphorical center of the house, and, therefore, its definitive isolation within the home. Thus was performed the process that J. P. Aron has called the evolution of the "alimentary topography,"[18] which would have its definitive ratification in our century. In this way, the kitchen, relegated to the place where food is prepared and separated from the place where it is consumed, precisely indicates the tendency toward differentiating work and service areas in the house from those of genuine and proper habitation.

17 See A. Corbin, *Le miasme et la jonquille* (Paris: Aubier Montaigne. 1982) and G. Vigarello, *Le propre et le sale: L'hygiéne du corps depuis le Moyen Age* (Paris: Seuil, 1985). Relating to the kitchen, see N. Chatelet, *Le corps a corps culinaire* (Paris: Seuil, 1977).

18 J. P. Aron, "Cucina," in *Enciclopedia*, vol. IV (Turin: Einaudi, 1978), 4. With the expression "alimentary topography," Aron designates the places where the *rite* of alimentation is accomplished. The variation in number, distribution, and importance of such places not only indicates changes in status and ways of living, but defines the degree of alimentary civility for a social group.

Living spaces adapted to moments of sociability, relationship, relief, and repose would constitute a discourse in itself as regards the compensatory function that comfort assumes in confronting the external world. It is even possible to draw a subtle line of originally unwavering demarcation between the spaces of domestic work; of feminine competence; and of domestic rest, which is of a markedly masculine character. In the first case, comfort is, for the most part, configured as an aid and alleviation of the labors of domestic toil. In the second case, it is configured as a restorative function. In short, something comparable to the "repose of the warrior." Thus, for example, the most comfortable furniture was intended for the use of males, which is quite clearly shown by their very rich and occasionally grotesque functional specialization, which, in the Victorian era, found expression in quite a vast range of furniture. We recall the reading chair, the smoker's chair, the siesta chair, the digestive chair, etc. The areas of the home were, moreover, classified into masculine and feminine areas.[19] The spaces for men were more comfortable than those for women for the simple reason that the most comfortable furniture was found in the former.

It must be said that this tendency weakened over time. In fact, a progressive specialization of living areas and furnishings occurred, and a greater simplification of furniture led to a new "heart" of the home: the parlor. The parlor constituted the most characteristic typology of the new style of middle-class life. This marked characteristic is accentuated by the presence within the parlor of the so-called "corner of the sofa," which constituted the "heart of the heart": an area that independently and compulsorily preordains the place in which conviviality should unfold.[20]

One may now ask whether there exists a connection between the development of the habitational microcosm and that of the urban macrocosm? In other words, are the compartments to be rigidly external and internal or, on the contrary, are there two interactive regions? Some reflections on the urban lifestyle can contribute to explaining many important aspects of what happens within quarters, especially middle-class quarters.

We can record Georg Simmel's notes on the city as an example in this sense. "There is perhaps no psychological phenomenon," wrote Simmel, "that is so characteristic and exclusive of the city as being *blasé*. . . . The essence of this disenchantment is in the obtuseness to the difference between things, not in the sense of being unaware that they exist, as with idiots, but in that the significance and value of these differences between things, and thus of the things themselves, are felt to be null, irrelevant. To the *blasé*, everything is of a uniformly gray, faded shade, and nothing merits being contrasted to other things."[21]

Anticipating D. E. Berlyne's[22] psychology of curiosity by fifty years, Simmel then confronts the theme of the relation between privation and satiety in perception; what is surprising is that he

19 J. Gloag, *Victorian Comfort* (Newton: Abbot, David and Charles, 1979).

20 See M. Warnke, "Zur Situation der Couchecke," in J. Habermas, ed., *Stichworte zur "Geisten Situation der Zeit"* (Frankfurt am Main: Suhrkamp, 1955).

21 G. Simmel, "Die Grossstadte und das Geistesleben," in *Jahrbuch der Gehestiftung,* IX (1903); reprinted in *Brücke und Tür* (Stuttgart: Koehler, 1957).

22 D. E. Berlyne, *Conflict, Arousal and Curiosity* (New York: McGraw Hill. 1960).

Design and Culture

treats the argument not only in terms of individual perception, but principally in terms of social perception. The large city, Simmel essentially says, is perceived, not apperceived. That is because there are too many, not too few, messages today. Thus satiety of perception leads to privation in apperception.

Examining a "large city"—Paris in Baudelaire's time—Walter Benjamin comes to conclusions very similar to Simmel's. But he doesn't stop here. In his attempt to "botanize the asphalt," in the sense of examining a city's life as meticulously as a botanist, he moves on to "botanizing the parquet," in the sense of examining internal life with the same meticulous care. In other words, Benjamin doesn't restrict himself to viewing the *flâneur* (idler) on the streets, but also within his home. So from Baudelaire, the external *flâneur*, he passes on to Proust, the internal *flâneur*. For Benjamin, there exists continuity between the streets and the internal world. The street and the internal world become part of a single labyrinth, the "labyrinth of merchandise" of middle-class society. That doesn't mean that Benjamin doesn't recognize the difference between working and private environments. On the contrary, he denounces the conflict between private and working environments, but without identifying the city *in toto* with work.

In the Baudelairean esthetic of the *flâneur*, the city is full of spaces that are absolutely extraneous to productive work—that is to say, spaces of gratuitous use. But the alienation that invalidates the private environment provides by its very nature, according to Benjamin, an intentional alternative to the working-place environment: "Under Louis Philippe," he writes in *Paris, the Capital of the Nineteenth Century* "the private person makes his entrance onto the stage of history. For the private individual, the living space is for the first time contrasted with the work place. . . . The private individual needs to be intimately lulled by his own illusions. . . . This gives rise to internal phantasmagoria. For the human being, this represents the world. In this he gathers in the distant and the past. His parlor is the stage of the universal theatre."[23]

Later in the same essay, Benjamin describes this internal phantasmagoria. The melancholy disorder of the city surreptitiously penetrates into the home, and there is found, to a minor degree, the same *blasé* attitude explained by Simmel in *Grossstadt*. It is the *blasé* universe of middle-class interior life: a universe enclosed in a "small box." Here the perception of the "diversity of things" also impedes the apperception of things. They are no longer objects, despite their material presence. There remain only the traces that we leave on them. The interior, Benjamin essentially says, is not only the universe, but also the care of the private individual. To inhabit means to leave impressions, and to acquire internally implies giving a certain relief to some perceptions. So we invent quantities of sheaths, bindings, boxes, and cases, on which are impressed the imprint of objects used every day. Thus the tenant's impressions are

23 W. Benjamin, "Paris, die Hauptstadt des XIX Jahrhunderts," in *Gesammelte Schriften*, vol. V-I (Frankfurt am Main: Suhrkamp, 1982), 52. See also W. Benjamin, "Das Paris des Second Empire bei Baudelaire" (1937), in *Gesammelte Schriften*, vol. 1–2, 511.

stamped within, and so arises the police investigations that exactly follow these clues.

Not by chance, Benjamin explicitly recalls Edgar Allen Poe, who is considered the first "physiognomist" of the interior life, as well as the father of the thriller genre. And that isn't all, for Poe opens a new interpretative avenue relative to comfort. For him, in fact, the display of conspicuous comfort is a form of "the display of wealth,"[24] an idea anticipating Thorstein Veblen's concept of "conspicuous consumption."[25]

As to the configuration of objects, the interior of a house is just a segment of a vast system of the material culture of society. But it is not a simple segment. Of course, external conditions that arise from the system to which they belong are decisive; yet, it would be absurd to deny every form of autonomous selection to the dwelling. Within certain limits, the consumer within a given habitational microenvironment can decide, as indeed happens, the generative modality of the segment of material culture that is assigned to him, the nature and position of the objects and the degree to which they fit his needs. For that reason, the consumer is compelled each day, more or less consciously, to judge the surroundings against his own model of happiness. One should not be surprised that an accurate investigation of the role of comfort in the habitational microenvironment calls upon a theory of material culture, as much as a theory of happiness—as much upon ergology (the study of material cultures) and eudeamonics (the doctrine of happiness).

Translated from the Italian by John Cullars.

---

24 E. A. Poe, "The Philosophy of Furniture (1840–45)," in *Selected Writings* (Harmondsworth: Penguin Books, 1967).

25 T. Veblen, *The Theory of the Leisure Class* (London: Macmillan, 1912). For a more detailed treatment of this aspect of Veblen's theory, see J. Dorfman, "New Light on Veblen," in T. Veblen, *Essays, Reviews and Reports* (Clifton: Augustus M. Kelley, 1973), 48 *passim*. On the (positive) role of ostentation in dress and furniture, see Q. Bell, *On Human Finery* (London: The Hogarth Press, 1976).

Design and Culture

The Design Museum:
Form Follows Funding
Barbara Usherwood

On 6 July 1989, Sir Terence Conran's long-cherished vision of a museum devoted entirely to industrial design became material reality. London's new Design Museum sits on the south bank of the River Thames, just downstream from Tower Bridge and at the very heart of Conran's substantial development site at Butler's Wharf, a £200 million scheme to transform acres of dockland warehousing into flats, shops, studios, restaurants, offices, and a hotel. Designed by Stuart Mosscrop and Richard Doone of the architectural firm Conran Roche, the museum, a converted 1950s warehouse, rises as a shining white, blockish building in angular ocean-liner style from the debris of half-developed riverside (*figure 1*).

The museum has been largely funded by the Conran Foundation, an educational charity that was set up in 1981 with capital derived from the stock market flotation of Conran's chain of Habitat home-furnishing shops. This new building is a much more ambitious re-incarnation of the first project funded by the Conran Foundation, the conversion of an old boilerhouse yard in the basement of the Victoria & Albert Museum into a venue that housed twenty-three design exhibitions between 1982–86. Stephen Bayley, Conran's long-time associate and dynamic fellow crusader in the campaign to increase design awareness in the British public, was recruited from higher education to run this Boilerhouse gallery and subsequently became the first chief executive of the Design Museum. Bayley resigned his post in the Autumn of 1989 and has been succeeded by the curator, Helen Rees, who was appointed in January 1990.

There will be few surprises for those acquainted with the esthetic associated with Conran's commercial enterprises: the Museum's retro-modern architecture; the monochromatic grandeur of the airy entrance hall, with its white walls and gray marble counters; and the carefully poised café-bar, selling basil and mozzarella baguettes. The entire museum is a paradigm of modernist style.

A small exhibition space at the entrance is devoted to graphic design, but the three main exhibition areas are housed on the first and second floors. The rhetoric associated with the first floor exhibitions is suggestive of a three-dimensional magazine. First, there is the Design Review, a space composed of the news and current affairs section of the museum, where new and speculative product designs are displayed. Adjacent to this section is the new Boilerhouse gallery, a space devoted to temporary exhibitions on

Figure 1
Entrance to the Design Museum.
Courtesy of the Design Museum.

design-related themes. This features section aims to reflect topical design issues in a thought-provoking way. Finally, the entire third floor houses the Study Collection of some 400 objects, plus computer databases. In addition to its display areas, the museum also has a reference library, a small lecture theater, and a restaurant.

At the end of a decade that spawned a shoal of new design magazines, books, periodicals, television programs, award schemes, and a fascination with design issues from the fundamental to the superficial, this new museum is a tangible representation of the subject in the form of the building, its exhibits, and its publicity. So, what is it saying about design? Which audiences does it address? Whose purposes does it serve? The following reflections will focus on these three questions.

Funding and philanthropy

As well as providing the bulk of the museum's capital funding, the Conran Foundation will also supply one-third of its annual running costs. The remaining financing will be generated by entry charges, company sponsorship, and a grant of £650,000 during three years from the Department of Trade and Industry. Margaret Thatcher herself opened the museum, thereby giving a very public show of political patronage.

Looking at possible motives of those who have provided the means for the museum's existence, obviously Sir Terence Conran has most to gain in the way of prestige. The launch of the Conran Foundation and the funding of this museum calls to mind a host of similar cultural benefactors, such as Gulbenkian, Mellon, Getty, Guggenheim, and Sainsbury. Perhaps the most striking difference is the circular nature of the funding in this case; commercial gains from Conran's own missionary-like efforts in bringing good design to British homes are being used to finance a Design Museum. The potential completion of the circle has attracted much press attention and will continue to linger as a question: To what degree is the museum being used to legitimate the buying of goods and services from Conran's commercial ventures? References are made to Habitat and its wares throughout the museum: chairs in the study collection, fabrics in the first temporary exhibition, and a Habitat carrier bag in one of the videos.

But these almost subliminal pieces of promotion are perhaps not as significant as the general promotion of a particular set of modernist design values associated with Conran. This fact is of particular interest at a time when some of his major business concerns are suffering setbacks. The Storehouse retailing group (which includes Habitat, Heal's, Mothercare, and British Home Stores) has been stalked by many predators following its underperformance, and the Conran Roche riverside flats at Butler's Wharf have proved difficult to sell in London's stagnant housing market.

In spite of Stephen Bayley's protestations that the museum is not a trade fair, its attraction for sponsoring companies is obvious; to be connected with an institution that advocates quality in design, tacitly or otherwise, means at worst a modicum of reflected glory and at best a validation of their wares. Perrier (UK) Ltd., for instance, sponsors the graphics gallery at the museum's entrance, which is now often referred to as Perrier Graphics. The company provided a collection of its advertising posters for one of the gallery's first displays, and a prominent Perrier logo appears on all information sheets associated with each new exhibition in the gallery. A more subtle sense of approval is suggested by the museum's use of Sony television monitors in both the Boilerhouse and the Study Collection. Various other Sony products have figures in the Design Review, but how "the latest products from all over the world" have been winnowed to the chosen few is not clear; we cannot tell whether they are included because they are examples of esthetic, functional, or manufacturing innovation, or because Sony UK is one of the museum's sponsors.

The Design Museum, therefore, holds particular attractions for company sponsorship and undoubtedly serves to fix Conran's position as an authoritative figure in the design world, as well as acts as a very public reminder of his philanthropy. However, its stated aim is "the advancement of the education of the public in the study of industrial and manufacturing art and design in its historical, social, artistic, industrial, and commercial contexts." According to Stephen Bayley, this educational aim has a specific objective: to provide a "framework of ideas to explain the everyday," which will produce "a better educated consumer . . . able to make more discriminating choices, thus forcing up standards from retailers to manufacturers."

There are echoes here of previous attempts to bolster British manufacturing industry by means of improving the design of goods (initiatives such as the early Schools of Design, the Great Exhibition of 1851, the Victoria & Albert Museum, and the Council of Industrial Design, among others too numerous to list) that have punctuated the course of design in Britain since the 1830s, most of which were sponsored, or at least sanctioned, by the British government. The present government seems to appreciate the dynamic, interventionist, and crusading role envisaged for the museum, as it sets out to improve the quality of manufactured goods (although Margaret Thatcher rightly queried the use of the word *museum* to describe its function). The government is backing the museum at a time when other bodies that were set up to improve design education, such as the Victoria & Albert Museum, art and design colleges, and the Design Council, are having to operate on reduced funding levels and are being forced to become more businesslike and more aware of the potential of private sponsorship; in other words, to become more like the Design Museum. It serves as a useful role model.

Audiences

Funding of £100,000 from the English Tourist Board's capital and a grant of £20,000 toward the cost of a ferry service from the London Docklands Development Corporation is evidence of the projected importance of the museum on London's tourist map. But the primary purpose of the museum is not simply to attract tourists. It aims to bring about a new relationship between industry and the public by trying to raise awareness: "It will increase popular awareness of design and its influence on everyday life, while persuading industry and commerce into a greater appreciation of the real benefits of making better goods . . . it will help to link the creative preoccupations of education with the realities of the marketplace." The museum, therefore, casts its net deliberately wide in order to capture a variety of audiences.

First, there is the role in formal education; the museum's Schools Program has been developed to dovetail with the requirements of the new National Curriculum, and students from many disciplines (design, design history, and design management specifically cited) are expected to benefit from resources that include study notes, worksheets, slide packs, and videos supporting the displays. The reference library is also intended for use by students, as well as "designers, journalists, researchers, people in industry and the general public" although there is seating for only ten readers.

Second, professional designers are expected to use the museum as a source of inspiration, to see new work in the Design Review, and to come to an understanding of "the product in its entire context."

Third, manufacturers whose products are on display in the Design Review are given the benefit of exposure in this "public clinic of unrivalled prestige and seriousness," as well as the opportunity to study products that have been successful in the past. Along with the London Business School, the museum is funding a Research Fellow in industrial design whose duties will include the coordination of talks and seminars for business and industry.

And finally, there is the general public. Of course, all of these audiences help to constitute "the public" and everyone is a consumer. However, the onus seems to be on a particular kind of consumer to help improve design standards. Stephen Bayley stated that the museum's first agenda-setting temporary exhibition "Commerce and Culture" was concerned with middle-class use. Does this topic imply that only the middle classes are sensitive enough to respond to the museum's educative efforts or articulate enough to demand improvements from manufacturers? Or perhaps this choice was simply a pragmatic recognition that the more affluent people are, the more likely they are to visit museums (and to buy consumer goods). Indeed, as with many other museums and galleries, only the affluent are likely to be able to afford the entry charge, refreshments, and the expensive book-catalogs that are essential to a full comprehension of the exhibitions.

Messages, methods, and arenas

Given the educative role the museum has set out for itself, the messages it promotes about design would seem to have great significance. Its very name is crucial in this respect, as The Design Museum implies that the boundaries of its scope are synonymous with the boundaries of the subject, although, in fact, the museum is only concerned with design for mass production. This narrow focus is perhaps not surprising in the light of its commercially oriented mission, but it does have the effect of excluding a whole range of activity. Excluded are engineering design, environmental design, craft, customizing, and one-off designs, among others.

The museum's Study Collection is further restricted to product design; arrays of chairs, bikes, telephones, radios, and cameras are chronologically ordered, and there is a small section about typography. There are eleven sets of study notes, most of which address these specific product groupings, but some are more general (for example, the Bauhaus and housework). Product design also dominates the Design Review, where an annually published tome will collate the contents of nine fast-changing exhibitions. Graphic design plays an important part in the promotion of mass-produced goods and has been given its own small niche in the Perrier Gallery at the entrance. Architecture, however, is described as "the mother of design" and seems to transcend the remit of the museum. Oddly enough, design for the fashion and textile industries is also neglected, despite the emphasis on mass production for personal consumption.

Perhaps the lack of fashion and textiles can be explained in terms of their traditional association with women; certainly there is nothing to suggest that the male bias in the study of design is about to be questioned or even acknowledged. Quite the reverse. *Nothing* in the Study Collection has been designed by a woman; the computer databases offer information on male designers from Alvar Aalto to Marco Zanuso. There is also an interactive computer game that privileges the male; the viewer is invited to design a toothbrush, and the surrogate designer shown on screen turns out to be a young man. Even in the videos of designers talking about their work, only two of the eight "talking heads" are women. An exhibition of Women Designers is planned for the Boilerhouse, but even this plan suggests, of course, that women are separate from the mainstream. However, the museum does not have a deliberate policy of exclusion or marginalization of women, but recognizing that such a bias has characterized the study of design and even the general parameters of what is worthy of study is important. Professional design activity and particularly product design have traditionally been associated with men and have been given priority over nonprofessional design activity and areas associated with women, such as embroidery, weaving, knitting, dressmaking, textiles, and so forth.[1] An unquestioning acceptance of a male bias can only serve to perpetuate this distortion.

The next question to consider is how design for mass production is being presented. We are told throughout the publicity material that disinterested esthetic appreciation will be eschewed in favor of a broader, contextual perspective; the aim is to avoid a celebratory attitude in which objects become fetishized and "false gods are put on plinths." However, this laudable aim seems to be undermined by a number of contradictory messages, not least the very form of the semipermanent displays where objects are plucked from their context and isolated for inspection (some are even in glass cases). Admittedly, the viewer is meant to use study notes and an

1   Cheryl Buckley has examined the patriarchal context within which the literature of design history, theory, and practice has been produced in "Made in Patriarchy: Toward a Feminist Analysis of Women and Design," *Design Issues* 3, no. 2 (1987): 3–15.

Design and Culture

audio guide to help to conjure up various contexts, but if the interpretive material is not used, this leaves a Pevsneresque array of design classics sitting on plinths, awaiting esthetic scrutiny. Another apparent incitement to focus on esthetics alone was given in an early brochure that proclaimed, "Industry has provided the most remarkable forms and images of the 20th century," an assertion illustrated by cropped photos celebrating the formal qualities of a Rolls Royce turbine fan blade and part of a circuit board.

In the case of the second Boilerhouse event, "French Designs," the entire exhibition emphasized the esthetic dimension. Designed by Phillipe Starck, this exhibition had first been shown at the Centre Pompidou in Paris. A range of objects chosen to "reflect social and economic changes as well as trends in design and manufacturing over the past 30 years" were all housed in identical perspex domes or boxes that stood on chunky wooden plinths. Some of the objects were actual size (children's clothing, Bic razors, a Cricket lighter), but, for the most part, they were models. Some were larger than life (a perfume bottle) but most were much smaller (the Train Grande Vitesse). This quirky parody of the museum exhibit was actually intended to give each object "equal physical and historical significance," but, in effect, this meant ignoring any context other than the esthetic. The celebration of pure form was enhanced by the fact that many of the models had no detailing whatsoever, and there was no contextual information provided. A display could not be more antipathetic to the stated aims of the Design Museum.

Another inconsistency is evident in huge photos of Charles Eames, Raymond Loewy, and other big-name designers peppered throughout the inaugural Boilerhouse exhibition. Stephen Bayley, who organized this exhibition, had also censured the adulation of designers. Those visitors who did not have the time or the inclination to read the accompanying text could have been forgiven for taking away the impression that the pantheon remains intact. Even the computers in the study collection contain mini-biographies of the Pioneers of Modern Design, and photographs of designers hang in the entrance to the Blueprint Café.

So, although the museum has some difficulty in moving away from a simple reverence for beautiful objects and their genius creators, its intention is to provide a broader perspective, and the question of how this goal is to be achieved needs to be asked. The study of design (however limited that concept of design might be) in its historical, social, artistic, industrial, and commercial contexts is an ambitious project if it is to be done with the requisite amount of methodological rigor.

In most museums, attempts to contextualize exhibits in permanent collections present a thorny problem; stories have to be fabricated around objects that have been collected on an arbitrary basis. Douglas Crimp, writing in the mid-1980s, addressed this fundamental issue: "The history of museology is a history of all the various attempts to deny the heterogeneity of the museum, to reduce it to a homogenous system or series. . . . faith in the possibility of ordering the museum's bric-a-brac persists until today."[2]

Theoretically, a new museum could avoid this problem by imposing criteria for the selection of material that would help rather than hinder any useful historical enquiry. Looking at the selection criteria for the Design Museum's Study Collection, however, we find that the artifacts chosen fall into one or more of the following categories:

- remarkable in terms of conception, esthetics, materials, engineering, technology, or function
- commercially significant
- innovative in the marketplace
- acknowledged classics of specific historical significance
- redolent of the social and cultural conditions that gave rise to them

A glance at these criteria reveals two potential and related areas of difficulty. The first problem is that, unless the precise basis for the selection of each artifact is made clear, we have no way of knowing how it is to be situated or its significance is to be assessed. Second, there is plenty of scope for what Fran Hannah and Tim Putnam have called *covert aestheticism*, where "taste operates as an unknown and therefore arbitrary determinant of what is selected as good or significant design," which leads to "indifferent design criticism rather than any kind of history."[3] Although Stephen Bayley has refuted the charge that the museum is a temple to either his own taste or that of Sir Terence Conran, the very phrase "remarkable in terms of conception, aesthetics . . . etc." presupposes a system of values that is never actually specified.

The Study Collection (*figure 2*) makes no grand claims to be either definitive or comprehensive; indeed, the partial nature of the

2   Douglas Crimp, "On the Museum's Ruins," *Postmodern Culture*, Hal Foster, ed. (London: Pluto Press, 1985).

3   Fran Hannah and Tim Putnam, "Taking Stock in Design History," *Block* 3 (1980): 25–33.

Figure 2
The Study Collection, including chairs produced in Italy by Magistretti, Deganello, and Kita. Courtesy of the Design Museum.

Figure 3
Product designs on display in the Design Review, including a new range of children's radios and cassette players made by Sony. Courtesy of the Design Museum, Phil Sayer, photographer.

Figure 4
The old British telephone kiosk and two proposals for its replacement, shown in the "Commerce and Culture" exhibition as part of a display that ridiculed the post-modern penchant for revivalist classicism in the urban environment. Courtesy of the Design Museum, Phil Sayer, photographer.

collection is obvious. However, much of the contextual information, particularly on the computer database system, is cursory, and the general impression is that the aim is simply to whet the appetite. Early publicity material promised information about the conditions and manner of production, but as yet this has not been evident. Moreover, there is a danger that the contextual information, such as it is, *could* be construed as presenting the definitive account, as there is no indication that history is a discussion and that meanings are unstable. The collection does aspire to raise public awareness of factors that influence design in mass production, but if this is to be anything more than a cabinet of curiosities, if it is to be of any real use to any of the targeted audiences, then, first, its methodology must be both sound and clear and, second, it should be made apparent that what is being given is only one of various possible histories of design.

The Design Review (*figure 3*) is concerned with current developments in design for mass production and aims to provide an international "shop window on innovation," so that popular reaction to new designs can be assessed. However, to enter into any kind of evaluative debate about innovative products the boundaries being pushed (stylistic, manufacturing, marketing, or technological) and the available options must be known. In addition, some clue must be given about how such a debate might be effected. Here is the future-oriented focal point of the museum, where the dual role as an educator of people at both ends of the production/consumption spectrum fuses into a single purpose: to help people to recognize, develop, and buy better goods. But what does this mean? Better for whom? Quite apart from patronizing notions of good design, which have characterized previous attempts to improve British manufacturing industry (and which the museum is at pains to deny), this question catapults us into a consideration of the social and ecological responsibilities of designers, manufacturers, and consumers. Perhaps this section is the most unsettling in the whole museum, in that the question is (unwittingly?) raised: How is it possible to reconcile the commitment to and need for innovation with the need to conserve resources?

The Boilerhouse is perhaps the part of the museum that is best equipped to fulfill the intention of moving the study of design away from objects and into the broader world of ideas. The space has been modeled on the flexible structure of a television studio, and the intention is to hold approximately six exhibitions per year, some of which will be initiated by the museum staff or invited organizers, and some imported from elsewhere. Its chief virtue is that it provides a forum for a variety of perspectives on designs and their meanings, thereby positing meanings as fluid and multiple rather than singular and fixed. Exhibitions are supplemented by talks and seminars on related issues, which take place in the small 56-seat lecture theater adjoining the main building.

Figure 5
The last exhibit in "Commerce and Culture" was both a celebration and parody of Stephen Bayley's vision of the future, showing access to knowledge centers from the comfort of your home. Courtesy of the Design Museum, Phil Sayer, photographer.

The very first Boilerhouse exhibition, "Commerce and Culture" (*figure 4*), is instructive to consider, first, because it was conceived as an agenda-setting exercise for the gallery, and, second, because it addressed an issue that is germane to the museum as a whole, namely, the blurring of the distinction between the commercial world and the role of cultural institutions. Here Stephen Bayley, the organizer and writer-editor of the accompanying book-catalog was aiming to look at the relationship between culture and commerce (variously called art and the everyday, art and trade, art and industry, art and life) in order to understand the influences on consumer choice in a world of rapidly changing values.[4]

His argument was, briefly, that art and trade were once indistinguishable but were forced apart in the nineteenth century by a "discriminating elite" who wanted to protect their tastes and values from being undermined by the tide of mass consumption brought about by the industrial age. However, the gap thus created is now closing as shops and museums, disseminators of commerce and culture, are encroaching upon each other's territory, thereby fusing two appetites that were once artificially separated: the desire for knowledge and the desire for goods. A vision of the future in which shops and museums actually elide into "knowledge centers—with everything available for inspection, comparison and for sale" was projected (*figure 5*). Bayley presented this as being a potentially enriching state of affairs and, thus, the logical inference to be drawn was that the Design Museum itself is a healthy and forward-looking expression of the fusion of cultural aspiration and commercial needs. Indeed, Bayley's title of chief executive is redolent of a commercial rather than a cultural institution.

Bayley used a perceived overlap between shops (those used largely by the middle classes, such as Habitat and Laura Ashley) and museums (such as the Victoria & Albert Museum) as evidence that commerce and culture are fusing. But is it not simply the case that those with wares to sell use every means at their disposal to engage public interest? Also, museums are hard-pressed for public funds and have had to resort to raising money in every conceivable way: company sponsorship, opening shops and restaurants, and selling facsimiles from their collections. Surely, where the possible fusion, or rather confusion, arises is when a museum accepts sponsorship from companies whose products are then directly legitimated by the liaison. However, the major problem that bedevilled Bayley's argument was the slippery use and lack of any definition of the term *culture*. The notion that commerce was ever separate from culture only makes sense if we think of culture as High Culture; if we think of culture in the anthropological sense, then commerce and culture are and always have been intertwined. This lack of intellectual rigor does not augur well for the future.

For all its faults, "Commerce and Culture" was a refreshing attempt to raise questions and present ideas in exhibition form, but

4   See the catalog *Commerce and Culture: From Pre-Industrial Art to Post-Industrial Value*, Stephen Bayley, ed. (London: The Design Museum, 1989).

Design and Culture

there is no easy answer to the problems this kind of communication poses. In this case, the exhibition turned out to be an abridged and more physically assertive version of the book-catalog, with a frenetic juxtaposition of visual and aural variety accompanying copious and indigestible amounts of text. Books, lectures, and television programs may be more suitable vehicles for the communication of such ideas.

Perhaps this direction was planned by Stephen Bayley; certainly his plans included sharing research costs for the temporary exhibitions with television companies, who would then presumably go on to make programs (and videos) on the same themes. Already, the exhibitions could be construed as sales pitches for the heavy and highly priced catalogs. This could be seen as a first step on the road to Bayley's vision of the museum as a knowledge center, with everything available for inspection, comparison, and sale, except that at this stage information and ideas about design are for sale rather than the artifacts themselves.

The Design Museum does offer an exciting opportunity to increase public awareness of design—a very broad area of activity that impinges upon all of our lives and which, at the same time, constructs and is constructed by our needs and desires. However, the ultimate educational objective seems to be to produce a more discriminating consumer who will contribute to increasing commercial success. This meager and shortsighted aim ignores the potential of the new institution. For, by examining the past in a scholarly, disinterested, and critical way, we can begin to make sense of the present and engage in a useful debate about the future of a world that, we now know, has frighteningly finite resources.

Yet small rays of hope flicker. There is evidence that the museum is willing to listen to criticism (to the extent that there was a trenchant critique by Robert Hewison published in the second issue of its own quarterly magazine), and the program of lectures and seminars may well provide an opportunity to widen the narrow focus suggested by the building and its permanent collection, although admittedly the audiences for these represent a tiny fraction of visitors. In addition, every new temporary exhibition will provide the opportunity for a more rigorous, scholarly, and communicative approach. Now that Stephen Bayley has gone, it remains to be seen whether Helen Rees, the new director, and her curatorial staff will be able to realize this potential and also pick a path through the minefield of vested interests.

Design and Immateriality: What of It in a Post Industrial Society?
Abraham A. Moles

An immaterial culture is emerging. It exists only because a heavily material base supports it and makes it possible. It is from the very outset a phenomenon—indeed, an epiphenomenon—resulting from technology. The future of design, then, for an artificial reality depends on the design of the hardware and specialized techniques, that are the fundamental constituents of an artificial reality and that contribute to the creation of what one could call *imago*—generalized images, not necessarily confined to a visual mode. Thus, a post industrial society (Bell) is a superindustrialized society, or one which has pushed to extremes the consequences of its industrialization.

It is true that we are surrounded by so-called electric phantoms, to use a phrase of Villiers de l'Isle Adam, which more and more are invading both our work and recreational environments. One of the problems posed to the human spirit is its capacity to exercise control over reality, while adjusting to the blurring of barriers between reality and images, or between real objects and their appearances. As we enter the age of *telepresence* we seek to establish an equivalence between "actual presence" and "vicarial presence." This vicarial presence is destroying the organizing principle upon which our society has, until now, been constructed. We have called this principle the *law of proximity:* what is close is more important, true, or concrete than what is far away, smaller, and more difficult to access (all other factors being equal).

We are aspiring, henceforth, to a way of life in which the distance between us and objects is becoming irrelevant to our realm of consciousness. In this respect, telepresence also signifies a feeling of equidistance of everyone from everyone else, and from each of us to any world event. At the same time, we live in an age of *communicational opulence.* We now have at our disposal more sources of communication and interaction than we will ever be able to make use of in our relatively short lifetime. This is the age of a social system of networks, decorated with the futuristic name of the "Information Society." Henceforth, the bulk of our effort will be spent more for manipulating information than for manipulating objects, which are now no more than products of far-out robots, controlled by abtruse programs, inaccessible models, and a ubiquitous creator.

Nevertheless, these new living conditions, which are also cultural conditions, and thus what one used to call the conditions for art, can subsist only on a spectacular hardware or material base.

This underlying structure is spectacular, most evidently, because of the astonishing omnipresence and sheer size of the machines and the specialized manufacturing plants making cars, video equipment, audio components, and so on. While generally unaware of the highly specialized, technical origin of such objects, the layman has to live with this material accumulation. But sheer size is not the most significant aspect of this material base. Rather, it is especially spectacular because of its complexity which stands as today's paradigm for technological advancement. A 3cm^2 microprocessor comprises more "things" than an automobile—more components, more functions, more connections, more relays, and, conceivably, more raw intelligence.

Yet, the structural complexity of today's hardware, which can be quantitatively measured, finds itself subject to one of the general laws of the universe, the law of entropy, or, simply put, the tendency of all conjunctions of things toward disorder. This irrepressible agitation of the physical world counteracts and eventually destroys the order imposed by the hardware creator. The consequences are overloads, short circuits, and equipment failure.

A maintenance society replaces a performance society
While transmitting and receiving messages and imagoes constituting an artificial reality, man encounters more frequently, like the *diabolus in machina* ("devil in the machine") of the religious era, the bug, the hitch, and the malfunction, largely random in nature, which erode the fundamental virtue that any mechanical aid or appliance must possess: reliability. All other factors being equal, the more our world is complex, in reality or appearance, the more it is fragile, and the more it is subject to mishaps. As a result, the hardware builder must adopt particular strategies or plans of action designed to control the demon of disorder. Such action gives rise to a *maintenance mentality*, which perfuses the world of support groups and technicians, for making "immaterials."

The creators of the new immaterial culture have devoted most of their effort to the permanent reproduction of what, for them, was once practically inconceivable—the transmission of sounds and speech over distance and the storage of data in memory banks. All this, which a century ago was hailed as "the miracle of communication," has become commonplace in our lives. From a social perspective, the inventors and the builders seem to have won the battle waged on the continual insurrection of nature against the complex pattern of circuits and transistors. They have learned how to incorporate a reasonable degree of reliability into an uncertain miracle, and have mastered the multiple and diverse causes of disorder through deduction and quantitative reasoning. The digital compact disc or the satellite numerical repeater are two noteworthy examples. *The immaterial civilization must be reliable;* otherwise, it could have no social impact and would be the subject of little or no debate today.

But the minimal reliability established by the industrial complex still does not inspire in the individual sufficient confidence to participate in an immaterial culture. He or she is reluctant to depend completely on telerepresentations being confronted by a heterogenous array of equipment that originated from various sources, was assembled at random, and offers uncertain compatibility. The situation of the individual, then, is different from that of the society at large, and consequently the meaning of the term "reliability" becomes more strict according to the scope of the human or material circumstances to which the word is applied. To live and experience a culture is to interact with innumerable, disparate forms of that culture, as well as to find oneself presented with a myriad of possibilities for successful—and unsuccessful—operation. The demands that the individual presents to society, therefore, are more important than the demands of society on its subjects, which is the situation we are faced with today.

The task of the designer is, precisely, to ensure reliability by mastering the factors that jeopardize it. Therefore, the first field of investigation of design for an immaterial culture is to furnish largely material assurance of the *universal reliability* of the systems that make it possible.

Design by a model or immaterialism of design?

A second direction of inquiry into the relationship between design and the immaterial culture is to investigate the impact of the stratagem on the designer's *task* in a computerized society. We used to say that the designer, an environmental engineer, was responsible for each of the systems he installs, as well as for their integration into the particular life-style of each person. Each of these systems required a material task of design, done in a workshop that until now, was hardly susceptible to automation. All this is changing, however, with the advent of computer processing and computer-aided manufacturing, which are modifying the phenomenological *nature of the design process* (Tuchny, Larroche).

It is useless to ask if design is an artistic activity or a scientific one; the etymology of the word "technology," or *techne* (art), provides a sufficient response. With respect to doing, the confusing etymology of the word "engineer" (the genius who drives the engine or machine) applies also.

The designer creates the environment of others. Until now the designer's vocation has been both conceptual and concrete. The workshop has been a place to perceive and build models destined to be copied for mass production. The question now, however, is how this vocation has been modified, for better or for worse, by the inexorable development of the immaterial culture. The design activity itself is changing because the designer's tools are becoming immaterial, as are the lives of those to whom the products are marketed. Design by holographic models may still be far in the future, but the

concrete activity of design even now partakes substantially of immaterial techniques, or usage of artificial representations, images, and
diagrams composed by image generating machines.

Affecting more than workshop activity alone, the trend
toward immaterialism includes all projectional conception in a
concrete model, a process which used to depend on a situation of
permanent interaction between conception and construction. The
dialectic game between the abstract (the idea, the mental vision) and
the concrete (the struggle with the material and disparate tools and
appliances) is giving way to work done essentially with computer-
integrated manufacturing at a computer desk. The designer's task
now consists of construction based on three precepts: (a) the work
order, (b) the rules of an exploratory program, (c) articulated in a
field of liberty defined by certain parameters—often of ergonomic
origin and eventually of creative fantasy. This suggests to the
designer, regarded as the master of the work, an ensemble of more
or less pertinent variations on which he will have to exercise his critical abilities, themselves controlled by functional optimization principles in the broadest sense. The designer, who assumes a more and
more important social role in a society where power is evanescent,
must confront the new fundamental idea of "Initial Form plus
Variations," in order to realize an often monotonous variation of
possible forms with respect to given parameters. This is what we
have called "variational creativity."

We are passing from a time of hands-on creation of a model
to one of an initial form plus a field of variations, which stem from
any already existing object, whether traditional or modern. Thus,
from this established model a whole series of new models is determined, with the intention of forever satisfying the avidity of the
consumer market. This process is done using the most refined and
the most abstract creative techniques, in order to express them in
programs, through creative methods (Alexander).

Not only the designer, but also the manufacturer of forms
and models faces this situation, but with a different perspective. The
manufacturer confronts a kind of creation in immateriality, which
encompasses the definition of the field of possibilities and its
methodical exploration, which, in turn, generates auxiliary criteria
for judgment. These criteria are then reapplied in order to furnish
yet another new field of possibilities. Henceforth, one expects no
longer to find drafting tables, sculptor's tools or carpenter's chisels
in the design room. They are being phased out by drawing and
image-creating machines that yield computer graphics, so that the
material objects themselves, as products of these images or of audio
and visual simulations, are, at a distance, mere products of the
imagination, and seem more *credible* than *real*.

From 1850 to 1950, industrialization was characterized by the
predominance of a system of drafted plans and diagrams, which
were essential to the materialization of ideas, and which caused a

proliferation of design patents. DeForge, in a noteworthy book, illustrated well this "kingdom of drawings" or technical diagrams, which were the rule in nineteenth century workshops.

For several decades the complexity and precision of drawings have rendered them amenable to both the computer's memory and the drafting table. Now, however, the draftsman and the modelist are disappearing from the finishing laboratory or the graphic workshop itself; the computer is supplanting them with its ability to generate, on demand, any view, profile, or cross section of any part or whole of the factory or machine in question. Furthermore, the implicit and intuitive relationship itself of a small part to the whole, or of a particular machine to the whole factory, is vanishing. In many complex systems the global design breaks loose, becomes accessory, indeed superfluous, because the whole changes with each moment of its construction. Certain parts are replaced by others and modifications are made during construction, even during the useful life of the product itself, because the conditions determining the integration of smaller parts into the whole are automatically taken into account by the computer. In short, the scale model is losing its significance; it serves only as a rough estimate or guide to the builder. It is only a palpable illustration of the concept involved and, most important, is no longer necessary. One could say that neither the designer, the engineer, nor the architect knows the system in all its exact detail, though any one of these persons could simply ask the computer for any piece of information concerning the function of the object under construction. Thus, we are arriving at a kind of conceptual immateriality of complex systems in the wake of those who create them in fragments.

The designer at the center of combinations of esthetic effects
Finally, it seems appropriate to consider the relationship of design with a fundamentally artificial reality, which is another systematic exploration of the field of possibilities and which will be one new sensorial combination, generated from a "new art," defined by the sensory parameters that it manipulates and the new esthetic arrangement it proposes. If, in the foreseeable future, art remains (for those unperfused to or allergic to the idea of chance) a programmed sensualization of the environment, the designer, as an environmental engineer, finds himself endowed with considerable ability to manipulate the new artistic matter, a step which transforms the designer himself into a neo-artist. Or, could the designer be called a meta-artist, the potential maker of new "art"? In this respect, our senses of the close range of those affecting us by contact (touch, smell, sensitivity to temperature, vibration, and balance) remain a relatively unexplored area of human sensoriality. We lack the means to evaluate objectively certain aspects of the real, which we could call *transduction* (to transform messages from one medium to another) or *interfacing* (to set up a partition of illusions for the

Design and Culture

projection of tele-images for example, a screen, a tactile sensor, a sonorous background, a simulated landscape, or a virtual actor). The immense technological structure proposed by the post industrial society seems precisely to have to fill quickly this gap. It is becoming the function of design to examine this new field of "programmed sensualizations" (what one used to call a "work of art" and what one could call from now on a "scene of esthetic action"). What would become, for example, of an electronic tactile detector combined with a Minitel or Compuserve system? In a purely philosophical sense, would the result be a by-product of the immaterial culture, or would it be a new event in the sphere of esthetic valorization?

The positions of design during the age of the invasion of immateriality

Any immaterial civilization will be heavily materialized because its immaterial products are necessarily linked to the mechanical infrastructure that generates, stabilizes, and governs them. By misinterpretation, a recent exposition celebrated, not an "immaterial world," but a form of the binomial object-images, forms, and support. This is another attitude of man vis-à-vis an artificial world—a world created by him as the only source of his reactions. Does such an attitude imply a danger of technological narcissism, at the moment when nature becomes inaccessible or restricted to parks with limited access?

Thus, every symphony has its compact disc; every audio experience its loudspeaker; every visual image its camera and video disc. Behind every outward image or symbol lies mechanical support, and if the immateriality of these images and symbols gives rise to a new approach to the relationship between human being and object, the analysis will be one of the individual's connection with the material support underlying the new culture of immateriality.

The real problem, though, resides in the kind of relationship man will establish with the new material foundation that he will consider simply as part of the decor of the environment, consequently that he rejects from his own field of consciousness, and thus forgets entirely for the benefit of the immaterial imago (which is slightly material in itself), which directs him and the *credibility* of which is becoming more important than its *verity*.

But since this same individual is constantly reminded of this material base by screens and terminals, the question is this: under what conditions of reliability will the material foundation be truly forgotten and replaced by the dubious, hazy, generalized images as only points of reference for a subsequent conscious activity?

These material supports reveal themselves only by their imperfections—by the necessity to plug in a computer, for example, and to turn it on in order to make it work. The infrastructure subsists in the fact that the elimination of the most insignificant contact—indeed, a telecontact—can extract all that the most advanced technology has put into a computer. The material supports remind us of our dependence on them, especially by such defects as the smudge on a poorly cleaned vinyl disc, the highrise apartment building that interferes with radio reception, or the interfering lines that intrude in our private telephone conversations.

As an individual, here and now, I could forget all the hardware, if only it were to reach perfection, something rarely attained in practice. Striving for that perfection and that absolute reliability is precisely the fundamental role of the one who *designs* the machinery of imagery, simulation, and communication; the standing of quality, without which no post industrial world could subsist, is always questioned, as is the fleeting "perfect moment" of my relationship with the world.

The role of the designer, then, is not so much to create "new" objects to serve as structural supports of an immaterial culture, as to insist on an environment of implacable stability. Before introducing something new, the designer must protect the status quo, which permits individuals to participate spontaneously and with little effort in the seductive immateriality of today's world.

Translated from the French by David W. Jacobus

Bibliography

Adam, Villiers de l'Isle, *L'Eve Future,* a science fiction poetical novel (Paris: Ed 10.18,1962).

Alexander, Christopher, *Notes on the Synthesis of Form* (Boston: Harvard University Press, 1974).

Bell, Daniel, *The Coming of Post Industrial Society* (New York: Basic Books, 1973).

DeForge, Yves, *Le Graphisme Technique* (Paris: Champvallon, 1981).

Moles, Abraham A., *Vivre Avec Yes Choses: Contre Une Culture Immaterielle* (Paris: Art Press, 1987), 1–28.

Moles, Abraham A., "Vom Design des Gegenstandes zum Design der Umgebung," *Design ist Unsichtbar* (Wien: Locker, 1981): 93–100, Moles on page 98.

Moles, Abraham A., "The comprehensive guarantee: a new consumer's value," *Design Issues 2,* no. 1 (Chicago: University of Illinois, 1985), 53–65.

Moles, Abraham A., *Theorie Structurale de la Communication et Societé* (Paris: Masson, 1986).

Moles, Abraham A., *Theory of information and Aesthetic Perception* (Champaign: University of Illinois Press [French edition, 1958]).

Simon, Herbert A., *The Architecture of Complexity* (Pittsburgh: Carnegie Institute of Technology, 1962).

Tuchny, Larroch, *Objet Industriel en Question* (Paris: Ed du Regard, 1985).

Expanding the Boundaries of Design: The Product Environment and the New User
Victor Margolin

While debates about the comparative merits of modern and post-modern style, Braun and Memphis, High Tech and High Touch, rage worldwide, more radical changes in designing are taking place. Most significantly, microprocessors are making possible more complex products with a widened range of functions, resulting in a new flexible relation to the user, who selects specific functions from a broad set of options by programming the product or making choices from a visual menu.

Consider the capabilities of the video cassette recorder. A person can have a program recorded off the air automatically and then can view it at any time. One can blip out commercials and stop, reverse, or fast forward programs to access any part of the tape, just as one does with a book or magazine. New picture-in-picture systems will even allow the viewer to watch as many as nine programs on the same screen.[1] Programs on videocassettes can also be substituted for those offered by the networks or cable companies. This is no different from what readers do with printed materials, but for video viewing it breaks the hammerlock of predetermined programs at set times that the broadcast and cable networks previously offered the viewer. The point here is not to make too much of this token user control, since it is the content of video programming that is ultimately liberating or confining, but to illustrate that a more flexible relation to the video medium creates the technological condition whereby a person can exercise a greater choice of content.

Today's product flexibility could not have been foreseen by those design theorists and reformers in the past who emphasized the appearance of objects as the central problem to be addressed. When curators at the Museum of Modern Art, for example, stressed the necessity of an object's form to articulate its function, they were thinking only of functions that could be embodied in a shape. The need to rethink the received issues of product form was noted in the 1950s by Tomás Maldonado, Gui Bonsiepe, and others at the Hochschule für Gestaltung in Ulm, West Germany. Focusing on the communicative aspects of forms, they were probably the first educators to incorporate semiotics and information theory into design training. The Ulm faculty recognized the importance of information in the product-user relationship. The symbol system designed by Maldonado and Bonsiepe for IBM data processing equipment was a

1   I have described the capabilities of commercially available products only. Researchers at the Massachusetts Institute of Technology's Media Lab and elsewhere are experimenting with "intelligent television," which will significantly enhance the flexibility of program formats.

good example, and other projects were initiated to clarify the instructional signs on the control panels of various kinds of electronic equipment. Even though the Ulm designers were dealing with less complex objects than those of today, their work remains important for its early emphasis on communication as central to product design.

Since the Hochschule für Gestaltung closed its doors in 1968, the number of functions that many new products possess has grown by large orders of magnitude, enhanced by the creation of microprocessors and software. In computers, software mediates between the user and the object. Since programmers first began to create software, software design and hardware design have been separate processes, for the most part. Product designers tend to concentrate on the shape and ergonomics of a physical object, while programmers design software that embodies complex sets of machine commands and capabilities. Despite the fact that machines and software exist in a symbiotic relationship, educators and manufacturers continue to bifurcate the design process. However, as the capabilities of new programming packages increase, there is all the more need to explore the ways that hardware design and software design relate to each other.

With the wider range and greater refinement of machine tasks, the process of giving commands is central to the user who has come to expect that the machine will take care of the work once it has been correctly instructed. In many instances, however, the user fails to make use of the product's full capabilities. This is certainly true of numerous software programs whose users do not take the time to explore all their possibilities. The disjuncture between expanded product capabilities and the user's limited ability to use them creates an unprecedented situation for designers, signaling the need for them to address the problem of encouraging and teaching consumers to make the fullest use of new products.

The increasing number of tasks that products can manage prompts the designer to shift radically from the traditional focus on form to the more flexible relation between the product and the user. The designer can no longer foresee all the ways that complex products will be used and must think in terms of multiple possibilities rather than a limited number of set functions.

While the concept of communicating product functions with the touch of a button or the shift of a mouse is relatively new, user participation in product definition actually has a considerable history. Objects with interchangeable components, such as hand tools, have a long tradition, but flexibility took on more polemical overtones with the design of furniture that had movable parts and was intended to give the user more choices by challenging the conventional expectation of a static form as the end result of the design process. An early example of such furniture was the "Living

Structure," a frame with movable platforms that could be adjusted according to user needs, designed by Ken Isaacs, who began developing this type of object in the 1940s. The Living Structure was followed by other designs such as Joe Colombo's "Additional System," a set of modular units that could be arranged into different combinations of chairs and couches. On a larger scale, the flexible "office landscape" design of the West German Quickborner Team subsequently became popular, as did the "Action Office" produced by the Herman Miller Company under the leadership of designer Robert Probst.

But the user relation to these objects and systems remained a physical one and the possibilities of exercising their flexibility were self-evident. The connection to products whose functions are not physically defined is different: the individual must become familiar with a lexicon of commands and functions that are either displayed visually on a screen, programmed through a keyboard, or activated by pushing buttons. Such participation is part and parcel of every complex object relationship. And as artificial intelligence and sophisticated sensing devices are incorporated to a greater degree in machine and software design to bring about more sophisticated human-machine interactivity, user participation will become an essential aspect of new products.

While ergonomists have traditionally concentrated on the physical interface between users and objects, a great need has emerged to learn more about the user's cognitive and emotional relation to products. Whereas designers like Isaacs, Colombo, and Probst thought of the user as someone who manipulated concrete objects, designers and manufacturers are now beginning to understand the user as a person who must relate to the functions of a product through a process of information exchange. Operating instructions, whether separate documents or inherent components of the software programs themselves, are central to product use, but user frustration is still all too frequent to take this aspect of design for granted. Yet, the process by which a person establishes a relation to a product is an important part of an even larger territory of design, that which I call the *product environment*. Few designers are prepared to understand this environment, although its importance is likely to grow in years to come.

The product environment

All the necessary conditions for acquiring the product, learning to use it, following its changes and improvements, providing components for it, and keeping it in good repair are part of the product environment.[2] The term "environment" denotes everything that surrounds the product and becomes part of its identity and value. For chairs and teapots, which have limited functions and require little or no maintenance, the environment is a narrow one, but that

2 The need to shift from designing objects to designing environments was first suggested by the French sociologist Abraham Moles and was the impetus for the concept put forth here. See Abraham Moles, "The Comprehensive Guarantee: A New Consumer Value," *Design Issues* vol. 2, no. 1 (Spring 1985): 53–64.

of a personal computer is wider and embraces many more elements, including the availability of peripherals and software, detailed programming manuals, telephone support systems, electronic bulletin boards, and repair facilities. The computer's environment is the set of elements that satisfies all the conditions for a satisfactory "living" relationship to it. This recognition that a physical object exists in an environment which contributes to its value may be compared to our understanding that our own well-being depends on a healthy natural environment.

For too long, designers, manufacturers, and critics have given inadequate attention to the product environment as a whole. But the design of the physical form is only one element within this environment, the parts of which must all work effectively to achieve the value of good or bad product design. Selected aspects of the product's environment should not merit good design awards if the environment as a whole is deficient in specific aspects.

For the user, the product itself and everything required to make it work are all of a piece. One element essential to high overall quality is efficient maintenance that can be provided without undue stress, either in terms of time or money. A cheap portable audio cassette recorder or an inexpensive telephone answering machine has a deficient product environment: it cannot be repaired for less than the cost of a new one. When something small goes wrong, the purchase price is wasted. As an antidote, Abraham Moles has proposed the concept of the "comprehensive guarantee," something like an insurance contract, that would bind the service provider, most likely the manufacturer, to do whatever is necessary to maintain an object's functions during a given period, even replacing a defective product if necessary. Moles perceptively points out that, in fact, people are not so much purchasing an object as a given set of functions on which they depend and which they need to maintain in the most efficient way possible.[3]

Too little attention has been paid to the design of product environments, even though the reasons to redress such neglect are many. Users depend more and more on product efficiency for their daily routines. Often even a simple backup system is lacking and a key machine out of commission can provoke a crisis. Certain objects have what Ivan Illich calls a "radical monopoly," meaning they are expected to be possessed by everyone. For example, few individuals would try to get by without a telephone and, in some circles, without a telephone answering machine. Likewise, many people would not be able to get to work without an automobile because public transportation systems do not often provide adequate backup for commuters. Thus, manufacturers cannot address every contingency related to satisfactory product use, but they need to anticipate as many as possible and think in terms of designing a product environment rather than a single object, in order to ensure user satisfaction.

3   See Moles, "The Comprehensive Guarantee: A New Consumer Value," *Design Issues* vol. 2, no. I (Spring 1985): 57–58.

The new user

Because of the fast pace of life and the constant press of obligations that people in industrialized societies experience, the increased functional capacity of many products has created rising expectations for more and better machine-provided services. Once people know what a machine can offer, they begin to imagine other functions that a machine with additional or expanded capabilities could provide. Encouraged by advertising rhetoric to know no bounds in their expectations, they push manufacturers to design products that are responsive to demands that are ever more refined.

Users expect products to function well because they have little time or money to budget for repairs or for the creation of backup systems. A writer who depends on a computer has a hard time when the machine is down because the files are not accessible unless a hard copy has been produced as back up. A commuter who needs an automobile every day requires the means for repair as well as the ability to borrow or rent another car. Therefore, the efficient performance of an automobile, backed up by a strong service support system, has become a major selling point for the buyer, while styling, at least in the range of small cars, plays a lesser role than it once did.

People must choose from an immense number of comparable products, as well as a wide range of functions offered by these products. So many options require them to have a clear sense of their needs to ensure that their time and money are spent efficiently to obtain the payoffs they expect. The danger remains that the user will perceive a new product as useful simply because it offers more efficient functioning, unaware that its acquisition will bring with it a set of obligations regarding service contracts, increased energy use, the supply of parts, and other factors not present with a product that requires no support system.

The future

Even though people find themselves in a web of relationships with objects that grow more complicated by the day, manufacturing is nonetheless in a transitional phase between the complex objects of today and the smart, more self-sufficient products of the future. Advances in artificial intelligence and sensor technology have demonstrated that machines can begin to approximate some human perceptual functions and change their operation in relation to such environmental factors as temperature, light, and sound. This technology is already leading to new types of designs, such as the "Smart House" in which more advanced utility systems will combine electrical and communication systems, for example, and will monitor and control energy flows throughout the house more effectively than the average home owner can do now.[4] Sensors in other objects will make them more efficient and accessible. Even as new technology generates products that are friendlier to the user,

4   See Ralph Lee Smith, *Smart House: The Coming Revolution in Housing* (Columbia, MD: GP Publishing, 1988).

however, their complexity increases the user's dependence on a specific product environment, which includes responsibility for proper maintenance. While such products enhance user autonomy by performing an expanded range of tasks and providing greater capabilities of communication and production, they also link the individual to an environment that is necessary to keep the product-user relationship in good order.

There is much that designers and manufacturers need to learn about the evolving relationship between products and users. In anticipation of satisfying a need, the user is actually purchasing an environment that promises a satisfying relationship to the product. It is the total organization of such environments that constitutes the next threshold for design. Only by recognizing this can manufacturers, designers, and the public shift their critical faculties to address the issue of product value more accurately.

Sources

All of the essays in this volume originally appeared in the journal *Design Issues*.

Volume 4, number 1–2 (Fall 1987–Spring 1988): Abraham A. Moles, "Design and Immateriality: What of It in a Post Industrial Society?" pp. 25–32; Victor Margolin, "Expanding the Boundaries of Design: The Product Environment and the New User," pp. 59–64.

Volume 5, number 1 (Fall 1988): Victor Papanek, "The Future Isn't What It Used to Be," pp. 4–17; Jorge Frascara, "Graphic Design: Fine Art or Social Science?" pp. 18–29.

Volume 5, number 2 (Spring 1989): Klaus Krippendorff, "On the Essential Contexts of Artifacts or on the Proposition that "Design Is Making Sense (of Things)," pp. 9–39; S. Balaram, "Product Symbolism of Gandhi and Its Connection with Indian Mythology," pp. 68–85; Martin Krampen, "Semiotics in Architecture and Industrial Product Design," pp. 124–40.

Volume 6, number 1 (Fall 1989): Tony Fry, "A Geography of Power: Design History and Marginality," pp. 15–30; Rajeshwari Ghose, "Design, Development, Culture, and Cultural Legacies in Asia," pp. 31–48.

Volume 6, number 2 (Spring 1990): Martin Solomon, "The Power of Punctuation," pp. 28–32; Gert Selle, "Untimely Opinions (An Attempt to Reflect on Design)," pp. 33–42; Yves Deforge, "Avatars of Design: Design before Design," pp. 43–50; Richard Buchanan, "Myth and Maturity: Toward a New Order in the Decade of Design," pp. 70–80.

Volume 7, number 1 (Fall 1990): Alain Findeli, "The Methodological and Philosophical Foundations of Moholy-Nagy's Design Pedagogy in Chicago (1937–1946)," pp. 4–19.

Volume 7, number 2 (Spring 1991): A Cheng, "Line," pp. 5–16; Takuo Hirano, "The Development of Modern Japanese Design: A Personal Account," pp. 54–62; Barbara Usherwood, "The Design Museum: Form Follows Funding," pp. 76–87.

Volume 8, number 1 (Fall 1991): Mihaly Csikszentmihalyi, "Design and Order in Everyday Life," pp. 26–34; Tomás Maldonado, "The Idea of Comfort," pp. 35–43.

Volume 8, number 2 (Spring 1992): Richard Buchanan, "Wicked Problems in Design Thinking," pp. 5–22.

Volume 9, number 1 (Fall 1992): Ann C. Tyler, "Shaping Belief: The Role of Audience in Visual Communication," pp. 21–29.

Volume 9, number 2 (Spring 1993): Rudolf Arnheim, "Sketching and the Psychology of Design," pp. 15–19; Clive Dilnot, "The Gift," pp. 51–65.

About the Contributors

Rudolf Arnheim is Professor Emeritus of The Psychology of Art at Harvard University. He has published widely on art, psychology, and crafts. Among his numerous books are *Art and Visual Perception* and *The Power of the Center: A Study of Composition in the Visual Arts.*

S. Balaram is Professor of Design at the National Institute of Design in Ahmedabad, India. His publications include *Mundane Things for Millions, A Different Design Movement,* and *Meaning with a Purpose: Mythological Rhetoric.*

Richard Buchanan is Professor of Design and Head of the Department of Design at Carnegie Mellon University. He is an editor of the journal *Design Issues* and coeditor of the book *Discovering Design: Explorations in Design Studies.*

A Cheng is a distinguished writer living in Los Angeles. He publishes primarily in the Far East and writes screenplays for Chinese filmmakers in Asia and the United States. His book of stories, *Three Kings,* has been translated into English.

Mihaly Csikszentmihalyi is Professor of Human Development and Education at the University of Chicago. He has published extensively on a wide range of topics. Among his many publications are several books with a particular relation to design, *The Meaning of Things,* which he coauthored; and *Flow.*

Yves Deforge taught courses in the history of technology and "culture technique" at the University of Technology in Compiègne, France. Before that, he was a consultant to various industries. He has published numerous works on design and technology.

Clive Dilnot has taught at the Carpenter Center for the Visual Arts and the Graduate School of Design at Harvard University. He is the author of many articles on visual culture and has been a columnist for *I.D.* magazine.

Alain Findeli is Professor at the School of Industrial Design, University of Montreal. A founder and editor of the journal *Informel,* he has published articles on design history and theory and has completed a major work on Moholy-Nagy's design pedagogy in Chicago.

Jorge Frascara is Professor of Graphic Design at the University of Alberta. He cochairs the Education Working Group of ICOGRADA (International Council of Graphic Design Associations) and has published widely on graphic design topics.

Tony Fry teaches in the Power Department of Fine Arts at the University of Sydney, Australia, and is Director of the Eco-Design Foundation. Among his numerous publications on art and design are the books *Design History Australia; Old Worlds, New Visions;* and *Remakings: Ecology, Design, Philosophy.*

Rajeshwari Ghose is the editor of *Design and Development in South and Southeast Asia*. She lives in Hong Kong.

Takuo Hirano is a founder of design practice and education in Japan. He proposed the G Mark quality design system and has taught at leading universities and technical institutions. In 1960, he started his own consulting firm where he continues to serve as Chairman. He is also a professor at the Tama Art University in Tokyo.

Martin Krampen is the author of *Zeichensysteme der Visuellen Kommunikation* and *Meaning in the Urban Environment*, the editor of *Icons of the Road*, and the coeditor of *Classics of Semiotics*. He lives in Germany.

Klaus Krippendorff is Professor of Communication at the Annenberg School of the University of Pennsylvania and is a design consultant. Books he has authored, edited, or coedited include *Content Analysis, Information Theory, Communication and Control in Society*, and *The Analysis of Communication Content*.

Tomás Maldonado is Professor of Environmental Design at the Politecnico in Milan, Italy. A former director of the Hochschule für Gestaltung in Ulm, Germany, his many books include *Design Industriale: Un Riesame, La Speranza Progettuale, Avanguardia e Rationalità*, and *Il Futuro della Modernità*.

Victor Margolin is Associate Professor of Design History at the University of Illinois, Chicago. An editor of *Design Issues*, he has edited *Design Discourse: History Theory Criticism* and coedited *Discovering Design: Explorations in Design Studies*.

Abraham A. Moles was Professor of Sociology at the University of Strasbourg, France, before his death in 1992. He was a prolific author of many books and articles on information theory, visual communication, action theory, kitsch, and other topics. These include *Théorie des Objets, L'Image: Communication Fonctionelle,* and *Psychologie du Kitsch*.

Victor Papanek is Professor of Architecture at the University of Kansas. His many publications on design include the books *Design for the Real World, Design for Human Scale*, and *How Things Don't Work*.

Gert Selle has taught design history, art education, and the aesthetics of daily life at Oldenburg University in Germany. His books include *Ideologie und Utopie des Design: Zur Gesellschaftlichen Theorie der Industriellen Formbebung* and *Design—Geschichte in Deutschland: Produktkultur als Entwurf und Erfahrung*.

Martin Solomon is a graphic designer in New York. His work has received numerous awards, and he has published extensively on the subject of typography.

The Idea of Design

Ann C. Tyler is Chair of Visual Communication at The School of the Art Institute of Chicago. Her design work has received many awards and has been widely published in various design annuals and magazines.

Barbara Usherwood is Senior Lecturer in Design History at the University of Teeside, England.